AVID

READER

PRESS

THE FIGHT
TO SAVE
THE TOWN

Reimagining
Discarded
America

MICHELLE WILDE
ANDERSON

Avid Reader Press

New York   London   Toronto   Sydney   New Delhi

AVID READER PRESS
An Imprint of Simon & Schuster, Inc.
1230 Avenue of the Americas
New York, NY 10020

Names and identifying characteristics of some individuals have been changed.

First Avid Reader Press hardcover edition June 2022

AVID READER PRESS and colophon are trademarks of Simon & Schuster, Inc.

For information about special discounts for bulk purchases, please contact Simon & Schuster Special Sales at 1-866-506-1949 or business@simonandschuster.com.

The Simon & Schuster Speakers Bureau can bring authors to your live event. For more information or to book an event contact the Simon & Schuster Speakers Bureau at 1-866-248-3049 or visit our website at www.simonspeakers.com.

Interior design by Lewelin Polanco

Manufactured in the United States of America

10 9 8 7 6 5 4 3 2 1

Library of Congress Cataloging-in-Publication Data has been applied for.

ISBN 978-1-5011-9598-3
ISBN 978-1-5011-9600-3 (ebook)

For Meda

Contents

*A bibliography is available on the book's website *

Prologue

Busted musical instruments don't play well. Cracked cellos, flutes missing keys, violins without tailpieces to hold their strings: they can't deliver notes on time, on key, or at all. Somehow, nonetheless, a composer managed to write a score for a band of old, damaged instruments collected from storage closets in Philadelphia public schools. This "Symphony for a Broken Orchestra" was performed by school children and musicians in December 2017. It was creative, chaotic, and oddly beautiful. But the point of the work was not to celebrate exceptional, against-the-odds art for its own sake, as if the instruments were just as good broken. The point was to make people care about the music students and teachers of the city's public schools. The performance raised money to buy instruments that work. "If you think about it," said composer David Lang, gesturing to a room full of damaged instruments, "this is a thousand children who could have music in their lives, who don't."

This book is not about Philly or music, or even public schools. But in its way, it tells the stories of other symphonies for broken orchestras. What's broken is our local governments in poor areas that once relied on blue-collar jobs. Forty years after the taxpayer rights revolution began limiting local government revenues, these cities and counties have run out of services to cut, properties to sell, bills to defer, and risky loans to take. They are now an unwitting test case for Grover Norquist's famous line: "I don't want to abolish government. I simply want to reduce it to the size where I can drag it into the bathroom and drown it in the bathtub." What we have learned is this: it is not just the government that we are drowning.

Yet something else is also true. In some of our poorest postindustrial places, people are fighting to make something beautiful from something broken. May these stories restore our will to help them.

THE FIGHT
TO SAVE
THE TOWN

"Aren't We the Government?"

The least visible way to steal gas from a car is to puncture the gas line with a bucket underneath. The owner ends up with an expensive repair, not just an empty tank. In Cave Junction, a town on the valley floor of Josephine County in Oregon, no one has money to waste on problems like that. When it happened to his son-in-law, Jimmy Evans had tired of that kind of trouble.

Evans, a fifty-something father of three, works at a popular butcher and meatpacking shop called Taylor's Sausage. He often covers the graveyard shift starting at three o'clock in the morning. He didn't have formal training in law enforcement, but nighttime patrols before work seemed like a way he could help. Evans and some neighbors started a group called Cave Junction Patrol to deter and interrupt crime. Eight years later, his "CJ Patrol" baseball cap has faded to match his long gray beard.

In church one Sunday in 2018, Evans heard a Harley roar past outside. "I've been doing patrol a long time," Evans says, "and so you know the sound of the vehicles. He's the guy who drops the drugs. When he comes through town, the whole place lights up with meth and heroin." It seemed like the engine slowed down by the woods behind the church. Evans knew who slept there. Her name was Maya.* She had bipolar disorder and lived on an old couch surrounded by a pool of clothes. The

---

* In nearly all cases, this book uses the full names of real people. Those persons identified only by first name have been anonymized.

man on the bike was a local predator, Evans explained, who had turned Maya into a prostitute after he got her hooked on drugs.

Excusing himself from church, Evans tried to identify the rider or see his license plate, but the Harley was gone. Soon enough, Evans heard another car park near the woods. He rushed out, thinking he could not "let this one go." He saw a pick-up truck near Maya's camp, and Evans approached to ask the driver what he was doing. The man told Evans that Maya was the mother of the baby in his backseat. The man had a restraining order against Maya, but he wanted to check on her. "It was the most beautiful baby ever," Evans told me later, going quiet.

Evans believed that he could get Maya a chance for recovery by catching the Harley rider. But if Evans had gotten the bike's plate that day, it is unlikely that much would have come of it. He had been through this drill before. He would call the sheriff's office. He'd get turned away because there was no violent crime in progress. Then he'd call the Oregon State Police, which had been patching in investigations and emergency response for the county. But their limited staff could not always dispatch for calls from Josephine County. Trying to confront the dealer or calling in his license plate put Evans at the limits of what he was willing or legally allowed to do. Any other efforts to catch, judge, or punish the man would turn Evans from a volunteer into a vigilante.

Revenue losses in 2012 had forced Josephine County officials to enact drastic budget cuts. They closed the public library and required local parks to charge admission fees. They shut down a wing of the county jail, eliminating its capacity to hold people for offenses like drunk driving and theft. More than one-third of county employees lost their jobs within five years. "I let one hundred and twenty-seven people go in one day," former County Commissioner Simon Hare said, recalling a layoff round that year. "It took me twenty-five minutes to do all of the signatures. It was really intense. I looked at every name. One hundred and twenty-seven families that'll never be the same." By 2014, Commissioner Hare had taken to quoting a song about the Great Depression, performed by the band Alabama: "Well somebody told us Wall Street fell, but we were so poor that we couldn't tell."

Back then, the county could barely provide any services other than minimal public safety and public works, plus state-mandated functions like holding elections. Even those ran on a skeleton crew. Funding evaporated for services related to public health, mental health, and child welfare. Despite the local history of catastrophic wildfires, most of the county had no publicly funded fire and ambulance services. Residents in those areas who wanted fire protection had to purchase it on a subscription basis from a for-profit company owned by a private equity firm based in New York City and a global firm based in Colorado. Hare had gone to business school before becoming commissioner. "They don't teach you how to reduce," he said. "They just teach you how to grow."

These cuts took place in the second-poorest county in Oregon. At the time of the cuts, one in five people lived below the poverty line and one in three relied on food stamps. The county's rural areas struggle with violence related to alcohol and meth addictions, and opioid use outpaces most of the country. Local common sense requires being able to distinguish a person on meth from a person on an opioid. Volunteers like Evans have trained to carry and administer Narcan injections to counteract an overdose. Ken Selig worked for the county as a deputy sheriff and medical examiner for thirty years. He is a father, so one of the hardest parts of the job was finding teenagers who had died of an overdose. He tried to tell himself it was a peaceful death, at least, as if they died in their sleep.

Across years of deep cuts to the county government accompanied by serious hardships, a particular kind of faithlessness settled in to Josephine's political culture. Between 2004 and 2016, county voters went to the polls nine times to consider revenue measures that would help revive law enforcement, reopen the library, and improve other services. Every time, a majority voted the taxes down. By 2016, the county's sheriff, Dave Daniel, was flummoxed. One argument in particular bugged him. "People say, 'Something really bad is going to have to happen before our citizenry starts supporting itself.' Really bad. Well it's already happened! It's come and gone, and it did not shake the tree at all."

Sheriff Daniel could have been referring to lots of "really bad" events. He might have meant one of the recent homicides, especially the murder of two elderly people by a stranger in their home. Or maybe Sheriff Daniel was thinking of the infamous 911 call in August 2012, when a woman reported a violent ex-boyfriend trying to break into her home. The 911 dispatcher had no one to send—the sheriff's department had no one on duty on weekends and the nearest state police officer was hours away. The dispatcher stayed on the phone for ten minutes, coaching the caller to hide or ask the man to go away, until the intruder broke into the woman's home and assaulted her. The following week, the sheriff in office at that time issued a press release warning victims of domestic violence with restraining orders to "consider relocating to an area with adequate law enforcement services." As the tragedies accumulated, local voters kept saying no new taxes.

Those events probably did shake the tree. Pretty much everyone agreed that crime was an urgent problem. Concealed carry permits for self-defense surged. That adaptation wasn't good enough, Evans explains, for the many retirees in town who "can't defend themselves the way they used to." Many people, including Sheriff Daniel, felt that as law enforcement in Josephine continued to dwindle, the county would attract more serious crime. Drugs would get worse, the sellers more violent. "If you don't pull out the dressers every now and then to clean out the house spiders," says local leader and activist Kate Dwyer, "you get black widows. There is a niche for a top predator." What residents did not agree on was whether new funds for government could help.

Meanwhile, state and federal lawmakers were losing their will to keep sending emergency funds to Josephine and other rural Oregon counties. They argued that people in Josephine needed to do more to help themselves by passing a ballot measure for new local taxes. It was not enough that sizable minorities had voted to approve levies in the past. Residents who supported new taxes had to find a way to start winning.

To solve their problems, residents would have to work together. But people in Josephine had been on their own for years—whether it was Maya battling addiction, or Evans trying to help her, or any resident worried about rising crime. Isolation started a vicious cycle that undermined the trust needed for cooperation.

There is more to say about how Josephine County got to this point. There is much more to say about the road residents are building to get past it. This book is about what happens when local governments and other shared institutions empty out in places where people still live. It is about what happens when residents fight to save their town.

FIRST BROKE, THEN FAITHLESS

The problem of citywide poverty

Josephine County is one of four places explored up close in the chapters that follow. I'll introduce the other three in a moment, but their stories and this book are rooted in a national problem. American poverty is stacking up in particular cities, towns, and counties. When local governments are populated mostly by low-income people, there is typically much less money for public services. Weak, broke local governments make it harder for residents to lead decent lives on low incomes or get their families out of poverty. Entire towns become poverty traps.

I'll shorthand this problem as "citywide poverty" or "border-to-border low-income" towns.* Incomes are depressed across much of the town, not just in small pockets. Sociologists can (and I hope will) develop a more refined metric for this idea, but for the purposes of this book I will use these two terms to refer to (1) a single municipality (whether a city, town, or village) or the unincorporated areas of a rural county government (2) that serves a population in which at least 20 percent of residents live under the poverty line, where (3) median incomes are less than two-thirds of the state median income. Combined, these metrics describe a local jurisdiction with widespread poverty as well as fewer people living at higher incomes.

Even before the Great Recession, citywide poverty was a growing problem. Between 2000 and 2009, there was a 31 percent increase in the number of municipalities, counties, and census-designated places where at least one in five people live under the poverty line. In 2020 numbers, the term "poverty line" stands for the hard reality of a family of four living on less than $26,246 per year—less than $2,200 a month

---

* In this book, I'll use the words "towns" and "cities" to refer to municipal governments.

in pretax income. The Foreclosure Crisis made matters worse, by divest-ing so many low- and middle-income homeowners of both their home and their only economic asset.

Places of citywide poverty vary. Some are big cities, small cities, or historic suburbs. Others are rural. Some vote blue, others red. Some are nearly all white, all Black, all Latino, or all Native American.* Some are the most diverse communities in America. Racial and eth-nic violence, segregation, and discrimination helps explain how some border-to-border poor places developed, and why they remain poor. Citywide poor places may have held their population or shrunk. They may have always been low-income, or were once known for a strong working class, or once had pockets of wealth. Some are literally poor from border to border, others still have a few comfortable blocks or neighborhoods with lovingly tended homes. Most have low rates of col-lege attainment, which makes it harder for residents to find a job with a livable income.

Citywide poverty is distinct from, but related to, the way people sort at bigger scales (the region) and at smaller ones (the neighbor-hood). Since 1980, the wealthiest regions of the country have seen in-comes increase much faster than the modest gains elsewhere, leading to stark regional inequality. In thirty-one states, one or two metropoli-tan areas account for more than half the state's gross domestic product (GDP). The most familiar example of this pattern is New York City, where the metro area accounts for 80 percent of New York state's total GDP. Most of the country is heading in the same direction. The Boston region drives more than three-quarters of the Massachusetts economy, though the state has 10,000 square miles with about 350 towns and cities. In Oregon and Washington, the metro regions of Portland and Seattle are thriving while huge areas of their states struggle. Same in

---

* This book capitalizes Black in order to acknowledge the global history, politics, and culture behind that term. I do not capitalize white, however, given the history of that term when capitalized as a signal for hate and subordination. I have chosen to use the word Latino rather than Latino/a or Latinx as a reflection of the predomi-nant self-identification my interviewees used in Stockton, Lawrence, and Detroit.

North Carolina beyond the Charlotte and Triangle regions; Iowa apart from Des Moines; Georgia outside Atlanta. Chicago's economic output not only drives the Illinois economy but surpasses adjacent Ohio's entire GDP.

Weak regions lacked the assets, good fortune, and strong networks needed to transform historic manufacturing centers into nodes of the knowledge economy. They never developed a nationally competitive hub for finance, insurance, law, and real estate services, as in New York City, Chicago, and Philadelphia. Some had colleges, but not the STEM-focused research universities of Boston, Pittsburgh, and the San Francisco Bay Area. Some regions had spectacular natural amenities, but they were too far from growing metros with growing paychecks to take off as major tourist destinations. They never had the luck of rearing business giants who came back to their hometowns (as in Seattle), nor the substantial government operations of cities such as D.C. or Atlanta. What is the future for the towns beyond the biggest metros in Pennsylvania, Kentucky, California, Texas, Maine, and many other states?

Many municipalities of citywide poverty are located in weaker regions, including in historic industrial areas carved up into dozens of small municipal governments. Each one must carry its own budget, elected officials, and employees. But citywide poverty can be found in strong, growing regions, too, which often have a mix of high-income and low-income suburbs. When wealthier suburbs use their land-use authority to block multifamily housing that low-wage workers can afford, these workers must crowd into low-income suburbs with cheaper housing.

Just as border-to-border poor municipalities are affected by the regions "above," they are affected by the neighborhoods "below." By definition, border-to-border poor cities encompass multiple poor neighborhoods. At least since the publication of William Julius Wilson's *The Truly Disadvantaged* in 1987, sociologists have shown how much neighborhoods matter. They shape safety, economic opportunities, and environmental conditions. With the rise of giant data sets and the computing tools to investigate them, economists and sociologists have confirmed and further explored how the neighborhood around a household can depress a child's *lifetime* income and educational outcomes.

Citywide poverty is not demonstrably "worse" (however one might define that word) than neighborhood or regional poverty. A household can face serious hardships whether it is rooted in a poor region, a poor city, a poor neighborhood, or all of the above. But the problem of local governments that serve high-poverty neighborhoods across most of their territory represents a specific and understudied pattern. Shallow tax bases in jurisdictions of high need depress revenues. Federal and state governments can and do share revenues with all local governments, including poor ones. But apart from a temporary bump during the COVID-19 pandemic, the state and the federal proportion of local revenues has been in decline for decades.

That means cities and counties become more reliant on revenues from local taxes, fines, and fees. If a city's housing stock and job base is in decline, those forces will drag down property values, which in turn drag down property tax revenues. Decreased investments in new buildings and renovations not only reinforce physical decline, they generate fewer permitting fees for local governments. Shrinking commercial districts generate fewer sales tax revenues. Same for revenues on other transactions that some states allow their municipalities to tax, such as payrolls, hotel stays, restaurant tabs, alcohol sales, real estate transfers, and business licenses.

When local governments have less money coming in, they can take out debt, raise local taxes and fees, lay off staff, and sell public land. They can (and nearly always do) defer improvements to obsolete infrastructure and technology, and keep using worn-out buildings, vehicles, and equipment. High-poverty cities and counties pay their employees less for work that is higher risk and more challenging. Many defer compensation for employees by offering pension benefits rather than competitive salaries, and then they can't save the money needed to meet those pension contracts. Their politicians try to bundle subsidies and tax breaks to lure big employers, but they compete with so many other local governments that the "winning" municipality typically gets a political victory but loses money over the life of the deal. Border-to-border places have become infamous for the worst revenue-raising technique of all—many have developed elaborate, regressive schemes of civil and criminal code enforcement for the purpose of extracting fines and fees from residents and drivers passing through town.

Each of these moves makes the city less livable for residents and businesses. In public services, as in so much of life, you get what you pay for, which drives the gaping inequality among cities. Decades into a process of fiscal decline, a local government will have no more loans to take, taxes to raise, services to privatize, or assets worth selling. As the city reduces or eliminates staff, local government seems less competent and more irritating. Infrastructure and public space decays. "It's death by a thousand cuts," says Reverend Joan Ross of Detroit, referring to the city's collapse in services. "It takes you a long time to bleed to death. But you do."

This book chronicles the human wounds left by decades of deep cuts to local government. Excluding education, broke local governments typically spend most of their budgets on emergencies and public safety alone. That would include police dispatch for violent crimes, under-resourced fire protection with aging equipment, emergency public works (such as repair of an erupting water main), and the maintenance of aging sanitation systems. School districts continue to manage education, albeit with terrible budget woes of their own, but many city and town governments are no longer pursuing a vision beyond reactive public safety. Containment, rather than betterment, defines the character of public services. People with choices choose to leave. For those who stay behind, this war of attrition makes them more trapped and more poor.

We have left local governments and other shared institutions to fade where people need them most. To achieve self-sufficiency—including the option to move to a place with better opportunities—poor residents need local governments that work. They can't afford to pay out of pocket for everything they need, including safe drinking water, sewage disposal, flood control, sidewalks, internet access, and good police. They may need libraries, buses to get to work, or community colleges to reach for better jobs. If those opportunities come at too steep a price, they cannot pay it. Yet among local government functions, only K-12 public school (about 6.5 hours per day for 180 days a year) is broadly guaranteed by law.

Depleted local governments do not mean that residents live without any government at all. On the contrary, the state is dominant in our poorest places. But it is not necessarily there to help. Other than local police and public schools, the face of government in urban and rural areas of concentrated poverty has increasingly become state systems—like civil courts enforcing eviction and foreclosure orders, criminal courts, prisons, child welfare systems. From afar, the federal government enacts tax, environmental, labor, or trade policies that many low-income households expect will reduce their incomes. Foreign policy actions affect immigrants' home nations, and immigration laws separate residents from loved ones. Actions by higher tiers of government have the power to trigger severe hardships in a person's life, including the loss of liberty, a child, a parent, a home, or a job.

In declining areas, residents look around and ask, "What is standing between me and the life I want?" They find answers. Across the political spectrum, it is easy to conclude that the problem is government action, not government absence. Low-income people have too many experiences of government that punishes, delays, or collects. They have too few experiences of government that prevents problems, invests in their future, or improves their quality of life. The far left and the far right, the poorest urban and the poorest rural communities, rarely agree about government's potential to improve. But they often share a deep cynicism that, as currently run, their governments have the public interest at heart.

Our smallest governments are at the frontlines of both the perception and the reality of American government. They affect people's safety, comfort, and life chances. They can create, protect, or destroy wealth. When they work well, city and county governments help children do better than their parents. When they do not, they help seal the economic fate now associated with childhood zip code. Local governments do not just reflect inequality. They help drive it.

LEARNING FROM FOUR PLACES

Discarded, Reimagined America

The chapters that follow are written portraits of places. For better or worse, the writer fell in love with her subjects. They reassured me that progress against the hardships of citywide poverty is possible.

Each town was a toiling labor colony of the First Gilded Age, a hometown of the mid-century middle class, and, by late century, a crater of postindustrialism. Each was once famous: for industrial prowess, for labor uprisings, for the booming West, for immigrant diversity, for wartime productivity, for working-class homeownership, and for the textiles, timber, shoes, food products, or cars that their people made. Their physical environments show this common heritage: neighborhoods with modest houses, shuttered mill buildings, contaminated land, and obsolete infrastructure. Their social environments do, too. Households are held back not just by lower levels of college attainment, but also lower levels of literacy. The same freeways, train lines, and rivers that once made these places good at moving products in the industrial economy now make them convenient for moving illicit drugs. Drug trafficking brings addiction and child neglect, as well as guns.

Marking their century-long cycle of poverty to prosperity to poverty again, this book brings these places together on the terms of their latest linked fate. The twenty-first century, and especially the Great Recession, has slammed these towns' residents and their government finances. If you look at a curve of the number of manufacturing jobs in the United States, it bounces up and down between 1970 and 2000, ranging from a high of 19.6 million jobs to a low of 16.8 million. Then in 2000 it crashes, diving to 11.5 million jobs by 2010. The manufacturing sector had continued to grow, but the number of manufacturing *jobs* had fallen steeply. Those job losses were concentrated in places where industry had flourished in the early twentieth century—hubs of steel production, coal mining, consumer product manufacturing, and related industries. The low-wage service sector became the main supplier of jobs for workers without college degrees. Labor economist

Enrico Moretti captured the result: "Today an American is significantly more likely to work in a restaurant than a factory."

Places of citywide poverty in the Rust Belt and Sun Belt took some of the hardest losses from the Foreclosure Crisis. Despite the historic economic expansion that followed the recession, 2010 to 2020 is referred to as a "lost decade" for state and local government finance, because those governments were never able to make up for deep, sustained losses after the crash. The places in this book, like dozens of other towns in America, had fallen so short of revenues by 2012 that their local governments began slashing their staff and budgets. Just before or during these difficult years, each of the places in this book went through a harmful cycle of weak management, if not corruption, which further stigmatized their governments at a time of peak economic vulnerability.

The fifty states reacted to local fiscal crisis in different ways. Some, notably California and Alabama, authorized their most financially distressed cities to file for bankruptcy. Northeastern states (including Pennsylvania, Massachusetts, New York, and Rhode Island) refined receivership programs in which state officials support or take over a city's finances. Michigan intensified its receivership program while also allowing its biggest city to file for bankruptcy. Other states, such as Oregon, took over specific public services that insolvent local governments could no longer afford. Most southern states did nothing, leaving local governments to cut their budgets and face their creditors in court. A few, like Missouri and Tennessee, arguably did worse than nothing, by further constraining their local governments without giving them better choices.

In the face of all these hardships, advocates in the four places profiled in this book found a way forward. This book tells the story of that progress in the 2016–2020 period. Leaders took advantage of post-recession growth to stabilize their finances. New leadership improved the reputation of their governments. Community groups sought new strategies to stop violence and heal its damage. Drawing on a heritage of resilience wired in town culture, local institutions went to the heart of the employment and housing challenges straining their families. Stockton, Lawrence, and Detroit pursued the moral imperative of distributing opportunity into communities of color in ways that earlier generations of working-class cities had failed to do. When the COVID-19 pandemic health and unemployment crisis hit these towns in 2020, the institutions and networks built in the years before became more important than ever.

The communities in this book are unique, distinct from one another and the rest of America. I am not claiming they are representative of other places, nor that they are progressing systematically faster than other places. I chose them for this book because I found them to be good teachers. In their particulars and in juxtaposition, these places demonstrate how chronic, citywide poverty emerges. The communities' differences (in terms of urbanization level, racial composition, and politics) help see similar problems from different angles, and distinct characteristics from one. Each place has advocates focused on four of the biggest problems in poor places: trauma from violence; mistrust of law enforcement; the skills gap; and unstable, unsafe housing.

While the places covered here run west to east, they are only in the political "blue" or "purple" states of the American north. Towns in so-called "red states" have good work underway too, and their challenges are comparable. Some of the most entrenched poverty and brokest, smallest local governments in America are in the Deep South, the Southwest, the inner-mountain west, the plains, and the solid red states of the Rust Belt and Appalachia. But pathways toward solutions in those places will have to be different. Their constitutions and state laws lock their governments in even tighter revenue and tax controls than other states, which means they lack the legal authority to do much beyond rudimentary services (often by contract) and business development. State electorates can reform those powers, but state-level reform movements are a subject for another book. So in the end, this book drops anchor in two conservative local communities, but none where citywide poverty is wired into state law.

STOCKTON (CHAPTER 1)

Satellite images of California show a network of water veins that carry the state's inland rivers to the San Francisco Bay and the Pacific Ocean.

These are the wetlands of the Delta, a region at the northern end of the San Joaquin Valley. The Delta hosts a giant water engineering system that transforms what would be floodlands into one of the world's most important breadbaskets. Stockton is a waterfront city on this Delta, set apart from the eastern cities of the San Francisco Bay Area by a long stretch of dry grasses across a mountain pass. Sometimes these yellow grasses look inhospitable, without a tree in sight. But when the sun hits them at the right angle, they look like another reason California is called the Golden State.

If you could trace Stockton's bloodlines like its waterways, they would fan across the globe. Across its history, the city and its region have drawn refugees and seekers from around the world, making Stockton the most diverse city in America. A representative group of twenty residents would include about eight Latinos, four Asian-Americans, four white people, two African-Americans, one Native American, and a multiracial child of one of the nation's highest metropolitan rates of intermarriage. The chronically low wages of farm work and food processing, the automation and offshoring of much of the city's manufacturing, and entrenched racial segregation have kept much of Stockton's population both poor and politically weak. During the Great Recession, Stockton faced a higher rate of foreclosures than any city in the nation, except Detroit.

Modern Stockton, home to more than 300,000 people, is a politically "purple" city in a conservative rural region. Until the Great Recession pushed the city into bankruptcy, which challenged business-as-usual city politics, Stockton's elected officials of both parties were beholden to real estate developers. They pushed the city to subsidize new suburban neighborhoods and redevelop the downtown, rather than to reinvest in the people or environments of older neighborhoods.

For decades, police and prisons were the city's main answer to the dangerous synergy of chronic economic stress, drug markets, and gun violence in the city's many poor areas. This approach will one day be as discredited as the era of treating pneumonia with bloodletting, or syphilis with mercury pills. Stockton is seeking better answers. For the first time, the city has a critical mass of leaders inside and outside government who are facing the high levels of exposure to local violence.

Trauma counseling now works to heal victims, witnesses, and survivors of violence. Community groups are reclaiming sidewalks and public spaces to allow people free movement outdoors. Their work is not only a humanitarian intervention, it is a public safety strategy. A community of people is finally trying, in the words of youth and racial justice leader Raymond Aguilar, "to really fix the broken pieces of what Stockton has become."

JOSEPHINE COUNTY (CHAPTER 2)

Southern Oregon, which includes Josephine, is one of the most beautiful regions in the United States. The Siskiyou Mountains lift some of the tallest trees on earth closer to the sky. Three wild rivers cut whitewater canyons above seams of gold and copper. Fertile valleys can grow everything from berries to hops, gladiolas to melons. The economy has boomed and busted twice, first on gold, then on timber. A new rush is now afoot: the region has proven ideal for cultivating marijuana. "It's the Climate," explains the sign across the largest town's main street. Rain and sun. More than 80,000 people call Josephine home.

Rural Josephine County has long attracted people looking for more than fertile land. They wanted to escape things: taxes, suburban materialism, child support debt, homophobia, arrest warrants, the urban cost of living, day jobs, nuclear annihilation, clothing, California. They came to find liberty, off the grid and in the forest. Since others did too, they found a freedom lacking social conformity. "We all celebrate to our own peculiar temperaments," a local publisher wrote in 1907. As a modern-day local put it, "Josephine County has very little racial diversity, but there is every conceivable way of being a white person here."

Josephine County, far West and far right, has managed one of the most extreme anti-government experiments in contemporary America. At first glance, the budget cuts to law enforcement and jails described earlier in this introduction may look like the changes called for by criminal justice reformers. But calls to "defund the police" accompany calls to shift resources toward other forms of violence prevention and conflict mediation. In Josephine, local officials cut law enforcement funding as an emergency budget measure following cuts to everything else too. To recommit to any public role at all in reducing crime has required nothing less than a grassroots, pro-tax social movement in one of the most anti-government counties in America.

LAWRENCE (CHAPTER 3)

Arriving in Lawrence, Massachusetts, on I-495 from Boston, you see the Merrimack River turn a broad curve through the center of town. Brick mills stand on either side of the river, with hundreds of symmetrical windows set under hand-built arches. The scale of the buildings conveys the city's former significance: if you stood one of these mills on end, it would be taller than the Empire State Building. Some of the glass in the windows is broken or boarded, but most of it still reflects the sky.

In the early twentieth century, those mills teemed, each like its own small city, with workers drawn from fifty-one nations. In the Bread & Roses Strike of 1912, mill workers rose up to help battle the dangerous poverty of the First Gilded Age in one of the nation's most effective labor uprisings. Elizabeth Gurley Flynn, one of the strike leaders, paraphrased Voltaire to remark on the advance of history in Lawrence. Referring to the clatter of Belgian immigrants' wooden shoes in the mills, she said, "Ever the velvet slippers coming down the stairs of history and the wooden shoes going up!" Yet the city's businesses moved and shrank so much that by the 1980s, there were fewer footsteps of any kind in the mills. The velvet-slipper set was back in charge. The people of Lawrence became low-wage workers in the Second Gilded Age service economy of the high-tech Route 128 corridor. Former President Trump and recent governors in Maine and New Hampshire have blamed Lawrence for the regional opioid crisis, stigmatizing the city as a place that needs more police to crack down, as Maine's former governor Paul LePage put it, on "Black and Hispanic" drug dealers.

Lawrence's population changed during the century, but the city never stopped earning its nickname the "Immigrant City." Puerto Ricans recruited as farmworkers to Massachusetts in the 1940s and '50s began to settle in Lawrence, establishing a Spanish-speaking home base that drew in later Puerto Ricans, as well as Dominicans. Some came straight to Lawrence to escape poverty, or U.S.-backed authoritarianism in the Dominican Republic. Others fled unemployment and the heroin and crack cocaine epidemics of the 1970s to the 1990s in New York City. Caribbean footfalls later carved space for other refugees and economic migrants from Central America and points south, earning Lawrence a second nickname as the "Latino City."

The strike tactics of Bread and Roses days are mostly unusable in today's economy. The city's population works for hundreds of employers in dozens of industries, scattered all across the region. Yet today, as then, Lawrence should be known for mobilizing its people to raise adult wages. And today, as then, Lawrence's leaders are forming strong, multiethnic networks among residents, then mobilizing those networks to make government better. In so doing, they have taken their city back from "machine politics" and transformed the work of the city's government: focusing it on the needs and futures of the city's residents, not on outside private interests.

DETROIT (CHAPTER 4)

I was not a fan of Motown before starting this book. Like most Americans, I could hum and sing along to classics like "Dancing in the Street" and "You Can't Hurry Love." But I thought Motown songs were just too sweet and . . . *peppy*. I began to hear those songs differently as I let Detroit's writers and people teach me the history of Black Detroit. In the Hitsville heyday of the 1960s, the city's most important Black neighborhoods had just been ground under by bulldozers. Discriminatory rents and wages had long gouged Black households, and the demolitions intensified desperate shortages of housing just as the city lost its industrial job base. Motown's romantic, vibrant beats were rebellious in their way—an insistence on Black joy and perseverance. Motown was a celebration of life, love, neighborhood, and family, come what may.

To hear this meaning in Motown reveals an even more moving truth about the music and the city still to come. In 1971, Detroiter Marvin Gaye left behind the defiant optimism of his Motown Gold hits to release "Inner City Blues." Human resilience, Gaye seemed to be show-ing, comes not just from celebration and gratitude. Resilience is rooted in mourning for that which has been lost. It encompasses self-respect. Gaye, and generations of the city's musicians and artists, offer nourish-ment for survival *as well as a demand for change*. That, I have gotten to see, is Black Detroit.

That fortitude has been more necessary than ever, as the city's housing markets cycled through a devastating era of exploitation in the 1970s, only to be outdone during the Foreclosure Crisis of the late 2000s. The Great Recession brought a decade of housing foreclosures (and a bankruptcy crisis) that turned over the ownership of nearly half of the homes in the city. Outsiders came buying, and today, in this symbolic capital of Black homeownership, a majority of households in the city are tenants. As has been true across most of the city's modern history, Detroit is better understood as a symbol of the African Ameri-can struggle to escape the debt peonage of the Jim Crow South and to secure basic autonomy through land ownership.

Detroit is diversifying faster than any other big city, but that future stands on the rubble of what Black Detroit has lost. So Detroit's resi-dents are drawing on a heritage of resilience to invent ways to block dis-placement and restore Black land ownership. As scrappy and insurgent as it has ever been, Detroit is reaching for a twenty-first-century vision of reconstruction and reparations.

Individuals and industries have long tied these places, and others of citywide poverty, together. Lines of internal migration have moved whole communities among these places, some on journeys that were hopeful, others that were desperate. The Ohio River, which originates just downstream from the low-income town of Braddock, Pennsylvania, later runs through the broke city of Portsmouth, Ohio, and on to Mis-sissippi. The Ohio served as a conduit for enslaved people "sold down the river" from Kentucky to face the cruelty of Mississippi cotton plan-tations. One or two generations later, some of their descendants fled the violence and entrapment of sharecropping by heading west to Stockton and California's Central Valley. Once there, they joined migrants from

Southeast Asia in a cannery strike for fair wages led by a subsidiary of the union at the helm of the Bread and Roses Strike in Lawrence. Today, the border-to-border low-income towns of Yazoo City in the Mississippi Delta and the rural areas of Kings County in California's Central Valley both rely on federal prisons as their primary job base. Andrew Carnegie built an early twentieth century anti-union steel empire in the Monongahela Valley, then established a philanthropic legacy that is chipping away at the margins of citywide poverty in towns across the country. A billionaire currently remaking downtown Detroit built his fortune in a mortgage industry that confiscated a generation of wealth in Sun Belt and Rust Belt cities alike.

This is a book about four places, for the sake of many others. At a time of faithlessness about the future, the people in the pages to come have helped me imagine—believe—that a time could come when we'd look back on the narrowing of racial, economic, and spatial inequality and describe how we did it.

"WHAT WOULD I DO IF I WON?"

Listening for Solutions

The road to this book began in the Great Recession and Foreclosure Crisis, which triggered the biggest surge in municipal bankruptcy and fiscal distress since the Great Depression. I did a national study of all the local governments that entered a state program for fiscal crisis, then looked in depth at several states' specific legal systems governing taxes, budget insolvency, and local government power.

Across these years of research, I observed one dynamic above all. These local governments were not just broke, they governed poor people. They were broke mostly *because* their people were poor. And their people stayed poor in part because they were broke. But state legal systems for local fiscal crisis were not designed for anti-poverty work. They tried to clear out some debt, shirk a few contracts, and generate some cash from selling the governments' properties.

I thought this book would be about the problem of citywide poverty and broke governments. Why, where, and how does poverty stack up within single jurisdictions? What happens when it does? What kinds of mistakes have local governments made trying to manage it? How do border-to-border low-income governments raise and spend money compared to mixed or wealthy ones? Advocates facing these issues already know what they are up against, but they did not seem to realize how many communities were in the same situation.

Those plans for a problem-centered book evolved in 2017 in Lawrence. I was at a fundraiser for a nonprofit where I ended up chatting with Joshua Alba, a wise twenty-something working at a youth arts program. "Anything top down will be an injustice here," Alba said. Policymakers "can't just come in and address the big issues quickly." But at the grassroots level, there was no obvious strategy. Alba told me he had considered running for city council, but he was wrestling with the question: "What would I do if I won?" He thought Lawrence needed a progressive city government platform, but wasn't sure what that looked like for such a poor city.

I wanted to be useful to people like Alba, whether they plan to run for elected office or want to fight for their town in other ways. A book that began with the (admittedly terrible) placeholder title *Living Places, Dying Governments* evolved into one called *The Fight to Save the Town*. Meanwhile, Alba ran successfully for the school board, where he is developing his own vision of a progressive platform for Lawrence. I came to think of this book as a way of sharing information among people already serving their towns and a way of recruiting others to join their work.

Alba was right about the limits of top-down solutions. The answers that people in border-to-border low-income places had found through trial and error were more valuable than those I could find by reading. So I went looking for people who understood the challenge of citywide poverty. Answers could not just come from local governments, because they were too broke and denuded of staff to accomplish enough on their own. Any fight to save the town in the United States today involves the private sector too; especially nonprofits working alongside government to make sure people in town have more choices and chances.

Such experts were easy to find. The research base for this book includes more than 250 interviews, primarily between 2016 and 2020.

The people I met with showed me around their towns, took me to community meetings and events, and reflected on their work. These experts included mayors and nonprofit leaders, cops and teachers, priests and parents, shopkeepers and artists, bankers and builders, coaches and counselors. Some have book smarts and others street smarts, but they all apply what they know to their community's problems. Some are elected themselves, while others work in coalition to keep elected officials accountable to residents.

To borrow the words of Lawrence-born poet Robert Frost, these advocates are moving even on this, "the darkest evening of the year." They "have miles to go before [they] sleep." No matter. These chapters are stories of journeys, not destinations. Pretty quickly, and also by chance in Lawrence, I found a good term to describe the core of what their work was all about.

NEXT GENERATION GATEWAY CITIES

Resident-Centered Governance

Lawmakers in Massachusetts (and, increasingly, in other places) call early industrial hubs "gateway cities," because they gave new immigrants a first home and job in America. I came to think of the term in a second, socioeconomic way as well. A gateway city also helps poor families build economic security and find a decent quality of life, whether they stay in town or move away. A gateway city is a good way to describe the alternative to a poverty trap.

What work is needed to turn declining blue-collar communities back into gateway cities? The American commitment to economic mobility turns on this project. The American commitment to equal opportunity depends on it too, because our poorest communities are among our most racially and ethnically diverse.

A gateway city neither pushes people to move, nor locks them into place. It gives them choices. Jessica Andors, a local leader in Lawrence, put it well: "Lawrence should be good enough to get a good start. It should be a healthy enough community that people can come in here, be welcome, learn English, retain their own language and culture, pass that on to their kids. And get a start, even if they do move out and go other places." It's not that she or others described in this book want their college graduates or most economically stable residents to leave town. These advocates are working hard to build the town's business community, improve the efficacy of the government workforce, role model the value of education for children, and reinforce civic engagement. But people should not be staying because they cannot afford to leave. And above all, they should not be staying because their hometown broke them with trauma, addiction, and hopelessness.

This book chronicles good work toward a gateway-city vision for Stockton, Josephine, Lawrence, and Detroit. It is about several of the most fundamental ingredients of flourishing and opportunity: mental health, personal safety, access to living wage jobs, and secure housing. It is about ways to put current residents at the center of governance— not some future population who might be recruited to live in the city, not outside businesses who might be incentivized to move to town, not suburbanites or tourists who might spend a few dollars in town, not contractors who want a piece of the city budget.

Education, of course, is central to gateway-city work, but this book is not about K-12 education. *The Fight to Save the Schools* is a book for another day. The way school districts are run and financed is connected to local organizing and town government to be sure, but in most states, school districts have much higher levels of centralized state funding and different management constraints. And K-12 education, unlike any of the other services explored in this book, is guaranteed by state law. There are legal grounds, not just political ones, to fight back when it is cut and minimized beyond recognition.

But the efforts described here do support schools and children. Even the best teachers and schools cannot save children from the migratory instability created by evictions, unlivable family wages, and traumatizing violence. This book explores what can be done outside a classroom in order for children to thrive inside. It asks what role local governments can play in preparing their residents—adults and children alike—for the higher skilled occupations for which the United States remains competitive in the global economy.

Because these stories of social change are true, they are not facile stories of brave leaders in red capes. Instead of waiting for transformative leaders or programs, the people in this book keep working at their challenges. Individuals matter—there are many described here in the admiring tones they deserve. Programs also matter. Some approaches to social problems are more effective than others. But when complex problems accumulate over decades, with no single villain to vanquish, they take time, networks, and experiments to solve. Although this book names individuals and organizations, it is ultimately about how they work together. It is about all the unnamed people who stand with them.

Nothing in these chapters will make a reader think, "They've got this." High-poverty places are up against ferocious headwinds mostly beyond their control: the widening income gulf between the richest Americans and the service workers their lifestyles demand; the federal and state anti-tax activism that has constrained government from creating the kind of middle class the United States enjoyed fifty years ago; two generations of disinvestment combined with racial and socioeconomic discrimination in public policy; the deceptive marketing and overprescription of opioids, which has led to a historic addiction and overdose crisis; the loans taken and pensions promised by prior generations of leaders; the easy availability of guns, both legal and illegal; and more. The hardships in these cities will overwhelm readers sometimes, as they did me.

They don't "got this," but as with the "Symphony for a Broken Orchestra" described in the Prologue, these places make me think: if advocates can do the work described here under their current constraints, what might be possible if outsiders did more to help? What might be possible if we reduced those headwinds and freed the capacity in these places? The point of the Symphony was not to get a standing ovation for triumphing over mangled instruments. It was to remind the public of the meaning and potential of music so they would give a damn.

So I think of the chapters that follow more like a "proof of concept" than a "how-to." The concept to prove is that progress is possible. To restore political will for action, we need to replace a discourse of lost causes with one about good causes. We have to look for improvement, not just transformation.

If the resident-centered networks described in this book could be summed up by a single photo, it might be one from a different border-to-border town. The photo depicts a blue message spray painted on the concrete walkway of an old pedestrian bridge in Braddock, Pennsylvania. The scene is gray and rainy. Pools of water reflect crisscrossing steel overhead and a chain link fence enclosing the sides. Braddock is one of the highest-poverty towns in the state, but the message does not say, "Welcome to Hell" or "God save us." In careful, looping blue cursive, it says, "we will grow." Braddock has been losing population for decades. Surely the person who wrote that knew the town was unlikely to grow its population or GDP. But I don't read the message to be about those metrics. I like to think the growth they had in mind was more like healing, changing, and learning. And whatever they meant, "we will grow" is a better way to live.

The people in this book are working together to make their towns better places to grow—for anyone who needs or chooses it as their home, for as long as they do so. If they choose to leave to seek new opportunities and experiences elsewhere, an American gateway city will have done its job.

OF HELLHOLES, CROOKS, AND HEROES

Stopping the Self-Fulfilling Prophecy of Decline

I hate to delay you from meeting Stockton, a city that embodies so much of American history. But I feel compelled to offer one last frame. It's my answer to this question: why is this a narrative book, rather than a data, law, or policy book?

The more I learned about these four places and those facing similar challenges, the more I came to believe that the way we talk and write about them is not only wrong, it is destructive. The prevailing narratives about high-poverty places fuel the cycle of poor and broke, broke and poor.

Our first distortion is to characterize America's poorest places as "dying," as if they were coming to the end of a lifespan. Cities have no inherent expiration date. The oldest on Earth are more than 10,000 years old. Yet academics and journalists describe hollowing cities and rural decline as if nature was just taking her course. Some of this eulogistic writing records memories of a place, as though it is already lost. It is a version of "ruin porn," a critical way to describe photography of vines growing over abandoned buildings, burned out cars catching the sunlight just so, swingsets with no swings. Such work may be art or historical documentation. Its melancholy nostalgia may be beautiful. But it is misleading and harmful if taken as a portrait of a place where people still live.

The dismantling of civil society does not matter where tumbleweeds have taken over. A ghost town needs no cops because it has no robbers.* But the United States has a much harder and more common problem today, in which shrinking governments are charged with protecting living people. Whatever their future, those communities have a present. Waves of residents may have left, but hundreds of thousands remain. Detroit is haunted by absence, but its population is still larger than that of Washington, D.C. It remains the biggest city in its state, like the troubled city of Newark. Cleveland and Buffalo have less than half their peak populations, but each retains more than 250,000 people. California cities like San Bernardino and Merced never depopulated; indeed, they have desperately tried to solve their fiscal problems through growth. Despite decades stuck in poverty, Helena, Arkansas, and Harlan County, Kentucky, still raise tens of thousands of school children.

Along with sad stories of urban "dying," writing and speeches about high-poverty cities often read like gritty true-crime drama, with corrupt politicians, drugs, and guns. "City of Ruins" and "Apocalypse, New Jersey" (headlines about Camden, New Jersey) or "American Carnage" (the theme of Former President Trump's inaugural address) are spectacles of this kind of writing. *Forbes* magazine and various click-bait blogs publish annual rankings of the "most miserable cities in America." In at least three of the "winning" places ranked by *Forbes*, I heard about people

---

* I do not believe that the best answer for robbers is always cops. But my argument in the text stands.

who had burned the magazine at a community event. They were trying to turn the moment into underdog solidarity to shake off the insult of more dehumanizing press.

If voters and policymakers think the problem with a poor place is that it's empty or mismanaged, they'll also assume heroes can turn the city around. Urban "pioneers" can repopulate it, they'll imagine, building "homesteads" that reclaim unused land. A great mayor can clean up city government, making good policy choices that lead the city back to prosperity. Benevolent CEOs can open warehouses or factories there and valiantly restore the job base.

Stories of hellholes, crooks, and heroes often have a veneer of empathy for the people living there. We feel sorry for them. But outlandish violence, with no acknowledgment of the people who care emotionally and physically for the wounded, makes a place seem unrecognizably dystopic. Stories of mismanagement make poverty and fiscal crisis seem self-inflicted. Outsiders take away an excuse for inaction, because action seems hopeless, dangerous, or foolish. This style of writing is tinged with voyeurism, as if written for readers who will never go to that place but feel curious about it. It gives a peephole through deep social divides. I think it is pitched particularly at high-income readers wanting to see inside low-income urban neighborhoods or rural areas known for intergenerational poverty. The wondering itself is not wrong—we'd be better off if social walls had many more holes in them. Better still if the holes were so big we walked through them to help and be helped. But any holes made by writing have to describe true pictures. That means more than bullets and blight.

Cities don't get eviction orders enforced by a sheriff, but our stories of urban and rural "death" function as a self-fulfilling prophecy of atrophy and attrition. Residents who believe a place is going to hell will want to get the hell out. Those who are less likely to stay are less likely to vote, invest in improvements, open businesses, or run for office. The same disinvestment sets in for outsiders, as state and federal taxpayers decide they are tired of subsidizing government services to try to slow decline that seems unstoppable. In interviews for this book, several people told me that their local government could not "cut its way to prosperity." They rarely bothered to say the corollary they took for granted: a local government can cut its way to further decline.

When so much stigma accumulates under a town's name that progress seems impossible, it not only promotes non-intervention, it also undermines every one of the more activist public policy solutions to urban and rural decline. Dystopic writing helps perpetuate a dynamic similar to the one Mitchell Duneier has called the "pernicious circular logic of the ghetto." Disinvestment, isolation, and segregation bring about deterioration and crime, which in turn help rationalize further disinvestment and exclusion.

Hellhole stories feed both the invention and failure of what I think of as *suitcase solutions*. Some commenters argue that when decline seems more like a trajectory than a rough patch, residents should move out of the city or region. Since no one seems to know "quite how to pick rural America up," wrote one editorial, "maybe it is time to pack rural America up." Rust Belt towns have heard such arguments for decades. Across the political spectrum, moving toward jobs is supposed to be built into American culture. But when people associate poor cities with high rates of crime and corruption, it is hard to motivate the largescale investments that would be needed to bring suitcase solutions to life, such as cash assistance to help millions of people move toward jobs. Without subsidies, telling people to buy their own way out of town is increasingly unrealistic when 39 percent of the country could not scrounge up $400 in cash in an emergency, let alone the costs of an initial place to stay or a security deposit in a job-rich area. And once they move, what family or friends will take care of their children for free? Who will care for their aging parents left back in their hometown? Leaving behind extended family, homeownership, and heritage looks like a high price to pay—especially for the "privilege" of renting an apartment on a floodplain outside Houston, or paying half of one's income toward an apartment fringed with black mold in San Jose.

Some people, especially younger ones and newer immigrants, will move to opportunity anyway—at a human cost. To see the suitcase strategy as practiced in real life, visit the rest stop off the I-80 freeway in Vallejo, California, at two in the morning on any day of the year. You'll see dozens of vehicles with sheets and shirts pinned in their windows so individuals, couples, and children can maintain some privacy while they sleep inside. Some have just finished work shifts, others will be starting them soon. All are scraping out a living in the San Francisco Bay Area. Some have no other home at all. Others, after a round of work shifts, will drive several hours to a small town with a weak job base in Northern California. People living in those cars are stuck without housing near their source of income, because local governments in job-rich areas are refusing to approve enough higher density housing. Those approvals are held back by the same racial discrimination and class bias that justified the abandonment of their hometowns in the first place. While the righteous battles continue to pursue higher density housing in growth areas, the people living in those cars should have other towns and other options.

Focusing on the ravages of concentrated poverty also undermines new maps and other *regional solutions* to place-based poverty. Several generations of academics, think tanks, and activists have argued we need to reorganize the territories that local governments serve. They have shown all the ways that local borders matter, because they determine which people and taxpayers are enclosed within a municipality or school district. These advocates fought for proposals to merge specific local governments together, or consolidate the rich and poor governments across a metro area into a single tax base. But by the time I went to graduate school in the early 2000s, dozens of these maps had been rejected by lawmakers or voters. The number of successful regional governments is so short I can list them on two hands, even as none of these really created a single joint government encompassing both schools and services. If representations of a region's people and government are all about conflict and chaos, why would a neighboring government work with them?

Stories about heroes set us up to think we wouldn't have to do anything as drastic as rearrange borders if we just had better decision makers. An expert can bring in some *spreadsheet solutions*, cutting costs or finding better deals without adding new funds or changing the rules of the game. If states intervene at all in local fiscal crisis, their go-to solution in recent years has been to appoint a fixer to take over a struggling

municipality's management. This person is typically chosen for technical expertise, whether or not they have the bedside manner to handle
democratic input from a community in distress. Indeed, these appointees are chosen in part for their thick skin, so they can make budget cuts
despite fierce opposition. To the degree the city's bigger problems relate
to chronic poverty, underemployment, and violence, selling a few assets
or renegotiating some contracts are marginal gains.

How about DIY-ing local services for a heroic rescue? I think of
this as the *substitution solution*. Private substitutes like churches, philanthropy, nonprofits, and volunteers try to take government's place when
it recedes. Indeed, broke cities create a natural experiment for the hypothesis that the private sector could do more and do it better if government hadn't already crowded in first. If only we had a thinner state,
this argument goes, charity and volunteerism would flower. The problem in broke cities is that private poverty precedes public poverty. The
level of need accumulated across so many years overwhelms volunteers
and local organizations. The terrible stigma and a fatalistic prognosis
that travel with concentrated poverty undermines nonprofit and other
private local institutions, not just government. The substitution that
emerges in these places can be a moving expression of human compassion, creativity, and resilience. But soup-kitchen level charity rarely
transforms lives or places.

Lastly, stories of hellholes waiting for heroes undermine the most
interventionist strategy of all: give the local government *more money*.
The right pejoratively calls this funding a bailout, the left calls it aid. Either way, dystopic stories feed a logic of tough-love fiscal rationality that
blocks money solutions. If a place is bleeding population or resources
for decades, shouldn't we reserve public investment for somewhere else?
Pay for success. Pick a winner. Don't throw good money after bad. We
treat cities and rural communities the same way Henry Ford II described consumer goods in 1955: "Obsolescence is the very hallmark
of progress." Public policy is rarely so candid. Yet a General Plan for
Tulare County in rural California once said openly what many officials
practice implicitly. That 1971 plan declared that its most impoverished
farmworker communities had "no authentic future" and thus should
not receive public investment in the water access they needed. The plan

was to neglect these places into nonexistence. Fifty years later, most of these communities carry on, still without reliable water.

Today, among those states that even bother to have a fiscal intervention program to help their local governments facing insolvency, all of them now emphasize spreadsheet solutions over new maps or new money. Substitution and DIY services are popping up in a creative but haphazard mishmash across the country. Stories of crooks, heroes, and hellholes are part of the reason so many people inside and outside these communities have stopped believing that progress is possible.

Our hypothesis that internal migration or tough love would solve regional concentrations of poverty was wrong. Regional governments, fiscal experts, outpourings of volunteers, and emergency aid never came to the rescue either. Some industrial and rural regions dutifully lost 30 to 60 percent of their population, even as millions of people still live there. Others are still populated, but crumple under the weight of poverty that is now intergenerational. Along the way, the residents and public servants who stayed have suffered the despair and violence associated with urban crack, rural meth, and everyone's opioids. They have lost jobs, homes, and loved ones.

Our failed politics added up to atrophy, which looks more like a bludgeon than a hospice program. Atrophy has yielded one clear result: multigenerational disinvestment in the living people rooted in so-called "dying places." Above all, that disinvestment in their people is the root of their greatest problems, *and ours*.

LOVE AND MISERY

Tools for a season of austerity

The book you have here is not an obituary, or a memorial to fallen glory. I have experienced sorrow in learning and writing it, but this is not nonfiction set to Springsteen's "Youngstown." I have also experienced anger, seeing up close how extreme wealth for some has been built at the direct and indirect expense of others. But I have tried not to write a screed either, because I still align myself with what civil rights leaders call the "call in," rather than "call out," tradition of social change. I believe in the better angels of American poverty, but so too, I hold on to hope for the better angels of American wealth. And anyway, seeing how big the loyalty, friendship, and purpose had to be to show up for problems this big, I felt another emotion sink in: I began to feel envy. So this book is, in its way, a tribute.

There is no disguising the hardship in these towns, and any attempt to whisk it out of view understates the urgency of the work needed. I have tried to stay close to a reflection by Justice Sonia Sotomayor of the United States Supreme Court. She was writing about her alcoholic father, but the sentiment seems just right for this book. "You can't say: This much love is worth this much misery. They're not opposites that cancel each other out; they're both true at the same time." A book that is true to these places must see both the love and the misery. They don't cancel each other out.

In Josephine County, I think a woman named Kate Lasky would agree with that idea. Lasky became the library director there in 2010, after the public library had shut down and volunteers reopened the main branch as a small nonprofit. In 2011, the circuitry failed in the main branch and half the overhead lights blacked out. She and the library volunteers debated what to do. They could use up their reserve funds to make repairs, but some volunteers thought they should start using flashlights instead. That would show people how defunded the library had become, they thought. Repairs, on the other hand, might suggest the library didn't need new funds. Lasky disagreed. She believed they could not progress by proclaiming, "Save us we're dying!" She thought it would feed into a destructive psychology she observed in town—a fatalistic acceptance that the needs were so dire that things could not get better. Even worse, the cuts to shared institutions seemed to reflect the view that residents didn't deserve more.

In a democracy, Lasky reflected, aren't we the government? "It's supposed to serve us," she said. "If it's us, and then we tear it down, what does that say?" Lasky took a stand. "We're going to invest in ourselves, no matter what," she said. The risk that people would think the library was "rich," she thought, was outweighed by the hope that a good library would help people in the community feel that *they* were rich. So they fixed the overhead lights. Then they fundraised to renovate the main library's reading nook for children. Then volunteers made 14,000 phone calls to voters on a ballot measure to restore public funding to the library and open hours at the rural branches. After years of losing at the ballot box, they won. It was just one of the victories heading their way.

So this book is written to celebrate and support a new generation of people-centered leadership like Lasky's. It is both for and about young leaders like Michael Tubbs, a city councilmember in Stockton from 2013 to 2016 and then mayor from 2017 to 2020. Tubbs grew up in Stockton, in one of the poorest neighborhoods in California. He was elected to serve his city at a time of acute crisis. His incumbent opponent had been arrested. A homicide surge had terrorized residents. The city had broken records for its foreclosure rates, then made national headlines again as the biggest municipal bankruptcy since the Great Depression. Tubbs and his coalition knew that underneath these challenges was an even harder reality: intergenerational poverty trapped in racially segregated neighborhoods traumatized by violence. But they had never given up on Stockton, and they refused to do so now.

On the night of Tubbs's mayoral inauguration, the region experienced torrential rainfall, with roadway flood warnings across Stockton. It didn't seem to matter. More than 1,000 people trekked to see his speech, and the arena was filled with cheering and tears of joy. "The energy they brought!" says city councilman Jesús Andrade, also a native son who returned to help heal his city. "The rain was symbolic—like the water was washing away the garbage, the stigma. It's a new era of leadership."

Change is hard, and sometimes four steps forward is followed by two back. I regret that Tubbs lost his bid for reelection in a narrow race four years later. But I think Andrade was still right. Those people at the Tubbs inauguration, and Tubbs's and Andrade's years in office, were all steps to set the city on a better path. A growing movement of people keep working at the city's challenges. Curtis Smith, a pastor in Stockton, put it this way as we discussed his candlelit walks at night to interrupt a period of peak gun violence: "In this season of austerity," he told me, "we have to hold each other up. We have to ask: 'What will this city look like if . . .'? We have to be that voice of hope. We cannot believe the narrative that has been written about us. We have to face the facts, but also *faith* the facts."

No one has a playbook for creating twenty-first century, racially equitable gateway cities. But the four communities that follow have helped me believe we could write one.

"I Won't Give Up On You, Ever"

Stockton, California

When Jasmine Dellafosse was a teenager at Edison High School in Stockton, ten of her peers were killed across a two-year period between 2010 and 2012. Judhromia Johnson, Jr., age seventeen, the football team's MVP, was shot while riding in a car on his way to practice. Fernando Aguilar, sixteen, and Edgar Alcauter, eighteen, were killed at a graduation party. Juan Juarez-Martinez, seventeen, was shot while riding his bike. Xavier Javier Plascencia, eighteen, was killed while walking on a sidewalk at noon on a Monday. Joe Xiong, fifteen, was shot, along with eight others who did not die, at a birthday party. Jorge Angulo, eighteen, was shot while sitting in a pickup truck with friends. Alejandro Vizcarra, sixteen, was shot in front of his home. Travae Vance, eighteen, was chased into a field and shot dead just months after his graduation from Edison. Searching for these youth, I found an eleventh who was no longer in school, an eighteen-year-old named Angelo Peraza who was shot in a car. There were also at least three other students at Stockton's Stagg High killed during that time.

When you search just about any one of these victims' names plus the word Stockton on YouTube, you'll find teen-made memorial videos with lyrics, photo montages, and messages of love to the dead. Once you find the first such video, YouTube's algorithms start queuing others—a channel for mourning made by surviving Stockton youth. I also came across a funeral home's online guestbook for Angelo Peraza's family and friends. He died in 2011, but the entries in the guestbook have continued. His mother, and sometimes other family members, use it to reach out to him. They wish him happy birthday, tell him about 49ers games. They try to report cheerful news from Christmas, but they admit that the sinkhole of his absence is biggest on holidays. Peraza's mother uses the guestbook like a grief diary, talking of the "life sentence" that she has gotten from his death, remembering and describing his skin, inputting poems about loss. She rearranges the words "I miss you" so she can say them again and again—sometimes with spaces between the letters, sometimes vertically, sometimes across the frame in a long diagonal as if she were marking time.

This is what trauma from violence looks like. Not the trauma handled in hospital emergency rooms, but the trauma that comes and stays for the people who emerge from that hospital alive, the family members who ran down hallways to find the ICU, the people who witnessed what it looks like when a human body takes a bullet. The trauma of Dellafosse, her classmates, their parents, their teachers, as death kept coming at them and erasing people they knew. That trauma that very likely preceded the shooters' capacity to pull those triggers.

But back in 2011, Edison High School did not have counselors equipped to help students and families process the trauma of their losses. Teachers gathered students in the library to let them cry, but "the only people who really helped us grieve through it were friends," Dellafosse said. After the first shooting, when they lost J. J., Edison principal Brian Biedermann told the local newspaper, "Nothing ever prepares you for this. There's no class, no training that teaches you to prepare for the loss of a student. I told the kids, just like you, I'm confused, hurt, don't know how to act. We just lost a family member."

In the aftermath of this violence, Stockton did what many cities do: punishment, fear, denial. They sent in police officers. They prosecuted shooters where they could. With just one counselor per 850 students, the school district spent about $3 million per year to fund a school police department, resulting in nearly 2,000 arrests of students between July 2012 and November 2016. Officers cited disruption, marijuana possession, truancy, and curfew violations for well over half of those arrests. There were no ceremonies to mark the death toll in the city, no public memorials in which outsiders expressed empathy, no sense that the killings had an endpoint where recovery could begin. Journalists publicized the rising body count, and city leaders answered with a recommitment to crime fighting—a two-step routine that treated the deaths as a sign of social depravity rather than suffering. When the homicide rate stopped breaking records, outsiders stopped paying attention at all.

Stockton then tried to forget. It had been doing the same since at least 1989, when a white man opened fire with an AK-47 at the city's Cleveland Elementary School, killing five children and wounding thirty-two others. All of the dead and most of the wounded were Cambodian and Vietnamese refugees, already traumatized by the violence they had fled. It was the worst K-12 school shooting in American history and remained so until the 1999 massacre at Columbine High in Colorado. But many people in Stockton and elsewhere have never heard of the Cleveland School shooting, says Dillon Delvo, who works to preserve Filipino history in the city. "Can you imagine Newtown forgetting what happened to them?" The failure to memorialize became a failure to treat the damage, and both carried a message to surviving youth and their parents: society doesn't notice if you die. There is no one but you to defend yourself and your families.

Delvo, Dellafosse, and many others in Stockton are coming to terms with the degree of trauma carried by the city's children and families, passing from parents to children. They are facing the humiliation and hopelessness created by racial segregation and intergenerational poverty. These efforts work to heal youth before they enter school charged with fear and armored in bravado. Advocates are working to de-normalize violence while normalizing mental health support, to teach coping skills and unteach powerlessness. They are cleaning up the fallout of mass incarceration and imagining a world beyond it.

This is the work of healing beyond the hospital and public safety beyond the police department. For the first time, Stockton has a critical mass of leaders who invest time and political capital in caring for the city's most traumatized people and neighborhoods.

At the moment Dellafosse said the word "ten" to tell me of her lost peers in high school, tears started rolling down her face. They fell on her shirt, which was printed with a photograph of her friend, another youth leader named Brandon Harrison. In the photo, Harrison smiles and wears a T-shirt that said, "HOPE DEALER," with a silhouette of Africa inside the letter O. He was gone too, killed at age twenty. Dellafosse was wearing Harrison's image to attend the arraignment of his alleged shooter.

Harrison had been part of that movement to stop the violence. In a speech to other youth in 2016 at a rally for "Schools Not Prisons," he called on his peers to summon the courage they would need. He asked them, *What kind of ancestor do you want to be?* He pushed them to resist becoming another generation suffocated by trauma, another generation without power or purpose. He called on them to be hope dealers. Healers. To honor his life, his loved ones keep that message close.

CITY OF ANCESTORS, CITY OF ORPHANS

Stockton's American Story

Stockton, this unfamous California city, looks like the world. One-fourth of city residents were born abroad. In this, the most diverse big city in America, first kisses cross color lines. Community potlucks are Black, white, brown, and multilingual. In 2017, more than 22 million people watched a homemade Fourth of July video of a spontaneous gathering on a residential street in Stockton. Two boom boxes traded off—one with Mexican music, the other with Punjabi music—as each group taught the other their dance moves. With the oldest Jewish cemetery in California and America's first Sikh Gurdwara, with a concrete modernist mosque and a bejeweled Cambodian temple, Stockton's people have long worshiped the free exercise of religion upon which America was founded.

Some families have centuries of ancestry connected to the region through the pre-colonial Yokuts and Miwok tribes, who lived along the Delta marshes in winter and the Sierra Foothills in summer. Some locals of Mexican and Spanish descent trace heritage back to Alta California before the Mexican–American War, when the city's namesake Robert Stockton conquered California soil for the United States in 1846.

Some local families date their histories to the Gold Rush. Chain-smoking under ornamental mustaches, fortune seekers from across the Americas, Europe, and China converged on Stockton as a transport depot to the gold mines. They would cram into stagecoach rides where, in the words of an appalled British writer in 1856, "for some incomprehensible reason, when stages meet, the recognition of friends is announced by enormously swearing at each other." The Transcontinental Railroad of the 1860s, that most ruthless and mighty of nation-building infrastructure, drew thousands of Chinese migrants to labor in lethal conditions to tunnel the Sierra Nevadas and, somehow, bridge western river canyons. These migrants built Stockton's Chinatown into *Samfow*, the "Third City" behind San Francisco and Sacramento. People say that nearly every Stockton family, rich or poor, has eaten dinner at New On Lock Sam, a local Chinese restaurant that dates back to 1898.

The Philippine–American War brought a fresh wave of newcomers, survivors of the death and disease caused by America's imperial effort to rule in Southeast Asia in 1900. Thousands fled their island nation by steamer ship to reach the Port of San Francisco, where they took an overpriced taxi ride to Stockton and delivered their men to California farms that hungered for stoop labor. Filipino farmworkers migrated among harvests across the west, but the small businesses of Stockton's Little Manila district gave them a permanent address. Each year, as labor rotations brought workers back to Stockton, they could rifle through boxes of collected letters, checking for news from their families across the ocean.

The Jim Crow Era drew migrants to Stockton from the American South. Thousands of African American children of slavery escaped the racial violence and debt peonage of sharecropping for the San Joaquin Valley, where boosters claimed they would find "[g]rapes as big as jade eggs and watermelons the size of small boats and cotton fields that didn't quit." The Dust Bowl followed: with eyes glazed over by loss and post-apocalyptic shock, survivors of the dark blizzards suffocating the Great Plains made it to western farm labor camps. Stockton's migrant camp is now a poor neighborhood known as Okieville. As late as the 1980s, lifetime Stockton resident Larry Johnson told me, "If you wanted a fight, Okieville was always the best place to go. Grandma, grandpa—anyone was ready."

One hundred years of systematic recruitment across Mexico—sometimes offering lawful immigration status, sometimes not—provided California's vast "industrial plantations" with a flow of yet unbroken newcomers. Later, lines of refugees fleeing gang violence and civil war in Central America and Mexico survived the border crossing to tend and harvest crops like asparagus, tomatoes, and almonds. From 1975 to the late 1980s, more than 30,000 refugees of the Vietnam War and the Khmer Rouge came from Vietnam, Cambodia, and Laos to Stockton and its region through resettlement programs. Silicon Valley has attracted the newest wave of prospectors, who left behind hometowns across the world in hopes of making a fortune, or at least a living, in California. They have not yet made it to pay dirt.

Stockton should be a symbol of the racial diversity at the heart of America's future. But so, too, it embodies the racial violence at the heart of America's history. Yokuts tribal villages were nearly wiped out by the Franciscan mission system, a calamitous malaria outbreak in 1833, and the "clearest case of genocide in the history of the American frontier." The Ku Klux Klan and others used bombing, arson, and lynching to terrorize Filipinos in the 1920s and 30s. Public officials assembled Japanese-Americans at a detention center at the fairgrounds in Stockton in 1942 before forced relocation to internment camps. Banks used racially restrictive covenants and mortgage redlining to bar non-whites from northern neighborhoods through the 1950s. City leaders bulldozed homes, business districts, and heritage sites in Little Manila, Chinatown, and Japantown in the 1960s, 1970s, and 1990s to make way for a freeway, a gas station, and a McDonald's.

Even though there are no plaques marking the city's redlining boundaries from the late 1930s, it is not hard to guess which streets enjoyed early public investment and mortgage lending, and which were marked as unworthy. Sidewalk canopies of ash, plum, pistachio, oaks, and redwood trees now shade those streets once color-coded as all-white and optimal for investment. Their sturdy trunks and arching branches reflect public dollars spent long ago. The redlined zones of Black, Latino, Asian-American, and mixed-race families, which were deemed high risk for investment, have sidewalks that are mostly a barren landscape of cracked concrete and scrappy grasses. These neighborhoods have a mismatched scattering of street trees, most of which are scrawny young things planted by nonprofits. By the time neighborhoods of all racial compositions could compete for public dollars for beautification and infrastructure, there were few dollars to go around. Between 1979 and 2016, the federal funding allocated to neighborhood development decreased 80 percent.

For decades, police stops helped enforce racial segregation in daily life. Gino Avila, a Latino counselor with Point Break Adolescent Resources, works long and high-risk hours trying to draw youth and men out of "the life" tangled up with crime. He describes his work as following the message of Saint Francis: "Preach the gospel. When necessary, use words." Yet Avila explains that he has been pulled over repeatedly by police when he's driving to reach his bank or the big grocery stores on the north side of town. Even when he shows his ID card showing his work for a well-known youth organization, officers have said, "You shouldn't be up here."

Stockton is a big city of 310,000 people, but its roots and setting make it feel more rural. Major dairy operations share the region with fields and orchards growing nuts, cherries, tomatoes, potatoes, grains, and beans. The city's canneries, tanneries, and warehouses feed transport lines that feed the nation. Two freeways and a railroad meet Stockton's inland seaport along the San Joaquin River, offering land and marine highways for moving goods between California's fertile interior and the metropolitan areas of San Francisco, San Jose, Oakland, and Sacramento, and global points beyond. At this strategic crossroads, the city built a manufacturing hub of farm machinery, construction materials, food packaging, and processed foods. Stockton has managed to hold on to some of these production lines, but this city that invented the Caterpillar tractor and Duraflame log has mostly lost its better-paid manufacturing jobs.

Like every other major city that went through a municipal bankruptcy in the Great Recession (including Detroit, San Bernardino, and
Vallejo), Stockton spent much of its modern history supporting the
American military. Shipyards and a U.S. Naval supply and communications facility in Stockton on Rough and Ready Island employed tens of
thousands of workers in World War II. The shipyards closed over time,
and Rough and Ready was decommissioned in 1995. Today, that land is
used for transportation and warehousing businesses, where lower-wage
workers sort and move imports and exports.

Stockton's region has gained jobs in the service sector, education,
and medicine, but its lower-skilled workers work more hours for lower
pay. Even in the national growth years of 2015–2020, unemployment
averaged 8.3 percent. One in four people younger than eighteen live
below the federal poverty line—a ratio that would climb dramatically if
corrected for California's high cost of living. Well over half of the tenants in the city pay more than 30 percent of their income for rent. More
than one-third of homeowners in the city pay more than 30 percent of
their income toward their mortgage.

Former city councilman Jesús Andrade called it a "badge of honor"
that Stockton has always made a home for California farmworkers. But
food systems don't pay those workers a livable income, which increases
poverty in Stockton. Farm labor entails seasons of sixty-hour weeks
of work in extreme heat or biting frost, interspersed with periods of
time with no income at all. The average annual income of farmworkers
employed by farm labor contractors (which is typically how Stockton
farmworkers find work) is about $18,720 a year. The living wage in-
come needed to support one adult and one child in San Joaquin County
is $42,000 per year. The San Joaquin Valley region has eight of the ten
counties with the highest crop value in California, as well as seven of the
ten counties in the state with the highest rate of child poverty.

Too many parents are gone from dawn to dusk to reach faraway
and low-paid jobs. Nearly one in ten working adults in the city commutes more than ninety minutes per day. Subcontractors' trucks and
vans come through South Stockton at four o'clock in the morning to
collect farmworkers or other manual laborers for the long drive to reach

regional fields or construction sites. Hospitals and universities in Silicon Valley, including Stanford University, run commuter buses and vans for their low-wage workforce departing Stockton hours before dawn. Some workers spend nights in the Bay Area with friends or family to avoid commute rounds. In a high-crime environment, parental absences for low-wage work create added dangers: youth look for other adults capable of protecting them from the streets, and they find people who promise that a job selling drugs will help pay their family's bills and grind less hard than life does for their parents.

Incarceration and homicide, not just long commute times, have made this city of ancestors into a city of orphans. The city's prime location along the West Coast's fastest freeway make Stockton a strategic node for the business of distributing cocaine, methamphetamines, heroin, and synthetic opioids. The city's homicide rate has been twice as high as California's figure for most of the past twenty years. The city has long been a capital of failed policies answering drug addiction crises with police and prisons. San Joaquin County (in which Stockton is by far the largest city) has one of the highest rates of incarceration in the state of California, ranking it eighth among fifty-eight counties in the state. It also has the fourth highest rate of transferring youths to adult criminal court after juvenile felony arrests, where they face longer sentences and stricter, more dangerous conditions of confinement that entangle them in gangs to survive. The city's police department ranked twelfth out of the 100 largest cities in the country based on the rate of civilian killings by police officers between January 2013 and December 2020.

"Some folks' empowerment is only held through guns, gangs," says youth leader Dillon Delvo. To help youth turn away from those instant but dangerous sources of identity and belonging, Delvo and others are teaching the struggle of the city's migrants from across the world. Youth can walk a difficult path with more confidence knowing their ancestors did it before them, he says. They can relate to other marginalized groups. "It's about self-love," Delvo says, "of being Filipino. Of being from Stockton. Of being an American." A boulevard and school in Stockton are named after El Dorado, the myth of a city full of treasure that helped drive the California Gold Rush. But the true El Dorado, Delvo says, is a community of "activism and people fighting for their rights."

"THE AIR JUST STOPS"

Stockton's Bankruptcy

On April 25, 2014, a local news station reported this: "STOCKTON (CBS13)—A man who was shot outside a Stockton movie theater on Friday night has died. The shooting happened around 10 p.m. at the Regal Cinemas 16 on El Dorado Street." The cinema is in downtown Stockton, part of a complex called City Centre (British spelling and all). The development has food businesses like a sushi bar and a Coldstone Creamery, with a plaza for open-air dining or takeout. A few blocks away, the city had built a riverwalk, a new marina, a minor league baseball field, a hockey and concert arena, and a new city hall to replace the city's historic but outmoded building. Public funding subsidized the renovation of a heritage hotel restaurant to host an upscale steakhouse, as well as a new hotel with cozy fire pits, a pool, jacuzzi, and ping-pong tables on an outdoor terrace facing the riverfront. All are lovely amenities.

Yet the shooting at City Centre represented generations of failed urban policy—a lesson learned by too many cities for too many years. Instead of trying to give their existing residents a gateway out of poverty, Stockton had tried to recruit new residents. Instead of focusing on the hard work of repairing its people and most neglected neighborhoods, the city had focused on repairing its downtown.

The City of Stockton developed the downtown improvements as part of more than $190 million in capital projects financed by bond debt between 2004 and 2009. City leaders longed for a revitalized downtown, as they had for more than fifty years. Leonard Gardner, in his celebrated 1969 novel *Fat City*, described Stockton's downtown at night to be a "phantasmagoria of worn-out, mangled faces, scarred cheeks and necks, twisted, pocked, crushed, and bloated noses, missing teeth, brown snags, empty gums, stubble beards, pitcher lips, flop ears, sores, scabs, dribbled tobacco juice, stooped shoulders, split brows, weary, desperate, stupefied eyes." By 2000, every block downtown had vacant or deteriorating buildings. Government offices brought some hustle-bustle during the day, but most workers cleared out anxiously before dark. One journalist wrote that renovating the waterfront was a "key to fixing Stockton's tenacious crumminess."

Imagining their point of view in 2000, it is hard to fault the city's politicians for seeking visible signs of progress, like construction activity, a ribbon to cut, and fresh public spaces. Redevelopment can make valuable improvements. It can clear and decontaminate blighted land to prepare it for new uses. It can construct facilities where people can live, earn a paycheck, have fun, dine, and shop. It can transform abandoned patches and strips of land (like an industrial riverfront) into open space with trails, bike paths, parks, and playgrounds.

These changes may be needed. But at the end of the day (including literally, at night), the built environment is only as safe and healthy as the activities there. Physical improvements can make property useable, but it cannot make it used. Redevelopment did nothing about the larger structural reason the downtown had been discarded. For decades, city leaders and big developers pursued a vision of growing the city with new, different residents. Developers had built new subdivisions, big box stores, and strip malls at the far northern edges. These developments were constructed on the cheap, with little to no investment in new parks, libraries, and other community facilities.

Former Stockton mayor Joan Darrah described this "uncontrolled development" driven by real estate and development interests who had come to "dominate the city" in the 1980s and 1990s. In a 1993 analysis of campaign contributions to city council races, the local newspaper found that all but one winning candidate had relied on real estate and development interests, with an average of 45 percent of their campaign funds coming from these sources. The anti-tax, small government politics of the city collected minimal fees and taxes on subdivision developments. Even before the Great Recession, developments were not bringing in the scale of revenues needed to fund the ongoing public investment they required.

Despite population growth, the city's government was still structured as if Stockton remained a small farm town. Before and in the years following the bankruptcy, city council members earned less than $16,000 a year—an expectation of the job that functionally limited those positions to people with other jobs or family income. A major raise in 2020 brought council salaries up to a still-low $29,400, and the mayoral job up to $90,000. By comparison, the city of Riverside (a comparable California city in population and demographic terms to Stockton) pays its council members more than $40,000 per year. In recent years, Riverside has collected and spent more than twice as much revenue per resident as Stockton.

In the early 2000s, with the San Francisco Bay Area's housing market soaring, boosters pitched Stockton as a bedroom community for middle-class workers with jobs in Silicon Valley. Like the city government, households moving to Stockton took out loans premised on climbing property values. The Great Recession destroyed that plan for both the city and its homeowners. Between 2006 and 2009, Stockton's housing prices fell more than 70 percent—with median home values plunging from nearly $400,000 to $110,000—which erased a decade of appreciation. Those losses undermined the city and its residents' ability to repay debts contingent on rising land values. By 2011, 56 percent of mortgages in Stockton were underwater. Reuters called Stockton "the town the housing boom broke."

As property values and household income tanked with the recession, so did city revenues to pay for services. Property tax revenues fell by 26 percent between the fiscal years of 2007 and 2011. Sales and use tax revenues plunged, given the local unemployment rate above 20 percent. From 2009 to 2012, the city cut nearly $90 million in spending. Just a few years after triumphant ribbon cuttings on the improvements downtown, the city could not keep up with their bond payments. As the city's bankruptcy judge would later put it: "Stockton committed its general fund to back long-term bonds to finance development projects based on an overly-sanguine 'if-you-build-it-they-will-come' mentality. They did not come."

Stockton had built its priorities around the formula Redevelopment > People. Movies played to row after row of empty seats, and to this day the hotel charges only about $120 per night for an upscale room with a river view. The steakhouse closed within a year. Prosperous residents were uncomfortable going downtown in the evening, and low-income residents could not afford $27 steak. The marina was mostly empty because it lacked amenities for working class boaters: pumping stations, showers, affordable restaurants, shops selling bait and sunscreen. "They only wanted yachts," says local writer and boater Paula Sheil, "like in a James Bond movie." When the arena opened in 2006 with a Neil Diamond concert subsidized by the city, many residents were irate. One asked me: "Who the fuck listens to Neil Diamond?"

The capital debts were not the only drain on city revenues. Mayors Joan Darrah (1990–1996), Gary Podesto (1997–2004), and Edward Chavez (2005–2009) were elected as small-government Republicans. But each signed unaffordable pension obligations that accumulated over time: uncapped retiree health care in the 1990s, pension increases in the late 1990s and early 2000s, and risky pension obligation bonds in 2007. By 2010, Stockton faced $148.5 million in unfunded liabilities for pensions and retiree benefits. Podesto also signed a twenty-year, $600 million contract with a multinational firm to take over the city's water, wastewater, and stormwater utilities—the largest water privatization deal in U.S. history—which opponents argued had set the city up to lose money over the long term and saddle residents with higher water rates. That deal did not stand up in court, but the city spent $5 million in legal and engineering fees to prepare and negotiate the failed deal, plus what was surely hundreds of hours of city staff time.

With steep monthly debt payments and falling revenues, the city had no choice but to slash spending between 2008 and 2011. Layoff notices went home with 20 percent of police officers and staff, 30 percent of the fire department, 38 percent of public works, 46 percent of library staff, and 56 percent of public recreation staff. Remaining employees took benefit cuts, as well as one round of unpaid furloughs after another. "It was a hatchet job," said Kurt Wilson, Stockton's city manager during the post-bankruptcy period. Between the layoffs, early retirements, and resignations by employees too scared to stay, there was no time to restructure staffing carefully. By mid-2012, city departments were pockmarked with random gaps, leaving employees with no managers, managers with no employees, and missing skill sets everywhere.

As crime rose to levels not seen since the early 1990s, cuts to policing drew the most attention. Between 2000 and 2012, Stockton dropped from a ratio of about 150 officers per 100,000 of population to about 110 per 100,000. The police union rented a billboard encouraging city residents to call the city manager to protest staffing cuts, displaying his cell phone number three-feet high. The bankruptcy judge reported grim trends: "In 2010, Stockton's violent crime rate bucked a nationwide drop and rose to rank it 10th nationally, with 13.81 violent crimes per 1,000 residents . . . Homicides were at an all-time record." The year 2012 then blew even that record away, with a devastating seventy-one homicides. Chief of Police Eric Jones described the "bunker mentality" that set in, as officers became only call responders and the city faced a "mass exodus" of officers to other police departments.

Officers adapted to staffing shortfalls with new policies, such as no dispatch for cold burglaries, car theft, or non-fatal collisions. "People were mad," Chief Jones recounted, "the biggest taxpayers complained about the focus on the high-poverty neighborhoods of the city. But the homicide rate was just too high." After his home was burglarized, Dallas Braden, a Stockton native and a pitcher for the Oakland A's, carried a bat to an anti-violence rally in the city in the fall of 2012. "Arm yourself or get out," he told a local news station. "It's the wild west and the boys in blue, they're outgunned." Chief Jones acknowledged that "cold burglaries are traumatic," but he felt the triage system was necessary with homicides spiking. "Death comes first," he says.

By 2012, Stockton had become a winner or finalist for accolades no city wants: highest rates of foreclosure, highest rate of citizen killings by police officers, highest rates of homicides, most miserable city in America. Even though the hardest impacts of segregation, poverty, crime, and foreclosure were always borne by specific neighborhoods, the city learned that its name, the word "Stockton," would stand for its worst statistics. The city had walled in its poorest neighborhoods with stigma and disinvestment, then realized that outsiders had built similar walls around all of Stockton. Governing the city's high-poverty areas through containment had always been morally wrong, but now it looked foolish too. A San Joaquin County Grand Jury Report put it well: "As the South Side Goes, So Goes Stockton."

At a six-hour city council meeting in February 2012, with the recession pounding city revenues while creditors pounded city leaders, Mayor Ann Johnston opened the meeting with a public prayer: "Lord, please help us." On June 28, 2012, the city council voted to file for bankruptcy. No one knew what to expect. Detroit had not yet filed its own petition, so Stockton was briefly the biggest bankruptcy in the state and the nation. "It was like two black eyes—you couldn't even see," said Jesús Andrade, later a city councilmember. Stockton had long faced the "bad press or no press" problem of being a poor city in a rural region, but the bankruptcy made it worse. Reporters from Sacramento, New York, Canada, Australia, and beyond "treated us like idiots, bumpkins," recalls Kathy Miller, a member of the city council at the time.

Residents panicked. "People needed to know what bankruptcy would mean in their lives. Would the street lights stay on? The traffic lights? Would their toilets flush? Would ambulances or police come if you called 911?" Miller took to YouTube in a series of videos to explain that the city could not pay its creditors everything owed and still offer basic emergency services. She would have to defend that position again and again, as she faced dozens of hours of legal depositions by lawyers for Wells Fargo and other creditors. They tried to prove that the city could have cut more services before shorting debt payments to creditors. Facing the Stockton public was nearly as bad. Citizens expressed their anger about service cuts, and retirees vented fears about cuts to health care benefits. "I got advice from staff about how I should sit at an angle so all the hate would bounce off me and I could protect myself," Miller said.

In the worst years of the layoffs and the bankruptcy, said District Attorney Tori Verber Salazar, "You could feel the air. It felt thicker and heavier, like after a car crash when the air just stops." Managers posted lists ranking staff for further layoffs, so employees in line to lose their jobs could prepare. Some colleagues lost multigenerational homes to foreclosure, Salazar said, adding to a feeling of shame. Community services director John Alita described the "fatigue, the shell-shock" that fell over his staff. His library director Suzy Daveluy put it more plainly: "Morale was in the toilet," she said. Alita nodded.

No one disputes how hard the bankruptcy proved to be. "In the end, the bankruptcy literally saved the city billions of dollars," said post-bankruptcy City Manager Kurt Wilson. "It still wasn't worth it." The city's fiscal straitjacket for the years during and after the bankruptcy made it hard to repair the damage that had been done. "Stretch a bit here and there? Can't do it," Wilson said. "Either we can afford it or we can't. It's not about what we deserve."

Redevelopment is expensive, complex, and politically tricky. Municipal bankruptcy is expensive, complex, and politically tricky. But any city can find people who know how to approach both of these challenges. Where could a city start to address problems like this one? By 2012, life expectancy in Stockton's high-income Lincoln Village was twenty-one years higher than that of downtown and South Stockton. They are about seven miles apart. South Stockton had urgent needs beyond bankruptcy.

MÁS TRANQUILA

Healing a Neighborhood

In 2012, at Stockton's low point, a social worker named Hector Lara accepted a new job running the Dorothy L. Jones Community Center in South Stockton. Lara had grown up an hour away from Stockton in a family of undocumented farmworkers from Mexico. He had left for college, secured his green card, earned two master's degrees, and spent several years working with low-income families caught up in the juvenile justice system. He had lived in Southern and Northern California. Now he wanted to be closer to home.

Lara didn't realize what he was up against. When he arrived, he was surprised to see that the Williams Brotherhood Park next door was nearly always empty, even though its nickname, CutiePie Park, suggested it had once been loved. He learned that a women's walking group in the park had disbanded after a series of daytime armed robberies in the city. A woman sitting on a bench by the playground had been grazed by crossfire on the afternoon of the last Christmas Eve. A few months after Lara's arrival, with about fifty people arriving at his community center to discuss public safety with elected officials, a man was shot in a drive-by shooting around the corner.

The park and Lara's center were also near an outdoor drug-dealing spot behind a store. According to court documents prepared later, the New Grand Save Market sold liquor, expired food, bags of chips near piles of rodent feces, and jars of "clean" urine that buyers could submit for drug tests. In a fenced side lot accessible through the store, men stood around selling drugs like bored retail clerks. Fred Sheil, the director of an affordable housing provider around the corner, described how he'd seen the store launder EBT cards, trading them for "40s and bowls of crack." The business was open to the public, so people could unknowingly wander in to what a court found was a "cesspool of unsanitary materials, fire hazards, and criminal activity." Robberies and shootings occasionally took place there.

New Grand Save had a neighboring park, church, and homes, but for years the police seemed to have adopted a tolerance policy to the store. As he showed me its outdoor drug market in 2014, lifetime South Stockton resident Larry Johnson explained that for a decade, "the only way to get a cop to come there was if there was a body down," as he gestured to the sidewalk where that body might lay. New Grand Save had become a symbol of the breakdown in trust with the police, Lara said, in which "the police would say: 'You don't call for service!' And the community members respond, 'Well, you don't show up! So why am I gonna call?'" The store captured the paradox of both "over-policing" and "under-policing" poor neighborhoods in the era of mass incarceration. Dangers like armed drug dealing were tolerated, even as the police conducted aggressive traffic stops and arrested residents for low-level offenses. Police seemed to focus on containing criminal activity in the neighborhood, rather than protecting its residents day-to-day.

Scared families prohibited their children from using Williams Brotherhood and other local parks after school. Yet indoor safe spaces were in short supply. The vocational high school next door to the Dorothy Jones Community Center had a nice gym, but it was closed after school and on weekends. The school had granted use rights for the gym to a nonprofit, but that organization didn't have the funds to staff it. Stockton was a tough place to run a nonprofit: its organizations took in a per capita rate of only $11.20 in charitable and philanthropic gifts, compared to a per capita state average of $47.17. The southside library closed, as library and recreation services lost 45 percent of their staffing between 2007 and 2015.

Even Lara's center was half-empty. It had been built in 2007 to house a medical clinic, but the city never found the money or a partner to occupy the space. The neighborhood was six miles from a hospital in a community with terrible health outcomes and poor access to transportation, so residents had pleaded with City Hall for years to open a clinic there. Local activist Virginia Gorman recalled her frustration working with the city in the early 2000s. "They thought we were stupid. They couldn't believe we'd ask for things like a clinic," she said. "They thought we needed another bail bondsman." The city secured funding to build the Dorothy Jones Center, but then ignored activists' advice to locate it on the main road. They tucked the center at the back of the park, so many residents didn't realize it was there. When Lara arrived, "the health clinic" was an empty shell.

Facing a gym that had closed, a clinic that had never opened, and a community chilled by mistrust, Lara turned to Amelia Adams, his predecessor at the center and an African American pastor in South Stockton. Lara explained that he had come to the neighborhood hoping to help prevent the kinds of harms he'd seen in years of social work in the juvenile probation and child welfare systems. Bossing families around never worked, he had learned, because it added to their experience of powerlessness. It made them defensive antagonists to the systems put in place to help. Care systems worked, Lara had learned, when families set their own goals and served as "experts in their own healing." Pastor Adams counseled him to scale that wisdom from families to the whole neighborhood. If residents could set goals and see them through, they would recover some of their self-esteem and ambition for change, which would in turn build momentum for further improvements. That advice marked a turning point for Lara, who set out to build relationships, enable residents to lead, and guide government officials to follow.

Lara was not the only one forging networks built on respect and engagement with residents. Michael Tubbs, a native son of South Stockton, graduated from Stanford in the spring of 2012 and returned to run for the neighborhood's seat on the city council.* Tubbs's cousin had been murdered in Stockton, and that loss had drawn Tubbs to reinvest his education back home. Tubbs was busy organizing in South Stockton—going door-to-door with youth to survey residents about their priorities for change, getting to know the network of activists and nonprofits, and hosting community events. His early speeches rallied neighbors to imagine that South Stockton could be reinvented as a safer place that gave children a future.

Tubbs and Lara learned that residents were already working to reduce violence and care for a neighborhood under siege. Small groups of church-based volunteers from multiple congregations were holding "prayer walks" and "night walks" on the most troubled blocks after dark, holding candles and flashlights as they walked sidewalks and spoke with residents. Their goal, as Pastor Curtis Smith described it, was to help people "live free" and end their "informal incarceration in their homes." Pastor Adams, Lara's counselor during his earliest days in Stockton, had started an "Adopt-A-Block" program through her church, the Open Door House of Prayer. Groups of Open Door volunteers walked door-to-door to bring necessities and companionship to elderly and vulnerable people scared to leave their homes.

An affordable housing nonprofit called STAND was helping, too, by acquiring dangerous drug houses to renovate the buildings and occupy them with low-income families. Virginia Gorman, one of the organization's founders and current leaders, had stuck by the neighborhood

---

* As a graduate of my own university, it may seem that my admiration for Michael Tubbs could be increased by my loyalty to Stanford. On the contrary, my admiration for Michael Tubbs has increased my loyalty to Stanford. I am proud that my university was part of his education.

through triumph and tragedy. In the late 1980s, when South Stockton was a regional hub for the distribution of crack cocaine into Sacramento and Bay Area cities, Gorman and her husband James, a Navy veteran, had worked with their neighbors, City Hall, and the police department to achieve a heroic drop in gun violence. The Gormans had stayed in the work even after losing their own daughter to an accidental gun death. When the youth who shot her did not have any family members show up for his arraignment, James Gorman's religious faith led him to call for mercy on the youth's behalf. The Gormans looked out for neighborhood children, using the STAND van for sports tournaments and regional field trips when the school district could no longer afford to take youth out of Stockton.

The Gormans saw the neighborhood as a home for families, not a collection of bad statistics. They knew their neighbors' jobs, such as nursing or working at PG&E, and knew which families had lived in South Stockton for multiple generations. Their daughter had wanted them to buy a home in a safer area on the north side. They did so after her death, but still lived in the South Stockton home where she grew up. "When you need a break from people hollering for help, you go away for a day or two," Virginia Gorman says. But the north side was lonely, full of people going in and out of their driveways without talking to their neighbors. "South Side is where all your friends and relatives are," she says, and a place to find meaning, not just comfort. STAND has grown into one of the most important nonprofit affordable housing providers in the city.

Tubbs won his race for a city council term starting in 2013. Working for a city mired in bankruptcy litigation, the council had few discretionary funds to spend. But elected officials, Tubbs believed, could use their position to bring people to the table. Despite deep cuts, schools, hospitals, churches, nonprofits, and government agencies were still working in South Stockton, and Tubbs worked to draw these entities together and rally their resources toward shared projects. They called this effort the REINVENT South Stockton Coalition, and Hector Lara became its first leader.

The Coalition's efforts had to cut across histories of mistrust and resentment, including deep racial divisions between the multigenerational

African American and Filipino households on the south side and relatively recent Latino residents. Tubbs and his generation had grown up
in multiethnic schools with a conception of a larger South Stockton
that was brown, rather than as separate neighborhoods or entities divided by ethnicity. Tubbs used common refrains: "I need you here," and
"I need you to put your ego at the door."

Youth working as part of the Tubbs campaign had canvassed neighborhoods, talking to residents about their priorities. The REINVENT
South Stockton Coalition ran an extensive community survey through
a series of volunteer-run block parties. Again and again, residents said
that South Stockton most needed three improvements: safe places for
children and teens to play after school hours, a medical clinic with mental health resources, and closure of the drug market at the New Grand
Save liquor store. Those projects became the early agenda for the REIN-
VENT Coalition, as well as for Tubbs on City Council.

By building relationships in the neighborhood, Lara got to know
the African American congregants at the Greater White Rose church
who wanted to engage youth in basketball leagues in the gym. He met
Latino parents ready to run indoor soccer. He helped open the gym,
and residents mobilized volunteers to staff it with weekday basketball
and weekend soccer. At their peak, volunteers ran twenty-eight soccer
teams for children ages four to eighteen, with basketball at the gym
every weeknight. A busy gym brought life to the park, where pick-up
soccer and basketball started again.

The reclamation of the gym soon grew into a larger effort for safe
parks and programs for youth. Jasmine Dellafosse (the Edison High
School graduate who opened this chapter) began interning with City
Councilman Tubbs and helping to build the Coalition while she was
in college. She organized summer literacy programs and book clubs.
She planned safe holiday events, like a "trunk or treat" Halloween with
decorated cars to replace the trick-or-treating. Back when he had been
a college student, Tubbs had worked with educator Ty-Licia Hooker
to establish a summer leadership academy for at-risk local high school
students. He passed this baton to Dellafosse, who helped build and lead
the program with Hooker. Based on his own history sheltered from
street violence by a busy schedule of summer and after-school activities

(and consistent with the parenting practices in wealthier places), Tubbs believed, "We can never have too many pro-social activities for young people."

On a Saturday in 2015, Dellafosse, Lara, and others in the Coalition brought together volunteers (including a dozen teenagers) and city workers to reclaim Williams Brotherhood Park. They painted over graffiti and filled six dumpsters with trash. Dellafosse's group eventually cleaned up twelve parks, with block parties and painting projects that began to attract up to one hundred children every other Saturday. At Liberty Square Park in South Stockton, they built a new playground. They painted scenes imagining pathways for their future, including a "college wall" to focus children and teens on education. "Through the artwork," she explained, "young people wanted to leave messages to show the children playing in the park that this is our community—we exist."

Volunteering at the gym and reclaiming parks were not just good deeds, Lara said. Taking back these public spaces, he said, helped the community heal from past violence. The public health literature had not yet begun using the term widely at the time, but what Lara had seen when he arrived in South Stockton in 2012 would now be called "community trauma." The neighborhood's social environment was torn up, with fragmented and dispirited social networks that undermined the neighborhood's ability to work together. This social unraveling had weakened residents' will to stand up to crime, as if the neighborhood had accepted violence as normal. South Stockton's physical environment of unusable parks, empty sidewalks, and dilapidated housing made people afraid as they moved through their daily activities. Easy access to alcohol, drugs, and guns in a context without enough work or educational opportunities made it hard for people of any age to imagine or sustain a healthy path.

Jesús Andrade, a former City Council member for South Stockton who grew up in the 1980s and 1990s in a public housing development there, describes how racial segregation and the conditions around him shaped his sense of himself. "You see fights, needles, blighted lots, dogs everywhere. You come home to where it's crowded and you have no space to unwind. Your dad, if he lives there, comes home after 7:00 with a shitty attitude because of his shitty job. And there is alcohol everywhere. You go to the north side and you see lush lawns, grocery stores. You have an inferiority complex and don't even know that. You think it's our fault we can't keep nice things." He felt unsafe on either side of town—whether because of crime near home or as a Latino face on the north side. Fear blended with shame and metastasized as fatalism.

When Williams Brotherhood Park and ordinary life began to open up again, the success helped disrupt the city's pattern of neglect and paternalism toward South Stockton. In the past, when neighborhood nonprofits and citizen groups tried to work on an issue with the city (say, to help reduce violence), the police or other city departments would say they didn't need help from residents—or didn't trust them to give it. "But when they had no staffing to do these things," Lara says, "they were reliant on the community to step up." That changed the dynamics with City Hall, Lara said, because as the budget began to thaw after the bankruptcy, City Councilmember Tubbs could demonstrate families' use of the gym to argue for a fair share of city funding. New leadership at the recreation department stepped up to help. When volunteers ran out of energy to staff the full operation alone, the city contracted with a nonprofit to help.

Lara, Tubbs, and others set out to open the health clinic at the Dorothy Jones Center. On the City Council, Tubbs gathered the data to make the case that South Stockton not only needed a health clinic to address its poor health outcomes, but also had thousands of residents with public or private insurance that would cover the costs of care. The Affordable Care Act had begun to fund mental health services even when patients had not been diagnosed with a severe disorder like psychosis. Tubbs and Lara negotiated with Community Medical Centers, a nonprofit provider that integrated mental health care with primary care. In 2016, Community Medical Centers opened a clinic in the Dorothy Jones space, with therapists on site.

Even with that important step forward, activists in South Stockton believed that no change was sustainable without shutting down New Grand Save. The store had long been a source of tension with the police and city attorney's office, which had led unsuccessful attempts to shut down the store through code enforcement in the past. Fred Sheil, STAND's executive director, said that when he and others pleaded with the city to get it done, government officials would tell them, "If we move him [the store owner], he'll just relocate somewhere else." People in South Stockton knew that a more prosperous neighborhood would not get the same answer. The city needed to reject the owner's business model and run up his costs, showing its commitment to fight predatory businesses wherever they arose.

Two shootings at the store in May 2016 reinforced that it was time to try again. In 2016, a deputy city attorney named Susanna Wood, in conjunction with police chief Eric Jones, saw the project through. Wood believed she could shut New Grand Save if she had the community's support, testimony, and patience across a prolonged court process. Lara could offer that. In return, he wanted the city to trust his coalition enough to warn them before police actions to collect evidence. Churches and nonprofits had outreach volunteers and homes nearby, and they did not want to be near the store during a police raid. With these open lines of communication, the city successfully obtained a court order closing the store as a nuisance that "substantially endangered" the public. The court put the site into a receivership to clean up hazards and code violations at the owners' expense, and to seek a legitimate commercial tenant for the property. With New Grand Save closed, more neighbors began coming out of their homes to volunteer and enjoy public spaces.

The abiding ethos at REINVENT South Stockton Coalition has been the same lesson Lara learned at Dorothy Jones. Like residents, city and nonprofit employees felt deflated by the years of challenges. Lara, Tubbs, and others worked to acknowledge these partners as professionals who cared about their city, reinvigorating their sense of trust in each other and pride in their jobs. "Our theory of change," Lara says, "is investing in people. We have to shift the language from people's problems to their assets." Restoring relationships allowed collaborations. Those collaborations yielded accomplishments. During Tubbs's term on City Council, he helped open the neighborhood's first bank, a credit union.

Tubbs drew the police and housing authority to work with the non-profit STAND to acquire and renovate five drug houses at an intersection used as an overnight drug market. With refreshed homes occupied by families paying affordable rents, the intersection became an ordinary, quiet residential area.

Tubbs helped initiate a San Joaquin Grand Jury investigation in 2014 of the City of Stockton's disinvestment in South Stockton. Activists found it therapeutic to see official recognition that City Hall had not served South Stockton "in any sustained and meaningful way." In 2016, 73 percent of city voters seemed ready to start correcting that history when they approved a sales tax measure to fund the reopening of South Stockton's shuttered library and restoring library and recreation services citywide.

In 2016, a national study found that Stockton tied for first place in health improvements, in large part because of the new clinic at Dorothy Jones and other work in South Stockton. Working as catalyst, a motivator, and a partner inside government, Tubbs moved public-private partnerships forward outside the real estate context where that term is typically used. As Fred Sheil put it, he was a "whirlwind of getting shit done." From ordinary teenagers to local moms, from public employees to youth leaders, people drew their networks towards REINVENT. Progress had begun to snowball. For decades, most Stockton youth who left for college had not come back, but the Coalition began drawing in local college students and summer interns to reengage. Locals called them boomerangs.

At lunch one day with Sheil and with Tubbs's successor on the City Council, Jesús Andrade, Sheil wagged his finger at Andrade, smiling: "I will be so glad when you and Tubbs leave and I won't be working six and a half days a week again! Where were you guys ten years ago?! You wait until I'm sixty-five and ready to retire?!"

For the first time, even bad news had to compete with good news. The city's first mayor elected after the bankruptcy, Anthony Silva, was arrested in August 2016 on charges of playing strip poker at a youth camp and supplying alcohol to a teenager. Photos of him in handcuffs reinforced the worst stereotypes and cynicism about city government.

But that scandal, so soon after the bankruptcy, helped to disrupt the old order of city politics. The bankruptcy broke the establishment's hold on Stockton and opened space for new ideas.

That new space included a bigger role for Michael Tubbs, then twenty-six years old. In November 2016, Stockton elected him mayor. He became the youngest big city mayor in America, as well as the first African American and second Democrat to serve as mayor in Stockton's history. He symbolized a new vision for a people-centered transformation. The REINVENT South Stockton Coalition was run by social workers like Hector Lara and youth leaders like Jasmine Dellafosse, not real estate interests. Tubbs and his coalition seemed to have internalized the real lesson of the bankruptcy and the Great Recession: growth and redevelopment are not anti-poverty programs. They had proven to be a pricey and failed substitute for residents' education and engagement.

Deeper progress would not come from a "poor us" story either, says Nate Werth, an early staff member at the Coalition. "We are not a Victorian ideal of charity," he says. "Parade out the orphans and hope you donate. We say, 'Here's the problem, here are the numbers, and here is the way we proceed.'" The orphans, he says, were ready to pick themselves up and build a new city: one that honors the city's ancestors by giving their descendants a chance.

It was the right goal, but they still had the hardest work ahead. South Stockton mother and activist Inocencia Cano told me in 2018 that her neighborhood had become "más tranquila." She relaxed back in her chair, describing her growing sense of ease coming and going from her home. But she was talking about outdoors. Stockton's people needed to feel "más tranquila" inside their bodies, homes, and classrooms, too.

FACING TRAUMA

Intergenerational Violence and Toxic Stress

Stockton had a root problem hiding beneath many others. Facing that problem was not a lost cause, but it would not be free either. "Childhood adversity" is the wonky way to describe this challenge, but people in Stockton cut to the chase to call it trauma. By 2016, a generation of research in psychiatry, public health, and neuroscience had started to discover how and why the biological effects of trauma drive a wider range of poor health outcomes, lower life expectancy, troubled schools, and broken homes. Trauma seemed to be driving violence too—both within families and in public. Stockton had people nerdy enough to know the emerging research and compassionate enough to act on it.

Childhood adversity has been defined by a common rubric since the 1990s. On the "adverse childhood experiences" (ACE) assessment, respondents got one point if they answered yes to this question: "During the first 18 years of your life, did a parent or other adult in the household often push, grab, slap, or throw something at you or ever hit you so hard that you had marks or were injured?" Another point for yes to this: "Did an adult or person at least 5 years older than you ever touch or fondle you or have you touch their body in a sexual way, or try to or actually have oral, anal, or vaginal sex with you?" Another point: "Did you often feel that you didn't have enough to eat, had to wear dirty clothes, and had no one to protect you, or that your parents were too drunk or high to take care of you or take you to the doctor if you needed it?" One point if your mother or stepmother was sometimes kicked, bitten, hit, or threatened with a lethal weapon. More tally marks if no one in your family loved you, if a member of your household went to prison, or if a member of your household was mentally ill or attempted suicide.

The original ACE questionnaire did not ask about experiencing, witnessing, or knowing of frequent fights, gun shots, injury, and death in a child's school or neighborhood. But a supplemental metric developed at UCSF and deployed across California now adds a point for this kind of "community violence." The new metric adds another point for deportations or migrations that separate children from their loved ones.

The first study of ACEs (based on a sample of more than 17,000 people in San Diego) launched hundreds of others. This work revealed the scope of child abuse and neglect. Nearly one-third of all violent crimes occur among family members. A major study of ACE scores in California found that 61.7 percent of adults have experienced at least one ACE, and one in six (16.7 percent) have experienced four or more. Distribution of these worrisome high scores by race is relatively even. But ACEs are not distributed evenly by income. People living below the federal poverty level and those with less than a high school degree show a much higher prevalence of ACE scores of four or more.

As people rack up three, four, even ten of these adverse childhood experiences, their odds of living a long life go down. A person with an ACE score of six or more has a life expectancy twenty years shorter than a person with a score of zero. The odds go up that they'll spend that shorter life in and out of hospitals. A person with an ACE score of four or more is at least double the risk of all but one of the ten leading causes of death in the United States, from heart disease to cancer to Alzheimer's. Such a person is more than five times as likely to suffer from depression than a person with no ACEs, and more than three times more likely to binge drink. The risk of social outcomes like homelessness skyrockets. A woman with three violent ACEs before her eighteenth birthday is 3.5 times more likely to be the victim of violence by an intimate partner. A man with that same ACE score is 3.8 times as likely to perpetrate intimate partner violence. Any person with three violent ACEs is more than eleven times as likely to be raped in adulthood. Trauma also drives a person's likelihood of spending time in prison— nine out of ten juveniles convicted of a crime had a traumatic event in childhood, and up to three in ten meet the criteria for post-traumatic stress disorder.

Like exposure to a toxin, the intensity and duration of trauma makes its health harms worse. Research confirmed again and again from various angles that the trauma *itself* creates health risks, not just by causing other problems that make people ill. That is, some patients who suffered in childhood also have other predictors for ill health, such as living in unhealthy neighborhoods without good access to health care, exercise, or healthy food. Other high-ACE patients adopt intervening coping behaviors (such as smoking or alcohol abuse) that increase their risk of disease. But *even controlling for these other negative health indicators*, serious adversity in childhood makes adults more likely to be ill.

Scientists have mapped the biology of these outcomes. The basic explanation is that surges of stress hormones like adrenaline and cortisol help make us safe. They evolved to flood the body in a moment of acute danger (the proverbial "being chased by a bear") to help us fight, flee, or freeze. They turn off our executive function, allowing us to act faster and more impulsively, therefore increasing our chance of survival. Minor elevation of these hormone levels and the increased heart rate they cause (say, jumping out of the way of a speeding car) is healthy and normal. More sustained adversity (such as adapting to parents' divorce, losing a loved one, or losing a home to natural disaster) is deemed "tolerable stress" where it is relieved over time by adults who help a child cope. But stress levels can become toxic if adversity is sustained and frequent, without adults to help a child feel safe and heal (such as abuse or domestic violence, or a caregiver with a mental illness). As California's surgeon general Dr. Nadine Burke Harris put it, toxic stress is "what happens when the bear comes home every night."

When acute enough, adversity can trigger post-traumatic stress disorder. But even shy of that diagnosis, trauma and toxic stress can cause impulsivity and hypervigilance, which undermine concentration and trigger overreaction to perceived dangers. They can cause avoidance, in which people become afraid to leave their homes, let alone walk on sidewalks or enjoy public parks. Trauma commonly triggers depression (vegetative symptoms and withdrawal from family and friends), as well as anxiety (sleepless agitation and debilitating fear). Nightmares and flashbacks are common, so people suffer from sleep disorders. They may resort to overeating or drug use to try to fill voids, replace thoughts, and temper anxiety. Trauma triggers social reactions too: weaponizing yourself or your home to be ready next time, and finding a network of other weaponized people to help protect you. Children, youth, and adults all learn to wear a mask of aggression to deter danger, until the mask is hard to take off.

It is both traumatic experiences themselves and the expectation of future trauma that tears at a child or adolescent's healthy development. Patterns of harmful events (such as seeing violence repeatedly or losing multiple loved ones) generate fear of future harms. Persistent feelings that a person is not safe and cannot reach for help from loving adults to become safe can blot out hope for the future, which increases the risk of truancy, self-harm, chronic anger, volatile relationships, drug abuse, and disassociation.

Even when a child or adolescent has not experienced violence personally, routinely hearing about shootings, stabbings, and other acts of violence in one's environment can trigger symptoms of PTSD. "Hearing about violent events this frequently," one study found, "confronts people with the stark reality that their community's capacity to offer safety and support may be shattered by violence and death at any time."

Elevated levels of stress hormones make it hard to sit still, control one's emotions, or work through challenges. Predictably, school performance goes down as a child's exposure to abuse and deprivations increases. Trauma can affect children's willingness to be away from their parents to attend school, because they can feel tense and anxious when they are separated from adults they trust. If loving adults do not help children understand what happened to them and why, they construct their own story. Combined with the natural "egocentrism" that is part of healthy child development, that story often situates the child as causing the harm they suffered: "deserving" physical abuse, "making" parents fight or divorce, or "attracting" sexual abuse.

People living and working amidst Stockton's poorest residents had seen these outcomes for years. Awareness of cycles of violence within families in Stockton dated back to the 1990s, when public health researchers in San Joaquin County focused on women struggling from severe mental health disorders and drug addiction. Frances Hutchins, the assistant behavioral health director for San Joaquin County, and other researchers learned that 97 percent of the women in local substance abuse treatment facilities had experienced domestic violence, sexual assault, and other forms of violence. The secondary health harm (substance abuse) seemed to be what doctors called a "maladaptation" to a first harm (the violence and abuse). Could counselors treat the addiction without giving other coping skills for the trauma buried beneath it? These researchers joined a generation of public health, neurology, and psychiatry researchers who answered "no."

In 2016, the major regional public health assessment covering Stockton identified trauma treatment and prevention as core health challenges. In the city's highest-poverty neighborhoods, the report found, more than one in six residents reported daily struggles with a mental health issue for at least fourteen days of the past year. The number of domestic violence calls is 37 percent higher in San Joaquin County than in California as a whole. More than 18 percent of adults across San Joaquin County (not even taking account of the spatial concentration in poor areas) reported needing treatment for mental health or alcohol/drug use. One of every three high school juniors reported clinical depression, defined as daily sorrow and hopelessness for two weeks or more. Fifteen percent reported current gang involvement, and more than one-third reported harassment or bullying at school. Yet San Joaquin County had about ninety mental health providers for each 100,000 people in the county, compared with 157 providers for that unit of population statewide.

Counselors in Stockton also observed the way that trauma seemed to be repeating itself across generations. Parents who have experienced violence, Stockton trauma counselor Gauri Sanchez explains, "parent *from* that violence." Sometimes that meant abuse; other times it meant that the effects of trauma on the parents (such as depression, hyper-reactivity, or substance abuse) affected their ability to nurture their children. Public health research confirms these intergenerational effects. One-third of people who were abused as children will themselves perpetuate abuse. Parents' own trauma can interfere with their ability to regulate emotions, manage aggression, and build healthy relationships. Traumatized adults are more likely to withdraw from children, or re-enact the abandonment or harsh discipline they experienced. Parents who struggle to meet their children's emotional needs are not providing those children with a loving adult to buffer them from other sources of trauma in the child's life.

Treating toxic stress and trauma has never been a lost cause for people of any age. The plasticity of children's brains make them especially vulnerable to traumatic events, but more susceptible to improvements, too. Above all, "buffering adults" can transform outcomes by offering love and reassurance, which release the counterbalancing hormone oxytocin. They can bring context and explanations to help children see they were not at fault. They can bring the physical relaxation of play, stability, and predictability.

Trauma-focused cognitive-behavioral therapy can help, as can increased economic security and hopefulness. Supportive relationships, nutrition, quality sleep, exercise, mindfulness practice, and other interventions can help people move past damaging events to reach "post-traumatic growth." Mothers who suffered abuse during their own childhoods have a lower likelihood of passing that on to the next generation when they avoid or manage anxiety or depression, undergo therapy, secure economic stability, or establish an intimate relationship that is "stable, supportive, and nonabusive." Patients can develop coping skills in their daily life, such as ways to bring themselves back into the present moment, away from traumatic recollections. Facilitators can help community members meet their neighbors to reestablish trust and mutual aid within high-crime neighborhoods. Years without violence can rebuild the expectation that today will be safe. Some trauma counselors used principles of *la cultura cura*, a healing framework rooted in indigenous traditions, such as *circulo de palabra* (talking/healing circles) to restore and rebalance families after harmful experiences.

Stockton's frontline organizations began to suspect that treating trauma in these ways was not just an act of mercy. Nor was it just a way to improve other health outcomes. Some organizations in the city came to believe that treating trauma was an anti-violence strategy, too. They believed that trauma helped explain why homicides had spiked in Stockton in 2010–2013, despite a nationwide decline in violent crime. The popular story of this spike blamed it on cuts in policing. But organizations near the front lines noticed something else. During those years, the age cohort most likely to commit crimes in the city (ages twenty-four to twenty-nine) had gone through childhood during the last cycle of peak homicides and drug-related violence in the early 1990s. The crack cocaine epidemic during these years, they hypothesized, had stuffed untreated trauma into many local families, whether they had been living in Stockton or a poor neighborhood somewhere else.

Simply describing the crack epidemic reads like a giant list of ACEs: peak rates of kids losing parents to violence, incarceration, or drug-related accidents; neglectful parents battling drug addiction; violent turf wars over drug sales territory; and intensively concentrated poverty, with widespread food scarcity and housing turnover. As those children became adults, Stockton carried the costs and risks of their traumatic childhoods. Statistics would suggest that those ACE-heavy childhoods would have cut off educational attainment and opportunity for many, while also making high numbers of the surviving adults now ill, struggling with mental health or substance abuse issues, or susceptible to family violence. Maybe, the advocates also wondered, some of those traumatized children had grown into one of the few adults who fueled the gun violence of the 2010s. Fathers & Families of the San Joaquin began to use the phrase "hurt people hurt people." This was not an excuse for ongoing violence. It was a plan to combat it: trauma treatment could serve as trauma prevention.

Treating trauma became part of a comprehensive anti-violence strategy in the Tubbs mayoral administration. "Toxic stress," "trauma," and "intergenerational trauma" became common phrases among his partners. Surely he was the city's first mayor, said Amy Portello Nelson, a staff member at the REINVENT South Stockton Coalition, who routinely asked for deliverables on ACE prevention and treatment. All children in the city, they believed, including children of color in the poorest neighborhoods, deserved the benefits of emerging science and health care.

Government agencies and community-based organizations built an ambitious network to treat trauma and toxic stress across the city, securing three major grants to support trauma-related work. In 2015, Fathers & Families received funding through 2021 from California's Victim Compensation Program to establish a trauma recovery center—becoming one of only six trauma recovery centers in California dedicated to serving the victims of violent crime. A partnership of health care providers, government agencies, community groups, and the REINVENT Coalition received an $850,000 grant for "Healing South Stockton" from the California Accountable Communities for Health Initiative. The project identified people living with high levels of trauma and connected them with therapeutic services. Leaders of the County Public Health department viewed the grant not just as treatment, but as violence prevention. Stockton also received a $400,000 grant from the Sierra Health Foundation for trauma-informed work with youth arrested for juvenile crimes who have a history of living in foster care or a documented history of trauma. By 2017, Stockton was held out as a model in California for its interventions in toxic stress.

The Community Medical Center at Dorothy Jones grew its trauma counseling practice, integrating ACE scores into its primary care and diagnostic work. The clinic is set up for "warm hand offs" between primary care and mental health support, says Alfonso Apu, their Chief Behavioral Health Officer. During primary care visits like diabetes care, he explains, patients often disclose or show signs of mild to moderate mental health problems like depression and anxiety. Getting them in to see a counselor that same day helps make sure the visit happens.

A typical patient there, says Apu, might be an African American or Latino already in his or her sixties with chronic disease, pain, or diabetes. He or she has never told anyone about adverse childhood experiences such as child abuse, sex abuse, loss of kin to violence. "When you normalize things," Apu explains, "and say 'it makes sense to me that you're struggling,' they say, 'oh you're saying I'm not crazy!' I tell them, 'You've been through so much. You've endured so much. How have you survived?' You focus on their resilience. You focus on the fact that they've survived horrible things. This has affected them more than they think. They realize: 'This is why I can't sleep, why I can't take my medicine.'" When therapists ease a patient's sense of shame and they start to open up, Apu describes, "Their bodies tell the story. The shaking, breathing, crying. My job is not to retraumatize them. I don't need to hear the details. I can teach them how to gain control of this moment. I can't take their memories away." He teaches them techniques to reground themselves, to reassure themselves that they are safe in the present moment.

But the Stockton vision for anti-trauma work stretched beyond mental health professionals trained to deal with trauma. "We're never going to have enough therapists," Lara said. The ethos became "No Wrong Door"—no matter where a person showed signs of crisis or revealed their backstory, Stockton should have people trained to help. A public education campaign anchored in South Stockton has taught

500 residents about the neurology of stress and trauma so they can better care for themselves and loved ones. Teachers, police officers, health workers, and others also needed to know how to recognize the signs of trauma, diffuse a triggered person's emotions, and direct people to appropriate services. Understanding the connection between trauma and its aftereffects (like hyper-reactivity, impulsivity, depression, and ADHD), those professionals could be more effective and empathetic in their ordinary work.

If a frontline worker is struggling with a person who is acting out and "non-compliant," Apu explains, they can refer that person to his clinic. "The conversations the systems have with patients are usually, 'do this, do that, take medication, stop that,'" he says. "As a behavioral health counselor, in one session I can assess that they've gone through recurrent trauma—sexual abuse, being a victim of a crime, hearing bullets all night." The focus shifts to what has happened to the person acting out and why. Apu was proud to report that police started bringing people to the Dorothy Jones Center and other mental health providers for clinical services in cases where it would not do any good to arrest them, take them to the county hospital, or mandate involuntary psychiatric commitment. With the police low on resources too, Lara is proud that this new option is not only more humane and productive, it is more cost effective too.

San Joaquin County district attorney Tori Verber Salazar and the city's chief of police Eric Jones have become leaders in this trauma-informed vision for the city. They are committed to, in Salazar's words, "attracting less business," because "if there is business, there is a victim." The DA believes that even if she can't muster a majority in the conservative county to understand that the "hit 'em harder" version of fighting crime doesn't prevent crime, she is trying to convince them that the county can't afford the astronomical costs of the older system, which she said runs hundreds of dollars to book a person, and "easily" a few thousand for a court proceeding on a misdemeanor. Salazar, like other law enforcement officials in town, now meets with local at-risk youth. "They are so bright," Salazar says, "just incredible kids. But they have suffered so much heartache. There are a lot of kids out here hanging on for dear life." As a fifth-generation city resident, Salazar feels that the city and system "need to accept responsibility for what we did to them," including the "off the hook racial disparities" in the criminal justice system. The DA's office is bustling with violence prevention programs alongside prosecution. Her city is changing for the good, Salazar says, as it—like so many of its children—climb out of its hardest hours. "We are a scrappy bunch of fighters," she says.

Chief Jones is training his police officers and staff to understand and handle people triggered by trauma or mental health disorders. He speaks publicly about repairing the damaged trust between the police department and city's neighborhoods of color. Racial reconciliation has to be part of reform in cities like Stockton, he says, because "you can't argue against the data on the history of policing in America." He worked with then Councilman Tubbs and other leaders in 2015 to secure funding through the National Initiative for Building Community Trust and Justice, which supports training and reforms to reduce implicit bias, enhance procedural justice, and promote racial reconciliation. These ideas, Chief Jones says, date back to two-hundred-year-old Peelian principles, that the police must earn the voluntary cooperation of the public to be able to secure respect and order. When officers go through a procedural justice training for the first time, he says, they are skeptical, suspecting that it is "politically correct, or the flavor of the week." But after doing it, Chief Jones says, "their feedback is so positive: 'Thanks for reminding me why I put this badge on.'"

While recruiting after bankruptcy was hard, the police department began attracting officers drawn to trust building and principled policing. Chief Jones changed police recruitment videos from "rifles and exciting things" to "community policing emphasizing humor and integrity." He built an award-winning officer wellness program to face the emotional and domestic toll of the hypervigilance that officers develop on the job, which itself creates risks to the public.

Stockton's reforms through the National Initiative for Building Community Trust and Justice grant were formally evaluated by the Urban Institute. The evaluation found that residents were more willing to cooperate with police, call for service, and share anonymous tips; residents felt better about safety and police legitimacy; police made fewer arrests; property crimes fell; officer-involved shootings decreased 80 percent in 2018; and police solved more cases. But I got a more spontaneous, informal version of those findings at a public meeting in South Stockton in 2018, when Lara announced an upcoming procedural justice training with the police department. One attendee at the meeting raised his hand and offered an unsolicited testimonial for the experience: "As a Black male, it was one of the most amazing things I've ever done. It made me proud of our community and the police department. It was an open dialogue—to understand them and for them to understand us."

Trauma counselors are now in place at the city's public high schools. Dellafosse ran a pilot with MindRight Health, a tech service that tries to meet youth where they are—at their phones—by having remote counselors check on them daily through texts and calls, then warn local counselors when a youth will need extra support. She also cofounded the South Stockton Schools Initiative, which organized one of the nation's strongest campaigns to demand that a school district shift resources away from its police department and toward counseling and restorative justice methods for diffusing conflict. Dellafosse has now become a statewide organizer for racial and youth justice.

For Tubbs, Jones, Salazar, and others, the idea was never that treating trauma substituted for other anti-violence strategies. Citywide, there was a wider vision of promoting public safety beyond the police department. In 2014, city leaders established an Office of Violence Prevention as a branch of the city manager's office. That office's civilian Ceasefire and Peacekeeper operations work to divert youth and adults from gang involvement and chain retaliation. In 2018, Mayor Tubbs recruited and secured private philanthropic funding for a partnership with Advance Peace, a diversion program that aims to reduce gun violence by providing monthly stipends coupled with intensive therapy, social services, and employment coaching to small groups of young men at high risk of committing violent gun crimes. He and other supporters of the partnership argued that the program was in the city's financial best interests. According to the Law Center to Prevent Gun Violence, which supported the program, medical care to treat gunshot injuries costs $49,164 per homicide, and police investigations cost $439,217 per homicide. The structure of the program as a fellowship for "active shooters," however, faced feverish opposition in Stockton among those who saw gun violence as rooted in moral failure rather than in social conditions.

Former Mayor Tubbs pushed for language in the city that moved beyond a police-centered view of public safety. "Because of understaffing of the police department," he says, "we were forced to rethink public safety." The city developed a "collective impact model," with schools, hospitals, police, and other partners taking ownership of safety and gathered at the same table. "Crime is a symptom of the deeper issues," Tubbs said, "and we have to solve them over time." Back when Tubbs had been on the city council, the REINVENT Coalition had developed a "Cradle-to-Career" vision for improvements. As mayor, with help from the nonprofit consulting group PolicyLink and other partners, he worked with the coalition to build an evidence-based plan with measurable indicators of success related to five community priorities: early literacy, violence prevention, affordable housing, healthy living, and successful transitions to adulthood. They inventoried public and private efforts pursuing these goals. That meant, for example, drilling down into exactly how many pre-care and after-care slots were available for each elementary school, compared to what was needed.

I saw the damage of intergenerational trauma in Stockton. But it is a space of intergenerational healing, too. I met two dozen social workers, counselors, and others at community organizations who had risen out of difficult childhoods. They were now caring for younger people to buffer the traumas of the next generation. That work seemed to provide meaning and love in lives that didn't always have enough of either.

Maria Alcazar, one of these counselors, spent her teenage years in a public housing complex in South Stockton. As a young woman, she witnessed the dangers of gun violence and the drug trade. Her brother, a young professional and local mentor, was killed walking by New Grand Save in 1999, when an intoxicated man accidentally fired his gun. Alcazar began working in a gang diversion program to steer teenage girls away from violence. About fifteen years ago, she walked into the cafeteria of a continuation high school, and a young girl named Yesenia Gomez looked her up and down and said, "Who the fuck are you?"

At that time in her life, Gomez tells me, "I was ditching school, drinking, using drugs." Her mom worked long hours and Gomez was sexually abused by a family member. "I was used to hanging around other broken people," Gomez continued, and "things weren't getting any better." She had barely been outside Stockton, summing up her isolation with the simple fact, "I had never been to the snow." Alcazar helped Gomez experience and feel comfortable in a social life beyond her neighborhood. It helped Gomez imagine she could be a role model for her own sister.

Along with another gang-diversion counselor named Gino Avila, Alcazar recognized Gomez for what she was: a scared, wounded child. Avila, a formerly incarcerated gang member who now wishes he could afford to remove the black widow tattoo on his neck, knows what it is like to mask vulnerability. Yet now, there are no tattoos mean enough to disguise these three people's loving natures and their affection for one another. "I found a father figure in Gino," Gomez said. "I just got married on a hillside near Lake Tahoe and Gino walked me down the aisle." Avila chimed in with a proud smile: "And I don't even do hikes!"

Alcazar and Avila are both in their second decades of serving their communities as counselors and trust-builders. Though she is extensively trained in trauma-informed care, Alcazar emphasizes that she is not a therapist. Instead, she says, her work is rooted in "kinship—just being kind, and genuinely doing and sharing what you know, and coming from a pure heart." I am no therapist either, but as I listened to her, I thought Alcazar's and Avila's support of Gomez lined up with the clinical definition of a "buffering adult." They helped Gomez contextualize and transcend her trauma. Gomez went on to earn her master's degree in social work and is now a case manager in the Stockton Unified School District, providing trauma-informed support for children who are missing too much school.

One day America will be ashamed of the era of making police and prisons our only answer to the toxic chemistry of guns, victimization, and chronic economic stress in poor neighborhoods. We could have done better. Stockton is trying to do better.

WORTHY

Healing for All

Back at the start of this chapter, I mentioned the death of Angelo Peraza, nicknamed Lolo, an eighteen-year-old who was killed in 2011. A memorial video on YouTube that his friends made for him has been played and replayed, and replayed again, more than 21,000 times. Its audio opens with a song one of his friends wrote for him, which begins with a tribute to Peraza. The song ends:

> Angelo Peraza, you will always be missed,
> My little homie Lolo, one of the realest.
> It got me thinking, am I gonna be next?
> That's why I drink this Remy bottle til there's none left.

When Peraza was killed, there were no counseling services available for the friends who wrote that song, or his grieving family members, unless they could afford private therapy. By 2016, such services were available in Stockton. But even then (until August 20, 2018) many families and survivors of color would have been disqualified. Changing the rules behind that disqualification marked one of the hardest and most important steps in saving Stockton's future from its past.

Victims like Angelo were loved. Is that pain diminished—is its destructive potential diminished—if they were arrested at some point before their death? The effort to answer that question "no" originated at Fathers & Families of San Joaquin County. The organization has since closed, but for years, its downtown space included a community center for elders, where any given day, one could catch lunch, dominoes, and partner dancing. Most of the staff at Fathers & Families focused on strengthening families through reentry counseling for formerly incarcerated adults. They worked with at-risk teenagers, including legal advocacy to humanize juvenile defendants during sentencing to protect them from adult prison. These efforts were mostly staffed by formerly incarcerated men and women. "This place rehumanized me," said Eduardo Crabbe, a staff member. "It brought my social status back. I'm now around public officials and others I couldn't have been around before. People don't judge me—DAs, sheriffs. I paid my dues. What can I do now? This place gave me a platform to help me give back."

In 2016, Fathers & Families led a successful application for state funding to expand into trauma recovery work. Whereas the clinic at the Dorothy Jones Center offers shorter-term counseling for a range of mental health needs and is funded through clients' medical insurance and the Affordable Care Act, the Stockton Trauma Recovery Center (TRC) provided more intensive, state-funded counseling for victims of enumerated violent crimes, including those who have been shot, stabbed, or raped; lost a family member to homicide; or suffered domestic violence, child abuse, or human trafficking. Using notification from the Stockton Police or referrals through their social networks in the city, TRC outreach workers went to crime scenes to help families at the peak of crisis and try to prevent retaliation.

The center provided no-cost, long-term therapy that started, at the outset, like urgent care. The day before I first met her, TRC counselor Trish Aguilar had spent her morning with a domestic violence victim who had fled her partner and was homeless. That afternoon she visited a mother who had just lost her son to homicide. "You need to sit there and talk to the person for two hours and talk to them about why they— why they don't need to die, because at first they want to die too," Aguilar says. Over the longer run, explained former TRC director Gauri Sanchez, the goal is to let clients "control their story" and direct their own care and goals for therapy, to restore their hold on life after a terrible event they could not stop. She gives an example of another client who had lost her son: "She is scared to go out. She comes into therapy, but every time she comes out of there, she's just kind of afraid on the streets, so [her therapist] has been saying, 'ok, let's go walk today during therapy.'" They focused on breathing, coping, taking steps.

Trauma Recovery Center counselors also helped clients access victim compensation funds, which are available in California (as in other states) to help survivors pay bills related to the crime they suffered, including funeral expenses, medical treatment, and residential security. Yet from the moment the center opened, its case managers kept running into a legal wall—a California rule that saw the phrase "crime victim" as inapplicable to a person alleged to be entangled with past criminal activity. TRC clients who had lost family members to gun violence were routinely denied victim compensation reimbursement on the grounds that the victim was at fault for being in the wrong place at the wrong time or had a criminal background.

This barrier dates back to the origin of victim's compensations funds, which were built on the notion that people could not be both victims and perpetrators. In April 1982, when President Ronald Reagan launched a federal reform effort to provide support for victims, he said:

> [The principles of freedom under law] will lose their meaning and our citizens will lose faith in them if we concentrate solely on punishing criminals and ignore the suffering of those upon whom the criminals prey. They should not be treated as ciphers on a statistician's chart. They are our fellow citizens—human beings who have experienced the tragedies of grievous personal injury, lost homes, ruined businesses, stolen belongings, and even the death of loved ones because some among us choose in cruel and violent ways to defy the rule of law.

As the rules implementing this commitment took place, they tried to divide victims worthy of this loving rehumanization from victims who had forfeited such care by hurting others. California's Victim Compensation Board, which collects fines and fees from federal and state offenders and distributes them to victims in the state, was authorized to deny a claim if the board's staff found that the applicant was involved in events that led up to the crime. The easy way to implement this practice was a quick online search. California maintains a database of persons convicted "or suspected" of gang membership or affiliation, imposing a blanket disqualification of people listed there, even without any specific information that a person's past affiliation or association was even still current, let alone connected to their victimization.

The database is not publicly accessible, but many youth killed or wounded in Stockton could have been tagged in it because of the high arrest rates and decades of racially discriminatory policing. His mother and sister would likely have been denied services even if Peraza's death had nothing to do with that incident in the car, or even if he was killed in crossfire. A 2016 state audit of this database revealed serious concerns with it, including that "law enforcement agencies could not always demonstrate that they had established reasonable suspicion that groups were gangs before entering them into CalGang," and that "law enforcement agencies do not have adequate support for some of the individuals and many of the criteria they entered into CalGang." In 2017, more than 100,000 people were listed in it, 93,000 of whom were Hispanic, Black, or Asian-American. In 2020, after reforms and leadership by Los Angeles County to address CalGang's racial bias, arbitrary standards, and ineffectiveness, the number of records in the database dropped to 45,000. But at least 90 percent of people listed were still people of color.

Marco, who spent several years as a youth justice organizer, said that learning about this database helped explain a lot of his experiences over the years. As a child, Marco grew up with conflict and violence at home, where his father battled alcoholism and drug abuse. Marco became preoccupied with earning enough income to move out. He got a fake ID that said he was old enough for employment and spent a summer in farm labor. That work left him wrecked with exhaustion, and anyway, there were few hours available if he stayed in school. He never joined a gang but worked with a couple of friends to become a dealer.

Even though Marco never joined a gang, when he was arrested and sentenced to juvenile hall, staff would look at his electronic records and identify him as a Norteño. Near the end of his probation, he was pulled over by police. They handcuffed him, patted him down, and conducted a search of his car. The next day they searched his mother's house. Marco felt re-traumatized by the experience. "The way they talk to you! 'So we got a shooter. So you're a gang member.' No, I'm not. 'So you're just hanging around guns? You're a Norteño.' But I'm not." Marco has a steady job now and remains on track to terminate his probation, and he's devoted to trying to expunge the record of his juvenile conviction. Yet if Marco was in fact listed in CalGang, he would need to navigate a petition process with local law enforcement agencies to remove his name from the database or wait five years after his last entry—even though he stresses that if he's in there, it was never correct to begin with.

In fighting for families in neighborhoods where social networks cross paths with illegal activity, Fathers & Families gave a lot of thought to the legal and symbolic force of the word "gang," which seemed to be doing the work at the Victim Compensation Board of converting victims into perpetrators. The term "gang" is used loosely, both in speech and in law, and it is routinely used to refer to scenarios ranging from large, multi-national organizations to a group of three teenagers selling drugs. The word strips children and youth of their innocence, even when they are more scared or traumatized than hardened. The city's young people, Fathers & Families staff would often say, come from Stockton's conditions. Victims seeking trauma counseling often were, or might become, those also in need of services to rebuild families after incarceration.

Faith in forgiveness and the promise that people can change was the point of the work at Fathers & Families. To give their client families the chance to heal, California law needed to change too. So that's what Fathers & Families did. They drafted a bill stating that "victims should be encouraged to access victim compensation services regardless of their own, or their family's, alleged gang membership, affiliation, or association, or their or their family's documentation or immigration status." That effort became AB 1639, titled the "Healing For All" bill. Missy Rae Magdalera, who worked at the TRC, said the expanded eligibility bill meant people cannot be turned away as "unworthy." That idea of "worthiness," she says, is at the center of everything. "Systems created a certain narrative about the people that we work with and deny them the things that they need in order to heal." Dozens of youth wrote letters describing the need to stabilize their lives and communities through trauma counseling and presented them at the State Capitol.

California's governor Jerry Brown signed the Healing For All bill into law August 20, 2018. It expressed a commitment that hurt people must be healed so they don't hurt people—including their children, including strangers, including themselves. But in Stockton, as in many American places now two generations into postindustrial job losses, addiction crises that fuel drug markets, and one of the highest rates of incarceration in world history, that principle had to go a step further: hurt people, *even ones who have already hurt people,* must be healed so they don't hurt others.

In a note to Marco, who had worked as one of the Healing For All bill organizers, I wrote that his work and life represented the virtues and values that world religions strive to teach: Redemption, Forgiveness, Mercy, Compassion, and Love. Marco wrote me back, "Those 5 are what happens when you heal." He is now working at a local business in a job he loves. His son is entering elementary school and plays a starring role in Marco's social media channels.

On January 21, 2019, California's next governor Gavin Newsom named Dr. Nadine Burke Harris as the first-ever surgeon general for the state. After a career running a health clinic in a high-poverty community, then a research and advocacy center related to childhood trauma, she had become the nation's leading public figure on the prevention and treatment of ACEs in childhood. She embarked on an ambitious campaign to cut childhood ACEs in half within a generation. How would she do it? Using the same basic components Stockton had come up with: trauma-informed care training across education and law enforcement, better access to mental health services, and improved training for health care providers. On January 22, 2019, the day after her appointment as surgeon general, she visited Stockton for a roundtable discussion with community leaders.

A MOVEMENT FOR OPEN WINDOWS

Progression, Regression, and the Work Ahead

On a visit to Stockton in 2017, I stepped into a restaurant for lunch on a street known as the Miracle Mile. In the 1920s, a developer built the

Miracle Mile as a pedestrian-centered shopping and restaurant district along Pacific Avenue, running north from the old segregation line of Harding Way. In more recent decades, the Miracle Mile has struggled to compete with car-centered malls farther north, but it has maintained its homey, humble atmosphere of small businesses. That lunchtime in 2017, the chatty owner saw me organizing my thoughts in a notebook and learned I was from out of town. As I stood to leave, she warned me solemnly: "Around here is ok, but don't go south of Harding Way." She reached out and shifted my messenger bag, which was already slung across my body with a cross strap, so it was in front of me. "And call me if you need any help, ok?" I had just spent the morning in South Stockton, so my first reaction was to feel sorry for her. South Stockton, I thought to myself, was where a person could find the city's mile of miracles today.

That is still true, though several years later, it is harder to feel bullish about the city. Mayor Tubbs and several key allies faced opposition from concentrated interests, then lost their bids for reelection in November 2020. A local blog, whose founder had a good-faith policy disagreement with Tubbs that metastasized into a vendetta against him, set out to oppose Tubbs and his allies. The blog, which had become popular for useful breaking reporting and sweet local stories about topics like traffic accidents and graduations, sprinkled in attacks on Tubbs's character and unsubstantiated allegations. In an expression, I think, of the lasting damage that decades of mismanagement and bankruptcy had done, Stocktonians' low expectations of their own government seemed to make local views that their mayor was bad more plausible than outsiders' views celebrating their leader as good.

Tubbs faced other challenges, too, such as the local (and national) rise in homicides during early COVID-19 pandemic lockdowns and layoffs. Local skepticism also ran high about universal basic income, which Tubbs had championed through a privately funded pilot program run in Stockton. He had spent more time away from the city than some people thought he should have, though those critics did not seem to acknowledge how much private philanthropy his rising external profile was bringing to the city's people. Tubbs's loss was compounded in May 2021, when the founder of Fathers & Families was arrested and charged with crimes that were so antithetical to the organization's mission that it folded, taking the important work of the Trauma Recovery Center with it.

But the good work in Stockton did not depend on any one official or organization, and it will continue. Lange Luntao, one of the Tubbs allies who lost his school board race, would have been the subject of this chapter if this book were called *The Fight to Save the Schools*. Luntao has been devastated by the setbacks in Stockton, but level-headed too. "This has always been a marathon relay," he said, "not a sprint. We need to get through these setbacks so we can get back into the larger fight." Under the motto "Heal, Grow, Change," Jasmine Dellafosse is working with Lecia Harrison, the mother of Brandon Harrison, a youth leader lost to gun violence, to build a program called Be Smooth that incorporates trauma counseling and rituals of grief and mourning to support youth and families.

For now, this book will head north from Stockton along I-5, which crosses into southern Oregon just east of Josephine County. The region likely has the worst rate of opioid overdoses in the west, though shortages of medical examiners make it hard to be sure. Just as Stockton has long been a distribution hub for food and manufactured goods, the city is a hub of the networks that move heroin and synthetic opioids northbound. In that way, Josephine is linked to the anti-trauma, anti-violence work underway in Stockton.

I asked many of the Stockton trauma counselors that I interviewed what they do to decompress after a day at work. These were some of their answers:

I go straight to my kids and hug them.

I take a shower, then lay on my back in the dark for a few minutes.

I drive the long way home through an orchard and focus on my breathing.

Their work is hard, but it defines a direction toward meaningful change for the people of this proud city. For years, Stockton was known for "broken windows" policing that showed zero tolerance for even small, nonviolent infractions. I think that today, Stockton should be known for developing "open windows" work that stretches far beyond the police department. That description honors the breezes that drift off the Delta waterways, a gift of the region's wetland ecology. At night, these breezes wash away the heat of summer days, making for pleasant evenings to leave your windows open and linger outside. For too long, there have been large areas of Stockton where residents could not comfortably come and go from their cars in the evening, let alone take a walk or sit on their porches. It is the counselors, social workers, and healers of Stockton who can give trust back to the city's people. It is this trust—not more prison sentences—that will help cool the city down, both from high temperatures and from violence.

This movement for open windows will take time. In a photograph that I love, a man had a message written in thick pen on his raised palms: *"Dear Stockton, I won't give up on you, ever."*

Man in the Arena

Josephine County, Oregon

Many other places in America would call Grave Creek a river. But it is small by comparison to the Rogue River, which the Grave joins in a torrent of whitecaps. The creek is named after a sixteen-year-old pioneer named Martha Leland Crowley, who died there of typhoid fever in 1846. Her fiancé marked her grave with a wooden headstone, which served for many years as a trail marker for the wagon trains following behind.

In 2009, a twenty-year-old woman named Caitlyn Strauser also lost her life at Grave Creek. Her boyfriend Joey O'Dell was wanted on drug possession and auto theft charges. According to a detective on the case, she was trying to persuade O'Dell to turn himself in. He had agreed, and the night before her death, they camped in his truck near the shore. The next morning they argued. Strauser ran. O'Dell caught up to her. In a methamphetamine-fueled rage, he killed her with a rock. He submerged her in Grave Creek to suggest an accidental drowning, then dropped her body at a friend's home.

People who loved Strauser, including her mother, heard what O'Dell had done. They also knew about his struggle with addiction and his own brutal past. When O'Dell was a boy, his father was fatally shot by a man protecting O'Dell's mother from domestic violence. His mother was then killed in an unsolved murder near railroad tracks when O'Dell was fourteen. In the aftermath of Strauser's death, with O'Dell on the run from the law, Strauser's mother and other locals spoke with him. Yet for weeks, they refused to speak with the police. The rural township of Wolf Creek, where Strauser and O'Dell lived, had long subsisted off the grid of just about any public services. Most residents preferred to keep it that way.

As many locals say with both pride and shame, rural Josephine is a "rough and tumble" place. On the cover of a history of the county, a sepia-toned photo depicts a pioneer couple standing two feet apart in front of a canvas tent. Wearing smudged overalls, the man is unsmiling beneath his beard. His wife's face is as stern as her woolen skirt. She is holding a thirty-two-inch rifle. "Maude and William Bigelow enjoy the natural beauty of Josephine County," the caption reads without irony. Maude's warning face portends the politics of the county's libertarian, conservative majority. But her photograph also captures the fierce independence of the region's lefty farm and forest communes. At the Magic Forest Farm, a housing collective founded in 1967, residents seem to capture Josephine's wider culture with the Farm's operating principle: "If you want a cup of coffee, go find an ax."

So it was that Josephine managed a radical experiment in local government downsizing. In recent decades, budget cuts eliminated most local public functions other than law enforcement, then leveled law enforcement, too. For years, the county ran by principles of independence: if you want a library, volunteer to fundraise private dollars to support one. If you want to reduce break-ins, volunteer to patrol your streets at night. If you want emergency law enforcement, sign up to take your neighbors' calls on your cell phone and dispatch with your own gun.

The remaining local officials, however, still had to govern. The words "Man in the Arena" float around as the screensaver message on Josephine County Sheriff Dave Daniel's desktop. He keeps it as a reminder of Teddy Roosevelt's speech celebrating the man who is not just a critic, but "who strives valiantly; who errs, who comes short again and again, because there is no effort without error and shortcoming." The sheriff has to be like that—a man who fights from within government, trying to hold on to at least a "night-watchman state" as politics and funding tighten around him. "We're driving an eighteen wheeler, and we've got ten wheels on right now, maybe nine," Daniel said in 2016.

Back then, Sheriff Daniel was bracing for even further cuts. The federal government had been sending special funding to Josephine and other "timber counties" in Oregon for more than twenty years, but those payments were sure to end. Federal funding dated back to an infamously polarizing environmental conflict: the battle over logging the old growth forests of the Pacific Northwest, where the endangered northern spotted owl nests in one of the world's most complex ecosystems. Recompense for the lost local jobs and public revenues could not go on forever, but neither could Josephine easily replace federal dollars. A 1990s tax revolt in Oregon cinched Josephine in a legal straitjacket by locking local taxes into an unsustainably low rate and requiring voting majority approval of any increases.

Given those tax laws, it wasn't enough that Sheriff Daniel and other government officials believed that the cuts to services had gone too far. To do something about it, they had to build a grassroots movement in favor of new taxes in one of the most anti-government places in America. You can still make your own damn coffee, they argued, but a local government needs a few jail cells and some trained patrol officers to dispatch for 911 calls. It needs the kind of investigators who can coax witnesses and family members out of the shadows in cases like Caitlyn Strauser's murder.

Josephine has become a pioneer county once again. Its residents have been called upon to restore the public law enforcement that their Gold Rush forefathers built 150 years ago. Or to let it go.

"TIMBER!"

Boom and Bust in the Pacific Northwest

When Martha Crowley and subsequent wagon trains crossed Josephine in the 1840s, the area around Grave Creek was governed by the Cow Creek Band, one of several bands of Umpqua Indians in southwest Oregon. The Umpqua and Rogue River watersheds offered abundant food sources, including deer, elk, silver salmon in the summer, steelhead in the winter, huckleberries, wild onions, and nuts. Coastal forests nurtured a rich Umpqua tradition of native plant medicine.

But within a few years, these tribes were in crisis. They lost more than half of their community from disease and conflict with a growing tide of white settlers lured by the 1851 discovery of gold in Josephine. In 1852, settlers accused the son of the chief of the Cow Creek Band of making an indecent suggestion to a white woman. The county had no local government or criminal justice system, but a vigilance committee—a group of white volunteers who arrested, judged, and punished alleged crimes—assembled. The chief's son was easy to recognize: he had the massive scar across his neck where settlers had tried to cut off his head for selling them a booby-trapped gun. Within four hours of the alleged indecent gesture, the vigilantes bound his limbs, tied a noose around his neck, and took him by horseback to a forested hillside. They lashed the noose to a tree limb, ignoring his threats of kinsmen's retribution, and ran the horse out from under him. They hanged the chief's son along his scar and threw his body into a bonfire.

The tribe never got its chance for retribution. At Grave Creek, the chief's son's death marks the conquest of Umpqua law and the era of vigilance committees. In 1853, the federal government coerced the Cow Creek Band into ceding 800 miles of territory. The chief himself was subsequently murdered. In 1856, after waging the Rogue River Wars, settlers forced tribal members on a 160-mile journey, a western Trail of Tears, to relocate to the Grand Ronde Reservation in northern Oregon.

Oregon legally established 1,642 square miles of land (an area larger than Rhode Island) as Josephine County in 1856. The county elected eight public officers, including its first government sheriff. The vigilance committees were retired, but bands of volunteers continued to patrol the region well into the 1860s. The rough justice of these frontier days was full of overreaction, impulse, manipulation, and error, with too many men hanged on too few facts. Like most western counties at that time, it took Josephine several years to replace vigilantism with a cohort of public law enforcement officers, a judicial system to protect the innocent, and a jail to enforce sentences less punitive than death.

Fast forward to 1978, and a man named Ken Selig started a career as one of those paid government officers. Fresh out of the Marine Corps and the police academy, he had come to the county with his new wife, the great-granddaughter of a Gold Rush–era postman who rafted the Rogue River to deliver the mail. Selig's thirty-three-year career as a deputy sheriff, followed by several years leading an armed neighborhood watch, maps the modern history of law enforcement in the county. During that career, he led the investigation of Caitlyn Strauser's murder.

Selig's first assignment in Josephine was as the resident deputy for the rural township of Wolf Creek, a service area that included Grave Creek. Selig's supervisor told him that as a dedicated local officer, Selig would be like Wolf Creek's chief of police. Locals seemed unimpressed. Driving down the main street in a cruiser on his first visit, several residents flipped Selig the bird. Two seemingly irreconcilable groups of people had made the township their home. They both hated law enforcement.

The first group, whom locals still call the hippies, came to town during a resurgent back-to-the-land movement in the 1960s and 70s. Josephine County landed on the cover of *Life* magazine in 1969 in an article about the Family of the Mystic Arts, a community that combined Christian fundamentalism with the "time of the tribal dance . . . as we go to live in tepees, celebrate our joys together, and learn to survive."

The Family of the Mystic Arts did not last, but Josephine attracted other more durable communes of people seeking life off the cultural grid. The woman's land movement, built on lesbian feminist ideals, took root in Wolf Creek. Leaders there published *WomanSpirit,* a magazine featuring photography, poetry, and essays of women building houses and infrastructure, growing food, making music, and forming domestic partnerships without men. Gay men established their own communal lands. A Maoist Sissy commune, which would later become a Radical Faerie Sanctuary, put down roots in Wolf Creek to provide an escape from the "repressive default world" of gender and sexuality. At summer gatherings, men from across the country could find the "verdant comfort of the gentle yet aged grandfather maple, his arms outstretched to embrace all his beautiful sprites and satyrs."

Just about a half-hour drive away from these communes, the melodramatically homophobic Roy Masters established the Foundation for Human Understanding. Perhaps the most nationally influential newcomer to Josephine in the 1960s, Masters started a radio show and retreat center to "de-hypnotize" Americans from liberal projects such as day care, which he viewed as a "dangerous" idea rooted in "radical feminism." For several decades, he counseled meditation tools as an alternative to doctors and argued that unbridled women cause divorce, stress, poverty, gay sons, and illness. Many locals in Josephine thought of Masters as a cult leader, but he influenced a generation of self-described Roybots who fought for slashing local government. Masters broadcasted a show that his son Mark Masters developed into a national hub of radical-right radio, which raised up Michael Savage, Laura Ingraham, and other leaders of anti-government populism.

Roy Masters would resist any association with the hippies, but the elder's retreat center put him closer to the communes than to the second big group living around Wolf Creek upon Selig's arrival. Many locals call this second group the "straight poor"—the second- and third-generation locals living on low incomes from blue-collar jobs. The timber industry had been rooted in Josephine since the 1920s, after their operations had emptied the forests of the Great Lakes region. Southwest Oregon's forested Siskiyou Mountains join with the Cascade and Coastal ranges to create one of the world's largest softwood forests. The oldest Douglas firs there had been growing for more than a thousand years. Full-grown trees are more than 200 feet tall, with stumps that could sit eight men across. Logging the big western trees was described as "more dangerous than war" in the early twentieth century. Even by the 1990s, the risk of death on the job was still eight times higher than in mining. Loggers relied on precision and experience. "Don't let anyone tell you this was low-skilled work," former Josephine County commissioner Simon Hare said, gesturing to an eight-foot saw hanging in his office.

Even at timber's peak, when Oregon was nicknamed the "flannel-shirt frontier," most jobs were not cutting trees. Most timber-related workers manufactured products made from wood, including paper, or trucked logs and goods out of the region. The wood-products industry aligned Oregon towns with the rise and fall of the Rust Belt.* But

---

* The fact that timber country is mostly "rural" and we think of the industrial Rust Belt as predominantly "urban" should only remind us how little those terms tell us about an area's employment. Nationwide, manufacturing jobs account for a large share of the rural economy, and rural manufacturing jobs have been especially vulnerable to automation and international competition.

blue-collar jobs in southern Oregon were mostly nonunionized and lower-paid, rarely offering the middle-class living associated with coal mining or manufacturing elsewhere. In part, that was because global markets for wood mill and manufacturing jobs came early. In 1928, a journalist named James Stevens traveled to South America on a ship carrying three million board feet of Northwestern Douglas fir. At an Argentine sawmill, he reported, laborers "toiled ten hours a day for unbelievably low wages" to cut and process the wood.

By the time Selig moved to the county, automation was eliminating jobs even as the industry boomed. In the earliest years of Western logging, it had taken a crew of half a dozen men a whole day just to cut the branches and fell the top section of a giant tree. By the 1970s, mobile steel towers replaced timber jobs known as climbers, fellers, and rig-up crews. Truck technology downsized jobs as well. A triumphant page of the 1978 Scholastic Press edition of *The Truck Book* for children exclaimed, "In the forest, logging trucks can quickly do jobs that once took lumberjacks many days of work!" But the king of automation was the "feller buncher," a machine invented in the 1960s that could cut, stack, and delimb trees. Modern feller bunchers do the work of ten to fifteen men at a rate faster than humans ever could, felling and stacking up to 200 trees an hour. During the recession of the early 1980s, which reduced demand for housing lumber, these technologies and others in the mills allowed "restructuring" of the wood-products industry to use fewer workers. In the 1980s, the Pacific Northwest's timber industry laid off 20 percent of its workforce, even though it *increased* production by 50 percent. These changes drove wages down. People in the wood-products industry who managed to keep their jobs took a 22 percent cut in real earnings between 1978 and 1990.

Back in Selig's Wolf Creek years, Josephine's incompatible rural subgroups mostly stayed away from one another and from the government. Selig learned early on that "the badge was a liability." A resident had taken a shot at the prior Wolf Creek deputy, as Selig was reminded daily by the bullet hole in his patrol car. But generally speaking, Selig thought residents didn't want to kill police officers as much as give them a bloody nose. Mostly, residents wanted to be left alone, particularly when it came to pot, alcohol, hallucinogens, and harder drugs.

One day Selig received a call from a payphone to the sheriff's office. "Hey, we just want you to know something," the caller told him. The caller and a group of friends had been sitting in a rural park smoking weed and drinking around a pickup truck, Selig recounts. A second, more rowdy crowd arrived. A drunk man in the second group grabbed a woman by her hair and dragged her across the parking lot. Another man in the park intervened and freed the woman, but her assailant pulled a knife and stabbed the man who had interfered. The bleeding man made it into a friend's truck and they rushed to the hospital. Once there, the wounded man refused to describe the incident or provide any names other than his own. The witness who had called told Selig that he and his friends had already cleaned up the blood, glass, and hair. But, the caller told Selig, "if you happen to have a car in the area, you might want to drive by."

The caller didn't ask for an ambulance or for cops to chase the bad guy. He didn't think of the place as a crime scene where photos or evidence could be important. He must have figured that a sheriff's car in the area could keep things quiet, but he didn't insist on it. In contrast to the city, where Selig says "they expect you, the cops, to solve almost all of their problems," in rural areas "people tend to solve their own problems, and it's not only by lawful means." A separate "common law" of crime governs their expectations, with locals saying they don't "subscribe" to the state penal code that the sheriff is sworn to uphold. Moral, or *malum in se*, offenses like rape and homicide could be matters for the police, Selig says, but locals did not believe the state should interfere when it came to legal, or *malum prohibitum*, wrongs, such as drunk driving, drug abuse, and theft. "Those people never spoke Latin," he jokes. "But that's the code they would operate under."

For a while, Selig got to be the kind of officer that community needed. That meant talking to people to understand their values, he says, and empathizing with their situation. It meant earning trust through meetings in coffee shops, helping with yard work, and looking out for older people. It meant small choices like taking a child home after she pedaled her tricycle onto the highway, without scolding her parents for failing to watch her. It also meant "negotiating" with locals. For crimes like drug abuse and DUIs, he explains, "You find another way. You take them home." Yielding to the local moral code rather than the Oregon Penal Code helped Selig gather information about who was committing violent crimes, including strong-armed robberies and the occasional homicide. In a rural setting at least twenty miles away from backup, "building alliances" was also a matter of personal safety. "If I needed help, there wasn't time," he explains, recalling an experience when he pulled over a motorist who became belligerent. A third car pulled up behind theirs, and Selig was relieved to see it was a local he'd once let go with a warning for driving with a suspended license. The man got out and offered to stand by in case Selig needed help.

It took Selig more than a year in Wolf Creek to convince locals that he wasn't going anywhere and could be trusted. But just a few years into his assignment at Wolf Creek, when the recession of the early 1980s forced a round of layoffs at the sheriff's office, the county's resident deputy program was dissolved. Selig transferred back to the county's more populous core. Any recession that affects property values and incomes hurts local government revenues, and this was no exception. But in Oregon's timber counties, the impact was even more severe. During recessions, construction demand for timber falls and logging on federal land slows. In an arrangement in place to this day, the federal government shares 50 percent of the net revenues from timber harvests on its property with Oregon public schools and counties that enclose federal forests.

At times in its history, that meant big revenues for Josephine, because nearly three-fourths of the forests in the county are owned by a federal agency. While the federal government did not otherwise pay a normal rate of property taxes to Josephine for its forest land (just as private owners in Oregon with land in pure "forest use" pay sharply discounted property taxes), the county came to rely on funding from federal timber harvests. This receipts system created a double dependence on logging on federal land: first, for jobs with private contractors hired for the clearcuts and mill work, and second, for revenue to pay for public services and government jobs. During recessions, incomes for households and for the government both crashed.

"Lots of timber, hire people," Selig explained. "No timber, layoffs." Until 1990, there were few constraints on federal logging other than the price of timber, and people expected that eventually the feds would "log it all." That had been the management approach to old growth forests owned by the states of Oregon and Washington, private companies, and local counties—all of which had clearcut nearly all their holdings by the end of World War II. In Washington, the state's Department of Natural Resources was nicknamed the "Department of Nothing Remaining." Old growth is not a renewable resource within current lifetimes. Even landholders who invest in replanting their property establish farm tree monocultures rather than forests. Herbicides and fertilizers try to hurry things up, but softwood tree farms take decades of growing time just to yield skinny young trunks.

The partnership between the federal government and local land-owners worked well so long as everyone agreed what to do with the forests. But in 1990, the two groups diverged, and the region's timber wars began. The face of these wars was the northern spotted owl, with its striped, forty-inch wingspan. As scientists discovered the teeming biodiversity of the forests of the Pacific Northwest, environmentalists moved to protect the remaining federal old growth. Only the Endangered Species Act offered a tool for ecosystem protection across such a large, multi-state area. The U.S. Fish and Wildlife Service listed the owl as a threatened species under the Endangered Species Act, and the next year, a federal court prohibited most of the clearcut logging of the birds' habitat.

Non-federal landowners had few old growth forests to log, but the rulings abruptly slowed logging on federal forest land, devastating the regional timber industry. Between 1989 and 1999, 45 percent of the sawmills in Oregon went out of business. By 2000, timber harvests on 24 million acres of federal land had dropped 90 percent from timber's heyday. Photographs of the owls and their featherball chicks dominated the news coverage so completely that the harms of automation and restructuring in the timber industry mostly escaped blame as codrivers of decline.

The spotted owl listing sparked a class and culture war. As one timber worker put it, "Some people think we're a bunch of dumb hicks who just like to butcher trees, but they can't get through a day without using wood somehow. Why should I be ashamed to provide something that everyone needs?" Both sides dug their trenches deep. Shops in the Pacific Northwest sold bumper stickers reading "Save a Logger, Shoot an Owl" and "Don't like Logging? Try Wiping with a Spotted Owl." Environmentalists printed T-shirts featuring the rings of a giant cut tree with an arrow pointing to an outer ring that said, "Loggers get a new job." In local politics, automation and globalization were recognized drivers of job losses, but somehow treated as natural, unstoppable forces. Environmental law, by contrast, was understood as a political choice, in which federal officials in power sacrificed Josephine's jobs in favor of abstract moral or scientific values. People across the political spectrum submitted to globalization and automation without a fight, but they picked sides, dug trenches, and fought hard when it came to environmental law.

Activists were right that the hour of obsolescence for old-growth timber jobs would come whether the ancient trees were cut or not— there were a finite number of them left. The question was whether the industry would die before or after the ecosystem was gone. But that argument was hard to make when timber industry workers were not the ones buying expensive doors and furniture made from old growth fir, or decks made of primeval redwood from Northern California. Behind the scenes, multinational timber companies headquartered in cities stood to gain most from a resumption of clearcutting the big trees, but in places like Josephine, the timber wars put wage-earning locals in conflict with college-educated activists and limousine liberals living somewhere else.

President Bill Clinton and Vice President Al Gore's Northwest Forest Plan in 1993 sought a compromise between environmental and economic objectives by putting $1.2 billion into five years of funding for job retraining programs, economic diversification, and local government services in California, Washington, and Oregon. The job-training programs showed gains, but they could not reach all displaced workers nor match the timber pay scale. These programs also struggled with the serious educational deficits in place: large numbers of dislocated forestry workers who sought job retraining came in with limited literacy and math skills. "Cussing at computers" replaced the work they knew.

Meanwhile, the tax breaks and federal deficits of the Reagan years had caught up to the local community college, which had to cancel its more expensive vocational-technology courses in the late 1990s at the Grants Pass campus.

Even though the federal government failed to smooth out the hardest edges for loggers and mill workers in the county, it did try to replace some of the public revenues lost by Oregon counties and school districts. In 1993, Congress began to grant direct subsidies for declining rural areas in forty-two states. Oregon's timber counties took home a full half of the total payments made nationwide—a wildly disproportionate share by any measure of population or need, but reflective of the intensity of the timber wars. With the subsidies, people like Ken Selig kept their job providing basic services in the county. But as the years dragged on, the funds for Oregon's timber counties came to be understood as an earmark at best and a giveaway to a low-tax county at worst. Federal funding has been saved through several late-breaking appropriations, but it has declined dramatically.

With this transition income, the idea went, timber counties could develop other industries and revenues. But postindustrial transition is never so easy. The region's population has grown, but not in ways that help much with tax and business receipts. The landscape attracts outdoor enthusiasts, and the county enjoys a small tourist sector related to river sports. A wave of retirees, especially from California, has moved to Grants Pass and its newer suburbs, which has kept the county's countywide poverty rate from rising steeply. A wave of so-called "YouTube homesteaders" bought land in the county's rural townships, learning online how to do everything from making laundry soap to repairing cars. But backwoods recreation, fixed incomes, and off-the-grid homesteaders drop few dollars into the local economy. Some say the county's best shot for economic recovery is to build a high-skilled service sector in medical services to attract more retirees, but significant workforce educational investments would have to come first. Taxing licensed marijuana farms is the next best hope.

There has yet to be a realistic, long-term transformation of the job base for the rural Pacific Northwest. The government never launched the full-scale Northwest Community Plan needed to go with the Northwest

Forests Plan. Or maybe it's not true to say there was no community plan. It was just an unspoken one: *move along now*. Move, that is, to a place with more jobs.

Many people did just that—unless they wouldn't or couldn't. Despite strong attachments to family property and regional landscapes, young people in particular have left in droves. Josephine's population is substantially older than state or national averages. More than one-fourth are older than sixty-five. Those who remain are less mobile. One in five families with minor children in Josephine live below the poverty line, and unemployment rates are among the highest in the state. Only 17.5 percent of the population has a bachelor's degree or higher, and 23 percent of the population aged eighteen to twenty-four has less than a high school degree or equivalent. Working-age adults remaining in the southern and eastern areas of the state now struggle against unemployment, drug abuse, and crime.

Jay Williams, a former mayor of Youngstown, Ohio, once explained that "[l]etting go of the past has been difficult for many people because the past was so good." It is hard to let go of the timber past in Josephine, too, though it is not quite right to say it was "so good." Rather, it was better. Timber and wood products jobs offered a modest working-class life rather than middle-class comfort, but working class at least meant working. Except for a small number of unionized jobs that were mostly in Washington State, the pay was never great. Many millworkers and loggers lived with seasonal unemployment and paltry benefits, as well as numb hands, chronic back pain, and deafness.

But logging offered challenging work outdoors, with skill sets that did not match other living wage jobs. The hours now required to make a living only intensified the loss. When Washington State passed a law setting a ten-hour per day, six days a week maximum on truck drivers' hours, many truckers could no longer clear enough profits to reach full-time minimum wage. And one logger-turned-trucker explained the other losses besides: "In the middle of winter, when the wind is blowing sideways, it's nice being inside the cab of that truck. . . . But when the sun comes out, you find yourself sizing up the trees and thinking about which way they would fall. It haunts you because you loved it so damned much."

Dave Toler, a county commissioner for Josephine from 2007 to 2011 and a rare liberal to hold office there, thinks that the local nostalgia for lost logging and mill jobs glosses over the poverty they brought. He thinks the longing is for something else that he can't quite name—a different type of family life maybe, or more conservative ideas about gender, or the lower levels of drug use, or maybe anger and fear over rising wealth, racial diversity, and education levels in Oregon's biggest cities. "You get people who never worked in that industry and think if we could just go back there, it would all be ok," he says. "There were a lot of changes since then that were not positive, but it's just a dream that timber would bring the old days back."

Toler's analysis seems true, but county visuals suggest a different story. The mountain peaks of Josephine County are still covered with forests. Resources like old-growth trees seem plentiful when living in their midst, even when they are rare for the planet. It's easy to see why locals feel land rich and wonder bitterly why they are cash poor. Antigovernment factions of county politics are fueled by the suspicion that distant cities and people in suits have locked local families away from their patrimony.

When that patrimony burns down in a catastrophic wildfire, becoming nothing more than a mushroom cloud of greenhouse gas emissions, both sides of the timber wars are devastated—and angry. Climate change has altered forest conditions and wildfire risk. In Oregon, drought conditions troubled seventeen of the twenty-one years between 2000 and 2021. The average annual temperature in the region is up by more than 1.5 degrees Fahrenheit, further weakening the trees' resistance to insects and fungal pathogens. Dry forests blighted with dead trees and disease mingled with dangerous wind conditions in the fall of 2020. One million acres of Oregon land burned, including thousands of homes and structures. The old timber wars flared again. Some blamed the environmentalist left for excessive conservation. Others blamed the political right for blocking environmental reform to slow climate change. A new flank in the timber wars revealed itself too, as the FBI and other law enforcement agencies tried to quash conspiracy theories advanced in the QAnon network that Antifa members started the fires.

The northern spotted owl remains threatened, due in large part to the thriving population of non-native barred owls. With less restrictive diets (which sometimes includes eating spotted owls), and faster reproduction, barred owls are better suited to the shifting forest climate of the Pacific Northwest and are driving northern spotted owls from their habitat. "Shoot an owl" is now an official task of some U.S. Fish and Wildlife Service employees, who have been tasked with reducing the population of the non-native species. Meanwhile, ongoing lawsuits over demands to resume large scale logging of old growth take no measure of the forests' primary ecological purpose. Their importance is far beyond nesting grounds: the more than one billion tons of Douglas fir biomass in Oregon's federal forests sequesters 573 million tons of carbon—an amount equal to about nine years of current emissions from the entire state of Oregon.

By the turn of the twenty-first century, northern spotted owls and full-time timber industry workers were both endangered. Despite decades of timber wars, neither population has recovered. It is easy in hindsight to wish that all sides had agreed to pay for labor-intensive forest thinning and selective burning practices. That approach would have managed wildfire risk and minimized the battles over clearcutting. But industry argued that clearcutting was the only cost-efficient way to log, and neither side of the timber wars proved willing to subsidize higher labor costs for the sake of either the families or the forests. And the United States has never enacted a federal climate change statute, let alone one that reinvests in timberland workforces to reduce wildfire risk and preserve forests' function of carbon sequestration.

Like many lagging rural economies, Josephine cannot build a path to recovery as a commuter town for a metro economy engine. The county is more than a five-hour drive from either the San Francisco Bay Area to the south or the Portland Metropolitan Area to the north. Josephine's political fate and economic history face north, to the Willamette Valley and Portland metro areas. Portland's early roots in the logging industry are memorialized by the Timbers major league soccer team, Stumptown Coffee Roasters, and a three-story-tall Paul Bunyan statue. Even Portland's hipster men's fashion of handcrafted work boots, coated canvas vests, and a beard style known as "lumbersexual" reflect the state's logging past. But timber is just a decorative identity in the big city, where a new economy has eclipsed the old. In Josephine, where the arm patch on the sheriffs' uniforms depicts a truck bed stacked with logs, the timber heritage seems to stand for an unfilled economic hole. Signs in Josephine calling for the secession of the timberlands of southern Oregon and Northern California into a new State of Jefferson seem to stand for a political hole, too.

GROWING POT IN A HAZMAT SUIT

Boom and Bust, Redux

First gold, then hops, then timber. Marijuana is Josephine County's fourth resource-based boom industry. As in the big timber years, the marijuana economy includes not just landowners, but also wage workers, including "garden gnomes" for cultivation and "trimmers" at harvest time. By 2005, the industry was attracting people for the tax-free living rather than the "earth values" that local marijuana culture had long represented. Profits were good, and a new subculture of pot producers started to blow their earnings on what some locals called the "three C's: coke, Costa Rica, and cruises." Marijuana production was a black-market affair until Oregon voters legalized recreational marijuana in 2014.

Illegal production and growing national demand hooked southern Oregon into drug distribution networks across the country. Locals watched with regret as grower culture began to shift from small "mom-and-pop" cannabis farms, explains local community leader Kate Dwyer, to "people with guns." Armed robbery of marijuana plants—and armed guards to prevent that—became increasingly common.

For many smaller growers, Josephine's "green rush" for marijuana is already over. Anya, a mother in the Illinois Valley, had moved to Josephine County from North Carolina. She and her husband were trying to shed a wage-earning life as bartenders, where each scratched out a living that barely allowed Anya to keep her child in preschool. Anya had visited Cave Junction on a road trip, and the couple decided to move there. They were drawn to the cheap cost of living, which meant they could "raise our own kids," rather than spend full-time hours at work while struggling to afford childcare. They wanted to make an income from their own patch of soil. Marijuana, they believed, would let them pay off their land. Their goal, she said, was simple: to own land, grow their own food, and raise their kids outside of a city. Pot cultivation was harder than they expected, including the way her husband had to sleep outside with a gun at harvest time to guard the plants from theft. But they made ends meet for a few years and had a second child.

Anya views high-quality, farmer-raised marijuana as a form of medicine, but she stopped growing it. Marijuana's price has plummeted. After legalization, the state tried to eliminate the black market by ramping up criminal penalties for unpermitted growers. New regulatory requirements (including security systems and complicated surveillance and tracking systems) made production more expensive. Pot growers lost the ability to sell to out-of-state buyers without risking a felony, causing a glut of supply sellable only within Oregon, which kept sale prices low. Small growers like Anya supported legalization but resented the way it was implemented to favor bigger growers with enough capital to comply with the onerous laws. Outsiders with capital have poured in, she says, using so many pesticides that their workers need hazmat suits. Wages, in freefall from dwindling grower profits, are too low for her to work on other people's plants either. The "shit old trailer," as she described it, where Anya lived with her family, had a busted door lock and a hole in the roof. She honors the years it gave her family as "a warm, loving home," including her son's birth in the living room. But during the COVID-19 pandemic, she left the trailer, and Josephine County, behind.

Anya is not the only one worried that Josephine's natural fertility is once again poised to make big capitalists rich but keep residents poor. Some public officials and residents worry that legalization could turn southern Oregon into a "Banana Republic" of large-scale pot plantations. That means aquifer depletion, soil contamination, and the pungent, skunky smell of budding plants. Low wages would trickle into local households, but the big profits would enrich owners living somewhere else. Rumor has it that tobacco conglomerates have started accumulating acreage in the region under different corporate names, so they are poised to enter the marijuana business upon national legalization. Between the falling wages for trimmers and the catastrophic wildfires of 2018 and 2020, receipts plummeted at the few restaurants and shops in the small town of Cave Junction. Rates of homelessness soared.

From his first days at Wolf Creek, long before state legalization, Selig learned that marijuana production was among the *malum prohibitum* activities that made locals wary of police. People wanted cops to stay out of their business and off their properties. Some locals threatened to punish people who spoke to law enforcement. And anyway, with locally based deputies coming and going in irregular cycles since the 1980s, many thought cops wouldn't help. If an officer failed to follow through, residents would be left on their own. If you tried to investigate a homicide in rural Josephine, Selig recalled, people would refuse. " 'It's not gonna bring them back, is it?' they would say, 'so I'm not talking to you.' " In popular culture, "stop snitching" is an urban phenomenon, but criminology research describes a rural version of the same pattern. Mistrust of government generates reluctance to disclose community problems to the state. Where a wrongdoer or his family is known personally, they can be sanctioned through "informal social control" rather than state justice.

Knowing this culture, Selig was not surprised in 2009 when Caitlyn Strauser's mother refused to speak with him for weeks after her daughter's murder. But during his years of community-based policing in Wolf Creek, Selig had earned the trust of locals there. In 1984 or so, Selig had mediated an armed confrontation between a gold miner named Skip and another resident: one claiming a right to dredge the lower Grave Creek, the other claiming that he owned a gold claim that gave him exclusive control of the creek. Neither was legally right, Selig said, but the immediate problem was that "tempers were hot, guns were drawn, and threats made." Arresting them, Selig explained, was "not an option and would have probably ended in my early demise." He worked to calm the situation and mediate.

Skip persuaded Strauser's mother that Selig was someone she could trust. Strauser's mother, it seemed, had lost faith that the "system will actually do what it's intended to do." She did not trust cops in general, so she needed to know she could trust Selig specifically. Would he be honest and follow through? Research shows that people care not just about law enforcement outcomes, but also about whether police treated them with dignity, respect, and fairness in the process. By spending years as a community-based deputy before the worst of the budget cuts, Selig had time to develop a reputation for community relationships and problem-solving, not just arrests and community control.

Strauser's mother ultimately agreed to meet with Selig and gave him her daughter's diary, which included descriptions of O'Dell's physical abuse and Strauser's fear that he would kill her. Selig and other investigators on the case also secured testimony from Savanna Albertson, a seventeen-year-old friend to Strauser and O'Dell. Albertson initially tried to protect O'Dell, but she later explained what she knew. O'Dell was convicted of manslaughter. His ten-year sentence was lower than he may have gotten in an urban setting but, Selig thought, more in line with Wolf Creek's sense of justice.

On June 16, 2010, just days after O'Dell's conviction, Albertson's boyfriend stabbed her to death in a state of meth-induced psychosis. The circumstances of her death tragically paralleled Strauser's, but they were deemed unconnected to Albertson's testimony.

"THIS IS NOT TV"

The Collapse of Government Services

The budget cuts Selig rode out during his first thirty years with the county were nothing like what came during his final years with the sheriff's office, when Caitlyn Strauser and Savanna Albertson were murdered. Between 2008 and 2012, with the Great Recession bearing down on government budgets, the federal subsidies for Oregon's rural counties entered the phase-out period described earlier in this chapter. Josephine still relied on these subsidies to pay for basic services, especially law enforcement.

At about the twentieth anniversary of the spotted owl compromise in 2012, the federal government terminated earmarks to Oregon's rural counties and schools. In June, the elected sheriff at the time, Gil Gilbertson, enacted dramatic cuts at the sheriff's office. He laid off all detectives. Same for the records staff, who answered the non-emergency phone line to report auto and property crimes so citizens could claim property crime losses for insurance. The number of dispatch staffers for 911 calls fell from 9 to 1.5 FTEs. People who called to report property crimes sat on hold for more than an hour or got redirected to a useless online reporting system. By law, dispatchers could not dispatch emergency medical personnel until law enforcement was on the scene, which meant that some wounded victims of car accidents waited for hours for aid. Savvy residents learned that the way to get emergency medical dispatch was to recharacterize injuries so 911 would send EMS from the fire department. One told dispatch that a gunshot wound was chest pain. There were few patrol deputies to send out anyway—their staffing dropped from twenty-three local officers to three. The sheriff's office dropped from eighty-five people to twenty-eight.

The hours of the sheriff's office fell to 8:00 am to 4:00 pm, Monday to Friday. Some residents felt it was a stunt to get more outside funding, but Sheriff Gilbertson told reporters that even during open hours, the few patrol deputies available could respond only to "life-threatening calls" and "person-to-person" crimes, such as assault and homicide.

The harms of these cuts became clear on August 18, 2012. At about five o'clock on a Saturday morning, when the sheriff's office was closed, a woman in Cave Junction called 911 as a violent ex-boyfriend tried to break into her home. Her call was transferred to the state police dispatcher. The caller told the dispatcher, "He put me in the hospital a few weeks ago and I have been trying to keep him away. . . . I've already told him I was calling you. He's broken in before, busted down my door, assaulted me." She told the dispatcher there was a warrant out for the man's arrest. But the nearest state police officer was hours away from the caller. The dispatcher reiterated four times, as if she was refreshing her browser to make it untrue, "I don't have anybody to send out there." The caller and dispatcher stayed on the phone together for more than ten minutes while the man continued breaking in. Presumably believing there was nothing else she could do, the dispatcher tried to offer advice that seemed irrelevant, if not insensitive, to the scale of the risk at hand. "You know, obviously, if he comes inside the residence and assaults you," the dispatcher said, "can you ask him to go away? Do you know if he's intoxicated or anything?" The caller replied: "Yeah, it doesn't matter. If he gets in the house, I'm done." After the intruder broke in, he choked and raped her.

The case offered tragic confirmation of an earlier public announcement Sheriff Gilbertson had made during a severe round of staffing cuts. He had warned victims of domestic violence with restraining orders to "consider relocating to an area with adequate law enforcement services." A domestic violence service provider in the county named Chris Mallette observed to NPR that the "whole system has crumbled, and we're the only ones left. And we don't have the badge, and we don't have the gun." But it did not mean women were relocating, she said. Instead, they were staying with abusers because they believed they were more likely to be killed or terrorized by their abuser if they left than if they stayed.

Even compared to the severity of urban domestic violence, domestic assaults resulting in severe injuries and assaults with a weapon are both more common in rural areas. Nearly one in five homicides in rural areas involve a current or former intimate partner. Yet rural areas have fewer law enforcement officers with domestic violence training, fewer district attorneys trained to prosecute domestic violence, slow law enforcement response times, and high rates of protective order violation. A study of rural and urban counties in Kentucky found that even the best rural law enforcement departments failed to serve restraining orders on their target offenders more than half the time. In the worst performing rural counties, 91 percent of restraining orders were never served at all. This checkered history of police efficacy at handling domestic violence matters has led many to argue that personnel other than police should dispatch for most domestic violence calls. Yet committed police abolitionists agree there must be someone who is trained and available for dispatch in a domestic violence emergency.

Budget cuts in county law enforcement affected property crimes as well as violent ones. Many Josephine residents have cynical stories from the hollowing out of law enforcement. The county already had the highest rate of auto theft in its region, and that rate doubled after 2013. Yet private cars are essential in a place where employment, schools, and groceries are clustered in towns far from rural homes. Anya needed her car for about two hours per day to get between her children's two schools, her job, and her home. After her car was stolen in 2014, it took three different phone calls across several days to catch a live person at the sheriff's office who would record it missing. She also told the local gas station owner, who asked around and learned that her car had been spotted off the side of a road, crashed and stripped for parts. Anya called the sheriff's office to ask if they wanted to investigate or remove it. The dispatcher told her, "This is not TV. We cannot investigate property crimes here." Dispatchers became as unpopular as they were scarce, and they were rarely helpful in their efforts to offer solutions other than officer dispatch.

It was hard to blame the dispatchers, however, when they did not have good options. Lily Morgan, a Josephine County Commissioner who had worked in 911 dispatch for Grants Pass, described how she was trained to not tell people what to do. "You can see your circumstance. I can't," she learned to say, especially if she had no deputy available for dispatch. "Don't be frozen. What do you need to do for your safety?" The work of being a dispatcher is heartbreaking, she said, recalling calls from burglaries in progress and fatal car crashes. "You only hear from people in their very worst moment," she said, "and you don't have any ability to do anything but send the troops and be calm for them."

Investigations into serious crimes also languished. Laurie Houston lost her twenty-one-year-old son Jarred in the fall of 2013 in Cave Junction, after a hit-and-run on a two-lane highway outside the town. Witnesses said the driver did not apply his brakes or attempt to stop, but the state police and county sheriff had limited time and resources for the investigation. "I won't let my son be swept under the carpet like he was nobody," Houston told a local reporter at that time. "He was somebody."

When these cuts went into effect at the county jail in 2012, the drop in staffing capacity required the county to close more than half the county's beds. Those closures eliminated the remaining patrol officers' capacity to hold people for offenses like burglary. The jail could no longer serve as the sobering or detox facility in town, to link drug users with treatment programs, drug courts, and other avenues for recovery. Alternative incarceration programs also closed, including a forest camp and community service program. Emergency mental health support was outsourced to a private nonprofit. The county shuttered its new juvenile detention center, which had housed juveniles convicted of person-to-person felony crimes. It also closed the non-secure juvenile residential facility for youth with no other safe home, cut all full-time employee positions related to both centers, and slashed home-based social services for juveniles.

The district attorney's office lost 40 percent of its staff. Ryan Mulkins, a deputy in that office at the time and a subsequent county district attorney, explained how during these years, an officer might issue a citation for an offense like drinking in a public park, but because there would be no consequences for it, the offender "would rip the ticket right in front of the officer and throw it on the ground." These "cite and release" policies lined up with some locals' views that *malum prohibitum* offenses shouldn't result in state involvement. But because those acts had not been decriminalized, the government just looked impotent and incompetent to those who had a stricter sense of law and order.

These cuts might look like steps toward progressive reform. Josephine did move its government away from using the criminal justice system to answer nonviolent crimes, addiction, and troubled youth. Somewhat inadvertently, Josephine moved toward a version of jail abolition. The county had advanced elements of all three of the stages of abolition, as defined by its advocates: a moratorium on building new jail cells, "decarceration" of some persons already in custody, and "excarceration" to reduce the number of people and problems (like drug addition, mental illness, and homelessness) that are tracked toward the criminal justice system. Activists in Josephine had also successfully stopped the state from siting a prison in the Illinois Valley. The county had developed jail release triage rules, closed juvenile and adult jail cells, and disinvested in police dispatch for minor crimes. Volunteers developed a well-functioning Local Public Safety Coordinating Council (LPSCC), which focuses on drug treatment and other collaborations to step-down criminal offenses and reduce incarceration. The county's mental health court reports impressive success with its program diverting people from jail into mental health treatment.

But events in Josephine bore little resemblance to the more transformative harm-reduction goals of prison or police abolitionists. The abolitionist vision has never been to leave violence unimpeded, but rather to prevent and treat violence as a symptom of the deeper diseases of poverty, racism, and mental illness. Divestment in criminal justice solutions, they argue, should be replaced with other violence prevention measures. This "Divest/Reinvest" principle calls for alternative systems of drug treatment, family support services, and restorative justice. The political left and the far right share ground about nonviolent activities that need not trouble the government at all. But they diverge about whether government should shrink overall (to get out of the business of trying to fight poverty), or simply change (to deemphasize police- and jail-based answers to poverty). In Josephine, as in all the places in this book, reforms have only tried out the first category. Disinvestment in police came with deep cuts to other services, and without reinvestment in alternatives to police.

"Every man for himself" never became the complete reality in Josephine, because the state of Oregon stepped up its own staff and resources during these years. The Oregon State Police, a law enforcement unit designed to focus on highway safety and statewide crime, doubled its staff focused on Josephine and took over all investigations of major crimes. But governors have long warned Josephine and other timber counties that the state does not have the funds to bail them out with more aid. State-level governmental task forces looked for new ways to help provide basic local functions like running elections, granting building permits, collecting taxes, and providing veterans' services.

Nonetheless, by 2014, after Josephine's patrol levels hit historic lows, a journalist reported a drug dealer "hawk[ing] meth and heroin along one town's commercial strip like they were Thin Mints and Samoas." Among the states, Oregon has the sixth highest rate of nonmedical use of prescription pain relievers, with a crisis-level 5.1 percent of its population misusing these drugs. Josephine County had the highest rate of opioid prescriptions in the state in 2012 per capita, with nearly two and a half times as many prescriptions given out that year as the county's total population, including children. Drug overdose mortality rates between 2001 and at least 2018 exceeded state rates, with peaks of three or four times the state rate in some years. Lily Morgan, who focused on drug treatment and crime prevention as Josephine County commissioner between 2016 and 2020, explained how meth never went away as a problem, even as opioid addiction rates rose. Many people in town, she said, use them both. "One's an upper, one's a downer," she explained, so locals used one "to not care"' and the other "to get up enough to get going."

A majority of voters would come to doubt whether Sheriff Gilbertson downsized his department effectively, as well as the wisdom of his public announcements revealing those changes. But no one could contest the underlying legality of the cuts themselves. The events related to a line of American law most recently considered by the U.S. Supreme Court in 2005, in the case of *Castle Rock v. Gonzales*. The "horrible facts" of the case, as Justice Scalia wrote in his opinion, concerned a mother named Jessica Gonzales, who had secured a restraining order against her violent husband. The order mandated that law enforcement officials "shall use every reasonable means to enforce this restraining order," including arrest for its violation whenever practicable. A few weeks after this order was made permanent, Ms. Gonzales's husband abducted their three daughters from her backyard where the girls were playing. Ms. Gonzales suspected him, and she called the police again and again that night. She went to the station in person with the order. She visited his house to try to find her children. In the early evening, she spoke to their father, who said he had her girls at an amusement park less than an hour away. At every contact, the police put Ms. Gonzales off and refused to investigate. About ten hours after he took the girls from their home, the father entered the police station and began firing a semi-automatic handgun. Officers returning fire killed him. "Inside the cab of his pickup truck," Justice Scalia reported, "they found the bodies of all three daughters, whom he had already murdered."

The case called the Supreme Court to answer the following question: Do we have a right to police assistance under the United States Constitution? The Due Process Clause of the Fourteenth Amendment provides: "No State shall . . . deprive any person of life, liberty, or property, without due process of law." Does that language oblige the government to protect our life, liberty, and property? As applied to the facts of the case, did the wife's restraining order give her a right to have the police look for her daughters and arrest her husband? No, the Court ruled. Alongside other cases, *Castle Rock* stands for the proposition that nothing in the Fourteenth Amendment, nor elsewhere in the U.S. Constitution, gives us the right to police protection. Indeed, nothing in the Constitution gives us a right to education, fire protection, or medical EMS either, or any kind of government services at all.

The U.S. Constitution is not the only source of law that could have given Ms. Gonzales or anyone else a right to state protection. States could grant some of these rights in their own constitutions and statutes, as they do with education. With respect to policing, Oregon has established a "mandatory arrest" law for domestic violence restraining orders, which obliges officers to follow up on an alleged restraining order violation. But even the strongest mandatory arrest laws are empty without police to enforce them. Budget-strapped municipalities cannot order employees like police to serve if there is no public money to pay them. Even without a legal right to police or emergency services, it is generally taken for granted that we receive them anyway. That is, we secure most basic services not through law but through politics. Democratic process and our representatives make the choice to fund critical government functions like emergency services.

When it comes to government, as with other investments, it takes money to make money. A city or county needs staff so that it can compete for resources from state and federal agencies. Grant proposals have to specify local needs and explain how new resources would be used effectively. Jim Shames, medical director for neighboring Jackson County and a state leader on addressing the opioid crisis, lived and practiced medicine in Josephine for thirty years. When people make funding allocations at the state level, he says, Josephine can be a "black hole" for a lack of data and staff. When the county misses chances to ask for help, it feels paternalistic to push it on them. It's just like with individuals, he says: "It's hard to help somebody when they don't want to be helped. . . . I know you need this even though you're not doing it for yourself."

Residents and local officials may not even realize what they are missing when government fades out. Shames cites the example of syphilis, a dangerous but treatable STD that has become a resurgent epidemic in Oregon and other places hit hard by drug use and homelessness. A nimble health system, Shames says, has to act immediately when it discovers a syphilis case, not just to treat the patient but to locate other connected cases. "If you have a gutted health department, if you can't get people treated right now," he says, "you may lose them for six months until they show up in jail or a hospital, and meanwhile they are infecting other people." If you don't pay for infrastructure maintenance, he says by analogy, "then at some point the bridges start to collapse." Preventable harms become irreversible harms.

By 2012, Josephine's sheriff's office had emptied out more dramatically than it had in generations. That May, the electorate considered a ballot measure that would have restored substantial funding for patrol deputies and jail staffing by nearly tripling the county property tax rate. The measure failed. Citizens seemed to be giving back the same answer to government that Anya had heard from a dispatcher when she asked if police could investigate her stolen car: "This isn't TV." A majority of voters decided that they would not give their government more money at a time when it seemed to be doing so little for them.

Opponents of that tax levy cried vindication for their anti-tax cause when, in the fall of that year, the *Grants Pass Daily Courier* ran an article scrutinizing Sheriff Gilbertson's resume. Although it found that the sheriff had accurately described most of his career, it left open some questions about the scope of the sheriff's past responsibilities. Tax opponents and other critics accused the sheriff of campaigning on an exaggerated military history. If he had lied about his past, these critics argued, maybe he had lied about everything else, too. Maybe the budget cuts were not as bad as he said. Maybe he could have come up with a better solution than cutting staff hours. Maybe the government could have kept people safer after all, without additional funds. Trust hit a new low.

"PEOPLE CAN'T LIVE LIKE THAT"

The Local Rebirth of Volunteer Policing

As disaffection and insecurity peaked, volunteers tried to replace their shrinking government. Ken Selig was one of them. He had retired during a big round of layoffs in 2012, after thirty-plus years with the sheriff's office. He had bought himself a motorcycle. He didn't get as much time for home improvements as he had expected.

Selig was among those willing to pay more taxes to the county, but he was outnumbered. "Actual law enforcement, as we know it today, is a luxury," he said. "When it's taken away from us, what do we do in the meantime? Do we become victims? And just eat it and say, 'Well it's not a crime unless the government says it is a crime?' " Selig was not ready to live in a county that had stopped investigating and trying to prevent violence. Rape, assault, home invasions, and threats with a gun are crimes, he said, whether the government responded to them or not. "Because people can't live like that."

So Selig, like others across Josephine, filled in for government law enforcement. His group, North Valley Community Watch (NVCW), began when an elderly woman called 911 to report that her front door had been kicked in. The dispatcher required the woman to confirm that intruders were still inside before sending out a deputy. Scared to do so, she called her neighbor, a contractor named Pete Scaglione, who grabbed his gun and entered her house. He found two men still inside. Deciding enough was enough, Scaglione called Selig to come up with a plan. They recruited volunteers, whom Selig trained with basic policing skills, plus investigative practices like collecting fingerprints and photographing crime scenes. If local and state officers were unavailable, neighbors could call Selig or Scaglione's personal cell phone numbers. One of them would dispatch with a second volunteer.

North Valley Community Watch was not the only volunteer policing effort in the county. Others sprang up in small rural townships and trailer parks. The retired manager of a marina helped form one group after his trailer was stolen. Another former sheriff's deputy established a Facebook page called "To Catch a Thief" to solicit and share citizen evidence, mug shots, and warnings to help deter and solve drug and property crimes.

In the southern part of the county near the town of Cave Junction, Jimmy Evans, the volunteer patroller who opened this book, got another model up and running. He and other founders structured Cave Junction Patrol with schedules of volunteers who drive around in pairs in their own trucks at night, aiming to deter crime, check on suspicious activities, and respond to calls for help from neighbors. Like Selig's group and others, CJ Patrol also offered no-cost security in the community by guarding local businesses or keeping an eye on homes whose occupants were out of town.

Depending on the group, the equipment used by volunteers included large amber flashers for their cars, spotlights, black vests saying "security," magnetic logos for vehicles, cameras, and notepads. One group carried plastic ties for making citizen arrests, another group prohibited them. Patrollers in every group outside of Grants Pass, however, typically carried their own gun.

State and national media took hold of that last detail, documenting Josephine's "armed patrols" and using suggestive words such as "posse." Locally, however, armed volunteers didn't seem so out of the ordinary. Open-carry is common, and concealed carry permits reached historic highs as law enforcement cuts intensified. Josephine is the kind of place where a sidewalk sign advertises SNOWCONES next to another sign with the silhouette of an automatic weapon and an arrow pointing toward GUNS. At the local farmer's market, some customers wear sidearms. At the office of a local newspaper in Josephine's Illinois Valley, due to accelerating threats and vandalism in former President Trump's anti-media climate, the publisher told me his staff are "never more than five to ten feet away from a gun in this office."

For the volunteer patrollers, it seemed obvious and nonnegotiable that they would carry guns for self-defense. "We're not vigilantes by any stretch of the imagination," Evans explains. Volunteers have had guns pulled on them, and "if we're under threat we'll protect ourselves and each other." Selig emphasized repeatedly that his group took pains never to function "like George Zimmerman." Evans and Selig are right that a weapon does not a vigilante make. Vigilante justice refers to arrest, citizen courts, and punishment—rough justice without state actors. As far as I can find, none of the groups, individuals, or incidents in Josephine involve citizen adjudication or punishment.

But voluntary policing is still risky. Hotheads make for combustible situations. In 2014, when a new CJ Patrol volunteer "pretended to be John Wayne" after dispatch to a burglary, shots were fired in both directions. "It was chaotic, mass confusion," Evans says with regret. Some people don't have the right temperament for the job, he says, like the guy who showed up to start his patrol equipped "with plastic ties to restrain people, and armor, like *Full Metal Jacket*." If they're not willing to turn "from John Wayne into Bob Dylan," he says, "they're not going to ride with us." Evans has been surprised to see who shows up to do the work and sticks with it: "Some of our best patrollers have been women," he says. "I thought we'd get strapping young dudes, but it's the fifty- to sixty-year-old women that kick butt. They're not afraid to do this stuff."

Evans's group developed rules, including a protocol barring its members from engaging in high-speed chases. "We'll speed up to get a plate," he says, "but no pursuit." As a father, he knows what is at stake for patrollers, bystanders, and "subjects of interest" if bullets start flying. CJ Patrollers approach people they deem suspicious, then introduce themselves and say things like, "Hey, we've had crimes around here and want to make sure you're ok." They ask for people's IDs. "We have a constitutional right to take photos," Evans explains. "They have a constitutional right to say, 'Fuck you, I'm not saying anything.' That's their right. We say, 'We're going to watch you.' They get mouthy and they leave."

CJ Patrol has maintained a policy not to get involved in conflicts like domestic disputes and bar fights, but Evans says, "The reality is that we have to get involved in all of it." When he saw "a man kicking a woman in the face" at 4 o'clock in the morning, for example, he intervened. "You've got to do something." Selig's North Valley Community Watch mediates disputes that are escalating dangerously, like the resident he talked down from violent retaliation after his dog was killed by the neighbor's son.

Some volunteers try to achieve more than crime prevention. For Evans, "patrol" is a combination of the social services associated with early twentieth century police, the anti-overdose medical services of modern EMS, and the humanitarian relief of a figure like Dorothy Day. He and other CJ Patrol members trained with a nonprofit to administer the anti-overdose drug Naloxone, and they carry it on patrol. They check occupied cars at night. They watch for body language to distinguish a person on meth from a person on heroin, or a person sleeping from a person who has overdosed. He recalled he and his partner's first job—a "boy and a girl" they'd found slumped over after an overdose, when they had to make sure they were alive.

Working with CJ Patrol has taught Evans about the world of people with no home to go to at night. Some sleep in their cars in downtown Cave Junction. Others without cars have to keep walking, sometimes all night when the temperature falls. Evans has developed a good sense of who's who. "Some are criminals, some are families," he says. His group carries socks and personal hygiene products, plus soup on especially cold nights. He has crowdsourced some modest funds and recruited volunteers to support a warming center for the homeless at night, and distributed small, insulated mobile shelters for winter sleep.

The volunteer turn in Josephine—in Selig's and Evans's cases at least—is a thoughtful adaptation to true needs. It may even be common. Paid private security has enjoyed a growing commercial market in the United States since the 1980s (and is common in Josephine as well). Deep local budget cuts have brought about a new realm of fully voluntary law enforcement that has moved far beyond conventional neighborhood watch. Sophisticated neighborhood patrols have sprung up in every city I researched for this book, including systematic overnight patrols in Detroit and 911 dispatch volunteers at substations in Flint. The United States has a long history of armed neighborhood patrols, including community-based guards organized by the Black Panthers in the 1970s and the Nation of Islam in the late 1980s and 90s. As in Selig's and Evans's cases, these groups described their work as a form of mutual aid—meeting the security needs of a community in the absence of state protection.

But what are the legal limits to the policing side of their work? Neighborhood watch volunteers do not carry badges. They act as private citizens and are bound by state laws governing firearms possession and citizen's arrest. Oregon law grants citizens broad authority to make arrests, using physical force if necessary, if they witness an event that they have probable cause to think is a "crime." Citizens can use their weapons to patrol their neighborhoods, defend private property (with the owner's consent), or defend another person against unlawful force.

In addition to community crime prevention groups, Josephine has a second category of volunteer law enforcement. Reserve (sometimes called auxiliary) police officers do carry badges and may work part-time or as volunteers. In some jurisdictions, they have the full responsibilities and constitutional limitations of paid police. In Oregon, county sheriffs have the authority to commission reserve officers to enforce state criminal and traffic laws. State law requires reserve officers to be armed. Because reserve officers are "deputized," they are in a contractual relationship with the sheriff's department. That makes them different from private security, like store security guards, who draw upon "merchant's privilege statutes" to detain suspects when a citizen's arrest would not be permitted.

Josephine's previous sheriff tried to expand the county's reserve law enforcement program in 2014, calling for citizen reinforcement after his staff was no longer able to investigate property crimes. Sheriff Gilbertson had long resisted volunteer patrols collecting evidence after burglaries, but he decided to recruit volunteers to train as investigators. Speaking on public radio, he acknowledged that such a program had fizzled in the past, but under the county's circumstances, he stressed emphatically, "I need help."

The distinctions among formal reserve deputy volunteers, good neighbors, and unaffiliated volunteers can get murky during an emergency with imperfect information. That risk became tragically apparent a few hours south of Josephine, in Northern California's rural Trinity County. In 2011, a California Highway Patrol 911 dispatcher took an emergency call from someone whispering "help me" before the line cut out. The dispatcher called the Trinity County sheriff, but he and his staff were hours away from the incident. The sheriff called James and Norma Gund, a couple he knew who lived near the caller's address. He asked them to check on the caller, telling the Gunds that the call was likely related to "inclement weather" and was "probably no big deal." The Gunds responded to the request and drove to the caller's house, where an assailant brutally attacked them. He had just murdered the caller and her boyfriend. The Gunds escaped but sustained life-threatening injuries.

The Gunds sued Trinity County and the office of the sheriff. The county argued, and the court agreed, that the Gunds became deputy law enforcement when they agreed to check on their neighbor. Based on that status, they were entitled only to worker's compensation, a much more limited remedy than they would have received for their tort claims of negligence and misrepresentation with malice. The case is a reminder that good Samaritans may neither appreciate nor be prepared for the risks they face.

Volunteer policing can also make it hard for ordinary residents to tell who is who, and that uncertainty is itself a risk. A retired police officer from California now living in Josephine, for example, blocked and pulled his gun on a vehicle that he suspected (correctly, as it turned out) of carrying a wanted man in the backseat—much to the terror of the driver and his girlfriend, who at that moment had less reason to trust the man pointing a gun through their window than the unarmed hitchhiker they'd just picked up. Gina Angelique, a longtime homesteader, was not happy about the meth user who drives behind her house with a Confederate flag on his Jeep, claiming he's on patrol. Just like she "doesn't trust a cop," because of the risk of a "power trip with the capacity for force," she doesn't trust her "patroller" either. She is not sure who he is affiliated with, if anyone. His presence made her consider getting her own gun even though that cut against her other values.

Sheriff Daniel sees Josephine's citizen patrols as "fallout" from having an inadequate law enforcement system, even as he was complimentary of their efforts. He was wary of some patrols at first, unsure of "how extreme they were going to go." He worried about dangerous situations, and the problem that "following suspicious vehicles can turn into harassment." But he thought the patrols settled into their role and formed a productive partnership with law enforcement. "The citizens can't do what we do," he says, given the risks of both injury and litigation. But so too, he says, "we can't do what we do without the citizens."

Local officials, and patrollers themselves, stress that volunteers are simply deterring violence and providing "eyes and ears" for the sheriff. David Sklansky, a scholar of private policing in the United States, observed this same claim made by paid private security as it grew into a big industry. Sklansky found, however, that this "augmentation" model can give way to the "displacement" of public police. In the paid private security context, wealthier neighborhoods may lose the political will to increase funds for the police if they feel as though they are already funding private security. In Josephine, the dynamic was different. The voluntary patrols lacked commercial incentives. They saw firsthand the risks created by dismantling law enforcement without anti-violence substitutes, because they bore those risks personally when they set out on patrol. Instead of undermining passage of new taxes, North Valley Community Watch tried to teach the public about the law enforcement funding situation. They invited the DA to meetings with their members, hosted local government candidate forums, and tried to open communication between citizens and government. The longer the patrols went on, the more volunteers wanted the sheriff's department improved and restored.

Selig and Evans were, in other words, the first to say that their efforts revealed limitations and dangers. The idiosyncrasies of volunteerism left an irregular patchwork across the county. Large areas had no patrol because no one has stepped up to lead or sustain such an effort. Even individual homes in a covered neighborhood can be "off the grid" of volunteers under models like Selig's, where he and his volunteers dispatched only to known, prescreened addresses and phone numbers. Households may be disconnected because they don't know any of the volunteers, or because they are engaged in illegal activities big or small (like marijuana plants on the property), which makes them guard their privacy. Yet the need for emergency dispatch may arise anywhere, not just in households where it is trusted. The problems of domestic violence, child abuse, and drug addiction loom: those who are vulnerable to crime will not always be in a position to opt in to emergency aid in advance. While dispatch of a specially trained social worker may be more effective than a police officer for many domestic calls, a pure volunteer-based system can leave victims disconnected from any help at all.

Beyond dispatches related to crime, such small numbers of people could not be the only ones addressing overdoses, homelessness, and mental illness. Evans told me the story of a local named Paula, whom he described as mentally ill and "self-medicating." She tried to keep moving at night, walking to keep safe, alert, and warm. Desperate with cold and exhaustion one night, she had punched in the glass of an abandoned burrito shack to shelter inside. The next morning, she showed up at Evans's work seeking help, her arms soaked in blood. There was nowhere else for her to go—not a shelter, not a health clinic, not even a public bathroom. So at dawn she turned to Evans, already midway into his shift at Taylor's Sausage. In some ways, he had become the best version of the old-style policing that, through trust, smooths the hardest edges of poverty and human crisis. But today, most counties in America have hundreds—if not thousands—of people facing hardships like Paula's. Very few even have one person like Jimmy Evans.

Josephine's patrols have also run into the limits of volunteerism over time. Volunteers come and go as life intervenes or they burn out. Group dynamics and personality conflicts turn some people off. At its peak, when the government cuts dominated local headlines, CJ Patrol had fifteen or so people—enough to provide free security to local businesses at opening and closing times. But soon, the patrol pool fell to six, sometimes eight. Just as he once retired from being a deputy sheriff, Ken Selig tried to retire from his years doing trainings and dispatch for the North Valley Community Watch. The high turnover meant repeating the same trainings again and again for new groups of volunteers, many of whom didn't last longer than a month or two. Selig's neighbors call him if they need help, but the organized watch has dissolved.

Problems like these could be alleviated with philanthropic or other support for volunteers. But other concerns are harder to resolve, including groups and individuals who threaten more harm than benefit. Concerned Fathers Against Crime mobilized nighttime volunteer patrols across the town of Grants Pass in the name of "homeland defense" after 9/11, answering the call of groups like the Promise Keepers to root out "al-Qaida sleeper agents" as a way to engage men in their community. Josephine has a strand of white anti-government activism, including an early chapter of the Oath Keepers that later became Liberty Watch. These groups perform community service projects that fill in for government (like evacuating and sheltering horses and livestock during a wildfire), but they also accumulate arms and military training to resist federal actions (such as the enforcement of environmental law) that they deem a violation of the U.S. Constitution.

As a practical, political matter, law-and-order conservatives in Josephine (which I think fairly describes Ken Selig as well as many elected officials there, such as Sheriff Daniel), are trying to hold ground in the county as against more angry, fringe elements of the populist right. In 2015, the Josephine Oath Keepers chapter issued a national summons to help a local mine resist federal regulation by the Bureau of Land Management. At least 700 volunteers passed through during the course of several weeks, many heavily armed and wearing "U.S. Patriot" vests. Tensions mounted, until the Bureau of Land Management took action that was perceived as a retreat. Participants in the standoff at the Sugar Pine Mine framed their actions as voluntary law enforcement to protect private property. In recent iterations, Josephine's spinoffs from the Oath Keepers are dominated by "preppers" getting ready for government collapse. The deaths at the Malheur National Wildlife Refuge standoff in 2016 and the January 2021 insurrection at the Capitol confirm the inherent risks of armed people who self-deputize as agents of an alternative understanding of law and politics.

The safety of Josephine's wider array of organized, volunteer patrols may rely in part on the county's lack of racial diversity. When self-appointed volunteers killed Black victims Ahmaud Arbery and Trayvon Martin in Georgia and Florida, the killings reconfirmed two separate strands of anti-Black bias: the assumption of Black criminality and the dehumanization of Black life required to kill a person suspected of a crime. The worst risks of race-based dehumanization showed up perilously close to Josephine in November 2020. In Jackson County, just forty-five minutes away from Grants Pass, a Black nineteen-year-old named Aidan Ellison was fatally shot in his car in a hotel parking lot at night by a white man who wanted Ellison to turn his music down. Both men were living at the hotel after a summer wildfire had burned down Ellison's workplace and the shooter's home.

But that same lack of racial and ethnic diversity in Josephine is helping to strangle the local economy. Josephine's best bet for new jobs and revenues is to grow the county's health and services sector. The county has marketed itself, especially to Californians, as an attractive, low-tax place to settle for retirement. Retirees need health and home care services, but those businesses cannot grow and thrive without a willing, trained workforce. The health and elder care industry, meanwhile, is among the most racially diverse workforces in the country. Josephine does not look like a safe and welcoming home for that workforce. In the Trump era, Confederate flags are open-carry in Josephine. There is no indication that there are widespread connections between anti-government activists in Josephine and alt-right groups trafficking in ideas of white supremacy, but many people of color would not wish to test Josephine's racial goodwill outside the limits of downtown Grants Pass. In 2013, a researcher at Oregon Humanities posed the question, "Why aren't there more Black people in Oregon?" Her answer was a long and blighted history of racial exclusion and violence in the state. For the patrols linked up with national "patriot" movements, the questions "protection from whom?" and "protection for whom?" loom large.

Ordinary ignorance and bias also stand in the way of recruiting these workers and new residents. I met an executive, for example, with a genuine compassion for the poverty and hardships in Josephine County. He mused about why neighboring Jackson County had much higher levels of racial diversity, particularly Latino families, compared with Josephine. "Maybe they go there for the public benefits," he said. Yet in fact, Josephine's population takes a much higher rate of food stamps, welfare, and Medicaid benefits than Jackson. What Jackson has that draws in diverse residents is a more vibrant, modern business environment offering jobs. In turn, Jackson more easily recruits employers too. Racial bias associating non-white groups with government dependence—rather than skills and job-readiness—makes Josephine less able to grow and support county businesses.

A final concern about the risks of private substitutes for law enforcement was captured vividly in 2014, when a fed-up father and his nine-year-old son wrote a satirical children's book called *Goldilocks and the Three BARS*. In Josephine, BARS stands for "Beyond Available Resources"—the term used when a 911 dispatcher has no law enforcement personnel to deploy. The book begins with three bears, who come home to discover missing porridge, broken furniture, and a sleeping Goldilocks. The bears (knowing how dangerous humans can be) call the sheriff's office, but get an automated message referring to part-time hours from budget cuts. They call 911, which also has no one to send. Goldilocks escapes, and other humans keep coming to steal from the bears. The final drawing features an angry bear wearing an ammo belt to restock his semi-automatic weapon. "To this day," the book advises, "if you are out in the woods in Josephine County, Oregon, you may see a bear or two. Be advised to turn and head in the other direction. Because if they suspect you of wanting to harm them or take their stuff, well, let's just say it's hard to know what they might do to you." The victim had become the danger. The public police might be beyond available resources, but armed self-defense might just be starting. Given increases in closed and open-carry weapons, the book was not just telling tales.

Volunteers like Evans and Selig were not vigilantes. But it was not simply their character that made that true. Despite the deep staffing cuts at the district attorney's office and the jail, Josephine County still had access to a government system of adjudication and punishment. Josephine's best volunteers helped protect residents, but they did not determine guilt and innocence. They did not hold or punish offenders. But by 2017, this outer boundary to the budget cuts was about to give way. Voters had to decide whether they wanted public jails.

TENTH TIME IS A CHARM

An Infusion of New Revenues, At Last

On a Thursday morning in October 2015, Sheriff Daniel responded to a call for reinforcements in a neighboring county. He drove seventy-five miles, fast, to reach Umpqua Community College, where a twenty-six-year-old man had shot a teacher and sixteen students. Eight students died before the shooter killed himself. Sheriff Daniel arrived to see what cannot be unseen.

After two days of forensics work and grieving families, he made his way back home, afraid for the students and teachers in his own county. "I wanted to protect our children," Sheriff Daniel said. "They're fairly out in the open right now. And with the things going on nationwide in the form of active shooters, things that happened in places just like this . . ." he trailed off. He began working with Josephine County's rural school district on a campus security plan—a rotating system of honorably retired law enforcement serving as school marshals on an undisclosed schedule.

Sheriff Daniel and the school district brought their school marshals proposal to the voters in 2016 as a special tax levy, which would have cost homeowners about five cents per $1,000 of assessed property value.

The levy failed. After the election, the sheriff shook his head and faltered as he described the levy's failure: "For a $300,000 home, that's $15 a year. So it was quite shocking to see the stand that people have in the county. They're really, and I—I guess to an extent I don't understand—but that one—that one was a fast ball that hit me right between the eyes. I was very much set back."

In any community in America, especially a progressive one, a levy to fund school marshals could have been controversial. But in Josephine, the levy was part of a pattern of rejecting any law enforcement improvements at all, whether for rural patrols, jail staffing, or juvenile justice program funding. Between 2004 and 2016, Josephine County voters went to the polls nine times to consider new taxes, ranging in amount, to support law enforcement. Each time, a majority voted the taxes down.

Raising local taxes is extremely difficult under Oregon law. The state was late to the anti-tax revolution started by California, but when Oregon showed up, it went for broke. During the 1990s, two statewide ballot measures locked assessed property values to a strictly controlled growth rate tethered to 1995 to 1996 property values. Each taxing district was also locked in to a permanent tax rate: the levies would stay fixed to whatever rates were being leveled at the time the measures passed in 1997. Because of the inflow of timber receipts, Josephine's rate was the lowest in the state—under sixty cents per $1,000 in real market value, compared to $2.50 per $1,000 in more than half of Oregon counties. Oregon voters thus set the year 1997 into state constitutional stone, a move that presumed the infinite availability of federal revenues from harvesting old-growth timber, a finite resource. Any new taxes would have to obtain majority approval in a local election.

New taxes are inherently unpopular in this region. For many locals, nostalgia for better days rides shotgun with blame, and carries one too. Strongly held views that citizens would be better off with less state law enforcement mingle with anti-tax sentiment to outvote the "law and order" conservatism of traditional Republican politics. The county's Republican Party now has vocal factions inspired by the Constitutional Sheriff movement associated with Arizona's Joe Arpaio, and moderate local officials face challengers from the far right who rail against taxes.

The secession movement to break the great western timberlands away from Oregon and California into a new fifty-first state called Jefferson argues that the road to recovery is control of natural resources, not new taxes.

A rural culture of self-defense does some of the work, too. A local resident I interviewed with strong libertarian views explains that armed self-defense accompanies low expectations of law enforcement. Local 911 dispatch, she said, reflects "the notion that you could pick up the phone and get someone to do violence on your behalf." Police, she says, are hired on behalf of people who don't wish to defend themselves, which is "more suburban than rural in the expectation of services."

By the time voters went to the polls in May 2017 to vote on a new levy for the sheriff's department, the next fiscal cycle threatened even deeper cuts to the capacity of the adult jail. A new round of lay-offs would mean that anyone arrested by the sheriff outside the city of Grants Pass (which paid supplemental taxes to fund jail beds for arrests by its own police department), could not be detained for anything less than a provable violent felony. After the deep cuts in 2012, which had reduced jail capacity by half, county leaders had patched together temporary replacement funds. But jail space in the county remained scarce. Between 2016 and 2018, the county still had to release one-third of the people booked to make room for more serious offenders. Rising numbers of people were never booked in the first place. Residents inferred that these changes were causing the rise in home burglary and car theft. After the cuts of 2012, the county's rate of recidivism doubled. Nearly half of all offenders arrested in the county were arrested again within one year.

After voters defeated levies again and again, it was hard to rationalize trying a new one. People against new taxes thought it was offensive to run another levy election. "They said, 'Are you crazy? We said no new taxes and we mean it,'" Dan DeYoung, a member of the County Board of Commissioners, recalled. People like DeYoung, who supported a levy, worried that running another one and losing "would be another notch in their belt" for the anti-government interests.

But try again they did. Kate Dwyer, a member of the rural school board and a tireless community activist, felt that residents had no choice but to run a new levy. Dwyer has lived in Takilma, at the south end of the county near Cave Junction, for nearly thirty years. She was twenty-four years old when she first arrived, a Long Island–born woman on a cross-country road trip with a group of girlfriends. The women visited Takilma, a hub of the commune movement, where two of them had extended family living in hand-built homes in a hillside forest. They arrived late at night. "I got here," Dwyer recalled. "It was dark, and I smelled the air, and I said 'Oh my God. This is my home. This is my home.'" She called her husband and "said 'we're moving out here, we're moving to Oregon!'" They did. They joined the Magic Forest Farm early on, and eventually bought their own home in Takilma through an interest-free, handshake-based, fifteen-year loan from a neighbor. Dwyer's husband worked as a hot glass artist, then took over a small business as a plumber. Dwyer made her living as a caterer, a library employee, and later as the head of a small community foundation in southern Oregon. They raised two kids in Josephine. Their family hosts free movies on a large screen in their unfenced backyard during the summer and potluck community meetings and parties at their handmade dining room table all year.

By 2017, Dwyer felt that her community was facing a dangerous crossroads. She feared that the levies would fail, but nonetheless felt resolute to fight for them. "What was the alternative at that point?" she stressed. Through her work with the local community development organization, she pushed for town halls in the south end of the county. "I picked up what we lovingly refer to as our telephone pamphlet, our phone book, and I called people in there because the people who have landlines tend to be older and tend to vote." She made calls for a couple of hours every evening for two weeks, telling voters about the levy proposal and inviting them to the town hall forums. If they could not make it, she collected their questions to ask at the event. Even if they said they planned to vote no, she called them back with answers.

Dwyer and other advocates for the tax levies came to understand that residents already agreed there was an urgent problem with crime. Trying to scare them into voting for government, therefore, was not working. Some counties facing similar jail cuts had published names and mugshots of people slated for release before the end of their sentences. Back in 2012, Josephine's former sheriff Gil Gilbertson had summarized that the people scheduled for release included "people charged with third-degree rape and sodomy, child neglect, endangering the welfare of a minor, encouraging child sex abuse, assault, robbery, drug possession and various property crimes." Voters had rejected the levy anyway.

What residents did not agree on was what to do about crime. They did not yet believe that their government was capable of making that problem better. Or maybe they did not believe that new taxes were necessary to help the government do better.

In one of the most libertarian, anti-government counties in the United States, the advocates for the new levies faced every argument against giving government more money. That included self-dealing: resentment that local politicians get paid too much and ride high on "junkets" to the state capital and D.C. Hidden stashes: the suspicion that there were other funds that could be used now in the county's time of need. Heroic alternatives: the theory that a good leader could come up with something other than new taxes. Bad priorities: the idea that fiscal problems could be solved by moving funds away from less worthy expenditures. Empire building: the concern that some departments or public sector unions were just amassing power. Self-indulgence by government employees: an assumption that employees should have made do with existing facilities and equipment. And the biggest one of all: a perception that government staff were lazy, dishonest, or incompetent.

Josephine's public officials had to answer all that anger and pessimism. At town halls across the county, Sheriff Daniel and Commissioner DeYoung listened and talked things through. Residents had real grievances and history with government—including the rising score of experiences calling for help from the sheriff's office and getting turned away. People vented decades-old frustration that the county had engaged in "petty pot busts." Residents had sensible questions about how existing taxes were being spent. The meetings were not always comfortable. Commissioner DeYoung recalled one meeting in particular where "everyone was packing a 45," and he felt that it was a "room full of people scared to death of something." Dwyer recalled a moment at a local church when "all these old ladies spontaneously shouted down" a relentless local anti-tax activist, yelling, "We're sick of you!"

Sheriff Daniel had to answer for his office's past management decisions. Some residents believed that Daniel's predecessor sheriff may have exaggerated or mismanaged the sheriff's department's budget woes. Residents, including Sheriff Daniel himself, believed that more could have been done to stretch and reorganize staffing to make up for the huge loss of funding in 2012. Many thought that some incidents— particularly the media spectacle over the mass release of inmates at the jail—were a political stunt. Sheriff Daniel tried to focus on earning trust back. "You do your best to start providing a better service," he says. "You don't say there are calls for service that we're just not going to go to," but rather, "we'll just do what we can every time."

At these meetings, the commissioner distributed a simple eight-page handout that his colleague Lily Morgan had written to explain the levy. They called it "Just the Facts." Using homemade, simple graphics, the pamphlet described the funds available for law enforcement and how they were spent. It presented what would happen to the county's services if the levy passed, and what would happen if it didn't pass. A colorful pie chart showed how Josephine's property tax revenues were spent, with more than 60 percent on public safety. It informed voters that while the county was suing the federal government about forest management practices, the commissioners had no power to make the federal government give them money.

The commissioners also brought the county's most influential anti-tax leaders to a small meeting where they could present alternatives to a new tax. Commissioner DeYoung said it helped to acknowledge those voices, and then to refocus everyone on the urgency of the present moment. "I like your ideas," he said about suggestions such as developing a cogeneration power plant in the county. "But can it get us a check by July 1?" DeYoung reassured the anti-government groups that he did not want to stop their voluntary patrols, but he emphasized the importance of a county criminal justice system to back them up. DeYoung asked the patrol groups to think it through. "When you get that guy captured over in your neighbor's kitchen, and you've got him down on the floor and you've got him all zip tied up, and you pick up the phone, where are you going to take him?" DeYoung asked. "Are you gonna go put him in your garage? Are you going to put him in the basement? You gonna take him for a ride in the woods? I want that jail to stay open so that you have a place to keep that person."

Restoring the library to public management was also on the ballot, which helped turn new and moderate voters out to the polls. During the budget cuts in 2007, the library had closed entirely. Kate Dwyer recalled the "stacks and stacks" piled on the floor in the library entryway and aisles. No library has enough shelves to house its entire collection, she explained, because "books don't belong on the shelves, they belong in people's homes." A group later came together to reopen the libraries as a new nonprofit, and the county transferred its book collections to them and gave them a lease on the library's buildings. But the staff, knowledge, and systems were gone. Dwyer and others learned how much harder it was to, as she put it, "reanimate the dead rather than keeping the living from flatlining." Fundraising for the library nonprofit was endless work. The new system had limited hours, few updates to the collection, and a narrow range of services.

The nonprofit library hired a new director, Kate Lasky, who worked with others to recruit dozens of volunteers (ultimately, more than three hundred per year). A volunteer-based staffing model lacked sophisticated expertise, but it built a base of advocates for the institution. Lasky and this volunteer army first attempted to restore public funding to the library in 2014, collecting thousands of signatures to get a levy on the ballot. The levy vote failed. Nevertheless, they decided to fundraise to rennovate a corner of the main library for small children. Some board members opposed the project, Lasky says, because they had told voters the library needed public funding. Now it might look like they hadn't needed it after all. Lasky pushed through, insisting, "We've got to keep improving, with or without voters." She and the board decided to keep focused on the 15,000 people who had voted for the 2014 levy, not the opponents. "You've got to focus on those who care," Lasky says.

In 2017, fueled by energy and affection for the library, leaders and volunteers tried again to pass a levy alongside the law enforcement vote.

They circulated charming photos of dozens of volunteers holding hands around the main library to give it a "hug." Lasky and other volunteers rang hundreds of doorbells and logged 14,000 phone calls—up to seven calls per voter to ensure people had cast their ballot. Lasky did not soft-pedal her views. In one blog post, she linked to a video clip of Voldemort when she referenced the levy's opponents. But she and others stayed on message that the library was a good part of life in Josephine. "It's human nature to want to thrive," Lasky says, reflecting on the campaign. "Not just to be in a state of hopelessness or allow your community to crumble."

The evening of the election, on May 16, 2017, Daniel, Dwyer, Lasky, DeYoung, Morgan, and others knew they'd done what they could. The sheriff went home, opened a book on the porch with his wife, and waited for the election returns. Across town at the Wild River Pizza & Brewery, Lasky and the library volunteers gathered. Daniel and Lasky both got the news by text message: 52.42 percent of the voters had approved the jail and juvenile levy. 52.6 percent had voted to re-open the public library. Voters had passed two other tax levies as well: one for the fire department and one for animal control. The Wild River pub broke out in cheering, jumping, and weeping. Commissioner Morgan got a text from a laid-off 911 dispatcher saying, "Is it really true? Do I get to go home to my job?"

The next morning, the governor's office called the County Commissioners to congratulate them, saying, "You guys are on fire!" Josephine's law enforcement levels are still among the lowest in the state, but government has gotten another chance to prove itself. The lesson from the successful tax campaigns was that need is not enough. Urgency is not enough. You've got to prove that government can help. You have to convince a critical mass of skeptical voters, one at a time, that government is competent, accountable, and necessary.

Carl Wilson, a Republican and Josephine County's State Representative at the time, has lived in the county for more than sixty years. He reflected on the road they had traveled. "In about 2008, we hit bottom and have been bouncing on the bottom since. Our services were barely adequate. No, they were just *barely*." He understands the May 2017 levy vote to convey that people had had enough of living with such depleted local government. "We've seen something, we've lived it, we're never going back," he says.

"THE (w)HOLE"

The Work of Repair

Emergency services are just one piece of what Josephine's residents—adults and children alike—will need for a chance at a good life. Ken Selig has learned an overarching lesson from his many years in Josephine. "If people feel they are wronged, that's where you lose trust," he explains. If that trust is lost, "you're not going to get any cooperation at all. And then everything else falls apart." But when you start to work together, strengthening the county's social networks to turn them toward progress, it is possible to start repairing the social compact between citizens and government. Kate Lasky and the library community invested in that work. So did Selig and Jimmy Evans, with their patrols, and Evans's homeless relief work. With people like Dave Daniel inside the government and citizens like Kate Dwyer outside, there were people "in the arena" doing their best.

Gina Angelique founded a performing arts and dance program in the Illinois Valley called RiverStars—one of the only extracurricular afterschool activities for kids in the county. A while back, Angelique complained to her mother, who lives in San Diego, about how hard it was to operate and fundraise in Josephine, where there is so little money to support the schools or youth. Most of the year, Angelique is only able to offer classes a few days a week. She and her fellow dance teachers collect part-time pay checks. Her mother sympathized, saying, "They don't deserve you."

Angelique thought of the kids she teaches. Many have parents who work as marijuana trimmers with incomes that have gone from low to unlivable in recent years. She knows the degree of drug use in many of their homes and the more serious harms besides. "Many kids here have watched their parents fight with knives, commit suicide, or even found their bodies hanging," she says. One girl in Angelique's class broke into tears when Gina asked the kids to "spread their legs" during a stretch.

Angelique knows seventh graders who can barely read, and she grieves the breakdown in critical thinking and open dialogue on hard topics. Her mother's comment about what the county deserves "struck something so deep in me," Angelique says. "Ok, I thought, I'm never leaving." She and others have ambitions for how the region can improve, while still giving people a way to live self-sufficiently on their own land. "I feel connected to how great this place could be," she says.

In 2019, Angelique and her dance theater group Dancefarm created a project called "Beyond Boom & Bust." In a video trailer for a performance called "The (w)HOLE," a lonely, mournful violin and cello composition follows a woman's voice alongside choreography and landscapes depicting Josephine's beauty, but also the pain imbedded in that land. The voice narrates: "When it gets to be more, you need more and you need more. It's like there's that hole that's inside. It's so vast and it's so deep. It's not a weed-size hole, and it's not an alcohol-size hole. And it's not . . . and it's not a heroin-size hole. It's not a meth-size hole. It's a god's-size hole." She pauses. A dancer named Kari Kvittem lies prone on the floor, seizing and gasping, staring up into nothing. The voice continues. "It is massive. It's a connectivity-sized hole. It's a love hole. There's nothing that's going to fill that hole except for love and connectivity." The narrator takes a deep, audible breath.

CHAPTER THREE

"Marching, Marching, in the Beauty of the Day"

Lawrence, Massachusetts

More than one hundred relatives and friends packed the event space at Northern Essex Community College to celebrate the first graduation of the teacher's aide training program. The seventeen graduates did not wear robes, but they had coordinated bright blue dresses that matched dozens of balloons. One graduate's young daughter wore head-to-toe silver satin and sequins. A coordinator of the program had filled mason jars with flowers for each graduate to take home. Another had printed each graduate's photograph alongside her heartfelt answer to the question: "Why do you want to become a teacher?"

Destiny Rodriguez had been chosen as the student speaker. Her interest in teaching came from several years working at the front desk of the local YWCA's shelter for teenage girls. Rodriguez saw herself in the girls there, many of whom had spent time in foster care and survived abusive relationships. Some were trying to make their way as single mothers. Rodriguez loved her YWCA job, but when her second child was born, she could not sustain the schedule and income. She returned to waitressing. "I was in a rut," Rodriguez said. Each month, she paid off whatever bills seemed most urgent and let others accumulate, bogging her down in debt. That's how it was with the local cost of living. "You work so hard and it's not enough," she said.

Her daughter was nine years old and her son just a baby when Rodriguez noticed a Facebook post announcing the paraprofessional teaching program. At $17/hour, a teaching assistant job would cover her biggest expenses—more than $13,000 per year in rent for her three-room apartment and at least $10,000 per year for daycare. Teaching could give her the sense of purpose she had felt at the YWCA, and she could align her schedule with her children's school hours on a predictable routine. And Rodriguez was ready to try school again. She had gotten her diploma in a cosmetology track at a vocational high school, but those were hard years for her family. Maybe, she thought, this could be a road to college.

Like her classmates, Rodriguez worked full-time hours during her year in the paraprofessional program. She attended class from 8 am to 1 pm daily, then picked her children up from school and daycare. Before 5 pm, she dropped them with her sister, mother, or friends so she could work night shifts. Some evenings she worked at WOW! Workout World, a twenty-four-hour gym in a Lawrence suburb, where she staffed the daycare or took an overnight shift at the front desk. Other nights, from 5 pm until 2 am, she waited tables at a suburban TGI Fridays.

Despite the hustle, she nearly lost her apartment three times. She fell short on rent money one month when the restaurant was slow and tips down, barely escaping an eviction until a local nonprofit came through with emergency funds. Then a blown pipe in her building flooded her unit. Old city infrastructure hit her next, when a natural gas line in her neighborhood exploded. That disaster displaced her family for a week, then left them without heat and hot water for several more weeks.

For more than a century, Rodriguez's hometown of Lawrence has been nicknamed the Immigrant City. The official city seal, dating back to 1853, includes a honeybee. A city of immigrants, the seal conveys, is a city of workers. For Rodriguez and her classmates, as for most residents, making an honest living has meant long hours with irregular schedules at low pay. Thirty percent of the workforce commutes more than an hour per day to reach suburban jobs. They care for other families' children and elders, staff foodservice and retail, clean homes and hospitals, and work in factories or warehouses. Parents who work these positions spend the overwhelming majority of their waking hours away from their children.

The scarce, insecure jobs of the postindustrial economy leave much of the city's workforce unemployed more hours each week and more months each year, living in households with more members who cannot find any work at all. Nearly one of every four Lawrence residents lives below the poverty line, and scant income must sustain a high cost of living, including the cars and gas needed to reach scattered jobs. The median monthly rent is $1,145. That number would consume half of a paycheck (even before taxes or utilities) for relatively "lucky" workers with a full-time job at a nearby company like Muffin Town. Factory jobs making and packing baked goods there start at $13.50 an hour, the state minimum wage in 2021.

In her graduation speech, Rodriguez described the way that she and her classmates had conquered "disappointment, failure, and aggravation" to make it through the program alongside full-time jobs and parenting. "I can't count the number of times I called it quits in my head," she said. But Rodriguez was proud to do her homework alongside her daughter when she could, modeling the importance of school. Rodriguez and her peers tutored each other. Native English speakers like her supported those still learning English, while peers with college degrees from Spanish-speaking countries helped others in subjects like math. The women babysat each other's children during work shifts. They exchanged encouraging text messages to keep in touch and on track. "That's my family now," Rodriguez said.

Another supportive network, the people who had built the program, also attended Rodriguez's graduation. Staff at the adult vocational school had written the curriculum to help students pass the state's paraprofessional exam. Community college teachers had brought that curriculum to life in the classroom. Case workers at the regional career center had helped secure jobs that accommodated the daily schedule. Social workers with the school district had recruited participants, coordinated apprenticeships in local schools, and sought emergency food and housing aid as needed. Staff from the nonprofit Lawrence Community Works had led coordination and fundraising for the program. This network had passed what locals call the "cell phone test." People pass that test, explained the regional community college president Lane Glenn, when they are listed as contacts in each other's cell phones. "We want everyone to be able to pick up the phone and get in touch with everyone else who makes things work here," he says.

Lawrence's public and private leaders have done what immigrants are known for: form tight social networks and look out for the people in them. Concepts such as "civic engagement" or "building community networks" can sound like empty jargon. The expression "it takes a village" is overused. In Lawrence, these ideas look like something real. They are the base of all other progress—on jobs, on education, on violence, on redevelopment of blighted land. No single program, institution, or industry can solve problems that big. No single household living on low or minimum wages can live well, let alone get ahead, without networks to depend on. So institutions and people give up, or they work together.

Massachusetts calls Lawrence and other mill towns gateway cities, to mark their heritage providing a first home for new immigrants. But strong networks are also striving to make Lawrence a "gateway city" in the other sense suggested in this book's introduction: a gateway to a livable income. Through efforts like the paraprofessional program, the city's networks are helping adults build the skills, connections, and experience needed for living-wage employment. They have focused in particular on the median incomes of parents with children in the city's public schools. Income gains for this group will do more than make Rodriguez and other adults better off. Gains will support the schools too, freeing children to focus on their education by relieving economic stress and upheaval in their homes.

This is not the first time that organizers in Lawrence invented ways to help lift their residents out of poverty. In spite of a local government that literally took up arms against its people—in spite of efforts to exploit ethnic differences among the poor to protect the stockpiled wealth of the rich—the Bread and Roses Strike of 1912 achieved a dramatic wage increase. That prior generation's methods, forming a union and striking against giant employers in a single industry, have little traction in a job market scattered across locations and industries.

But Lawrence's Latino, Afro-Caribbean, and white leaders are reinventing the pan-ethnic cooperation that once powered the city's picket lines and are applying it to the modern economy. They are forging strong networks among residents and institutions, then focusing those networks on making City Hall more effective and accountable. The work at the core of the Bread and Roses Strike, and again today, is to put government and its partners to work for the city's people, not for outsiders' private interests. The city is as broke as it has ever been, but unlike a century ago, its public and private leaders are part of the movement for change.

"I have my high school diploma, but I never attended a graduation," Rodriguez told the crowd at the paraprofessional graduation. She halted across her words to hold back her emotion. The audience let their tears fall. "This will not be my last one."

UNDER AMERICA

The Rise and Fall of Shared Prosperity

The Everett Mill, a giant mill along the Merrimack, had an oversize entry built for horse-drawn wagons. Those doors are sealed now to serve as the wall of a modest diner called Coco's Café & Catering, which sells coffee, pastries, fried eggs, and Puerto Rican *tostones*. On this spot in 1912, a battalion of militiamen armed with bayonets burst into a picket line, driving back striking workers in one of the most violent episodes of one of the most effective labor uprisings in American history. The strike began upstairs, on a Friday in January, when 200 Polish immigrant women stood still at their looms to protest a wage cut. Their "ancient call for bread," as poet James Oppenheim described it, began in tense silence. Soon, 15,000 immigrant strikers marched outside those doors, blocking scabs and singing labor songs in their new English words.

Everett's mill workers were among the weakest, poorest people on earth. "My people are not in America," a Lawrence priest wrote of his flock at that time. "They are under it." In the late 1800s and early 1900s, Everett and other Lawrence mills had "inhal[ed] rawboned farmhands" from fifty-one nations. On so-called "coffin ships," more than two million desperate refugees had fled the Irish Potato Famine of the late 1850s, which killed twice as many people as would die in the American Civil War. Soon came exiles of poverty, job losses, and persecution in Quebec,

England, and Germany. Others followed from Italy, Poland, Lithuania, Russia, Syria, Turkey, Lebanon, China, and beyond. Assembled in the Lawrence mills, these migrants produced one of the world's largest supplies of spun cotton, worsted wool, and other textiles.

Each morning in early 1912, the Ayer Mill's ornate clocktower, with glass faces just a few inches smaller than London's Big Ben, called the city's people to work. Twenty-eight thousand people walked to the mills. From machine accidents to anthrax exposure, conditions in the textile industry killed one-third of Lawrence mill workers before their tenth year on the job. The deafening machines, the floor vibrations, and the constant vigilance required to avoid injury left workers shaking by the end of their shifts.

Conditions in the city's housing were just as bleak. Workers lived with what one report in 1912 called the "chain of the Ds": "Darkness and dampness and dirt, dirt and discomfort and disease; death." Sewage exposure led to relentless intestinal illnesses, the lack of indoor light cost residents their eyesight, and smoky stoves in windowless apartments caused respiratory disease. The mortality record of the city's tenements "reads like battle statistics."

Government as we know it was not yet invented. Minimum wage and workplace safety regulations were just ideas described in socialist speeches. Child labor was legal for fourteen-year-olds and common before that age. Infrastructure was rare and primitive. Giant pipes shot colored dye and wool scouring waste straight into the city's waterways. An innovative water treatment system filtered Merrimack River water before it entered local taps, but the system was no match for the effects of 250,000 upriver people's untreated sewage and industrial waste. Everyone knew the city's feeble fire brigade could not stop the kind of catastrophic fire that had leveled nearby cities. "The sticks are all laid for a most superb bonfire," a 1912 report observed sarcastically of Lawrence's crowded wooden tenements and piles of flammable trash.

The First Gilded Age economy generated the dehumanizing conditions in Lawrence, but also the extravagance of a growing American elite. The richest one percent of the country controlled half the nation's wealth. At the start of 1912, average wages in Lawrence mills amounted to $315 per year (and national per capita income was little better, at $340 per year). Yet patricians in Washington, D.C., attended a single party that year that cost $35,000 (again in 1912 dollars), thrown by a hostess wearing jewelry worth $500,000.

With the 1889 publication of Andrew Carnegie's "Gospel of Wealth," philanthropy was coming into vogue. But Billy Wood, Lawrence's biggest mill owner, mostly opted out of the trend. Wood was the tenth wealthiest man in America's First Gilded Age, but one of the few among his peers (including Carnegie and John D. Rockefeller) who did not establish a national philanthropic legacy.

Early in 1912, after sixty years of debate about whether textile mill conditions were unconscionable, the state of Massachusetts took a small step for the state's workers. A new law reduced the maximum work week for women and children from fifty-six to fifty-four hours. The mills could not run without them, so mill owners implemented the law by cutting all workers' time by two hours. Owners could have kept weekly earnings steady to compensate for several years of rapidly accelerating machinery, which had lifted profits while endangering and exhausting mill workers. They cut pay instead.

When the reduced paychecks hit Everett Mills on January 12, 1912, workers decided they were not willing to work to death for wages on which they could barely live. Despite record-setting low temperatures across the Northeast—so cold that portions of Niagara Falls had frozen in midair—textile workers walked picket lines for more than two months. Marches featured American flags, even as opponents called the strikers an "undigested lump" of immigrants. The city government, though as broke as its people, sent militiamen and police. "We will either break this strike or break the strikers' heads," the mayor said. The state dispatched armed militia, including a company of college students excused from their exams at Harvard. The U.S. Marines sent sharpshooters.

Women helped lead the strike, on the picket line and at the podium. Elizabeth Gurley Flynn, twenty-two years old but already a leader of the Industrial Workers of the World (IWW) union, worked with Margaret Sanger and Helen Keller to shelter the city's children in labor-sympathizers' homes in New York City and Barre, Vermont.* As the strike dragged on, with picket lines chanting that it was "better to starve fighting than to starve working," Lawrence's children were protected from violence. They were nursed back to health from, as Sanger put it, a "pale, emaciated, dejected" state. Facing cavalry, billy clubs, bayonets, and rifles, female strikers "threw pepper in the faces of police and militia, cut their suspenders with scissors, or sent them flying off horses jabbed by hat pins." In particular defiance of the social norms of her era, one woman flashed her breasts at police and dared them to shoot her.

At a 1912 Congressional hearing about the Lawrence strike, witnesses debated whether the fact that some workers could afford to add a smudge of molasses to a meal of plain bread demonstrated the desperation of their poverty or the "luxury" of their wages. They debated whether ten hours of mill labor per day, six days per week, was too long for fourteen-year-olds. Education was important, one reverend testified, but the "education" children could get working in the mill would typically be more "congenial to the child" compared to "where it is uncongenial, as it is in school." A girl named Carmela Teoli testified about leaving school at age thirteen to work and help support her family. She lasted two weeks in a mill before she "got hurt in my head," she told them. "Well, how were you hurt?" one congressman asked. "The machine pulled my scalp off," she answered.

Opposition to the strike characterized it as a mob led by "foreign operatives" who were waging "a war against lawfully constituted authority." The strikers' answer was clear: "[W]e were not considered foreigners when we meekly consented to being robbed of our labors and opportunities." The union rallied Irish and Scottish immigrants, who had longer histories and better jobs in Lawrence, to remain on strike with recent immigrants.

After workers went without pay for more than two months, mill

---

* This was the same Margaret Sanger—nurse and women's advocate—who would later establish Planned Parenthood, and the same celebrated Helen Keller, the disability activist and socialist leader, with whom Flynn would work for decades to defend the free speech rights of labor activists.

owners capitulated to a 15 percent average wage increase, not just for Lawrence's workers, but for the textile mills across New England. The settlement required translation into twelve languages before the vote to approve it. Following the rally proclaiming victory, strikers brought roses to the cemetery and to the jail, to mourn their dead and honor their leaders. But the "Bread and Roses" name later given to the uprising was not because of these bouquets. It referred to the strikers' claim that they should be able to live a life beyond bare survival. The phrase was first published in a 1911 article by suffragist Helen Todd and woven into a poem by James Oppenheim later that year. Oppenheim's poem describes "marching, marching, in the beauty of the day," because, *"Our lives shall not be sweated from birth until life closes; Hearts starve as well as bodies; give us bread, but give us roses."*

The mills' massive machines started up again. The Ayer Mill clocktower again tolled the eleven-hour factory days. Mill jobs had not changed much. That first week back, a man was fatally crushed by an elevator at the Everett Mill. But some conditions were different. One worker said of the strike: "We are a new people. We have hope. We will never stand again what we stood before."

Yet xenophobia and anti-communism grew in the years following. Traffickers of ideas about Nordic supremacy and eugenics merged their case with economic arguments that immigrants suppressed wages. By 1921, these ideas and backlash against the Lawrence strike had yielded an anti-immigrant literacy test and a quota law that stalled immigration from all nations beyond western and northern Europe. Most of the strike's leaders, including Elizabeth Gurley Flynn, spent years in prison for espionage convictions related to labor organizing. Strike leader Big Bill Haywood fled a politicized conviction during the First Red Scare in 1921, taking refuge in Moscow. He died less than a decade letter of alcoholism, homesickness, and diabetes, survived by a Russian wife with whom he shared no common language.

Textile mill owner Billy Wood, once the second highest earning man in America, also reached a dismal end. In the years after the strike, Wood lost a daughter to illness and a son to a car crash. In 1926, grief-stricken and facing an indictment for tax fraud, he walked alone onto a beach in Florida and fired a gun into his mouth.

Lawrence did nothing to celebrate or acknowledge the strike for decades. Yet the Bread and Roses Strike helped lead society toward decency in American jobs and housing. Hard-fought legal reforms sought during the strike and the decades following reduced inequality and laid the foundation for the modern middle class. Lawrence built its first public playground, and Massachusetts adopted America's first minimum wage law. Locally and elsewhere, housing codes brought sunlight, air flow, plumbing, and garbage disposal into tenements. Laws required employers to invest in safety features for machinery. Taxes cut into the extremes of hoarded wealth, allowing local governments to invest revenues in water treatment and sewage disposal systems. Fire protection became a public service, rather than an opt-in subscription. Regulations reduced child labor and expanded public education. The Works Progress Administration and other New Deal programs during the Great Depression built civic infrastructure in Lawrence, including two bridges, a municipal airport, a major city park, and many sidewalks. Racial discrimination kept the direct benefits of improved jobs and neighborhoods limited to white people, but the regulations from this era modeled America's legal bulwark against destitution.

This activist, people-oriented government shared the wealth of the First Gilded Age with its industrial workforce. The Lawrence mills remained hubs of textile and shoe manufacturing, including as major producers of military blankets and uniforms during World War I. Following World War II, the city remained, as one former resident put it, "rich in the aroma of leather, fabrics, and machine grease. . . . [T]here were no McMansions, but there was broad prosperity, great hope and generations of upwardly mobile, accomplished citizens."

Broad prosperity, however, did not last long enough. In his closing speech to the Bread and Roses Strike in 1912, labor leader Big Bill Haywood had said:

> You, the strikers of Lawrence, have won the most signal victory
> of any body of organized working men in the world. You have
> won the strike for yourselves and by your strike you have won

an increase in the wages for 250,000 other textile workers in
the vicinity . . . You have won by your solidarity and brains and
muscle.

Haywood's words inadvertently foreshadowed losses that started in
the 1950s. "In the vicinity" described a loophole, and Lawrence fell
through it. A program of federal regulatory exemptions, infrastructure
investments, and tax subsidies lured textile production away from the
northeast and to the American South, a region desperate for jobs and
a modern industrial economy. Laws there permitted companies to pay
minimum wage to skilled workers (even though minimum wages fell
below subsistence levels) and less than minimum wage to new employees. Southern state regulations impeded union organizing and wage
protections, while their towns offered tax relief and incurred unsustainable debt to build and furnish new textile plants and train workers.

Lawrence lost 18,000 textile jobs by 1953. One in five Lawrence
workers could not find a job in the 1950s, despite a booming national economy. As he watched Massachusetts's textile industry shrivel,
then-Senator John F. Kennedy admonished Southern officials about
their fiscally reckless subsidy packages. He warned that soon enough,
"their newfound (industrial) benefactors" would abandon the South
too, hunting bargains farther afield. That's exactly what happened, and
Southern states now wrestle with blighted mills and depopulated textile
towns. Profits flow to shareholders and cheaper goods flow to American consumers, but the textile industry has hemorrhaged domestic jobs.
The Gap, Inc., was manufacturing its brands in forty-two countries
by 2003.

The Lawrence heritage in fabrics was reduced to remnants. The
Ayer Mill's grand bell tower first rang on October 3, 1910. No one recorded the date in 1955 when it rang for the last time. A publicly traded
textile giant named Textron bought the American Woolen Company,
which owned the mill. By the end of the 1950s, Textron had closed all
of its northeastern facilities, including the Ayer Mill. Ownership of the
American Woolen Company changed hands through various restruc-
turings. For most of the late twentieth century, its business consisted of

an office in Florida that imported blankets manufactured abroad, until it was recently reborn as a producer of luxury woolen goods made at a mill in Connecticut.

At some point after the Ayer Mill closed, someone stole the tower's 4,850-pound copper and tin bell, presumably to scrap. The 1950s marked the beginning of three decades of "disinvestment"—a bloodless word for the bloodletting of American cities, in which residents and businesses moved to suburbs and the Sun Belt in droves. Buildings, incomes, and morale in older cities began to decline, then to collapse.

In the thirty-five years after its closure, the Ayer Mill clock tower filled with several stories of pigeon droppings infested with mice. When a hazardous waste company emptied it out in 1991, the restoration created a plume of dust so big that locals thought the tower was on fire.

SCABS, WELFARE QUEENS, AND CRIMINALS

The Racial Narrative of Lawrence's Decline

Lawrence's population could have hollowed out from the 1960s to the 1990s, as disinvestment drained the city of jobs and capital. Many northeastern industrial cities lost residents faster than they could replace them. Although businesses and homeowners did leave Lawrence across these decades, the city was not abandoned. A new generation of immigrants and their children, mostly from Puerto Rico and the Dominican Republic, chose Lawrence as their home.

These newcomers represented the city's best hope for the future. The Bread and Roses Strike stood as a reminder that if people failed to stand up for one another in spite of their racial, ethnic, and class differences, inequality and discrimination would trap them all in poverty. "Among workers there is only one nationality, one race, one creed," strike leader Joe Ettor had said. "Do not play the aristocrat because you speak English, are habituated to the country, have a trade and are better paid. Throw in your lot with the low-paid. You must either reach down and lift them or they will reach up and pull you down."

Ettor's lesson was lost on white city officials, who by the 1980s seemed to view Latino immigrants as they viewed the empty mills—a problem to solve. When they could afford to, they handled the mills with wrecking balls and the people with police. When budgets were tight, they handled both with neglect. This disinvestment from the city's new population damaged Lawrence's ability to attract new jobs and alleviate local poverty over the longer run. As in all postindustrial places, it was this disinvestment in people that did the most harm. It made hard problems harder.

Dan Rivera was one of the early Latino newcomers to Lawrence. His childhood in Lawrence in the 1970s and 80s wasn't so bad. He figures he lived pretty much the same way that poor children had for decades. He played sports at the Boys and Girls Club, rode bikes in parks, delivered papers for the *The Eagle-Tribune*. He joined the Boy Scouts and later the military, and those organizations gave him the male role models he needed as a child who had never met his father. As part of a growing number of Latino families from the Caribbean in a city still run by white people, Rivera saw discrimination as part of daily life. But he felt fortunate to have grown up alongside other children like him: "It helped that there were a lot of us. I wasn't one brown kid in a sea of other kids."

Life was easier in Lawrence than it had been in the Bronx, where Rivera lived until age five. Rivera remembers fun times in New York, like going to daycare with his big brother by jumping across tenement rooftops. But those years were grinding, vulnerable ones for his mother, who worked as a seamstress in basement sweatshops in the Garment District. All around them, New York City's conditions were disintegrating: half a million jobs lost in part to factory closings, peak overdose rates as the heroin epidemic swept the city, historic rates of white flight, and homicide rates heading toward record-breaking highs in the 1980s. After a terrible fire left Rivera's sister with third-degree burns the night of her first communion, Rivera's mother moved the family to Lawrence. She was following a well-worn Caribbean trail established in the 1940s and 1950s, when agricultural businesses in Western Massachusetts first recruited Puerto Ricans as farmworkers after their island's coffee and tobacco growers lost their land to American sugar companies. Subsequent generations of Puerto Ricans, followed by Dominicans, made their way to Lawrence in search of a hometown that offered not only jobs, but also familiar language, music, food, and culture.

For Dominicans like Rivera's mother, moving to Lawrence from New York was a small adjustment compared to the move that had brought them to the United States. Rivera's mother was born in the Dominican Republic during dictator Rafael Trujillo's thirty-one-year reign of terror. Trujillo rose to power as a military leader during the American occupation of the island nation from 1916–1924, then took control of the island via a coup d'état in 1930. "He was our Sauron, our Arawn, our Darkseid, our Once and Future Dictator," writes Dominican-American novelist Junot Díaz, "a personaje so outlandish, so perverse, so dreadful that not even a sci-fi writer could have made his ass up." After Trujillo's assassination in 1961, a popular uprising in the country restored free elections on the island, but the U.S. military again invaded in 1965 in the name of anti-communism. With the Dominican military under U.S. command, they brought a Trujillo officer to power for another twelve years of brutality, censorship, and land confiscation.

Rivera's mother and more than 400,000 other Dominicans fled the island from 1961–1986 with visas issued to pro-democracy Dominicans by the U.S. government as a strategy to quiet the island's democratic resistance. This political migration became an economic one too. Decades of terror and corruption had turned a nation of small farms over to large-scale industrial agriculture and peonage. New waves of migrants chose to "flee the cane" in rural areas and seek lives beyond the crowded shanty towns of Santo Domingo. The Dominican flight to the United States embodied what journalist Juan González called the "harvest of empire."

In Lawrence, Rivera's mother found some of the remaining textile and manufacturing jobs. She sewed for what is now Brooks Brothers, assembled auto parts for the P. T. Brake Lining Company, and stitched ultrasuede jackets and skirts for the Samuel Robert Company, a brand favored by Jackie Kennedy Onassis. Rivera says he can spot a vintage Samuel Robert piece "from 100 yards." His mom's jobs were hard and hardly paid. Whether for her bosses or her children, she was always working.

Compared to Lawrence's recent past, the years of Rivera's childhood were troubled ones. Wages fell for the remaining textile and shoe manufacturing jobs. A shoemaker called Lawrence Maid Footwear hung on longer than most, but during the 1970s, the size of its workforce fell from 2,200 workers to 750. A video of the factory at the time depicts its workers, mostly women, stitching this or that particular seam on endlessly refilling stacks of leather in large, half-empty halls echoing with the jackhammering of sewing machines. Lawrence Maid paid workers just above minimum wage for jobs that demanded a notoriously fast pace. The company offered the kind of minimum-wage, high-injury positions that sociologists call "bad jobs"—the kind that only look good in hindsight when they're gone and the alternative condition of "no jobs" is clear.

Lawrence's falling wages and rising unemployment were not exceptional. Starting in 1979, low-wage workers across the country were heading into decades of steady wage decline that, by 2013, had cost those workers 5 percent of their real (inflation-adjusted) wages. Middle-wage workers also had stagnant pay for the majority of that time period, apart from a small lift in the late 1990s. The situation was even worse for Latinos in Massachusetts. Their median household income fell by 40 percent during the 1980s. Alongside this steep fall in wages for Massachusetts Latinos, the income of high-wage earners nationally began to take off, leading to a 41 percent increase by 2013.

From 1940 to 1980, two out of every five white residents left Lawrence. In a masterful history of Lawrence, Llana Barber documents how push factors (including an infamous urban renewal project that destroyed a low-income white neighborhood) displaced some residents. Newer homes and larger lots, in towns free of immigrants, pulled other white residents to the suburbs. The city sank to its lowest population in 1980, but that number climbed again as the Dominican community refilled the city. Between 1980 and 1990, the Dominican share of Lawrence's population increased fivefold, growing from 3 to 15 percent by decade's end.

This racial transition, and the harsh policing that city officials applied to it, turned violent in August 1984. Two days of racial conflict erupted in Lower Tower Hill, a formerly French-Canadian neighborhood that had become about half Latino. The triggering event remains unknown, but the first day drew 200 to 300 people divided into white and Latino groups. Throughout two nights, they threw rocks, set trash barrels aflame, and launched Molotov cocktails, while white rioters chanted "U.S.A., U.S.A.," "Who's American? We are," and "Go home! We were here first." Latinos fought back, but their protests and confrontations were directed primarily at the police. "We can't even ride a bike because they say it is stolen," one young Latino protestor said. Another explained, "police officers treat us like animals."

After the streets calmed, Latino leaders again pushed the city to hire bilingual police officers and firefighters to improve communications with new immigrants. Only two of Lawrence's ninety-six city police officers were Latino in 1984, despite long-standing concerns about the city's aggressive and humiliating policing of Latinos. One white religious leader suggested that if it was difficult to hire more bilingual, Latino officers and firefighters, the city could teach its existing staff some Spanish. The remark seemed to capture the city's own stance: better to gather white officers for Spanish class ("Let's start with 'Hola!'") than learn to recruit Latino officers conversant in both languages.

Life in most of the city went on as usual, even as news coverage depicted a city in flames. The coverage, along with a state of emergency declaration and a curfew, reinforced the outside view that Lawrence was falling apart. Hate crimes and white nativism grew across the 1990s and 2000s, targeting Latinos as perpetual foreigners who belonged in some other country. Meanwhile, observed historian Llana Barber, Lawrence city officials resisted characterizations of the incident as a white race riot, because they worried Lawrence would become known as a "racist backwater." Officials leveraged the event to secure increased police funding and militaristic equipment from the state.

These events, changing racial demographics, inequality between the city and its suburbs, and steep manufacturing job losses converged to reinforce anti-Latino narratives of Lawrence's decline. It was correlation without causation: Lawrence had been hemorrhaging jobs for decades before the biggest surge of Latino immigrants to the city, but Puerto Ricans and Dominicans took the blame for rising unemployment, poverty, and crime. Victorious mayoral candidate Kevin Sullivan stoked this prejudice against the city's newest immigrants with his 1985 campaign slogan: "Giving the city back to those who built it."

Latino leaders such as Félix Mejía expressed the impossible paradox facing Latinos: "If you work, you're taking the job away from someone else. If you don't work, you're on welfare." The new Latino population, which included Puerto Ricans, Dominicans, and Cubans of African descent, battled both the "undeserving poor" script that characterized anti-Black racism as well as the "perpetual foreigner" script that described anti-Latino, anti-immigrant sentiment.

Strategic discrimination against ethnic minorities was an old story in Lawrence. Vilification of early Irish workers in the city had once helped rationalize low wages by blaming workers' living conditions on their culture. Nativist voices at the *Merrimack Courier* blamed the Irish for crime and called them the "most vicious population of Europe." In 1856, the *Lawrence American* described a political parade "of the most noisy Irish rabble . . . comprising some 500 ragged, dirty-faced, filthy urchins culled and dragged forth from the rum-holes, grog cellars and shanties" of the Irish neighborhood. It could have come straight from this anti-Irish script when, a century later in 1986, an assistant principal at a Lawrence junior high school joked that there were no Puerto Ricans at a St. Patrick's Day event "because they were 'all outside stealing our cars.'"

Rather than connect ethnic white families to later newcomers, Lawrence's immigrant history intensified the anti-Latino sentiment as descendants of white immigrants "argued that their immigrant forebears made it in America without help." Such claims overlooked the federal regulatory protections, education funding, housing subsidies, and infrastructure investments made during the New Deal and postwar periods. "They forget, too," one Latino resident said, "the riots, protest, strikes, demonstrations, that make up part of [European immigrants'] history."

Even Latino immigrants to Lawrence started to believe the story that new immigrants were scabs reducing wages, welfare queens living off of taxpayers, or criminals stealing from workers. Nelson Butten, a community leader who had emigrated from the Dominican Republic as a young man, recalled conversations with his grandmother, who had immigrated to Lawrence when it was still a mostly white city. She would give Nelson an earful about how easy it was to find jobs in Lawrence before, as he recalled her saying, "Latinos came, and started stealing, and started doing this and doing that." He tried to argue with her and come up with alternative explanations for the city's unemployment rate. "If it is true what you are saying, if Latinos are so bad," he would say, "why did American factories go to Mexico, to the Caribbean? They follow us!" His grandmother never had an answer for that, but she never gave up her suspicion of newcomers, either. Her views helped Nelson understand a lesson he learned from a mentor in Lawrence: "History is made of myth and facts." Latino immigrants to Lawrence, Nelson says, "need to share our stories, because otherwise someone is going to make them for us."

Lawrence's fact-based history challenges one of the most powerful myths told throughout the 1980s: that taxpayers in suburban growth areas had been "bailing out" struggling cities like Lawrence for many years. Lawrence's suburban expatriates, Barber documents, never canceled or disavowed the activist government that helped build their middle-class stability. They simply took it with them, relocating government subsidies to favor suburbs over cities. The 1980s political culture labeled the decline of industrial American cities as their residents' and leaders' own fault. Using the language of fiscal rationality and tough love, the federal government started defunding "noncompetitive" places branded as mismanaged and corrupt.

Yet in the suburbs, federal money still flowed. The Massachusetts suburbs of the Route 128 area, including those around Lawrence, pioneered a suburban agenda that would transform Democratic Party politics away from its "roots in the labor union halls of northern cities, and toward white-collar suburbanites in the postindustrial metropolitan periphery." As the job base relocated to these areas and white flight intensified racial segregation, an ambitious state law in 1969 (dubbed the "Anti-Snob Zoning Act") had tried to open all Massachusetts towns to a non-zero level of multifamily housing development. But during the next twenty years, only about 8 percent of Massachusetts municipalities met their benchmarks under the law, and most that did were already the most diverse, dense cities. Since then, the Route 128 suburbs have continued to fall short of Anti-Snob Zoning Act benchmarks.

Suburban liberalism had taken an individualistic turn, concerned less with dismantling the structures of poverty and more with protecting low-density neighborhoods, open space, and corporations.

The politics that helped trap lower wage workers in cities like Lawrence became an anti-tax agenda as well. State voters, persuaded by anti-tax activists funded in large part by technology companies, enacted Proposition 2½, one of the earliest and most dramatic property tax overhauls. When the law first hit municipal budgets in 1983, it devastated poor cities' ability to generate revenues. Lawrence took deep cuts from these tax changes. For a few years, the state softened some of those losses with higher state aid, but as a share of the state budget, local aid peaked in 1988 and has fallen ever since. During the boom years of the 1990s, the state legislature cut taxes more than forty times, until by 2002, Massachusetts ranked forty-seventh nationwide for the rate of state/local taxes and fees as a percentage of personal income. Contrary to its reputation as a high-tax state, Massachusetts charged the eleventh lowest state income tax rate in the country, placing it just behind Utah.

Lawrence's government lost revenues fast, resulting in dramatic and abrupt cuts to city services in the early 1980s. The city closed its only pool, canceled after-school and summer programs, laid off firefighters, and cut more than 30 percent of the police department. The city slashed its school district budget, cutting nearly one-fifth of spending per pupil despite rising need for bilingual education. In 1989, the Massachusetts governor gutted a special line of funding for the state's gateway cities, including funding for adult education in English as a second language. City staff started taping plastic over the windows inside City Hall's public meeting chamber to save on winter heating costs. Trash became a chronic problem, due to a collapse in funding for garbage removal and no enforcement efforts to stop illegal dumping. "People ask: If the city doesn't care about me, why should I care about it?" recalled city nonprofit leader Juan Bonilla, describing how falling city services dragged down personal responsibility, too. "I'd think, 'This place is a dump—there's nothing good here. I don't care.'" For him and other children of his generation, the goal was not to improve Lawrence. It was to escape it.

Government investments in research and development also moved toward Lawrence's suburbs, bringing private capital in tow. Just five miles away from Everett Mills, along South Union and then North Main Streets, is downtown Andover, once Billy Wood's hometown. Andover is home to the Phillips Academy boarding school, where annual tuition and board fees for one student are $16,000 higher than the median income for a household in Lawrence. Andover is also one of the principal towns of the "Massachusetts Miracle" of the 1980s, when the state built up its financial services and technology sectors to replace lost industrial jobs. Government research dollars in defense and communications, not just market forces, drove this transformation, which helped make Andover one of America's wealthiest towns.

Middle-class flight and development incentives in the suburbs made it hard for businesses in Lawrence to compete. With falling wages, newer Lawrence families like Dan Rivera's didn't have as much disposable income to spend on restaurants and shopping. The city's historic commercial center on Essex Street hollowed out, and the consumer dollars and sales tax Lawrence families did spend flowed to the donut of suburbs surrounding the city. Essex Street soon sold little more than inexpensive goods, such as actual donuts and imported synthetic clothing. Essex Street was never a ghost town commercial district, but it became a low-rent corridor with periodic vacancies. The immigrant entrepreneurs who ran its small shops didn't have the capital to restore aging historic buildings.

On one visit to Lawrence, a white woman who had spent her childhood in the city before moving to the suburbs tried to capture the change for me. When she had been a child, she recalled, Essex Street was decorated with wreaths and lights for the Christmas holidays. In the 1980s, she said, after "everyone left," the Essex holiday tradition was lost. I learned later that she was wrong. City workers kept hanging wreaths and lights every year. Lawrence homes added new traditions, with exuberant, colorful light displays. Feeling sorrow (or scorn) for the city from a distance deprived expatriates like her of information about Lawrence's good qualities even during its hardest hours, including the legacies preserved by the city's newer guardians. Christmas was never canceled.

John J. Buckley, who served as mayor on and off for twenty-two

years between 1952–1986, invested in futile efforts to draw suburbanites back to the city. He used federal and state aid to try to redevelop
the downtown by razing nine blocks north of its central green space
in 1978. Planners promised the demolished neighborhood's predominantly Latino residents that they would have access to new housing
there. But Mayor Buckley and business interests changed course, deciding to make the new development only middle-income. Echoing a sentiment common among central-city mayors of his generation, Buckley
said: "Lawrence cannot afford to be a city of the poor and the elderly."
The reality turned out differently: Lawrence remained a city of mostly
poor and elderly people, but they were even worse off as their city demolished their homes and funneled public dollars toward failed real
estate developments.

Many suburban landowners continued to make money in Lawrence,
often in ways that hurt city residents. The steady inflow of homeseekers
into Lawrence from New York City and the Caribbean kept rents high
across the 1980s, leading to a wave of speculative real estate investment. Rent dollars flowed to an increasingly absentee set of landowners
who reinvested profits elsewhere. Deep budget cuts to housing code
enforcement weakened the city's ability to hold hard-to-reach absentee
landlords to habitability standards. Rents crashed in the early 1990s,
however, and some landlords could not find profitable buyers or renters
for their properties. Arson offered an answer: if fire destroyed a building, its owner could recoup insurance payouts. After taking insurance
money, landowners could hold their land for future value, sell it for a
junk price to be done with it, or stop paying taxes and abandon it to
become the city's problem. In 1989, a businessman invented another
use for underutilized property: to avoid the costs of waste disposal, he
bought an old mill and filled it with tires, construction debris, and other
waste from his businesses. Then he abandoned the mill.

Lawrence became known as an arson capital, but the city's depleted
fire department did not have the staffing to investigate suspicious fires.
Residents lived amidst the blight of hazardous charred buildings and
squeezed into a diminished supply of usable housing. To this day, Lawrence residents pay some of the highest home and auto insurance rates

in their region because insurance companies are neither generous nor stupid. The city government bore the cost of legal processes to condemn property and eventually demolish trashed structures.

Inbound commuters continued to occupy most city jobs, such as teaching, policing, and clerical work. Government employment did not require city residence. In the mid-1980s, Latinos held only around 2 percent of the city's jobs, even as they were on their way to comprising 42 percent of the city's working-age population by 1990. An antiquated city council system of at-large elections effectively blocked Latino voters from electing any representation to the council. City hiring, as one state representative put it at the time, was "rotten with patronage."

Lawrence's government dug in. In an executive order by Governor Michael Dukakis back in 1977, the state had established goals for equal opportunity in public employment. Lawrence entered into a voluntary agreement with the state to accelerate Latino hiring, but the city made meager progress even as it hired new employees. Describing the message that the negligible number of Latino public employees sent, one state official said, "Nothing speaks louder than zero."

In March 1991, on the occasion of David Duke giving a speech in Boston, a journalist visited Lawrence to film a Boston TV news segment called "Ethnic Tensions in Lawrence." The reporter narrated: "Close to half the population in Lawrence is Hispanic now . . ." followed by a pause, "and growing." He interviewed a Latino man in the following exchange:

LAWRENCE MAN: People are mostly from Chicago and New York.

JOURNALIST: Chicago?! There are no jobs here.

LAWRENCE MAN: Alright, to be honest, there ain't shit around here. I mean, Lawrence is not a place you could just come and move, just like that, because this place sucks.

JOURNALIST: But why are people coming here? Why are all you guys here?

LAWRENCE MAN: We're here because probably there ain't nowhere else to go.

The journalist's voice cut in with a somber overlay: "To many white people, these are the faces of trouble, come to Lawrence." The reporter interviewed Lawrence's mayor Kevin Sullivan, who explained: "I'm willing to say that everybody here is welcomed, but you better come here to contribute. If you don't come here to contribute, then the City of Lawrence is going to make it very rough for you." But as to David Duke's visit, the mayor said: "The Southern bigotry that Duke represents has not, would not, manifest itself up here in any way." Yet the reporter and mayor had conveyed that Lawrence's Latinos were to blame for the city's problems. Those problems, the mayor made clear, called for punishment and containment of newcomers.

Dan Rivera was serving in the U.S. Army in Iraq and Kuwait when that news spot aired. In 1993, he made his way back to Lawrence to earn his college and business degrees. In 2009, he would be elected to the city council. Four years later, he would become the first Lawrence mayor in half a century to build an administration focused on improving job access, income, and quality of life for the city's residents—including its Latinos—rather than policing or trying to replace them. But before Rivera could win either of these elections, Lawrence would need to stop scapegoating its newer residents so it could face its real problems. That would require a grassroots effort to transform immigrants from a dozen nations into a political network.

"WE'VE BEEN ASLEEP"

The Birth of the Latino City

In 1992, a woman named Nancy Rodriguez walked her children to her usual North Lawrence bus stop for the first day of school. The school bus didn't come, so she figured she must have been late that day. But the same thing happened the next day, then the next. She went downtown to the school district offices and learned, alongside other confused Spanish-speaking parents, that public-school buses had been eliminated in the most recent round of budget cuts. Already overwhelmed as a single mother, she struggled each day to secure enough income to keep her children fed and housed. Yet Rodriguez needed the buses back, so she made time to organize other parents to appear at public meetings to try to reestablish school transit. They were too late. Again and again, district officials asked, "Where were you when we made the decision?"

Rodriguez learned an important lesson: local governments were making decisions that affected her family. She needed to get involved in those decisions. "We've been asleep," she would say. "We really need to start paying attention." It wasn't that Rodriguez needed to be involved in spite of her poverty. She needed to be involved because of it. Her margins were too thin to take additional hits or miss any chances. This time it had been public service cuts, but next time it could be a redevelopment that would displace her family's home. She might miss a job opening, or an adult education program that could work for her schedule. She needed to build a network of relationships that could teach her how public decision-making worked, how to find jobs, how to be active in her children's education, how to advocate for herself, how to find advocates who could vouch for her.

Rodriguez had little time to implement this lesson herself. Within two years of that no-show bus, she fell ill and then passed away. But Rodriguez's story remains alive with Luz Santana, one of a generation of Latino and Latina leaders in Lawrence who have spent their careers working to integrate residents like Rodriguez into the social and political fabric of the city. Santana came to Lawrence as a young mother from Puerto Rico. She spent her early years in Lawrence unemployed, then secured a coveted job as a factory worker. When her employer closed the factory and laid her off, Santana made her way to college, then into a job as a social services caseworker. Today, she is cofounder and codirector of a major nonprofit educational organization and the author of several books. From her own life, Santana could appreciate Rodriguez's insight that ethnic silos kept Latino residents isolated, powerless, and poor. And if Latinos could not make it out of poverty, Lawrence couldn't either.

Across the late 1980s and 90s, Santana and other Latino leaders set out to address two problems at the heart of the city's challenges. First, to improve the basic economic security of Lawrence families, they needed to start reaching Latinos with existing government anti-poverty programs. Second, they needed to seat Latinos in positions of government leadership to direct city investments toward the betterment of—not displacement or confinement of—Latino families. They needed inclusion in existing programs, but also the power to change them.

Santana was an early caseworker at Centro Panamericano, one of Lawrence's first bilingual social services agencies. For years before founders Isabel Melendez and Jorge Santiago built Centro, social services had failed to serve Latino families with ladders out of unemployment. Most caseworkers could do little more for monolingual immigrants than issue or deny eligibility for public benefits, rather than coach and advocate for their clients. By reaching Spanish speakers, Centro helped achieve what ethnic clubs had once done for earlier immigrants, helping them to find jobs, housing, and English classes.

Centro also gave Santana and other future leaders their first white-collar job, and with it, a stepping stone toward higher education and better opportunities. As the share of Lawrence's population employed in manufacturing fell between 1970 and 2000, the region gained jobs in education, social services, and health care. Writer Jeanne Schinto described how the transformation had changed Everett Mills: "Where rows of textile workers used to toil for hourly wages, there is now a honeycomb of little blue cubicles." By 2000, services (mostly in the private and nonprofit sector) commanded nearly 40 percent of the city's workforce.

As labor organizers had done during the Bread and Roses Strike, Centro and other Latino organizations helped create ties among Puerto Ricans, Dominicans, and smaller immigrant groups from Latin America. White Lawrencians lumped these groups together as "the Spanish," but the machine's hold on the city could survive only if new immigrants competed amongst themselves. Uniting these groups, however, was harder than it might seem. Puerto Ricans and Dominicans had historically competed for jobs and investment both on- and off-island. The Afro-Latinidad population from the Dominican Republic and Puerto Rico faced colorism and anti-Black bias from both white people and lighter-skinned Latinos. Lawrence residents from Latin America struggled more with immigration status than Puerto Ricans (who were

U.S. citizens) or Dominicans (many of whom came through special visa programs connected to U.S. foreign policy goals in the Dominican Republic).

Centro's diverse mix of caseworkers and clientele helped nurture a pan-Latino identity. A common colonial language enabled shared communications like *Rumbo*, the city's first bilingual newspaper. Centro founder Isabel Melendez started the Semana Hispana festival in 1979 to celebrate common and distinctive elements of each group's food, arts, and culture.

During her years at Centro, then later as a leader of a nonprofit, Luz Santana tried to share the lesson that Nancy Rodriguez had learned: effective democratic institutions require people to understand and shape the systems around them. Whether involving parents in their children's education or helping jobseekers navigate the hiring process at a new business, Latino leaders built residents' confidence and knowledge. By doing so, they could improve their families and their city.

Electoral returns followed. Latinos began winning elected offices, including an at-large seat on the school board in 1991, a city council seat in 1993, and a state representative seat in 1998. Local Latino activists spurred the federal government to prosecute a civil rights lawsuit that removed voting barriers, established a ward system, and raised Latino turnout in 1999. Two additional voting rights lawsuits in 2001 curtailed gerrymandering and blocked the last-minute implementation of a voter ID policy that would have discouraged Latinos from voting.

As Santana worked toward her master's degree in the 1990s, three students in MIT's urban planning department were doing the same. In class one day, a professor assigned a newspaper feature arguing that Lawrence was struggling, while the nearby city of Lowell was succeeding, because Lowell had a "can-do" spirit that Lawrence lacked. A student named Kristen Harol left class riled up. Her grandfather had worked in Lawrence as a shoe salesman, and she had spent time there across her childhood. The story that Lawrence's people were not pulling hard enough on their bootstraps, Harol said, didn't match her experience. She vented her irritation to classmates Jess Andors and Tamar Kotelchuck, who had also been skeptical that Lawrence's biggest problem was a bad attitude. As New Yorkers, Andors and Kotelchuck had not grown up amidst the Massachusetts stigma against Lawrence.

To find out why Lawrence was lagging, the three students teamed up with a Lawrence native and community building expert named Bill Traynor. They raised summer grant funding to join Lawrence Community Works (LCW), a community development organization. This group had not come to Lawrence as missionaries intending to "save the city." Instead, like most newcomers to Lawrence across its history, they had come to find good work. Lawrence's mills, river, and canals gave it "good bones" for an urban planner to love. The city had compelling people and a rich history. When they arrived, however, city officials offered them a "who's-who" list of government and nonprofit leaders. Every person on the list was white. Though they too were white, Traynor and the women from MIT recognized that the city's segregated power structure was part of the problem. The establishment's alienation from the city's Latino majority, they observed, made it ineffective in its most critical roles, including schools, policing, and job programs.

Traynor, Andors, Kotelchuck, and Harol worked to support and earn the trust of Latina leaders from the Centro and LCW communities, such as Isabel Melendez, Luz Santana, and Ana Rodriguez—all of whom modeled a people-centered vision of change for the city. The new team at LCW had intended to focus on the city's physical environment, especially the need for decent affordable housing. But through the organizing networks established by Centro and other local groups, community members told LCW they needed youth programs more urgently than housing. So these young urban planners, with no youth development training, spent their first summer in Lawrence running a fly-by-the-seat-of-their-pants program for children featuring baseball, art projects, and field trips.

Andors, Kotelchuck, and Harol, along with Maggie Super Church (a fourth MIT classmate they recruited to join them), later became the new leaders of LCW and a sister organization called Groundwork Lawrence, which transforms contaminated land and waterways into parks, playgrounds, and waterfront trails. Groundwork's current deputy director, Lesly Melendez, singles these women out as key building blocks of the city's progress. Instead of acting like saviors telling other people what needed to be done, she said, they tackled one issue at a time in partnership with residents. For twenty years, they have been in the partnerships behind the scenes of nearly every good-news headline from Lawrence.

Over the years, LCW and Groundwork Lawrence came to see that the disengagement Nancy Rodriguez had described so well, which Centro and other Latino leaders had mobilized to address, was not just one problem on a long list. It was *the* problem—the one at the center of other hardships. As Andors and Traynor put it in an article for *Shelterforce* magazine, it had become "too hard, too scary, too boring and too unnatural for people to find ways to get to know and learn to trust their neighbors, or take part in public life." Civic life stagnated, with old, underfunded, and understaffed plans for the future. Lack of accountability to the local public perpetuated "friends and family" hiring and contracting patterns that excluded Latinos.

The antidote to this alienation, staff learned at LCW, was to help residents identify problems in their communities, brainstorm solutions, and actively implement them. LCW began setting up three-part group dinners called NeighborCircles, held in a volunteer host's home. These dinners connected residents in a one- or two-block area to learn about one another's families and histories in Lawrence, while also organizing a joint project to improve their area. NeighborCircles groups made improvements such as getting four-way stop signs at a busy intersection outside a nursery school, cleaning up a local park, boarding or demolishing a blighted home, chipping in to buy a shared snowblower for the block, lobbying the city for a new street light, or organizing a block party.

For Jess Andors, the NeighborCircles on her own block helped nurture relationships among her son and other children, and between her and other parents. One neighbor bought a snow shovel for his truck, and even though he moved to a different block, he still comes by after snowstorms to clear the back-alley driveway that linked his former house with those of his neighbors. Their block functions some days as a form of communal childcare, with one family's trampoline complementing another's basketball hoop, one family offering snacks one day and another the next, parents trading off with supervision to cover each other's work shifts. One day her son counted the number of children in elementary school on his block for me: "Nine," he said, listing their names. I'd already met four of them by sitting at the Andors' kitchen table for less than two hours.

Nelson Butten, who ran the NeighborCircles program and served as a co-director of LCW, described the difference it made for projects to spring from local families, rather than from nonprofit staff. He recalls early days of cleaning parks with outsiders from an AmeriCorps program, after which volunteers despaired to see blown trash and overflowing barrels in the park again. Because volunteers did not introduce themselves or involve residents, park users assumed they'd be back. LCW's model, he said, meant the community took responsibility for protecting the progress they had made. NeighborCircles forge community networks, not just improvements. Acquaintances and friendships at the block level help people feel safer and rely on one another for mutual aid.

Groundwork Lawrence also uses its projects to nurture local leadership and social connections, rather than relying solely on outside experts or suburban volunteers. Groundwork's campaign to improve the Spicket River began in 2002 with just twenty resident volunteers at a river clean-up. Despite anti-pollution investments through the Clean Water Act, the Spicket was still sullied by its days as a wastewater channel. In 1921, Robert Frost had described it as a brook "thrown / Deep in a sewer dungeon under stone / In fetid darkness still to live and run." Lesly Melendez, an early volunteer, remembers standing in the river in wader boots and thick gloves, removing trash in the pouring rain. It was dirty work, she recalls, but so too, "it was a blast." The event forged friendships across a "small group of people who all care about the same thing." The annual Spicket River Cleanup is now one of the city's biggest community events.

The gains from events like the river cleanup were not just physical. LCW and Groundwork Lawrence cultivated a next-generation Latino leadership for Lawrence, including Melendez herself. The daughter of Puerto Rican factory workers at the Lawrence Maid Footwear factory, Melendez grew up amidst the city's hard times. Throughout her childhood, a barbed wire face shrouded in black fabric surrounded a giant area near the central hospital. She and other children would peek through tears in the fabric to see a giant hole, where toxic soil had been removed from the site of a long-gone mill that had manufactured paper for *National Geographic* magazines. The land was still too polluted for use as anything other than a parking lot, but through a decade of work at Groundwork, Melendez and others remediated the rest of the site as a butterfly meadow with a spiral trail. Connected to that meadow, they built a three-mile waterfront path for walking and biking called the Spicket River Greenway.

Reflecting on their early years in the city, when there was so much to learn about the technical sides of redevelopment and finance, Church would later note, "We were just making it up at that point, if we're being honest. It's useful not to know how difficult the problems you need to solve are." LCW and Groundwork had embraced the entre-preneurial spirit of Caribbean culture, taking on bold projects despite scarce resources and weak government. Caribbean food and music and the occasional costume party drew people toward their work.

Before the Great Recession, a person could almost be optimistic about Lawrence. Activists in the city had accumulated an impressive list of big and small victories. Several mills were in the process of redevelop-ment, new parks and playgrounds teemed with life, and more residents were working together through the city's nonprofit institutions.

It would have been good to be in Lawrence on New Year's Eve in 2001. Church, Melendez, and others wanted a civic event for the new year, and they wanted to kick off an effort to clean up the city's canals. The city's hydroelectric system, including its canals, had been sold to an Italian multinational company, which had determined that it was no longer profitable to keep water flowing through the canals. They low-ered the water level, leaving rainwater to stagnate with murky vegeta-tion. The canals became a "place to dispose of evidence, to throw trash." Once they became a portfolio asset rather than a public good, Law-rence's canals could be abandoned by managers from none other than Italy, a nation known for treasuring an urban canal district of its own.

That New Year's Eve, Groundwork and LCW gathered a group of children and families from the surrounding low-income Latino neigh-borhood. They cut the tops off clear, 1-liter soda bottles, decorated them with colored tissue paper, and tied them together with strings. When the darkness of New Year's fell, they tromped in snow boots to the edge of the North Canal. They passed around hot cocoa, teasing each other about the low-budget production and freezing temperatures. They lit a votive candle inside each bottle and took turns launching them into the water. Their laughter fell quiet. As the lanterns floated in the dark, they saw something beautiful. They had made it.

Later that night, they tugged the bottles back to shore. Years of work cleaning up the canals had begun. Today, you can walk alongside them on tree-lined footpaths or read at a bench on the waterfront. The canal water reflects steel bridges, lamplight, and sky.

GOVERNING "THE CITY OF THE DAMNED"

The Hollow Prize of Leading Lawrence

While Centro, LCW, and Groundwork have never been explicitly political, they supported the grassroots connectivity that ended up educating people about city government and elections. The city elected its first Latino mayor, a Dominican-American, in 2009, an event that made national headlines. A new generation of leaders could finally face the racial discrimination that had justified two decades of disinvestment in the city's Latino residents.

Maybe if you were not part of making it happen, it was hard to see the progress in Lawrence. Or maybe Lawrence's reputation as hopeless was too baked in, or the bias against Dominicans and Puerto Ricans too ingrained. Whatever it was, in 2012, a *Boston* magazine headline dubbed Lawrence "City of the Damned." After a recitation of woes related to budget cuts, rising unemployment, troubled schools, and rising crime, the reporter accused that the "once-proud 'Immigrant City' has become an object lesson in how to screw things up." Portraying Lawrence as a bastion of corruption and drug dealing, the reporter found only a white Catholic priest and a recall proponent for the city's mayor as counterforces for good. Lawrence, the article said, was the "most god-forsaken place in Massachusetts." The article itself—independently of the events it described—humiliated the city.

No doubt, new challenges battered Lawrence in the years immediately after Mayor Lantigua's election in 2009. Across the nation, those were terrible years to be a smaller postindustrial community's mayor. One might call it a "hollow prize"—a term coined in the 1970s to describe the electoral victories of the first generation of African American mayors of big cities.* Those mayors took office at a time of historic challenges: steep manufacturing layoffs, slumping property values and tax revenues from white flight, police killings, and anti-police riots.

Lawrence's first Latino mayor faced comparable challenges when he was elected in 2009. Willie Lantigua took office just as dramatic public revenue losses from the Great Recession hit U.S. cities. He inherited a cumulative budget deficit of $24 million in 2010, with an additional deficit of more than $3 million expected in 2011. "A regular pattern of overestimating revenues, under budgeting expenditures," an official assessment of city finances explained, had combined with understated financial commitments in collective bargaining agreements plus "significant cuts in local aid" from the state. The city's tax base was weak and the city's infrastructure remained old and needy, but Lawrence residents were too poor to bear tax increases to fund shortfalls. During Lantigua's first year in office, he and the city council saw no choice but to lay off forty police officers (about one-third of the department), plus more than twenty firefighters and thirty-six teachers. The city police staffing ratio dropped to 1.4 officers per 1,000 people, well below the statewide average of 2.5 officers.

The state of Massachusetts intervened, appointing a fiscal overseer to work with the city's financial team and guide its return to solvency. In 2011, the city's schools were put into a state receivership for "chronically underperforming" districts. There were school management

---

* A related concept, known as the "glass cliff," would have also fit the bill for that era. It captures the fact that women and people of color are dramatically underrepresented in executive leadership—except when businesses and organizations face a crisis and seek transformative change. Deborah L. Rhode, *Women and Leadership* (New York: Oxford University Press 2017), 63.

problems to be sure, but "anyone that knows anything about schools" said Sean Cronin, the state fiscal overseer for Lawrence from 2014 to 2019, "would say that Lawrence Public Schools would be better off with more money." School buildings were in "awful shape" and required capital investment, and they needed better funding for operation and instruction.

Mayor Lantigua struggled to stabilize Lawrence during these hard times. He was known for keeping the city's old patronage system for government jobs alive, and he was accused of misuing campaign funds and other improprieties. His breaches of the public trust were no worse than many predecessors, but put under the magnifying lens applied to him as the first Latino mayor, they embarrassed those who had fought to break the hold of the city's white machine politics.

When the *Boston* magazine article bashed Lawrence as "damned," it ignored the outside economic forces besieging the city, the long-term structural budget problems inherited from past mayors and state legislatures, and the growing record of progress from LCW and other institutions. Leaders in Lawrence did not deny the city's problems, but grim portrayals only deterred ambition and involvement in the city's civic life.

Jess Andors and resident leaders at LCW protested the article at the magazine's offices. They worked with future Mayor Dan Rivera (who was on the city council at the time), teachers at Lawrence High School, and Maggie Super Church at Groundwork Lawrence to organize a civic event to reject the article's fatalism. They gathered at Pemberton Park, and students from Lawrence High School marched over the middle bridge for a rally called "We Are Lawrence." Organizers brought signs to pin on people's backs, styled like numbers for a marathon. The signs said I AM DAMNED_____ and participants filled in the blank with sharpies: EXCITED. OPTIMISTIC. ANGRY. The rally drew hundreds of people, including students wearing an acrostic poem that used the letters CITY OF THE DAMNED to list hopeful words about their city. "We Are Lawrence" became a social media organizing node for supporting local businesses through group "cash mob" outings and sharing good news.

Empowered by organizing and pride, and unwilling to accept defeat or self-loathing, a social movement in Lawrence cleaned up, then reinvented, city government. In 2014, Massachusetts senator Elizabeth Warren swore in Dan Rivera as Lawrence's new mayor. Rivera chose a more tactful song ("America, the Beautiful") than Lantigua's choice of "My Way" for his 2010 swearing-in ceremony, and his tact served him well as mayor. But Rivera's job was no easier than Lantigua's. The national economy had thawed, but the job market was still trapping Lawrence's population in low wages and patches of unemployment. With an ongoing budget overhang from past pension commitments, along with a population too overstretched to generate more taxes even if the city had the power to levy them, Rivera had to cut his way to balanced budgets.

Governance problems loomed too, such as the accumulation of $20 million in unpaid taxes, including from some landowners who had not paid their property taxes since the early 1980s. Years of budget cuts had diminished the city's ability to take legal action against tax nonpayment, so some of the city's biggest property owners had gotten accustomed to using the city for interest-free loans. Landowners racked up property tax debt and betted against the city's administrative capacity to pursue the taxes, let alone penalties. Mayor Rivera opposed levying additional taxes on his low-income city, so he instead got serious about collecting unpaid taxes from people who could afford to pay, adopting strategies such as withholding permits from scofflaw businesses. Using lawyers from outside the city, he cracked down on seemingly untouchable local businesses, including some with multigenerational ties and extensive real estate in Lawrence. Rivera also became known for tight management of contractors and city service departments, rewarding good employees, thinning out unproductive ones, and demanding decent work from service contractors.

As would also happen in Stockton, however, the city's low-information, high-cynicism electoral environment punished Mayor Rivera for his efforts to improve government. In 2015, a group called the Foundation for Transparency in Government tried to recall the mayor, claiming he was ineffective and untrue to his campaign promises. The group included at least one business who resented having to pay back taxes, as well as disgruntled employees the mayor was trying to fire. Signature collectors for the recall campaign allegedly offered people free turkeys to sign. The recall failed, and Lawrence under Mayor Rivera's leadership went on to double the city's collection rate on delinquent taxes.

Early in his first term, Mayor Rivera learned some issues were simply beyond his control. This included the addiction crisis that had been building across New England since 2012: soaring rates of prescription opioids like Oxycontin cultivated severe addictions that sought replacement fixes in street heroin and synthetic opioids like Fentanyl. Locational and transportation advantages that had once made Lawrence a distribution hub for textiles now made it an urban center for moving heroin and other opioids through New England. Demand poured across the state line and into Lawrence.

Overdoses drained city emergency resources, as drug sales and injections took over several parks and sidewalks. Tent encampments with addicted exiles from New England grew up under Lawrence bridges. Residents railed against the number of "New Hampshire plates" they saw in town. "They are not coming here for the shopping," one resident told me, with her eyebrows raised: "Or, at least, it's another kind of shopping they want: pharmaceutical shopping." So many people were dying of overdoses and drug-related deaths on his streets that Rivera said he felt like a "wartime mayor."

In 2016, this overdose crisis brought Lawrence national attention. A smartphone video, which went so viral that it was reported twice in *The New York Times*, showed a woman who had collapsed of a drug overdose on the floor of the toy aisle in a local Family Dollar store. Standing beside her in Disney Princess pajamas was her daughter, so small that her age would still be counted in months. The toddler wailed as she tried to lift her mother's limp arm and unmoving head. High on Fentanyl, the mother had driven into Lawrence from her nearby hometown of Salem, New Hampshire.

The woman depicted in the Family Dollar overdose video later faced a child endangerment charge. She struggled to get clean and regained the right to visit her daughter, now living with an uncle. She later told the *Times* how much shame and damage the video had caused her and her daughter, and how distorted it was to judge her with no knowledge of the dark road that had brought her to that point and her effort to survive an addiction. People in Lawrence could relate. The opioid crisis has brought their little-known city to national attention for statistics on drugs and drug-related crime, without any broader context or plan of support.

As regional politicians faced pressure to act, Lawrence became a popular scapegoat. In 2016, Maine governor Paul LePage blamed Lawrence and its Latino population as a driving cause for his state's overdoses. "The heroin-Fentanyl arrests are not white people," he said. "They're Hispanic and they're Black and they're from Lowell and Lawrence, Massachusetts; Waterbury, Connecticut; the Bronx and Brooklyn." New Hampshire governor Chris Sununu picked up the tactic, guesstimating without any evidence that 85 percent of his state's opioids came from Lawrence. Then–President Trump in a speech blamed the "sanctuary city of Lawrence" for New Hampshire's drug crisis, dog whistling a purported link between immigrants and drug dealing.

Rivera did what he could to restore police staffing levels, but they did not return to 2009 levels until 2019. And anyway, Lawrence could not solve the regional opioid crisis without neighboring states' investments in addiction recovery. With so much demand, Rivera said, "every time you put a drug dealer away, somebody else steps up to sell." He advocated for more beds in six-month residential treatment programs, which Lawrence can't provide directly. By analogy, he tells the story of a pothole that periodically opens on a New Hampshire street that runs into Lawrence. New Hampshire governments never get around to filling it, he explains, and Lawrence residents who commute across the state line for work call the mayor's office to complain. So Rivera made sure the Massachusetts public works teams took care of patching that road. Lawrence "just can't do that with homelessness and drug addiction," he says. All alone, the city cannot dig its region out of problems that big.

Jess Andors often thinks back to a boy that she met in middle school in 1999, during her first summer in Lawrence. He struggled to manage his temper, and she had suspended him for a few days from LCW's youth program. One afternoon, she visited his home to talk with him and his family. She found him on his front steps, and as they talked, he picked at paint chips and nibbled their chewy surfaces. Odds are it was lead paint, which tastes sweet. Ingesting lead is extremely hazardous to child development, causing aggression, hyperreactivity, and attention deficits. By the time the opioid crisis was raging in New England, that boy was in his late twenties and tangled in street crime as a drug dealer. Andors will never know if lead poisoning drove his specific fate, but it is fair to assume that lead abatement during his childhood would have been cheaper than the cost society would now pay to remedy or punish any harms he caused.

To this day, national press outlets rarely mention Lawrence unless reporting on the opioid crisis. Gun violence and drug usage threaten local safety to be sure, but I never managed to see drug dealers dropping baggies into open car windows at red lights, as police told *The New York Times* is common. Andors describes how those who see the city through the eyes of the police see only the crime. But which Lawrence you see, she says, "really depends on who you walk with." Through the eyes of LCW, "you're going to see a lot of poor but very hard-working immigrant families who are trying to send their children to school, and buy a house, and start a business, and learn English, and get computer skills, and get a better job."

I saw that side of Lawrence during my time there. I also noticed more people than I'm used to holding hands as they walk in town— parents and children, couples, maybe even friends. Several Sunday mornings, I saw little girls in matching dresses and hair bows, and little boys wearing ties, walking with their families to church. One day, just an hour after an Andover resident had told me that her friends were too scared to go to Lawrence day or night, I sat down in a Lawrence cafe near a Latino family of three. The parents called their child "mi amor" as they chatted in a mix of English and Spanish. The mother had to leave before the other two. As she stood to go, the father said, "I love you." She answered, "I love you more." I remembered the *Boston* magazine article calling Lawrence "the most godforsaken place in Massachusetts." It was not God, I thought to myself, who had forsaken Lawrence.

EVERYTHING ELSE FLOWS
FROM THERE

Sewing a City

As a city of families, Lawrence was particularly rattled by a tragedy in December 2016. A man walking his dog along the Merrimack came upon the body of a beheaded teenager washed up on the river's bank. Investigation and prosecution later revealed that the murder was an isolated, singular case by a high school peer. But for months following the event, its mystery was both terrorizing and tragic. It was the kind of winter that could isolate people in their homes, bunkered and afraid.

By that point, however, Lawrence was more than twenty years into a sustained, systematic effort to open lines of communication, trust, and accountability in the city—among neighbors, with government, across institutions. Across that winter, as had been true for years, Lawrence residents kept working and organizing to protect one another and their children. Every week, every month.

In March 2017, as the investigation into the teenager's murder continued, a group of fifteen or so adults gathered to discuss public safety in the city at Our House, LCW's community center. One resident volunteered to facilitate and take notes at an easel. In a combination of English and Spanish (with participants helping to translate), they talked through the lack of information about the killing. "We need more of an explanation of what happened. My son goes walking to school every day alone. We need the full story from law enforcement!"

Everyone there seemed to be a parent, and they all talked through their larger fears, experiences, and priorities. "I've lived in New York City and in San Juan," one mother said. "They are a lot tougher than Lawrence. But in small communities," she said, pantomiming a rumor mill, "everyone knows when big things happen." She was worried that since 2014, the opioid crisis had increased local gun violence. She felt afraid to let her teenage son walk home from school. Others also described the struggle to keep children safe. "I had to purchase a cell phone for my kids so I'd always know where they are," one mother said. "You have to teach them things when they are too young to hear it. I taught mine never to run if he hears shots. Just lay down on the ground." They honed in on specific issues and places they worried about: a school near a street with drug dealing, a park where people injected drugs, the need for more free programs to keep youth safe after school. Broader safety concerns came up too, such as inadequate sidewalk snow removal that required children to walk to school in the street, and the lack of traffic controls on the lower-income north side of the city.

The poised, bilingual mother who had volunteered to facilitate for the group took notes on the oversized pad and turned the discussion toward action. "Who is responsible for our public safety problems?" she asked. The group brainstormed four answers: the police department, parents, society, the mayor. "It's our responsibility to take our city back," one said. One shared the phone number for an anonymous tip line to report crimes to the police. One pointed out the mayoral election coming in six months, and suggested they ask the candidates for a town hall about public safety. Another encouraged people to engage critically with the candidates: "Look at the national election! You can't just listen to what a person says. You have to know what they can actually do." One shared his experiences with calling his city councilmember, who in turn asked city employees for more attention in his district.

Free-floating anxiety about a sinister crime had become a way to share experiences among strangers, then discuss discrete, concrete actions of civic engagement. This discussion happened as part of an event called the Mercado, held on the third Tuesday of every month (including online during the COVID pandemic). About forty adults, from which the smaller public safety conversation emerged, gathered for the in-person Mercado that I visited. After an initial chance to make name tags and chat over a generous spread of appetizers, Mercados begin with an LCW custom. For one minute, measured by a cheerful staff member with a timer and a large bell, participants rush through the room trying to greet as many people as possible. The instructions suggest that people can exchange names with a hug, kiss, or handshake, but (at least before the COVID-19 pandemic), Caribbean culture motivated attendees to forgo handshakes in favor of warm smiles and hugs. At the ring of the bell, everyone returns to the standing circle, where each person is invited to say something "Nuevo y Bueno."

At the meeting I attended in March 2017, we heard from a young man who had an admissions interview set for college, a lady whose arthritis was mild enough to allow her to make it to the meeting, a man whose mother received a remission prognosis for her cancer, and a mother who was glad her son was going to live at home when he began college. When a little girl wearing a school uniform and a flowered headband announced it was her birthday, the group burst into song. Everything was presented in both English and Spanish—people spoke in both languages themselves (sometimes practicing shyly), or spoke in one language with another resident translating. The discussion doubled as a conversational language class.

Mercados at LCW also includes a Mini Marketplace, "El Mini Mercado." Each person may offer something she can do for others, or express a need that another attendee might help with. The idea is for people to find non-monetary ways to help one another. The assistance might be small, such as loaning a neighbor a grill. More substantial trades can also emerge, for example a plumber who fixes a sink for a family in exchange for that family adding the plumber's child to their walk to school sometimes. I heard offers for help with drafting a resume, babysitting, and applying for work at this or that business.

At the last and longest stage of the evening, community members suggested discussion topics and broke out into groups to tackle them. The public safety breakout session that night in March was just one of several groups, including one planning a public march to defend undocumented immigrants, and another learning about a new employment training program in town. As each group broke out into separate meeting spaces, we could hear a teen program practicing a dance show upstairs. Groups chose their own facilitators and reported out summaries in a closing circle.

In urban planning, terms such as "public participation" and "community-based" can become jargon. Sometimes they mean little more than a couple of public meetings, which are treated as a mandatory box to check or an annoying drag on time-to-completion. For others, the process of gathering community input is a way to make any given project more effective over the long run, because the project will reflect community priorities and launch with resident stewards. In Lawrence, these efforts seem to be the heart of the work, a mode of self-governance rather than "urban planning."

Crime fell dramatically in Lawrence in 2018 and 2019, reaching twenty-year lows. I will have to leave it to criminologists to analyze whether the kind of organizing at LCW and its partners helped drive this crime reduction. But a networked community at least offers a better way to live. Neuroscience and public health research have demonstrated that social connections are ends in themselves, not just means to some other outcome. Two-time U.S. Surgeon General Dr. Vivek Murthy gathered this evidence in a recent book. Murthy explains that we have a neurobiological need to be connected to other people. Loneliness and social isolation increase toxic stress levels and shorten lives. They also build on themselves, because being alone generates hypervigilance about perceived threats, which in turn makes us act defensively to low-level threats and further distances us from the people around us.

As described in Chapter One, areas with high rates of gun violence tend to increase social isolation by trapping residents indoors and keeping parks, sidewalks, and porches empty. Low-income immigrants living in places of concentrated poverty particularly need networks of support and information, as they wrestle with challenges like language isolation, racial or ethnic discrimination, fear of crime, lost social status or career identity, and separation from family and friends.

As if he were writing a grant for LCW, Murthy argues that the deepest gains in people's health and well-being come not from having intimate partners and supportive friendships, or attending events and joining social groups. Instead, he writes, "[t]he real therapeutic synergy occurs when we come together with others to take action to achieve a common goal." Our brains reward us for finding a larger purpose outside our immediate self-interest and working with others to achieve it, which means that physiologically, "*doing good makes us feel good.*"

Strong social networks also deliver supportive relationships that we need when things go wrong—whether it is neighbors who share food and water after a hurricane or a friend who helps a person make it through a period of addiction or family violence. By basing those networks on blocks or neighborhoods rather than ethnicity or religion, techniques such as LCW's NeighborCircles and Mercados connect people who might not otherwise meet or trust one another.

"We help people with civic engagement and participation," Juan Bonilla, LCW's chief operating officer, says. "Everything else flows from there." When a community development organization takes this approach, he explains, it ends up with some projects related to the physical environment (such as affordable housing rehabilitation), and some related to social services (such as English classes or family budgeting workshops). But neither kind of project is the place to start. The community networks drive decision-making, because organizing generates other gains along the way, such as new opportunities, mutual aid, and trust across cultural or racial lines. Taking care of a city, Bonilla explains, requires "an ecosystem—an environment of collaboration where we hold each other accountable." The city does its best for residents and, therefore, can ask that residents do right by the city and one another.

Even though LCW and Groundwork are non-political organizations, it is not an accident that Lawrence's government is getting better. Their form of network organizing helps communities understand what government does now, what it could do better, and what it feasibly cannot do. It helps people demand—and also acknowledge—improvements in government services. We are now decades into social science research demonstrating that when people are engaged like this, government works better. Residents who helped build and maintain a park will work to defend it, whether from budget cuts or drug dealers. When people shape government through participation, they might actually need less of it. When people withdraw, they will get less from their government even as they need more.

Jess Andors cautions, however, against treating LCW's organizing techniques as models ready for export to other cities. She says NeighborCircles, for example, might not work in New York City, where the deeper anonymity of big city life might deter people from opening their home to neighbors before having met and built trust with them on neutral ground. Community organizing would not work the same way even in the nearby mill town of Lowell, she adds, because a higher share of immigrants to Lowell are refugees of war or dictatorships, rather than economic migrants. For those whose life experiences have taught them that speaking out at a public meeting can "get your brother killed or your head torn off," as Andors put it, civic engagement will require a longer trust-building phase. The lessons to take from Lawrence, she says, are the foundational principles: "Meeting people where they are, listening to people's stories, honoring them, finding ways that they want to be involved and things that they care about."

Do that, LCW and Groundwork show, and even the most complex projects can yield wider community benefits. The kind of public interest redevelopment that LCW and Groundwork undertake is highly technical, requiring complex financing, costly land decontamination, and compliance with layered regulations. These organizations have developed affordable, owner-occupied duplex buildings; transformed two blighted mill buildings into attractive, affordable housing units overlooking the river; constructed new playgrounds; and more.

At the site of a former textile dyeing facility along the Spicket River, for example, several cycles of property abandonment and corporate restructuring had left behind not only toxic pollution, but also costly legal chaos. Dozens of people during a dozen years at the state, the city, LCW, and Groundwork worked to clean up the site, both legally (by clarifying and updating its ownership) and physically (by decontaminating its soil). But in the end, it was the site's neighbors who got to reimagine and design it as a park, then put it to good use with a continuous line of community events. Residents gained a basketball court, playground, riverside picnic tables under striped awnings, and open space edged by trees. By connecting neighbors to one another, envisioning and maintaining that park has also generated indirect gains for civic education, governmental accountability, and access to services.

The park's neighbors, most of whom are Latino, decided to name it Dr. Nina Scarito Park, in honor of an Italian-American obstetrician who, locals say, delivered more than 20,000 babies in Lawrence. Susan Fink, a widely admired city administrator who has worked on community development since 1995, spent years helping to finance and construct the park. Fink was moved to see it named in honor of the doctor who had delivered her own daughter. Outsiders might malign Lawrence like it is a megacity crime hub, but from below it feels like a small town. "Once Lawrence gets under your skin," Fink told me, "you love it and you want to be part of it."

"WE CAN'T ALL BE ZOILA GOMEZ"

No Adult Left Behind

I'll come around to Zoila Gomez later in this section, but for now, I want to touch back on the Bread and Roses Strike. One of the most famous photographs from the strike depicts workers starting to cross a bridge over a frozen canal to picket at the Pacific Mill on the other side. Despite temperatures far below zero, police and security guarding the mill turned fire hoses on the strikers, drenching the front rows. The photo showed the old way to get a raise: form a union and strike, facing down grave dangers and impossible odds.

I find it symbolic that the bridge in that photo has been relocated (as a historical artifact preserved for its innovative engineering) to a branch of the Northern Essex Community College. The new location shows a new way to get a raise: higher education and workforce training. Just as the 1912 strikers had to invent a new script for labor organizing, contemporary networks in Lawrence have had to work together—pooling individuals and institutions into collective strength—to invent new methods for lifting people to a living wage.

In 2013, a group of leaders from city hall, Lawrence public schools, the local community college, LCW, and major city employers began meeting to compete for a funding stream from the Federal Reserve Bank of Boston called the Working Cities Challenge (WCC) Initiative. The program required intensive community collaboration, in keeping with research on recovery in postindustrial cities. Meaningful networks across institutions were not necessary back when big employers dominated civic life in early industrial hubs like Lawrence. Company leaders not only exerted influence on local government, but also on hospitals, churches, and charitable and arts institutions. As these companies and their leaders moved away, however, they left behind a vacuum of power amounting to a "civic and social crisis." Weakened and isolated institutions intensified the harms of lost population and lost jobs.

As part of their Working Cities discussions, Lawrence's leaders identified priorities and set out to achieve an audacious goal: a 15 percent increase in median income of the parents of children attending the city's public schools. Income gains, they hypothesized, would not just help adults. Gains would also support schools, by relieving the economic stress and upheaval in students' homes. Fifteen percent was the increase it would take to align median incomes with the actual cost of living in Lawrence, so in the spirit of entrepreneurs, they set out to do what needed to be done. As it happened, this percentile represented a poetic echo of the city's past that the Working Cities group did not notice: 15 percent was the average wage gain achieved by the Bread and Roses Strike.

By focusing on wage gains among public-school parents, leaders committed to the more impactful, more challenging work of social mobility for legacy residents, not newcomers. But this metric made their job harder because income data would exclude the higher-paid Boston commuters moving into newly renovated loft housing in former Lawrence mills. Few of these commuters had children, let alone students in public schools. Derek Mitchell, who helped set this goal as the head of an economic development consortium called Lawrence Partnership, explains that most traditional measures of progress for poor cities drive gentrification by rewarding cities when they add high earners to dilute poor ones, or displace low earners entirely. They evaluate the number of square feet a city fills and the change in the city's rents. "But you've got to have a place where immigrants and others can afford to live," he says. "In the statewide context, if you can't afford to live in Lawrence, where the hell can you live? Instead of investing in bricks and mortar, with a trickle-down impact, how do we invest in people? In upward mobility? In local capital?"

The region's job market had changed dramatically in the past thirty years. Way back when, local manufacturing consultant Marko Duffy remembers working at a company that nickel-plated parts for cowboy boots and saddles. "I used to work with guys who'd reek of booze at nine in the morning, guys from Southie," he says. You didn't need to be sober, he explains, because the technology of any given job was simple: "You just had to keep pushing that button." Times have changed. Duffy cites steering wheels as an example. Once they consisted of metal rings with spokes and a pump horn; now a driver can answer her phone from one. Advanced technology like that requires exacting precision and rigorous workplace audits. Workers require specialized training, educational credentials or certifications, and English language skills. Lawrence's Merrimack Valley region doesn't make steering wheels anymore, but it still has factory jobs in fields like aerospace, where the details can be life-or-death matters.

To label this challenge as crossing a "skills gap" is controversial—both on the ground and in the academic literature. People in postindustrial cities sometimes take offense at the term, noting all the tasks that purportedly "low-skilled workers" know how to do that people in more educated places can't do. Some skills are undervalued in today's economy, but are skills nonetheless, such as the operation of technical machinery, self-reliance in car and home maintenance, the social skills to navigate a high-crime environment, or the radical self-sufficiency and thrift required to survive on a paltry income. Researchers agree that postindustrial areas often have at least a "skills mismatch" between what workers in an area know how to do and what employers in their area need. With companies moving and employees changing positions more often, fewer employers find it worthwhile to provide extensive internal training. The burden for specialized training has shifted to educational institutions and the students themselves. Given the wide array of technologies used by companies and the cost barriers of education, prospective employees are not acquiring the skills they need. In cities such as Lawrence, public and nonprofit agencies are left to fill the gap, but they are doing so on minimal budgets that require maximal collaboration.

As in many industrial towns, these heightened skill requirements mean that most Lawrence workers are no longer as competitive for regional manufacturing jobs. Instead, the city's workforce has shifted into the low-skilled service industry, which offers low pay, insecure tenure, and long commute times. The gap between the cost of living and local wages has widened, trapping families in debt and poverty across decades. As far back as 1999, while she was a graduate student at MIT, early LCW leader Tamar Kotelchuck cataloged how gains in income during the Massachusetts Miracle (in the 1980s) and the Route 128 tech boom (in the 1990s) were passing Lawrence by, trapping its residents in declining wages. She quoted an economist at Merrimack College who put it bluntly: "Lawrence is the sinkhole in the lawn that must stay wet so the rest of the region can stay dry." That is, the service economy wants workers, but it does not want to pay them a living wage. So that workforce has packed into Lawrence, which hosts some of the only neighborhoods in the region that allow multifamily housing affordable to low-wage workers.

The problems facing Lawrence on jobs and wages are formidable, and typical. Places with higher shares of residents with a college degree experience greater population and economic growth—that is, "skills predict growth." Dozens of empirical analyses of declining cities have since confirmed that higher human capital (as measured by degree attainment) helps to insulate cities from economic decline or supports their recovery. Getting out of the low-wage rut of service jobs, says labor economist Enrico Moretti, requires improved educational attainment rates, above all.

Lane Glenn, president of the Northern Essex Community College, knows the research on higher education and wages. He's tired of people pretending that poor cities can get around it. "The voices you hear saying, 'Not everybody needs a bachelor's degree,' their kids have bachelor's degrees," he says. He's tired of the paternalism implicit in thinking poor city residents can get ahead without those same credentials. Sure, he acknowledges, some occupations, such as plumbers, electricians, and technicians, require vocational training rather than a college degree. Glenn thinks community colleges should continue to partner with vocational schools to make those opportunities accessible. But the surest path into the middle class, he says, is still a college degree. Glenn has set a personal goal of helping to more than double Lawrence's college attainment rate, from 11 percent up to 25 percent. "That's ambitious," he says. "That's a huge needle move, it really is. It's going to take years."

But when it happens, he says, "I'll feel pretty darn good about that, then somebody else can pick it up, take it from there."

Glenn and others in the city have led an intensive college preparation drive at the local high school and have mobilized to expand two small regional colleges into downtown Lawrence to serve additional students. Everyone seemed to agree that Lawrence needed more strategies. The high cost of living forced most adults without a college degree to put "jobs" before "careers." To keep up with their expenses and erratic job schedules, most adults in Lawrence cannot afford to pay college tuition, even at community college, or clear enough consistent time each week to maintain a class schedule. This means that being a "low-skilled worker" is a permanent status, not a temporary stop on the way to something better.

The Working Cities partners focused first on "eds and meds." Education and health care both offered good jobs with headroom for advancement. Both fields struggled locally to find and retain the workers they needed, which drove up their operating costs. The Lawrence Public Schools needed more bilingual teachers who would be accessible to immigrant parents. Meanwhile, Lawrence residents who would have loved to become teachers, some of whom had the necessary skills, were stuck in factory and service jobs. By moving more Lawrence residents into teaching careers, the city could improve residents' incomes while also improving their schools. The city's central hospital also needed more Spanish-speakers on staff, and it was struggling with a high turnover rate among certified nursing assistants and medical assistants. Lawrence residents already working in lower skilled hospital jobs wanted these better positions.

Instead of trying to wing it through those challenges based on generic research from other places, Lawrence's leaders turned to their networks of residents to figure out the barriers to entry in education and health care jobs. LCW assembled and trained teams of parents who had children in the public schools. One team surveyed other parents about jobs in education. Did parents want to work as teachers or teaching assistants? If so, what kind of education and training schedule would be feasible? Based on their findings, LCW and a network of local partner institutions created the paraprofessional program described at the outset of this chapter. With a feasible schedule and a cohort to foster support and community, each group would move not just toward a certification for a pool of jobs, but also toward an eventual BA.

Another skills assessment team worked on the health care side. In response to their findings and the hospital's training needs, the community college developed a training program with a schedule that can fit around workers' existing hospital jobs. The program keeps workers earning their current paycheck while moving toward better jobs. Other specialized training programs are underway to lift residents into entry-level jobs in construction and IT. Some of the jobs fed by these programs are better paid than those in the low-skilled service sector. Others have different virtues: better schedules to accommodate parenting, more rewarding work, more stability, or greater advancement opportunities.

With funding from the Federal Reserve Bank of Boston, the Working Cities network also built an "intake valve" to recruit new parents in the public school system into regional training and educational opportunities. Since every public-school parent (by definition) has to go through a school enrollment process, they tied these functions together. The Family Resource Center (FRC) was born, run within the Lawrence Public Schools district but linked tightly to other institutions. Parents come through the door to enroll their children in school, but then find a hub for improving their own economic and educational opportunities. FRC staff are trained to look out for parents having trouble enrolling a child on the public computers—an entry point to identify parents who might benefit from adult literacy classes or basic technology training. Through intake interviews with social workers, parents learn about local opportunities for job training and social services. Posters and handouts in the FRC advertise job training programs, resume review workshops, food banks and farmers' markets, and intensive job counseling services. The FRC leads workshops and trainings for parents on topics ranging from avoiding truancy to child nutrition. Families without consistent housing can work with a homelessness case worker. It was the FRC that coordinated and advertised the paraprofessional program, where Destiny Rodriguez enrolled to get on a track toward college.

The institutional network in Lawrence is also developing new ways to ensure that language alone is not a barrier to employment. An ambitious effort at Northern Essex Community College called the Programa Internacional de Educación Superior (PIÉS) helps new immigrants transfer degrees or higher educational units they may have earned abroad before moving to Lawrence. PIÉS has created a program, for example, that transfers units from the Autonomous University of Santo Domingo in the Dominican Republic, which happens to be the oldest university in the Western Hemisphere, founded a century before Harvard.

Regardless of the steady progress in higher education, the city also needs strategies to improve wages for residents who don't have the backgrounds and skill sets needed for college classes. Vargas helps to explain this problem with a story from his own past. Back when he was a student at Lawrence High School, Vargas remembers, he saw his best friend get into a fight at a party. Vargas knew he was expected to protect his friend, but he didn't. Vargas is in his thirties now, established as a husband, father, and homeowner, but he often reflects on that night. "What would have happened if I got in that fight? What if I had gotten suspended? I could have gotten hurt or I could have hurt someone." He sees the incident as typical of the way children growing up in cities like Lawrence have to "outwill their circumstances." "You have to make good decisions all the time," he says, but you have constant opportunities to make bad decisions. And given the alternatives, "bad decisions" to stray from education and lawful employment don't always seem morally wrong. Meeting Lawrence's people where they are means looking out for people who have not quite managed to "outwill their circumstances" every time, but are ready to try again.

So Vargas, Glenn, and others in town think a lot about non-college pathways out of poverty. They want to make a path for people who are, as Vargas puts it, "rough around the edges" or missing valuable skill sets. That might be an auto mechanic who doesn't speak English but can disassemble and reassemble a transmission, he says, or a woman who dropped out of high school to have a baby and now works for poverty-level wages in a nail salon. Lawrence also needs a path for residents whose confidence in themselves or the world around them has been, for now at least, broken by hardships like family abuse and street violence. Some residents need coaching and support to persevere through challenges, while others need a chance to start over after serving time in prison or battling an addiction.

As in many historic manufacturing regions, the Lawrence area still produces jobs that aren't pretty, but pay decently and need doing. Manufacturing consultant Marko Duffy reflects back on his own career, which started with years of manufacturing chemicals and fabricating metal. No one is born wanting to go into manufacturing, he says. "I didn't decide I wanted to stand in puddles of 'that ain't water' or to say 'if we heat this to 195 degrees it might work.' I didn't want to work in places that smell like that, or to stand in one spot all day." After working long hours indoors, he would step outside and think, "When did it snow?" But across Lawrence's history, he says, there have been steady, accurate hands ready to do hard work well, and he tries to help businesses see that potential in Lawrence's Latino population. Duffy is now helping to lead a project to support local advanced manufacturing businesses at hiring and training bilingual managers, who in turn can hire an entry-level workforce still learning English. These efforts help close what Mayor Rivera called the "access gap"—the difference between the jobs that Lawrence residents are qualified to do and the jobs they actually get.

I think if you could unite the adult educational reinvestment in Lawrence under a single motto, it would be something I heard from Abel Vargas, the head of the local workforce development agency for several years. He used Zoila Gomez, a respected local immigration lawyer, as a benchmark for his work. Gomez came to Lawrence from the Dominican Republic as a single mother of two. She worked full-time wage jobs through eleven years of college and law school. Vargas deeply admires her talent, endurance, and determination. But he is a realist. "We can't all be Zoila Gomez," he says. The goal of the adult education work in Lawrence—by his local agency, the community college, LCW, the Family Resource Center, local businesses, and others—is to help more residents afford the local cost of living while also moving into better work over the long run. That means supporting them at being a parent, a student, and a provider all at once. It need not be as hard as it was for Gomez. It cannot be that hard if Lawrence is to be a gateway to better jobs for a broad cut of its people.

At one point, I talked with Zoila Gomez. We met for a glass of wine with Maggie Super Church, one of the early leaders at Groundwork Lawrence and LCW. Gomez and Church had worked together to lead transition planning when Rivera took office as mayor. The evening we met, Gomez had spent her day counseling her clients at a jail and an immigration detention center. She deflected my admiration for her work and my questions about her against-the-odds path out of poverty. She wanted to talk instead about why she had never moved to Boston, even though many colleagues had told her she should do so to advance her legal career. She had never left Lawrence, she explained, because she had clients who appreciated her, a tight network of colleagues, and friends like Church. That, in the end, is what had gotten her through higher education and into meaningful work. She and Church clinked glasses. Gomez said, "We have something special here that is getting lost in other cities."

BELIEVE

Crossing Over to a Living Wage

Destiny Rodriguez, who opened this chapter, made it through the paraprofessional program (despite the long hours and housing pressures), thanks in part to an apprenticeship. She was teaching back at her own middle school, which itself was healing. In spite of everything she had gone through, she was moving forward in life. Her job at the school was to work one-on-one with struggling students. Some had behavioral issues or ADHD. Others would "just lose hope," Rodriguez said, and withdraw from school. One young boy in particular really stuck with her. He acted bored and goofed off in class, and at first, he stonewalled her. But soon he learned that Rodriguez had gone to that same school and still lived in his neighborhood. He asked why she carried a backpack and learned that she too was in school with homework. Something changed at that moment, Rodriguez recalled. He sat down and began to read aloud with her.

That boy helped Rodriguez realize that she wanted to work with middle and high school students, despite the additional challenges. The little children, she said, were sweet and affectionate, still happy with their teachers and school. Rodriguez sought the rewards of turning youth back to school after they'd soured on it. She wanted to raise their expectations of themselves. From her own experiences, she felt that "you have to teach the child that you have now, not the child that you want." She wanted to be the kind of teacher who met youth wherever they were developmentally and emotionally, "instead of trying to make them different and fighting your way through."

Youth had all kinds of backstories, she knew, including missing parents, or trauma and violence at home. Even in the ordinary case, she said, "us as Latinos . . . we're sent off to work. You know, even as children. And we're taking care of our siblings in order for our parents to work." That, she explained, "weighs a lot on our children." In her graduation speech, she articulated the hope she had for her classmates and the profession of teaching. "It takes a big heart to shape little minds," Rodriguez told them. "One word, one question, just one second to stop and remember that our children are humane, and they deserve kindness, empathy, sympathy, love, time, and a teacher who encourages their success when no one else would."

In fall 2019, a few months after I attended her graduation, I met Rodriguez at a downtown cafe. Owned by a local family, the El Taller cafe and bookstore had all the seductions of youth and urban vitality, even as it felt uniquely Lawrencian. The baristas, with big smiles and bigger tattoos, took orders for fresh food ranging from Puerto Rican specialties to "yoga bowls," from banana mango oatmeal cookies to "bee sting" lattes. Shelves displayed books to browse and buy, mostly by writers of color such as Martín Espada and Michelle Alexander. The walls hung art for sale by Lawrence High School students, and a colorful painting announced the wifi password. Every weekend, on a corner stage inlaid with upcycled timber, the cafe hosted open mic nights, poetry slams, and concerts. One of the owners' sons had inlaid factory tools in the benches and created barstools from giant spools of thread. One of the ornate sewing machines on top of the bookcase looked like an interior designer found it in an antique store. Not so—a local told me that it had been his grandmother's. It just seemed right that the cafe was owned by a married couple with immigrant roots in both Ireland and Mexico.

Despite the pleasant chatter in our surroundings, that day was not a happy one for Rodriguez. She suppressed tears, looking away from me and turning her back to the bustling cashier. Rodriguez had been offered her dream job as a teaching assistant back at the middle school where she had apprenticed, but a sudden hardship ensnaring her brother and boyfriend held her back from accepting a new job. She was still working as a waitress. She wanted to live up to the hope I had seen in her graduation, and she still felt driven to make it through college and become a teacher. In spite of the vicious headwinds she was facing, Rodriguez wished to thank me for a gift I had given her daughter, who is the same age as my own. Rodriguez handed me a lavender gift bag with matching tissue paper. Inside I found a ceramic mug that has become a prized possession and motivating force in writing this book. The mug said one word in black, uncompromising letters, surrounded by friendly, colorful flowers: BELIEVE.

After Rodriguez left, I stopped in El Taller's bathroom, where staff had left a marker for people to write messages, poetry, and song lyrics on the orange walls. One of the larger messages said, "Mija, you've got this!!!" I texted a picture of it to Rodriguez. I know it is naïve to think things are that simple. The fiercest challenges facing both her and her city are mostly out of her hands. But I think that she and others in Lawrence have figured out the most important thing. They are trying to be there for the people of the city as they are, instead of, in Rodriguez's words, "trying to make them different and fighting your way through." That, I think, is what it means to be a gateway city.

Today, Rodriguez is working at Lawrence Community Works and taking classes toward her BA. She lives near Dan Rivera in South Lawrence. He and the city council had stabilized the city's budget by 2019, when Lawrence was released from ten years of state fiscal oversight. By the end of his time as mayor, more than half the city's police officers were Latino. A formal evaluation of the Lawrence Working Families Initiative found that its coaching, training, and placement assistance helped place more than 200 parents in jobs, increasing their wages by an average of 25 percent—well over the 15 percent increase its partners intended. Rivera recently moved on to become the head of MassDevelopment, a public agency working statewide on economic growth and jobs challenges. A new mayor has picked up the baton. As far as I know, Rodriguez and Rivera have not met. But it seems like only a matter of time before they cross paths, or even work together on progress for their city.

Do Not Bid

Detroit, Michigan

I f you start at the riverfront downtown and travel five miles up the
center of Detroit, northeast along Woodward Avenue, the neighborhood of North End will be to your right. About half of the homes
on many blocks are occupied, often with tended front yards. Another
quarter or so of the lots have grasses and trees, without buildings. When
my family stayed in North End during the summer of 2017, one of the
vacant lots had a pit bull on a long chain. He was guarding a pile of sal-
vaged lumber. In the afternoons, a thirty-something African American
woman renting a house across the street sat on her front porch studying
for a nursing certification exam. She told me that the owner of the dog
and the lot with the lumber lived on the other side of town and came
by to feed the dog.

Oakland Avenue Farms is just around the corner. The farm has orchards, vegetable beds, picnic areas, and hoop houses. Public murals
and sculptures make the space seem like a park. The adjacent stretch of
Woodward is less scenic, but it has a popular joint called Asian Corned
Beef that sells cheesecake egg rolls. It's part of a strip mall in Highland
Park, a separate city contained within Detroit where 58 percent of the
children live under the poverty line and one-third of the housing is
vacant. That section of Woodward is near the George Ferris School,
a stately brick building built in 1911 with classrooms facing a garden
atrium. The school closed for declining enrollment in the 1990s, before
scrappers stripped it, lookie-loos took thousands of photographs, and

an arts entrepreneur bought it for $2,000 in 2014. He has been trying to raise the extensive financing required to renovate the building.

Keep going up Woodward, and you'll pass the former Highland Park Ford Plant, which operated the world's first assembly line in 1913. The plant produced 15 million Model Ts before 1927, then tanks, auto parts, and aircraft engines until 1974. Turn right on to Seven Mile Road at Dutch Girl Donuts, in business for seventy years until 2021. Naughty locals called late-night donut runs "getting a Dutch girl." Pass Pingree Farms, a youth agricultural education center where goats wander around yoga classes in the barn.

At this point, you'll be in the neighborhood where James lived for more than thirty years. His mother, a daughter of the Great Migration, bought her home there with her wages from suburban retail jobs. James sets the neighborhood as a six-block rectangle north of Seven Mile and east of the I-75 freeway, a piece of the larger area locals call by its zip code: 48203. He defines the neighborhood by National Bakery, a business that made bread and desserts for forty years. The signage is still there, with a hand-painted cup of steaming coffee on the shutters, but the site is now vacant. James grew up in the neighborhood, as did his two sons and his older daughter. His mother, his grandmother, and a few cousins lived there, too. During his childhood, back before crack cocaine came to town, he said, "our whole block was filled with homes. Our whole block." For several years in the 1990s and again in the early 2000s, he bought and ran a carwash near National Bakery. He and his wife used their income to buy and fix up neighborhood homes to live in and rent out.

Even though James spent most of his life investing in the people, houses, and economy in his pocket of 48203, it was a hard place to live. "I have seen everything," James says in a quiet, unassuming voice. Most people he knew well in high school are now dead, in prison, or recently released from prison. James has tried to support incarcerated friends, serving as an "outside voice." They lean on him for news and conversation, for leads about jobs and housing if they get out. James is African American, so it was striking when he described his high school friends this way: "I am the only one who is still free."

If James is rare, he's also typical. Like 120,000 Black homeowners in Detroit during the past six years, he owned and lost his land in the city. He lost his first home, as well as a second property he rented out, through exploitative land contracts. Fine print in those deals allowed the sellers to yank their houses back after he was late with a payment—seizing not just the properties, but the value of his renovations. He later bought another home, which he fixed up for his family with a working furnace and fresh carpets. Subprime terms in his mortgage took that one at the height of the Great Recession. A speculator bought it at an auction then burned it down to collect insurance money. James's mother lost her property to a tax foreclosure soon after.

These losses cost the family their land, their homes, and thousands of dollars in transaction fees and renovation investments. His grandmother still lives in the neighborhood, but after James's foreclosures, he gave up on Detroit and on homeownership. He moved his family to a rental in an adjacent city called Eastpointe. The town used to be called East Detroit, but in 1992, it changed its name. The city council wanted to disassociate with James's hometown and try to tie its future to the wealthy Grosse Pointe suburbs.

Urban theorists call Detroit a "shrinking city" for its falling population—64 percent lower than at the city's peak. City boundaries enclose vacant land totaling twenty square miles, a void about the size of Manhattan.* But Detroit should be known as a shrinking city in a second sense as well: a collapse in homeownership. In the past fifty years, the number of owner-occupied homes fell from 900,000 to 171,000. The Great Recession drove a 25 percent fall in the number of homeowners in the city between 2000 and 2010. This symbolic national capital of homeownership—and Black homeownership in particular—is now a place of record-breaking housing displacement. The majority of

---

* At 139 square miles, however, Detroit is not "too big," as many portrayals suggest. The city's total land area is smaller than Sun Belt and southern cities, such as Houston, Phoenix, Louisville, and Nashville.

Detroit's residents, including 53 percent of its Black residents, are now tenants. From 2014 to 2018, landlords evicted an average of eighty tenants per day. About 10,000 people a year live in tents, shelters, or blighted buildings.

That is the paradox of land in Detroit: a displacement crisis in a city known for surplus land. Inequality, not poverty alone, has driven this crisis. The city's real estate market has been remade by consolidation and speculation, with fewer owners accumulating bigger land portfolios. Several billionaires, all of whom are white, are leading the largest privately financed and privately owned downtown transformation in American history. The resurgent downtown and cheap land has attracted outside buyers. Some are bidding on single parcels, others on properties by the dozen.

Some of Detroit's outside owners intend to bank land for future value. Others have found an income stream in the business of leasing property at inflated prices to a population without better alternatives. One-third of residents live below the poverty line. Desperate housing seekers offer a profitable combination to slumlords willing to engage in the following business model:

- Buy dilapidated property from a public auction for a negligible investment (a median price of $1,300).
- Do little or nothing to fix it up.
- Sell or rent it a bit below median Detroit rents of $820 per month to people who can't find a better deal.
- Evict tenants for nonpayment of rent.
- Repeat until the building is so ruined that no one will pay to live there, then abandon it and pass the demolition costs to the city. Or stiff the city on property taxes and wait three years until the county forecloses. Under a new corporate name, consider purchasing the property again, cleansed of its back tax debt, at the public auction.

This cycle is the latest phase in Detroit's century-long history of exploiting vulnerable families of color seeking homes.

James cannot afford to get his land back. The city cut a deal with a real estate company and Amazon to open a distribution center at the empty state fairgrounds at the edges of his old blocks, which has driven a speculation rush. The Amazon facility will be operated mostly by robots, but Amazon expects more than a thousand low-wage jobs there. In anticipation of a new supply of tenants and buyers, land prices nearby are now about four times what they were before the Great Recession.

But Detroit and 48203's history is not finished. Leaders are inventing new ways to slow Black land loss and protect small-scale homeownership. They are reforming laws and practices that made it quicker and cheaper for bulk buyers to acquire land than it was for single-lot buyers to do the same. They are updating local government systems whose weaknesses enabled a tax foreclosure crisis. They are buying land to secure present stability and future wealth for residents. Detroit is well on its way to a "comeback." This movement wants to make sure that when that happens, the word "Detroit" will still symbolize a place where African Americans and working-class people of any color can make a living and a life.

An eastside mural, not far from James's old blocks, captured these efforts well. Artists Jonny Alexander, Ellen Rutt, and Ouizi painted it on a house built without windows on the sides because its neighbors were tucked in close. The neighboring houses are gone now, so the side wall offered a giant canvas. The home with the mural had been put up in an auction with a family still living inside, after a foreclosure that should have been illegal. Activists with a group called the Tricycle Collective were trying to ward off speculators who'd buy the land and evict the family. They needed more time to help the family inside get their house back. In old-timey font styled like letterpress stationery, amidst potted flowers exploding in vibrant color, the mural conveyed a giant message:

"This is a HOME: DO NOT BID!"

If only that mural could have been painted on the entire City of Detroit.

"CITY OF HOMES"

The Stories of Detroit's Decline

In an aerial image of Detroit from the 1940s, thousands of simple frame houses pack the street grid. The city's radial boulevards, built extra wide in an homage to the car, fan out in diagonals from the downtown core at the Detroit River. Multistory buildings rise up here and there, but otherwise the boulevards cut through low-rise neighborhoods. "Detroit was, above all, a city of homes," writes historian Thomas Sugrue.

Helicopter photography shows how many of these homes are gone now. Buildings dot rather than line some neighborhoods. During the summer, the vacancies look green, whether they are tended as gardens, overgrown with grasses, or mowed bare. Comparing a contemporary image with the one from the 1940s, anyone would want to know: *What happened here?*

Mainstream culture offers facile, inaccurate answers to that question. The most common one is summed up by an award-winning video for the song "Detroit '67," by an indie group called the Sam Roberts Band. The video features two band members dressed like film noir cops in suits with loose ties and Ray-Bans. They stroll Detroit streets through a montage of blighted buildings and vacant land. They photograph a dead body in an abandoned structure, as if investigating a murder.

We're meant to find the detectives in the video hot, but also sad. They drink away their misery in a rowdy cop bar, singing about the what-happened-here mystery. The lyrics ask: "Does anyone here tonight remember those times? Can anyone here tonight just tell me what they felt like?" Happy film clips flash: bustling boulevards, Motown musicians, let-out time at a factory, labor and civil rights protests, an ice hockey goal, 50's jitterbug dancing, waterskiing at Detroit's Metropolitan Beach.

The lyrics suggest what destroyed this carefree past: "Someone call the riot police, there's trouble down on Twelfth Street." Footage from the week of July 23, 1967, cuts through in color: fire bursting through the windows of multistory buildings; National Guard tanks, guns, and nightsticks; Black people carrying merchandise out of stores amidst smoky chaos; a Black man yelling and throwing punches; police officers with a dozen Black men, hands up against a wall. Giant fire hoses do their best to save buildings, but as the video closes, soldiers and police officers shake their heads in disbelief as they survey the rubble-strewn streets.

Our narrators are purportedly compassionate, drowning their sadness for Detroit with whiskey shots and beer chasers. But this story is one of blame. The video tells the tale that journalist Charlie LeDuff says he and other white children learned growing up in Detroit's suburbs: "Blacks went crazy and burned the city down." This story situates the events of 1967 as an explanation and an excuse for white flight, deindustrialization, and the destruction of a great American city. This, I think, is the white gaze on Detroit: nostalgia and loss for the happier, whiter past; the explosive summer of 1967 as the start of a bleaker present with rising crime, fire, and physical deterioration. "Some look ahead," Sam Roberts sings, "I'm going back." The video is hipster MAGA. No matter that it is written by stars who are probably liberal.

The historic footage in the video is real, but the assembled story is false by omission. In one line, Detroit poet Tawana "Honeycomb" Petty gave a fuller, more truthful answer to the question of how her town lost so much wealth and so many people. "My city got a black eye," she writes, "for loving Black people." Detroit has been a refuge for African Americans in the shadow of slavery and racial violence since the city's founding. Black history on that land helps explain Detroit's history, and Detroit's history helps explain Black history nationwide.

African American roots in Detroit date back to enslavement in French farms along the river in the 1700s. Formerly enslaved people founded the Second Baptist Church in 1836, then turned the sanctuary's basement into a shelter for a stream of 5,000 people escaping slavery on the Underground Railroad. Detroit was the last stop before crossing the Detroit River by boat into Canada, where slavery was illegal. Detroit's codename on the railroad was "Midnight" because the city's safehouses marked the last hour before the first day of a new life. On an October day in 1863, Sojourner Truth and other Black abolitionist leaders in Michigan gathered at Second Baptist to rally volunteers to fight with the Union Army. Two-thirds of the 1,400 men who enlisted had fled the South to settle in Detroit, but they willingly returned to southern battlefields. Ten percent would not survive the Civil War to return north.

A 1921 photograph hand-captioned "Colored Waiting Room" depicts Detroit's growing role as a home for Black refugees. The picture shows African Americans wearing their Sunday best in a Jacksonville, Florida, train depot. They are headed north, about to leave behind the debt peonage, public lynchings, and racial terrorism of the Jim Crow South. Detroit's Black population grew more than 700 percent between 1910 and 1920, and it nearly tripled again in the next decade. Henry Ford's 1914 promise of a "Five Dollar Day" (nearly double the prevailing wage) helped recruit Black workers, which allowed Ford to grow in spite of wartime deployment and new restrictions on European immigration. Black workers needed jobs, so they accepted the most hazardous roles. At the Ford Rouge Complex, Black workers made iron in blast furnaces or poured that iron into molds for auto parts in the thirty-acre foundry. If these workers could evade tuberculosis, deafness, dismemberment, or death, they could earn a steady income. That labor force allowed the Ford Company to make cars from scratch: to take in raw iron ore, coal, and limestone and turn out finished cars from nearby assembly lines.

Most white landowners in the city were unwilling to sell or rent housing to African Americans. Rather than living "down South," Black Detroiters remarked, they lived "up South." Immigrants streamed into the city from around the world for industrial jobs, but they learned that "if they were white, no matter how difficult circumstances were for them, life for their children would be 'all right.'" Segregation cut across daily life, from the bleachers at Navin Field (which became Tiger Stadium) to the baseball teams themselves, from the taxis to the grocery stores.

Second Baptist Church's neighborhood, called Black Bottom, had an "ethnic hodgepodge" of Jewish, African American, and other groups. The area had been named for its rich soil, but because it was one of the only neighborhoods open to Black homeseekers, the neighborhood tipped Black and its name became associated with its racial identity. Landlords in Black Bottom charged African American tenants a steep

premium, setting their rents at up to 150 percent of what white tenants paid for the same units. Yet housing shortages meant that tenants
could be found for the most dilapidated buildings. Despite government
pressure to install plumbing, by 1926 about a third of Black Bottom
homes still had no toilet. Many were too old or makeshift to keep out
rain and snow. Imagery illustrating Petty's poem might include a photograph from the eve of the Great Depression, which shows five African
American children in an alley behind a row of shacks. Their family had
just been evicted. A single chair sticks up behind them on a pile of possessions no taller than they are. When families crowded into apartments
to reduce costs, landlords criticized Black caretaking standards as an
additional justification for rent gouging.

Pent up demand meant white landowners could also sell land at a
premium to non-white buyers, but mobs often blocked these transactions. In 1925, a man named Dr. Ossian Sweet and his family bought
a bungalow home on Garland Avenue. Sweet was a physician at Dun-
bar Hospital, a training hospital for Black patients and doctors. After
threats of violence, the Sweets sought protection as they moved in. Police patrolled and family came to help defend the home. Several hundred people gathered around their corner lot. On the second night, the
mob shattered three of the home's windows with rocks. Sweet's brother
Henry panicked and fired a rifle into the crowd. He killed a white man.
All ten adults in the house were put on trial for murder.

During Sweet's testimony, he described opening his door to pull in
his brother, who had arrived to a crowd screaming threatening epithets.
"When I opened the door and saw the mob," he testified, "I realized
I was facing the same mob that had hounded my people through our
entire history. . . . I was filled with a peculiar fear, the fear of one who
knows the history of my race." As a five-year-old growing up in central
Florida, Sweet had watched a mob chain a Black teenager he knew to
a tree and light him on fire because they suspected him of murder-
ing a white woman. The town newspaper reported: "By midnight, the
town was as peaceful as ever." In closing arguments at Dr. Sweet's trial,
his defense lawyer Clarence Darrow called the jury to see the fanatical
violence that had run from slavery to Sweet's Jim Crow childhood to
1920s Detroit. A white homeowner, Darrow stressed, would never face

charges for defending his family from a mob. After a hung jury and second trial, charges were dropped against all the Sweet defendants. The case was one of the first orderly, law-based trials of an African American who killed a white person in U.S. history.

Some white Detroiters chose to sell land to Black buyers at fair prices. A white abolitionist named Shubael Conant forbade racially restrictive covenants on any parcels subdivided from his land. Black families purchased these lots, building up a prosperous enclave called Conant Gardens that was known for vegetable gardens in backyards and flowers in front. Working-class African American families also found affordable land for sale in the 1920s and 1930s in a neighborhood called West Eight Mile. Local authorities had never invested in running water, electricity, and streetcar stops there, but owning land helped families raise food and maintain shelter to survive the Great Depression.

West Eight Mile, however, was also emblematic of the discriminatory lending that withheld the full benefits of homeownership in Black neighborhoods. On survey maps created by the federal Home Owners' Loan Corporation in 1935 to help assess risks for real estate lending, every Black neighborhood in Detroit was classified as a "hazardous" investment. These "redlining" practices disqualified homes from Federal Housing Administration (FHA) insurance, which in turn meant that households and developers could not borrow to finance construction. Without access to insured mortgages, families in West Eight Mile borrowed on unregulated markets, built their homes slowly over time with scrap materials, or left their property vacant until they could afford construction. Nonetheless, residents improved their homes when they could, and planted gardens on undeveloped parcels.

In 1941, based on West Eight Mile's hazardous designation, the FHA refused to insure a development for white buyers located next door. The developer proposed a two-block-long, six-foot-high concrete wall to keep the neighborhoods apart. The FHA approved the developer's loan and the wall was built against West Eight Mile's organized opposition. In a photograph taken that year, four African American children pose for the camera in front of the wall. One girl is holding a white baby doll. The wall, the children, and the doll are a startling premonition of Chief Justice Earl Warren's opinion in *Brown v. Board of*

Education. The opinion described how segregation generated a "feeling of inferiority as to their status in the community that may affect their hearts and minds in a way unlikely ever to be undone." Among other research, the opinion cited a 1940s psychological study of the attributes and life chances that children assign to dolls of different races. The Birwood Wall, which still stands today, conveyed that Black families were separate because they were not equal.

Seregation and mob violence against Black households moving across color lines continued, even as Black Detroiters rose to national fame. On June 22, 1938, Black Bottom's own Joe Louis defeated Max Schmeling, the German boxer celebrated by Adolf Hitler as a symbol of Aryan strength. When Louis defeated Schmeling in two minutes and four seconds, front page headlines cheered the victory in giant font. But Louis called out the hypocrisy of this adulation, saying, "White Americans—even while some of them still were lynching black people in the South—were depending on me to K.O. Germany."

Two race riots against Black Detroiters mortified the city during World War II, generating images used in anti-American propaganda in Germany, Italy, and Japan. In February 1942, when housing authorities opened wartime housing for Black families adjacent to a white neighborhood, a white mob assaulted the new tenants with rocks and neighbors posted a giant banner reading WE WANT WHITE TENANTS IN OUR WHITE COMMUNITY. Yet police arrested more than one hundred African Americans and only three white individuals. It took two months to move anyone into the new apartments, and more than 2,000 state and federal troops and police deployed to protect them.

The following year, a white mob started a race riot at the city park on Belle Isle, trashing nearby Black businesses and swarming street cars to assault Black men. One infamous photograph shows an African American man whose face has been badly beaten, soaking his suit and tie in blood. He had collapsed in the arms of two anguished white tourists to Detroit who had intervened to save his life. Some white Detroiters were killed as a race riot ensued, but half of the total deaths were Black Detroiters killed by police officers; nearly all of the arrests and criminal convictions were of Black Detroit residents.

Postwar, a new wave of African Americans moved to Detroit, as

Black veterans gave up on their hometowns in the segregated South after experiencing military dignity. In the Second Great Migration from 1940 to 1970, Detroit's Black population quadrupled in size while housing options remained narrow. By the late 1940s, approximately 80 percent of Detroit's residential parcels outside Black Bottom contained racially restrictive covenants in the deed. When the McGhee family bought such a house in 1944, a brick home with a second story and a covered porch on Seebaldt Street, a neighbor sued to void the sale. He alleged that the seller had not realized his light-skinned buyer violated a covenant that stated the following: "This property shall not be used or occupied by any person or persons except those of the Caucasian race." In *Sipes v. McGhee* in 1947, the Michigan Supreme Court upheld the enforceability of this covenant, finding that they lacked sufficient reason to overturn "[a] recognized rule of property." So instead, the Michigan Supreme Court focused on whether to uphold the trial court's finding that the McGhees were not white. The neighbor seeking to enforce the covenant had testified, "I have seen Mr. McGhee, and he appears to have colored features. They are more darker [sic] than mine. I haven't got near enough to the man to recognize his eyes."

The NAACP and Thurgood Marshall convinced the U.S. Supreme Court that the family's race was beside the point. Courts, they argued, should never enforce discriminatory covenants. The McGhees moved in. But the ruling did not prohibit private parties from obeying covenants voluntarily. Social pressure to comply with covenants, racial steering by realtors, and cross burnings continued to segregate Detroit until the 1968 Fair Housing Act created legal tools to fight discrimination and harassment by private actors.

Covenants and other means of segregation intensified overcrowding and gouged Black families financially. But the dense, mixed-income vitality of Detroit's Black neighborhoods had the virtue of building up Black-owned businesses and culture. Paradise Valley, Black Bottom's commercial district, gained a national reputation for shaping four decades of music, from boogie-woogie piano to big-band jazz and swing. Blues, writes city historian Herb Boyd, "emanated from every keyhole and peephole." John Lee Hooker, the son of a Mississippi sharecropper who started his music career in Detroit, created a new generation of the Delta Blues with his electric guitar and rough, elemental voice. A segregated Black middle and high school in Paradise Valley developed a celebrated music program. The area's rich music culture later helped generate Motown and its legendary, Black-owned recording studio, Hitsville U.S.A. Touring celebrities like Louis Armstrong, Duke Ellington, Ella Fitzgerald, and Billie Holiday performed at Black-owned venues. They could stay in the Black-owned Hotel Gotham, which poet Langston Hughes called a "minor miracle." Instead of relying on dingy hotels with broken windows and furniture, Hughes wrote using all caps, Black entrepreneurs could "OWN and MANAGE" hotels and treat Black guests with dignity.

But just as Detroit headed into the dramatic job losses of deindustrialization, the city bulldozed much of the Black wealth, housing, and cultural heritage built up during segregation. A true history of the city of homes should show Mayor Edward Jeffries issuing the Detroit Plan of 1946, which slated Paradise Valley and Black Bottom for redevelopment. City officials justified Black Bottom's demolition based on its deterioration and its reputation for vice—both of which were byproducts of racial discrimination. For most of the neighborhood's history, traditional lenders excluded Black businesses, leaving them to obtain capital by overpaying loan sharks or collecting cash from illicit operations. Music, dancing, gambling, prostitution, and drinking (especially during Prohibition) helped draw mixed race crowds to spend money at Black businesses. Paradise Valley's exclusion from credit markets saddled it with dilapidated housing and an under-the-table economy that, in a vicious cycle originating in and returning to racism, was used to justify its destruction.

City officials did not finalize the Detroit Plan until 1951, and demolition then took more than a decade. Slow attrition across these years further devalued Black-owned businesses. After demolition crews leveled thousands of units of housing, the Chrysler and Fisher freeways took their place, allowing suburbanites to access downtown jobs at highway speeds. A middle-class housing development also replaced Black Bottom, and Paradise Valley's land was cleared for Ford Field and part of Comerica Park, two privately owned, publicly subsidized sports stadiums. Black families moved into the Twelfth Street area. The area had celebrated jazz venues, but the vibrant cultural center of Paradise Valley was never re-created.

Detroit lost more than half of its manufacturing jobs between 1947 and 1977, including 82,000 defense-industry jobs. The federal government subsidized industry and infrastructure in suburbs and smaller cities across the Midwest and the Sun Belt. Bombings of European cities such as Liverpool, Dresden, and Rotterdam during World War II had demonstrated the risks of concentrating military-industrial manufacturing in single cities. Firms relocated to areas without African American residents, or those with Jim Crow hiring practices that blocked Black access to new jobs. Seniority rules and racial discrimination made job losses in Detroit steepest for Black workers. Black unemployment nearly doubled between 1950 and 1980. Meanwhile, Michigan law authorized relentless postwar suburban expansion, making Metro Detroit's job base the most decentralized of any big city in the country.

Following these jobs to the South or to the suburbs was not viable for Black Detroiters. On childhood trips to see her mother's relatives still living in Alabama in the 1950s, Detroit-born Diana Ross recalled how her family had to move to the back of Greyhound buses when they reached Cincinnati. At rest stops from that point on, her family had to use the "horrible and smelly" rest rooms and "rusty and dirty water fountains" marked "colored," just in view of newer, cleaner facilities marked for whites only. Detroit's close-in suburbs did their part to block African Americans from leaving the city. Dearborn's mayor from 1942 to 1978 made a spectacle of his segregationist, racist views, encouraging harassment of Black homebuyers and bragging that he kept an eye out for new Black residents so he could provide police and fire protection that was "a little too good," with harassing wake-up calls at nighttime.

Black Detroit organized against these abuses. The Detroit chapter of the NAACP, one of the biggest in the nation, took on civil rights battles in schools, police reform, restaurants, voting, and employment. Aretha Franklin's father, a preacher and civil rights activist, organized 125,000 marchers in a 1963 Walk to Freedom, where Dr. Martin Luther King Jr. debuted his "I Have A Dream" speech. Elijah Muhammad built Temple

No. 1 of the Nation of Islam there, where he trained Malcom X to become a minister. The League of Revolutionary Black Workers and other labor activists in the late 1960s organized to demand that government shift its focus from the well-being of industrial corporations to the well-being of industrial workers. In writings sold in radical bookstores, in speeches at rallies, and at workshops hosted in living rooms or factory break rooms, activists imagined a society that put education and opportunities before buildings or company stock prices.

In 1965, activists James and Grace Lee Boggs warned that the city had reached a dangerous crossroads. African Americans had become a majority in cities like Detroit, but remained walled out of city government. Black youth faced impossible unemployment rates. Urban police had become a "growing occupation army," they wrote, which was "empowered to resort to any means considered necessary to safeguard the interests of the absentee landlords, merchants, politicians, and administrators . . . who themselves are afraid to walk its streets."

These tensions exploded on July 23, 1967, when police raided a Black social club hosting a homecoming party for a returning veteran from Vietnam. The death toll of forty-three (with thirty killed by law enforcement) was comparable to the deaths in the 1943 race riots, but injuries and property damage were worse. For the first time, the Detroit Fire Department telegraphed 3-777 to all its stations, a code created in World War II to recall all firefighters to duty. More than two thousand buildings were burned or looted. Seventeen thousand federal, state, and local law enforcement and military troops deployed in the city, sometimes restoring order, sometimes brutalizing civilians. For years, Detroit's writers and historians have called these events a "rebellion" or "uprising" rather than a "riot," given the degree of discrimination and police violence facing the Black community. A newspaper founded after the rebellion opened with a summary of the problem:

> We are still working, still working too hard, getting paid too little, living in bad housing, sending our kids to substandard schools, paying too much for groceries, and treated like dogs by the police. We still don't own anything and don't control

anything . . . In other words, we are still being systematically exploited by the system and still have the responsibility to break the back of that system.

In the years following, the Detroit police dug in. The department formed an undercover unit in 1971 known as STRESS ("Stop the Robberies, Enjoy Safe Streets") that became infamous for excessive force. The STRESS unit alone killed twenty-two Detroiters in less than two years, ranking the city first nationwide for the number of police killings of civilians per capita. STRESS tactics polarized city politics. The multiracial left (including Black police officers) protested police brutality. White conservatives held pro-police rallies. The mayoral election of 1973 pitted the white police chief John Nichols (a staunch defender of STRESS) against Coleman Young, a member of the Michigan Senate and the Black son of a barber in Paradise Valley. Young vowed to reform the police and abolish STRESS, which he called "an execution squad." Ninety percent of Black voters chose Young. Ninety percent of white voters picked Nichols. Young won.

Young's election, not the 1967 uprising, marked Detroit's most dramatic demographic turning point. The Black share of Detroit's population grew from 44 percent in 1970 to 67 percent in 1980. Suburbs resisted regional cooperation with Detroit's new management. Starting in the 1970s and consistently as late as 2018, suburban voters and officials blocked public transportation to link the city with its suburbs. These decisions forced low-income Detroiters to sustain the costs of private cars to commute toward low-wage jobs in the suburbs. By 2011, Detroit families spent nearly one-third of their incomes on transportation, despite the fact that more than 20 percent of Detroiters could not afford to own or share a car.

Anti-busing activism to block school integration proliferated in Detroit's suburbs through grassroots groups like Mothers Alert Detroit (MAD). Implementing *Brown v. Board of Education*, the federal trial court found that the Detroit Public Schools had engaged in decades of unconstitutional school segregation. Housing segregation, the court found, had reinforced school segregation, dividing neighborhoods and cities by race. Because Detroit schools were now mostly Black, these courts found, a desegregation remedy would require creating new school catchment areas that would cross city boundaries across the Metro Detroit region. Antibusing campaigns fought these decisions, and in 1974, a U.S. Supreme Court transformed by appointees of President Richard Nixon (who opposed school busing) ruled that federal courts did not have the power to enforce this desegregation remedy. In *Milliken v. Bradley*, the Court agreed that Detroit's students had been illegally segregated in violation of their constitutional rights. But the court found that Detroit could only desegregate within its borders—an increasingly meaningless remedy as the city became predominantly Black.

Coleman Young served as Detroit's mayor for twenty years. The *Detroit Free Press*, which conducted a systematic analysis of city finances from 1950 to 2013, called him the "most austere Detroit mayor since World War II" for his management of the city's budgets and debts. Apparently that reality ran contrary to most Detroiters' assumptions, leading the *Free Press* to call its piece "How Detroit Went Broke: The Answers May Surprise You—and Don't Blame Coleman Young." Any stereotypes that Young had overspent on welfare programs cut against political science research on municipal spending. When a city is at least 50 percent African American, it spends approximately half as much on redistribution as when a city is only 5 percent Black.

Like all big-city mayors of his generation, Mayor Young faced bruising challenges across the 1970s and 1980s: recession, deindustrialization, racial conflict, depopulation, the heroin epidemic. A corruption and real estate scandal the mayor called "Hurricane HUD" hit the city too. Housing legislation in the 1950s and 1960s aimed to increase low-income homeownership, including in urban centers and among working-class African Americans. In a grim preview of modern-day events, private and public profiteers distorted the laws to harm the people they were designed to help. Speculators took advantage of federal housing programs to buy dozens of derelict properties and flip them for sale at inflated values. A *Detroit Free Press* survey found that real estate speculators in Detroit earned 59–69 percent profit as a percentage of investment.

Scholar Keeanga-Yamahtta Taylor, in an exceptional history of this scandal, documented how low-income Black women in particular were subject to "predatory inclusion" in these homeownership programs, which granted them access to mortgages but on more expensive, higher risk terms. Real estate agents typically showed them only one home option and pushed them to sign a purchase agreement on the spot. Mortgage bankers sought these women as customers, because if they defaulted on the mortgage, the house could be flipped again. Lenders' losses were backstopped by the government, and each sale fed brokers with commissions and fees. More than one hundred speculators, contractors, appraisers, and government officials were later indicted for bribery, doctored paperwork, and other acts of fraud. Owners on fixed income could not afford payments as well as the emergency repairs their dilapidated homes required. Foreclosures spiked between 1968 and 1971. By the mid-1970s, Detroit had 15,000 abandoned units tarnished by legal histories that made properties hard to resell.

In the aftermath of this displacement disaster, and having watched President Ford let New York City continue its fiscal freefall into a 1975 bankruptcy petition, Mayor Young believed that retaining manufacturing jobs was the only way for Detroit to survive. Hoping to build a future by holding on to the industrial titans of the past, in 1980 Detroit gave General Motors $200 million in tax incentives to build a new assembly plant. They condemned and demolished 1,300 homes and 140 businesses (plus churches and a hospital) in a neighborhood called Poletown to make way for the plant. After the resistance vigils yielded to bulldozers, the new, automated assembly plant created only half of the promised jobs, and General Motors proceeded to shutter two of its older plants in the city. The deal left city residents and leaders bitter and disillusioned.

But for all the hardships of those decades, ordinary, better changes were happening in those years. A more complete visual montage might show students in seminar rooms at Wayne State University, which held some of America's first Black Studies classes. Groups of evening roller skaters took to Detroit's quiet streets across the 1980s. There could be images from Cass Technical High School, which continued to graduate accomplished figures ranging from the Pulitzer Prize–winning historian Heather Ann Thompson to contemporary music icons such as Big Sean, Jack White, and Regina Carter. It might show the intimate art deco space for jazz at Baker's Keyboard Lounge, where karaoke nights in front of packed houses feel like auditions for *American Idol*. Starting in the 1990s, a man named John put carpet on his front porch for acoustics and welcomed blues musicians to play for crowds outside. "John's Carpet House" expanded into a grass field where twenty years of free Sunday concerts have played to an audience sitting in lawn chairs or dancing. Eastern Market continued to host a giant, multibuilding farmers' market on Saturdays. The cheese shop DeVries & Co. celebrated its 125th anniversary in 2012 and kept on going. Upstairs in a studio loft, stars like Eminem rehearsed and recorded with Luis Resto, one of America's most important producers.

Detroit has remained a hub for progressive organizing. The Allied Media Conference, based in Detroit since 2007, hosted the first national convening for the Movement for Black Lives in 2015. The city also remained a home for vulnerable people and a testament to Black resilience. A blues artist named Son House, a creator of the Mississippi Blues tradition who moved to Detroit, had helped countless African Americans carry the sorrows of the Black South and the Great Migration. Caregivers at the New Light Nursing Home in West Detroit eased House's own passage, carrying him through Alzheimer's disease. Wearing clothes staff had embroidered with his initials, he died there in 1988.

Against the odds, a thriving Black middle class developed, and they helped shape and maintain the city several decades longer than their white peers. Sunnie Wilson, a Black entrepreneur, boxing promoter, and gregarious host, established the Forest Club in 1941, which was bigger than the original Madison Square Garden, with a 107-foot bar, a bowling alley, and a performance space that doubled as a roller-skating rink. Urban renewal in Paradise Valley put the club out of business, so Wilson opened a hotel in the Twelfth Street area until the neighborhood's poverty put the hotel out of business. Wilson adapted again, creating seventeen years of nightlife downtown with Sunnie's Celebrity Room. As downtown emptied, the once popular nightclub could no longer afford its electricity bill, so for one final summer, in 1987, Wilson moved four tables out to the sidewalk. Staffed by Wilson and his last waitress, the club's candlelit tables remained full until winter.

Detroit was known for "dying," but it never stopped living. Like most bad summaries of what happened in Detroit, the Sam Roberts Band missed the real story. Pre-1967 Detroit was pretty, but pre-1967 Detroit was also ugly. Post-1967 Detroit had tragic, ugly parts, but there was beauty too. Racism and the resilience needed to survive it are not as easy to photograph as fires and looting, but they defined Detroit's modern history and its present poverty. Since this telling of Detroit's history began with a poem by a Black woman, it seems right to end with one too. Lucille Clifton was not from Detroit, but she captured the contested stories we tell about the city in her poem "why some people be mad at me sometimes." She wrote:

> they ask me to remember
> but they want me to remember
> their memories
> and i keep on remembering
> mine.

"THE WATER IS WARM"

The Fresh Start of Detroit's Bankruptcy?

In the 1990s, when a man named Shannon Smith was a child, his dad would drive him through Detroit's neighborhoods. They avoided the city's freeways, including the lidless tunnels that had paved over Black Bottom. He wanted Smith to imagine the neighborhoods as they had been. He pointed out homes owned by people he knew. Black self-governance, Smith's father emphasized, was a sacred responsibility. Once Black Detroiters had lost the right to govern, he warned, they would lose part of their culture too.

Smith absorbed these recollections with a twinge of doubt—it was hard to believe the old days had been so golden. Having grown up in the city, he could not imagine away the depopulation and blight. In high school, he walked to school in the middle of the street on winter mornings because the sidewalks were unlit. Like other kids in Detroit Public Schools, success meant leaving the city. Smith could have fulfilled his childhood dream of wearing a suit for a job in New York or Chicago, but in 2012, after his graduation from the University of Michigan, he returned to Detroit for a job at the Federal Reserve. He had kept a worried eye on his peers from childhood. He felt compelled to bring his college degree back home, where only 18 percent of people had a degree beyond high school. If he and other Black Detroiters did not take responsibility for the city, he thought, "what will our future look like?"

The city was at a low point. French photographers Yves Marchand and Romain Meffre were bringing the city's blight to international attention. Outside reporters and busloads of tourists visited the city's graffitied ruins. More than 700,000 people still lived in Detroit, but in the previous decade, the city had lost 25 percent of its population—a staggering rate of loss second only to New Orleans in the aftermath of Hurricane Katrina. Recent years had pummeled remaining residents' incomes. Starting in 2000, the American manufacturing jobs base began a "prolonged collapse," losing five million jobs by 2014. The 2014 manufacturing jobs total was lower than at any time since 1940. Metro Detroit lost 400,000 jobs, a wildly disproportionate share of these national losses. Detroit's unemployment rate nearly quadrupled between 2000 and 2010, until more than one in five Detroiters was unemployed. A Detroiter with a four-year college degree was more likely to live in poverty than the average American with a two-year college degree.

The city also faced a cash flow crisis driven by the Great Recession. Total tax revenues sank between 2007 and 2013. Municipal income tax revenues fell 15 percent. Sales tax revenues fell 29 percent. The foreclosure crisis drove a 35 percent drop in property tax revenues from 2011 to 2013. Michigan's own fiscal challenges led the state to reduce its revenue sharing with the city. The state cut aid to Detroit by nearly 31 percent. These reductions were not worse than statewide averages, but nor had Michigan softened the recession's blow to its biggest city.

The recession also triggered unpayable contract obligations to Wall Street creditors. In 2005 and 2006, Merrill Lynch, UBS, and other banks had sold Detroit a series of complex financial deals that purported to help the city meet its pension obligations. These deals included interest rate swaps designed to protect the city from rising interest payments over time. When the Great Recession tanked interest rates, these deals bound Detroit to a high interest rate on its debts. The deals also included trigger clauses requiring immediate "termination payments" to the banks if the city's bond rating fell below investment grade. That, foreseeably, is what happened as the city's finances deteriorated. In the court opinion deeming Detroit eligible for bankruptcy, the judge put it this way: "[T]he City lost on the swaps bet. Actually, it lost catastrophically on the swaps bet." Some lawyers and financial analysts believed these deals were doomed to default and had unethically (if not illegally) worked around the city's debt limits. Either way, Detroit faced the prospect of about $300 million in termination payments to the banks.

The problem of the termination payments sat on top of the underlying debt problem of unfunded pension liabilities. How to quantify this debt (since it would come due over such a long time horizon) was contested, with totals ranging from $1 billion to $3.5 billion. The city's average annual retirement benefits were relatively modest: $18,000 per year for non-uniformed retirees and $30,000 for police and fire retirees. Other retiree benefits, including health insurance, amounted to an additional $4.3 billion. But the city faced the pension cost drivers plaguing cities nationwide, such as increasing lifespans, the spiraling costs of health care, and the failure to fund pension promises as they accrued. Detroit's population loss aggravated these pension problems: by 2013, the city had twice as many retirees as there were current workers. This "pension overhang" meant a shrunken number of taxpayers were paying for pension promises made on behalf of the service needs of hundreds of thousands of people who no longer paid city taxes. Some pensioners were now paying taxes to some other Michigan town, or to some other state entirely.

This basic problem of population loss bogged down the city balance sheets in other ways, too. The assessed value of taxable property in the city had fallen by 77 percent during the fifty years before the bankruptcy, as the drain on residents weakened demand for property. Seventy-two sites qualified for the federal Superfund program for the worst cases of hazardous waste contamination. Detroit entered bankruptcy with 78,000 abandoned and blighted structures, each representing an average demolition cost of $8,500. Where demolishing obsolete or dilapidated structures to clear lots for reuse costs more than resale value, landowners don't bother. At that point it becomes cheaper to abandon land. That abandoment then passes the costs of demolition to taxpayers. Vacant land represented an opportunity to green the city with parks and farms, or to build rain gardens and other "green infrastructure" to prevent flooding. But blighted land had to be cleaned and repurposed first.

Losing people, however, did not alter the city's territory for public services. Many neighborhoods were emptier but none were empty—they still needed snow plowing, lighting, and emergency services. The city still needed bus routes to help its low-income population reach jobs, groceries, and churches. Sixty-one percent of employed city residents worked outside the city. Recession-related unemployment and deteriorating social conditions drove drug trade. In 2011, the city's violent crime rate was the second highest in the country among cities with more than 100,000 people. The investment of public resources in answering poverty with mass incarceration had only increased the need for services, as high rates of prison admission in Detroit neighborhoods more than doubled the risk of major depressive disorders and general anxiety disorders. The city's police department was under federal oversight from 2003 to 2016 because of its record of excessive force, unlawful detentions, and a disastrously high rate of shootings of citizens—an average of sixty-nine per year in the five years before federal intervention. High rates of trauma in the city showed up in a range of health metrics; such as the fact that Detroiters were 50 percent more likely to die of heart disease.

Despite the rising need for care and services, the city reduced spending dramatically in the years leading up to bankruptcy. Detroit cut its public workforce by 36 percent between 2002 and 2009, then laid off at least another 2,700 employees before 2013. The city closed fourteen of its thirty recreation centers plus more than two-thirds of its parks, then stopped maintenance and trash collection at most of the open parks. By 2010, only 35,000 of the city's 88,000 street lights were operational, and 27 percent of its roads were in poor condition. City ambulances broke down so often that only about one-third of them were in service at any given time. Some had driven more than 250,000 miles. Archaic IT systems for payroll and finances required painstaking data entry.

As the city administration weathered steep layoffs, its ability to enforce its tax laws fell away. Unpaid income taxes in fiscal year 2011 totaled $250 million. Failing to pursue collection processes may have helped some low-income Detroiters without income to spare, but it was also a giveaway to those who took advantage of weak tax enforcement. As recent U.S. history has shown, failure to pay taxes is not the same thing as inability to pay taxes.

The state government in Lansing could not muster the political will to restore pre-recession grant levels to Detroit. But nor could Michigan leave its largest city to default on its bond payments. In 2011, then-Governor Rick Snyder and the state legislature enacted Public Act 4, a controversial law expanding the authority of state-appointed "emergency managers" to intervene in local finances during a fiscal crisis. Once Detroit came under emergency management, 57 percent of the state's African American population had state-appointed emergency managers running their city or their school district, or both. A majority of Michigan voters believed that Public Act 4 had gone too far. In a referendum in the November 2012 election, voters overturned the law. But in a lame-duck session the next month, Governor Snyder enacted Public Act 436, a slightly revised version of the same law. A few months later, the governor appointed Kevyn Orr as Detroit's emergency manager. Selecting Orr, an attorney who had led Chrysler's 2009 bankruptcy process, made clear that state officials believed the city had no choice but to restructure its debt in bankruptcy court. Orr filed the city's Chapter 9 bankruptcy on July 18, 2013.

Just about every decision in the city's bankruptcy process was hard fought. Commentators, activists, and creditors (who hired fleets of lawyers and public relations teams) told different stories about who bore the blame for the fiscal crisis, and thus who should pay for it. In one story, the villain was Wall Street, blameworthy for having sold Detroit debts loaded with risks that only a mathematician could quantify and only a banker could love. In another, city politics and unions were to blame for having made unaffordable contracts during the years of population loss without saving money to pay for them. A third narrative blamed the state for building up suburbs that drained the city's population, then reducing aid to older cities. All of these stories were true. The collapse in state aid and the termination payments on the swaps deal had triggered the short-term debt crisis that necessitated bankruptcy. The failure to fund pension promises had imperiled the city's fiscal health for years into the future. But it was state investment in the suburbs that helped drain the city of population and taxpayers, which made every fiscal problem, especially pension debt, worse.

Filing bankruptcy exposed Detroit's assets to liquidation and its pensioners to poverty, but when it was all over, the "near miss" list was longer than the actual losses. Retiree health care benefits were cut dramatically, but the Affordable Care Act and Michigan's ACA exchange at least allowed retirees of any age or preexisting condition to find coverage. Pension payments took cuts, but smaller ones than feared. Testimony, activism, and court findings exposed the dehumanizing collapse of the city's services and the modesty of most Detroit pensions. These accounts sparked leaders in philanthropy and state government to triangulate a deal called the Grand Bargain, which generated funds to protect most pensions. That deal also saved the city's world-class art collection from court-ordered sale. Creditors might have sought to put the land on Detroit's iconic island park at Belle Isle up for sale too, but Orr shielded the park with a long-term lease to the state, which has invested $50 million in park restoration.

No municipality exits bankruptcy without debt, but the goal of the litigation is to reduce or rearrange the schedule of that debt so the city can keep up with monthly payments while still affording basic services. Detroit's bankruptcy plan transferred valuable land and assets to creditors, but it was designed to hold back enough money in the city budget going forward that Detroit could rebuild services and invest in growth. That growth, in turn, would help the city keep up with pension and other debts. The city's bankruptcy judge, Steven Rhodes, read an oral opinion from the bench when the litigation was over. Debt and the suspension of the city's democracy had been painful, he said, but Detroit now had a chance to rebuild. "I urge you now not to forget your anger," he said to the city's people. "Your enduring and collective memory of what happened here, and your memory of your anger about it, will be exactly what will prevent this from ever happening again."

After the bankruptcy, city government began a slow reconstruction.

Carry-over staff had been demoralized by layoffs, years of low expectations, and inadequate tools and training. New staff were charged with overhauling departments and systems. In 2016, I spoke with Carol O'Cleireacain, a deputy mayor charged with modernizing the city's income tax collection to offer basic services like electronic filing. I commented that she must have been proud of the difference she was making. She paused and looked at me. "Do you think that's true? Thank you. No one except my husband tells me that." She wasn't the only one who seem to need a boost. On my way out, I stopped in one of the city building's bathrooms. Someone had left a pad of Post-its and a pen near a blank wall. Staff had written a dozen encouraging messages to each other on pink squares that decorated the wall. "You're stronger than you think," one said. O'Cleireacain and others surely got the thanks they deserved when figures came out showing a 15 percent increase in the city's income tax revenues between fiscal years 2014 and 2018.

In parallel with the city's fiscal restructuring, another set of changes also gave rise to talk of a Detroit "recovery." In 2011, a "skyscraper sale" downtown had attracted Dan Gilbert, the founder and CEO of Quicken Loans and other companies, the owner of the Cleveland Cavaliers, and one of the fifty richest people in the world today. Gilbert had grown up in the Detroit suburbs, but his father had owned a bar on Woodward Avenue in the 1960s. By the end of 2012, Gilbert's real estate companies had purchased and renovated fifteen buildings in Detroit, populating them with 7,000 employees he moved out of suburban facilities. These renovations marked the first major real estate investment in Detroit's downtown since the 1970s.

Leaving buildings vacant in the suburbs looked like a comeuppance for Oakland County, which had become one of the wealthiest counties in America as Detroit shrank. Oakland's chief executive from 1992 to 2019, L. Brooks Patterson, had risen to prominence early in his career by fighting a desegregation order in suburban schools, and he built a brand out of bashing Detroit with remarks like this one: "I made a prediction a long time ago, and it's come to pass. I said, 'What we're gonna do is turn Detroit into an Indian reservation, where we herd all the Indians into the city, build a fence around it, and then throw in the blankets and corn.'"

Gilbert's investments restored Detroit's downtown architectural treasures. Within a decade, his companies owned more than 18 million square feet of real estate (about one hundred buildings) in Detroit. Gilbert seemed to be proving that a massive capital infusion, which created a critical mass of people and jobs all at once, could restore a city core. He announced to other investors that, as a businessman put it, the "water was warm." Near the area nicknamed Gilbertville rose Ilitchville, a redevelopment area built around sports and entertainment. Mike (now deceased) and Marian Ilitch, also Forbes-ranked billionaires with Detroit roots, grew a portfolio of at least 250 properties, as well as the Detroit Tigers and Red Wings teams. Their piece of downtown area is anchored in the Little Caesars Arena, named for their pizza empire, where the Detroit Red Wings hockey and Detroit Pistons basketball teams play. State and local taxpayers invested $398 million in demolition, construction costs, and incentives for the arena and adjacent redevelopment. A third billionaire, Matty Moroun, also assembled a giant portfolio of real estate at fire-sale prices, but his speculation seemed mostly to buffer his other existing businesses with land he could control. But eventually he—and his son, after Matty's passing—also began to renovate some buildings.

By 2017, one could say with confidence that downtown was coming back. Downtown was hip: you could grab a colored chair and sink your bare feet into a sand pit cheekily called "The Beach," even though its closest waterway is a fruity drink at the bar. It was classy: in restaurants ranked among the best in the state, you could get your fries scented with truffle oil. Some changes felt generic, like the many cafes and shops playing ubiquitous retro music from white stars like David Bowie, Fleetwood Mac, and the Pixies, in a city that remained a vibrant capital of music made by African Americans. But with cranes in the air and morning lines at the coffee shops, it seemed like the city had done what so many other depopulated Rust Belt cities had tried, but failed, to do. *Detroit was growing.*

Still, it stood to wonder: who was this new Detroit for? Development deals in Gilbertville and Ilitchville held back the new property tax revenues they generated to pay back debts incurred in the city's infrastructure and capital investments there. It would take years before significant new downtown revenues would reach schools and services in the neighborhoods. The brand identity of the recovery was a single Detroit, but when it came to tax law, there now seemed to be two of them: "downtown/midtown" versus "neighborhoods."

Many believed there were "two Detroits" in social, racial respects too. The neglect, social isolation, and educational disinvestment in the city's people had gone on too long for them just to step in to service jobs. On a summer day in 2017, I watched a twenty-something African American woman holding a baby and wearing cut-off sweat pants and worn-out shoes linger nervously near the hostess pedestal of a new restaurant downtown. She exchanged curious glances with a waiter carrying cocktails served in chilled copper mugs with sprigs of rosemary. The hostess was a white twenty-something wearing red lipstick and an asymmetrical linen top. When she was free, the woman with the baby stepped up and asked for a job application. The hostess answered that there was a PDF on the website. The jobseeker paused, waiting, as though she needed more information than that. She said her thanks and left. The two women had spoken to each other with stilted, nervous politeness, as though they came from separate worlds. Neither woman said in words what their faces seemed to express: "A job here is not going to happen." Detroiters often put it this way: downtown won't trickle down.

Imani Mixon, a Black writer in Detroit, grew up on the East Side but commuted to white suburbs for elementary and high school. Parents of her white school friends rarely allowed their children to visit Mixon's house, even for her birthday parties, for fear of crime. Mixon moved to Chicago for college. She returned to Detroit after her graduation and was shocked by how much the city had changed. "I've never seen so many white people in Detroit in my life," she said, as daytime workers, restaurant patrons, and new residents bustled downtown. The suburbs had moved back in. Sometimes it was a bit rich to see so many shirts, hoodies, signs, and swag celebrating the city with phrases such as "Made in Detroit." Mixon had "spent a lot of time in white spaces" for her education, so she still felt comfortable downtown and midtown. But other members of her family no longer felt at ease in those areas. Some family members joined the tide of "Black flight"—the stream of middle-class families moving to suburbs. They were tired of waiting for improvements to the schools and other neighborhood services.

Shannon Smith's father passed away in 2013. He did not live to see his downtown bustling again, or the bankruptcy that gave the city budget room to breathe. But nor did he live to feel the loss in those changes too—the way that the cultural, social, and business life downtown seemed like it was for the same people who had turned its suburbs into gated communities to keep Detroiters out. He didn't see how many assets the city lost in the bankruptcy, or the way the City of Detroit lost its authority to govern Belle Isle, the DIA, and its regional water system.

During the years of the bankruptcy, Smith was volunteering for Councilwoman Raquel Castañeda-López's office in southwest Detroit. Later he would help lead city efforts to support small, minority-owned businesses and run for the school board. He wanted to help make the city better, like his dad taught him to do. When Detroit's first mayor elected after the bankruptcy was also its first white mayor in forty years, Castañeda-López and Smith observed a sense of defeat—the stigma against the city internalized as a story that, as she put it, "I guess our people couldn't do it." So they worked to celebrate and foster the strong community that had gotten the neighborhoods through decades of disinvestment—organizing donations for a grass-cutting collective to buy a lawnmower to mow empty lots, people chipping in to fund repairs for elderly neighbors, and mutual aid efforts for grocery runs and transportation. Castañeda-López recalled happy moments of progress too, like her niece reacting to new streetlights by singing the Disney song from *Tangled*, "I see the light."

Smith and the councilwoman facilitated some difficult conversations about the city's racial and social change. Public projects like new bike lanes raised tensions, heightening a sense among long-time Detroiters that the city was putting the needs of new twenty-somethings above those of low-income families. When people are struggling to survive or don't feel safe, Castañeda-López explained, it's hard to talk to them about this or that small improvement for the long term. Castañeda-López and her office started an effort called "Detroit, Our City," which convened conversations between long-time Detroit residents and newer ones. Participants shared stories about journeys to the city of Detroit or their families' local history and talked about the deeper values behind being a Detroiter. People, she emphasized, were "craving" these spaces as a way to feel less isolated. Her office also coordinated District 6 Tours, in which residents led tours of their neighborhood for people from different neighborhoods of the district, followed by a group lunch. The amount of trauma in the city, she said, made this work hard but essential.

At the moment of the bankruptcy filing in 2013, wrote reporter Nathan Bomey, "Detroit hit rock bottom." But he and others believed that filing bankruptcy also meant "Detroit finally had hope." If we read these lines to refer to the City of Detroit, as a government, Bomey was right. But if we read them to mean the People of Detroit, the ones who had lived through the city's poverty and bankruptcy crises, I think he was wrong. As Smith could see on his driving tours of the city, and as he and Councilwoman Castañeda-López heard every day in her constituent office, many of Detroit's people had several more years to fall.

FORTY-EIGHT PERCENT

A City of Tenants

A stunning 48 percent of Detroit's residential units (120,000 homes) went through a mortgage or tax foreclosure, or both, between 2005 and 2015. The rate of homeownership among African Americans in Wayne County plunged eleven points after the recession, transforming Detroit into a majority renter city by 2016.

The mortgage foreclosure crisis of the Great Recession slammed Detroit. During the subprime lending frenzy of the early 2000s, Detroit had been targeted by practices known as "reverse redlining." Lenders marketed subprime loans with high-risk or predatory terms to residents in neighborhoods where residents did not have access to better loans. Discrepancies in subprime lending and subsequent foreclosures were not explainable based on income or credit rates alone. Black and Latino borrowers were more likely to receive costly subprime loans even after controlling for income. Nearly half of the mortgages originated in Detroit in 2006 were subprime, high-cost loans.

Door to door salespeople targeting seniors older than age sixty-two also slathered the city in reverse mortgages, resulting in the highest rate of foreclosures on these loans of any American city between 2013 and 2017. Nationally, as in Detroit, predation in Black neighborhoods to find vulnerable borrowers resulted in a reverse mortgage foreclosure rate six times as high in low-income predominantly Black zip codes as in low-income, predominantly white ones. Homeowners used the loans to fund maintenance costs or other expenses, and lenders profited on fees and insurance that cost as much as $15,000 plus interest payments. Lenders targeted Black neighborhoods in Detroit and other places with high numbers of "cash poor, land rich" homeowners with equity in their home but low levels of income. Like many subprime loans, the fine print of reverse mortgages included interest rate jumps, balloon payments, or other hidden costs that doomed borrowers to default.

As land values plummeted after the recession, more properties developed a "value gap," in which the property value is less than the cost of the repairs it needs to be habitable. That gap made it impossible to access the regular mortgage market, because (by definition) mortgages are loans in which a property is the collateral. Small purchase prices also made mortgage loans effectively unavailable—banks typically won't bother to write mortgages under $50,000. Good mortgages became unavailable in much of Detroit. Homebuying became an all-cash affair, in a city full of residents with no cash to spare.

But the same could not be said of outsiders, who were flush with cash. As global real estate investment in subprime mortgages reached a dead end, capital shifted into bulk land speculation, single-family rental markets, and land-installment contracts. The glut of mortgage-reverted property had created a pipeline for bulk buyers, often backed by private equity firms seeking new investments. With the unequal recovery from the recession, land in poor towns became seductively cheap. Demand grew in all kinds of broke towns, from Ohio to Pennsylvania. Buyers began to gather in Detroit.

Some sought to hold land for strategic resale or development purposes in the future. Others bought land for more immediate gains. If a buyer didn't bother to invest in repairs to make their properties safe for tenants, Detroit's homes offered a profit stream. A buyer could get land for a nominal price (a third of properties sold for less than $500, and the median price was only $1,300), then put them out to rent.

Even with overall population loss in the city, foreclosure rates pushed so many residents into rental markets that the number of tenants in the city remained stable. Downtown redevelopment pushed central city rents skyward alongside falling federal funding for Detroit's affordable housing programs. Average rents in the city spiked—from 2005 to 2016, they increased 25 percent. Detroit is consistent with sociologist Matthew Desmond's findings that in weak land markets, median rents in the poorest neighborhoods are not much lower than citywide medians. Speculators could clear a profit with just a few months of rent, even if they ended up paying legal fees for an eviction.

Government in Detroit, meanwhile, was still reeling. The city's tax assessment office had lost so much staffing that each appraiser was responsible for nearly 7,000 parcels (double the state's recommended ratio). Thirty years had passed since the last citywide site visits to check for changed circumstances on the lots. But in earlier days of government dismemberment, lax assessment was matched by lax enforcement. The city estimated that it was owed $131 million in unpaid property taxes in 2011. The bankruptcy settlement focused on the lax enforcement side, requiring the city to kick its tax foreclosure pipeline back into gear to deter nonpayment and close the gap between the taxes owed and the taxes received. This wasn't wrong—tax laws without enforcement are regressive, because absentee owners stiff cities more often than residents do. Anyone preserving or stockpiling land in Detroit owed their share of taxes to pay for services. And any self-respecting city has to try to move vacant, abandoned property into the hands of new owners ready to reinvest in the city.

The problem with renewed enforcement was that the city restarted tax collection without fixing the administrative systems that make tax collection fair. A majority of Detroit homes (and by some measures as high as 84 percent of them), legal scholar Bernadette Atuahene found, had such distorted assessments that they violated taxpayer rights granted under the state constitution. The lower the property value—and thus the poorer the occupant—the more likely the assessment was excessive and unlawful. As the saying goes, it's expensive to be poor.

Another problem made the assessment distortions even worse:

Detroit has one of the nation's highest "effective tax rates" (the property tax payment as a percentage of market value). Like other poor, broke cities on the top-five list (including Bridgeport, Newark, and Milwaukee), Detroit applies a relatively high tax rate because otherwise its low land values make it impossible to afford basic services.

At the time Detroit boosted tax collection, Wayne County was also teetering financially. This fiscal turbulence mattered to Detroit homeowners, because the county functions like a collection agency for Detroit property taxes. If a landowner falls behind in Detroit, the account kicks over to the Wayne County treasurer's office, which applies hefty interest rates and fees to the tax debt. If a landowner fails to catch up within three years, the county can commence tax foreclosure proceedings. After a period of notice, the county takes title to the land, after which it can put the property up for sale. At its annual foreclosure auction, the county tries to sell foreclosed land for at least the amount of back taxes due. If that fails, a second round of the auction offers a $500 starting bid.

The majority of parcels put through the post-bankruptcy pipeline of tax foreclosure had been owned by banks or other landowners who had abandoned their property. But the auctions also put occupied homes up for sale. They became a "pageant of misery," write scholars Joshua Akers and Eric Seymour, as tenants or owner-occupants gathered desperately in a ballroom near a casino to try to stop their foreclosure through tax payment plans, or buy back their homes. Legal aid attorney Marilyn Mullane recalled the tension in the ballroom when an occupied home went up for auction. Detroit residents at the auction, Mullane recalled, often tried to bid on their own homes with their last few dollars. "Sometimes a woman would stand up and face her opponent, and say, 'Please don't take my home. This is all I have.'" Bidders might back down, and the ballroom would erupt in cheers. Other bidders kept going. Auctions always included residents weeping or yelling.

In theory, there were programs designed to protect individuals from foreclosure due to hardship. The federal government funded the Hardest Hit Fund to stabilize homeowners hit by the recession. Michigan received its share, and in turn allocated $52.3 million for homeowners in Detroit. But the state agency administering the program set unrealistic eligibility requirements, and most Detroit applicants for relief were turned away. So the City of Detroit lobbied for permission to use the funds for blight demolition instead. This choice enraged community groups, who wanted Detroit to prevent the displacement that drove blight rather than just wreck homes after families had lost them.

An owner who lost his or her home to a foreclosure faced the dilapidated rental market for housing. Landowners with properties too defective to secure tenants discovered that they could offer them to homeseekers in a second way too. After the Great Recession, land-installment contracts started reappearing across Rust Belt cities. In Detroit, land-installment contracts showed up with predatory features, such as interest rates as high as 11 percent, steep late payment penalties, and trigger clauses that could convert the contract into a lease. These terms alone can make these contracts exploitative, and further danger lay in the way a seller can write one for a home that needs extensive repairs to be safe, then shift the costs of repairs and taxes to the tenant/buyer. That means a buyer might invest in the structure, plumbing, or heating system, only to be forced to gift those investments to their seller as a penalty for a late payment. Worse, default on land contracts is generally treated as an eviction, without the legal protections of a foreclosure. After a protracted battle to regulate these instruments in Texas and New Mexico, where they were gouging low-income Latino households, Texas is home to a number of LLCs now peddling land contracts in postindustrial cities. Like any contract, these instruments can be written to advantage either party; needless to say, Detroit's vulnerable buyers are not the ones writing them.

Legal aid attorneys and researchers observed a predatory new business model across the city. Local scholars Joshua Akers and Eric Seymour gave it a bleak name: the "eviction machine." In a multiyear study tracking homes purchased at the county foreclosure auctions, they identified the regional landlords and real estate investment speculation groups operating this business model of "milking" properties for rent, flipping them to other investors, selling them through eviction-prone land contracts, or booting occupants and holding land for future gains. When the cheap, fast-moving process of bulk buying landed a speculator with a dud piece of land they could not profit from, he or she could stiff the city on taxes and abandon it. By using various limited liability companies (which one report accused of sometimes having shameless names such as "Exit Strategy April 2013, LLC"), speculators could even "tax-wash" their inventory: withhold taxes, abandon a parcel, then use a new alias to buy it back at the auction for $500. One landlord, Akers and Seymour found, ignored property tax bills totaling as much as six figures while still collecting rent.

So it was that in 2017, Detroit hit a new bottom. The United Community Housing Coalition (UCHC), Detroit's biggest legal aid organization for housing problems, played an automated message to direct calls. After a greeting and an option to hear hours and location, the message enumerated the many ways to lose a home in Detroit. If every single owner or tenant in Detroit had known to call UCHC for help and the phone system kept data on callers' selections in 2017 and 2018, the results would have looked something like this:

"If you are calling because you are facing tax foreclosure, press two."

> Between 2003 and 2017, tens of thousands of people in the city would have pressed two. About 150,000 Detroit properties were sold at an auction after a tax foreclosure—in a city with a total of 384,840 properties. In 2011 alone, 45,000 parcels went through tax foreclosure. A devastating 41 percent of them were occupied. Nearly 30 percent of the auctioned homes were occupied in 2015, and even after improvements, nearly 3,000 occupied homes still went up for auction in 2017.

"If you are calling because you're in need of help with mortgage foreclosure or a land contract problem, press three."

> Another 70,000 households would have pressed three to try to renegotiate a mortgage to stop a foreclosure between 2005 and 2011. Nearly 30 percent of the city's residential properties went through a mortgage foreclosure in that window. Another wave of mortgage foreclosures followed between 2013 and 2017. As the mortgage market dried up and the land contract market

grew, the number of known, new land contracts began to ex-ceed the number of new mortgages in the city. Land contracts are highly unregulated and hard to track, but they grew more in Detroit than in any other city and were disproportionately concentrated in Black neighborhoods.

"If you have a court judgment for eviction and need to find housing, press four."

If every tenant evicted in Detroit had called UCHC and pressed four, their phone system would have crashed. From 2014 to 2018, the city averaged nearly 30,000 eviction filings per year. Countywide, more than one in five tenancies ended up in evic-tion. By 2019, nearly half of Detroit households spent at least half of their monthly income on rent alone, propelling eviction trends forward.

"If you have an eviction hearing pending, need a motion filed, or have other landlord problems, press five."

Thousands of Detroit tenants might have pressed five for "landlord problems" relating to dreadful conditions in their units. An estimated 24,000 homes in Detroit lack safe, reliable electricity, heating, plumbing, and/or basic kitchen facilities, or they have holes and cracks that plague the unit with leaks or vermin. Flaking lead-based paint as well as airborne lead from nearby demolitions drive the highest rate of lead poison-ing in Michigan, with nearly 9 percent of Detroit's children testing positive for lead poisoning in 2016. In one ZIP code, 22 percent had lead poisoning. Asthma rates, which are driven by the dust, mold, and pests in unsafe housing, were three times higher among Detroit's children than national averages. An aging housing stock and disinvestment in properties, one report found, gives most tenants "few options but to choose between toxic structures."

UCHC was not able to take on all housing-related problems. If they were, the phone tracking system for Detroiters would have included other options too, such as these:

"If your water has been shut off, press eight."

Between 2014 and 2019, 141,000 people faced water shut-offs, as the city restarted aggressive bill collection with a shut-off penalty without effective waivers in place for people who could not afford to pay. In Detroit and its region, households below the poverty line pay an average of 10 percent of their monthly income on their water bills, more than double what is considered affordable.

"If you are living in a vehicle or an abandoned property, press nine."

In 2017, an average of about 3,800 people were unhoused each night in Detroit.

"If you have lost your home and no longer know where to send your child to school, press ten."

As the school district reorganized and consolidated to adapt to population loss, state policy on charter schools, and budget cuts, 195 Detroit Public Schools closed between 2000 and 2015. These closures combined with the high eviction and foreclosure rates in Detroit to drive extreme school turnover rates, which in turn harms child and school academic performance. During the 2015–2016 school year, 60 percent of the public and charter school children in Detroit attended at least two schools.

The final choice on the UCHC voicemail offers a dial by name directory. With all this land loss, displacement, and housing churn,

Detroit needed an army of housing lawyers and counselors. But anyone who pressed the option for the UCHC directory would have found only about thirty names there. All of the city's nonprofits are overstretched trying to help with one of the most ruinous housing crises in America. Less than five percent of Detroit tenants have anyone to represent them in eviction court.

For at least the first several years of the city's "restart," it failed to put up protective shields around assets that did not have much market value, but still had use value to the city's people. The city failed to anticipate or guard against a fundamental problem: in an era of this much inequality, in which residents are some of the poorest people in a nation where some people have tremendous wealth, residents cannot compete with outside money. That money did not just move toward the so-called "urban prairie" of vacant lots. It moved toward homes.

Early on, it was hard to see how vulnerable land ownership had become. "In Detroit, the city can grow," an entrepreneur told me in 2016, still flush with optimism about his recent move to Detroit from Manhattan. "In New York City, you have to crush things to grow." I understand what he meant, and it seemed true for land: Detroit had empty spaces that could still be used. Resurgent growth did involve the rehabilitation of some abandoned buildings, where fewer people were immediately displaced by the changes. Maybe it all could have been that way—growing only into the vacant spaces without touching the occupied ones.

But the Detroit housing crisis taught me that market growth doesn't always work that way. The cheapest, fastest properties to renovate, use, rent, or sell are often the best ones. Market demand moved toward occupied homes, or vacant lots that had been cleared and tended as urban farms. Housing laws to protect vulnerable tenants failed to protect them. Tax administration practices facilitated land turnover from low-income owners to speculators. Even in Detroit, *growth still crushed things*.

In a major study of the tax foreclosure crisis in Detroit, law professor Bernadette Atuahene warned that Detroit had become a "predatory city." Its administration relied on raiding scarce funds from its poorest residents to pay its bills. She was referring to actions and omissions by the government itself. But by 2017 or so, predatory also seemed like a fair description of the overall housing market in Detroit.

FIGHTING LAND LOSS

Angels' Night

Where do you start to stop a housing crisis of that scale? Detroit teaches that you get to work. Here are some of the people and organizations who did that, sorted by five categories of activism: expose, defend, pressure, reform, restore.

Expose

"Detroit has had more homes foreclosed in the past ten years than the total number of houses in several suburbs—or all of Buffalo, New York," said the lead of a *Detroit News* article in 2015 by Joel Kurth and Christine MacDonald. The article, like a handful of other transformative long-form investigations, assessed the scale of the crisis, identified its causes, and taught those mechanics to the public. With data and people-centered stories, journalists humanized the hardships and confusion of foreclosures to drive energy, resources, and expertise toward reform. In parallel, Detroit-based scholars dug into the legal and policy dimensions of the crisis in order to find a path to reversing it. Sarah Alvarez and Candice Fortman built an innovative news service called Outlier Media, which distributed information and scam warnings to the city's most vulnerable residents.

As a big city with major press outlets and research universities (which is rarely true in places of citywide poverty), Detroit has become the most important city in the Rust Belt for exposing the predatory real estate practices that have grown from rising inequality. In spite of the fast-moving nature of the crisis, scholars and graduate students at the University of Michigan and Wayne State University researched, evaluated, and recommended reforms to the city and partners.

Research and reporting were especially critical in Detroit. As city government hollowed out in the years before and during the bankruptcy, land administration became an understaffed, obsolete system. Large-scale repeat buyers could afford the research, relationships, and delays needed in that setting. Small-scale landowners and buyers could not. But this kind of information did not, on its own, equal power. As press about the price of Detroit's land raised the profile of the foreclosure auctions, drawing new investors toward them, advocates had to be there to defend occupied homes.

Defend

Michele Oberholtzer moved to Detroit as an aspiring writer about a decade ago. She took a day job at a mapping and land data company called Loveland Technologies, where her role was to bike around the city to homes listed in the foreclosure auction, snap a photo of them, and mark them as occupied or unoccupied. The sight of a white woman on a bike taking a photo of their home with an iPad brought many occupants out to investigate, and Oberholtzer soon found herself bearing news that many homeowners or tenants were hearing for the first time. She started coming equipped with basic information about key dates and resources to help landowners fight for their homes. It was her "radicalization moment," she says. She and a biracial group of other women built the Tricycle Collective, a nonprofit that crowd-funded $120,000 to help families with young children defend or buy back properties facing tax foreclosure.

Oberholtzer decided to start preventing foreclosures as a full-time job with the United Community Housing Coalition. At the Tax Foreclosure Prevention Project, UCHC provides counseling and workshops to help owners and tenants understand the legal process, pay their bills where possible, and use available channels to fight for their homes. Oberholtzer says she can't stand her own paperwork—administrative tasks for herself back up at home and in her inbox. But she developed a tolerance for long days of what she rebranded as "radical paperwork": tracking down details and filling out forms. She is not a lawyer, but any poverty lawyer would recognize the endless but essential work of helping people fight for themselves through government bureaucracies. Like other staff at UCHC and Michigan Legal Services, she pinned a heart hand-cut from felt to her clothes to remember what the paperwork was all about—homes and families.

A team including Oberholtzer, Ted Phillips of UCHC, Marilyn

Mullane of Michigan Legal Services, and others at both organizations developed a system for buying occupied properties in the foreclosure auction and returning them to their occupants. These early, improvised efforts to fight for homes one-by-one evolved into the Make It Home program, a partnership with the City of Detroit. By combining UCHC's client intake services, lines of legal authority held by the City of Detroit, a pool of philanthropic dollars, and zero-percent interest land contracts, the program allows residents facing foreclosure to buy their homes back via a payment plan. This public-private effort keeps the cost of the property limited to auction prices, which have ranged from $2,000 to $5,600 for Make It Home participants. In 2017–2019 alone, Make It Home successfully kept 1,100 occupied homes out of foreclosure. A foreclosure moratorium put in place during the COVID-19 pandemic then helped by pausing the auctions. An accompanying repair program made grants to households for urgent repairs to roofs, plumbing, furnaces, and the like. Oberholtzer moved into a position at the Mayor's Office in 2021 in hopes of further reform and collaboration to address the city's housing crisis.

Pressure

Detroit activists, many of whom are united under the Detroit People's Platform, have channeled their compassion and justifiable anger over the housing crisis into protests and campaigns to prevent foreclosures. Grassroots organizations in Detroit aligned in 2017 to form the Coalition for Property Tax Justice, led by legal scholar and activist Bernadette Atuahene, who built a research foundation to understand the tax foreclosure problem. Through virtual "People's Forums," rallies, and public hearings attended by as many as 500 people, these activists are pushing the Mayor's Office to develop a system for tax rebates for low-income homeowners overcharged by the city. Their work is now propelled by involvement and advocacy from local politicians, including U.S. Representative Rashida Tlaib and City Council President Mary Sheffield.

Meanwhile, under the slogan "Nobody Moves," Detroit Eviction Defense (DED) has drawn activists together weekly at St. John's Church to organize pressure campaigns, protests, tenant education materials, and free legal clinics. In partnership with the Urban Praxis Workshop, an academic research collective, DED organizers have proactively identified the addresses of homes likely to be in exploitative land contracts to help tenants know and pursue their legal rights.

At times, the fight against land loss in Detroit has been more confrontational than city officials might wish, but in keeping with the urgent stakes of housing activism. After centuries of discrimination, exclusion, and exploitation, many low-income residents of color in Detroit are fed up with private markets and public systems. DED has developed campaigns against "vulture developers" and other major buyers at the Wayne County foreclosure auction, whom their partner researchers have accused of writing predatory leases and land contracts for unsafe homes. After a Property Tax Justice Coalition meeting in 2017 in which the group decided to hold a protest outside the private home of the Wayne County Treasurer, I asked coalition member Monica Lewis-Patrick about the choice to let a protest become personal in this way. Lewis-Patrick's nationally recognized advocacy to bring down Detroit water bills has put her on the front lines of city poverty, so she had a clear answer to my question. "Today," she told me, "I met with a woman who has been sleeping in her car with her two babies for months because of a tax foreclosure by his office. It's them I'm worried about."

Reform

Under pressure from writers, voters, and activists, the city took steps to build an administrative system capable of protecting residents without letting scofflaw landlords and absentee speculators avoid their city taxes. The city had to, in short, build means-tested relief from property taxes.

The Wayne County Treasurer improved the notice systems for foreclosure and enrolled more than 23,000 eligible households in repayment plans by 2016. State, county, and city officials then established a property tax exemption program for qualified, low-income homeowners for their current-year taxes, as well as a payment plan to catch up on past debts. As a result of these efforts, the number of tax foreclosures fell 94 percent between their peak in 2015 and 2019.

The city government also tried to improve the accuracy of its property value assessments. In 2014, his first year of office, Mayor Duggan started a new citywide reassessment of land values—a lot by lot process that took three years and cost $10 million. This made over-assessment less likely going forward, but in 2020, a major investigative report by *The Detroit News* and the investigative reporting service *Reveal* found that the city tax bills between 2010 and 2016 had already over-taxed homeowners by an average total of $3,800. The article profiled the owner of a modest brick bungalow she had purchased in 2011 at a tax foreclosure auction for $4,800. Her tax bill that year, however, assessed her house as worth $57,000, yielding a bill of $2,600. In theory, she and other homeowners could use an appeal process to protest their tax bills, but few knew about this option or had the wherewithal to pursue its cumbersome paperwork. The fight for retroactive justice for homeowners in her position is ongoing.

A series of bills proposed or enacted at the City Council has taken on other dimensions of the housing crisis. In 2018 and 2019, City Council President Mary Sheffield sponsored a series of "People's Bills," one of which made it easier to qualify for Detroit's homeowners property tax assistance and exemptions. She began to advocate for a Right to Counsel ordinance in eviction court, which would fund representation for low-income tenants in eviction court (as is now the law in San Francisco, Los Angeles, and New York City), but this legislation was put on hold due to the pandemic. Councilmember Janee Ayers spearheaded a successful effort in 2019 to pass a "fair chance ordinance," which bars larger landlords from conducting criminal background checks until late in the application process, and then bars them from refusing prospective tenants purely on the basis of a nonviolent offense. In a city where an estimated 15 percent of adults have felony convictions, in a state that has spent as much as one-fifth of its general fund operating its prisons, fair chance reforms like this are a form of restorative justice.

City Councilmember Castañeda-López has been involved in many of the efforts to address the unaffordable water rates and the property tax foreclosure crisis. "The poorest of the poor," she says, are the ones who sustained the city as it lost population, whether they stayed by choice or not. The city, she said, cannot allow a "revitalization" that drained their resources or skipped their needs.

Restore

Most Detroit residents who lost homes in the housing crisis cannot get their properties back. But leaders in the city are nonetheless trying to turn the tide on Black land loss in Detroit. They are working to keep more land *in use* by local people, rather than stacking up in outside owners' investment portfolios. Visionary problem solvers such as Storehouse of Hope, Detroit Justice Center, and the Detroit People's Platform have begun to use community land trusts to allow owners to pool resources to purchase homes at auctions, then establish collective ownership and management structures.

In 2020, leaders in the city's urban agricultural movement invented another model of restorative justice. Tepfirah Rushdan, a director of Keep Growing Detroit, explains the problem they are trying to solve this way. Black farmers across the city are cultivating farms on abandoned lots and successfully selling produce from that labor, but they lack formal legal title to the land. The land may eventually be sold or auctioned out from under them, causing the farmers to suddenly lose a source of food and income, as well as their investments. The obvious solution is for the farmers to buy the land, but two things stand in the way: a few thousand dollars in hand, and the complicated, technical process of buying a lot owned by a public agency in Detroit.

Neither problem seemed hard to solve. "This is crazy!" Rushdan said she and her partners felt, seeing what small sums could secure farmers' investments. Even a fish fry, they thought, could fund purchases. With COVID-19 crushing Detroit with hospitalizations, job losses, and food insecurity, Rushdan worked with Jerry Ann Hebron of Oakland Avenue Farms and Malik Yakini of the Detroit Black Community Food Security Network to create the Detroit Black Farmer Land Fund to raise funds for land purchases and to provide technical assistance for Black farmers to acquire the parcels they had been farming.

On Juneteenth in 2020, the Detroit Black Farmer Land Fund launched as a GoFundMe page. It quickly blew past the initial $5,000 fundraising goal and eventually raised $65,000. Organizers put out a public call for applications from farmers and created a name-blind selection process. Thirty farmers received good news in October. In 2021, they did it again, raising $30,000. It has not been easy to work with the city in securing clear title to abandoned land, but their volunteers are working through the process, lot by lot.

The farmers seeking to buy property, Hebron says, are not asking for much. "We just want to be able to have a quality of life that we can sustain for our family, be healthy, create a great environment in our community—that's it." Indeed, it's the modesty of the Detroit Black Farmer Land Fund that is most striking. For a relatively trivial amount of money, the Fund is helping to line up the city's land with the needs of the city's people. After two centuries of Black land loss and racial discrimination in Detroit, the Black Farmer Land Fund puts a question in stark relief: *Why aren't we doing this for thousands of residents of color in Detroit tomorrow, before it's too late?*

As of the time of writing, Detroit's housing crisis is ongoing. Foreclosure moratoria put in place in 2020 and 2021 during the COVID-19 pandemic gave homeowners through March 2022 to catch up or enroll in the payment plans. An estimated 2,400 owner-occupied homes are at risk of foreclosure when the process reboots, as are thousands of tenants living in homes that have fallen behind on taxes. Campaigns to reimburse landowners for past overpayment of property taxes remain active.

But I think the city's government and advocates have stepped on to the right side of history. When you step on to the right side of *Detroit's* history, that's a proud place to be. Detroit is a city of radical imagination followed by hard work. I thought about this on Halloween in 2018, when the City of Detroit hosted an ordinary holiday celebration called "Halloween in the D." In the 1980s, Halloween in Detroit had been known for "Devil's Night," a dangerous, nihilistic pattern of arson before Halloween. International reporting on these fires attracted tourists to watch and participate, deepening both the stigma and the problem. Devil's Night brought days of mortal danger to neighbors and firefighters each year. But starting in 1995 and for more than a decade thereafter, Detroit overcame this pattern through "Angels' Night," a breathtaking volunteer mobilization led by City Hall and neighborhoods. On the nights before Halloween, up to 50,000 volunteers patrolled their neighborhoods,

guarded vacant properties, and illuminated the porches and yards of occupied homes. Groups of orange-clad volunteers rode bikes sparkling
with fairy lights. Youth competed in poster contests with themes such
as "Detroit: Yours, Mine, Ours." Angels' Night efforts put Devil's Night
to rest, and after a few quiet years the city laid Angels' Night to rest too.

Outside the city, no one noticed or reported on that story. Fire and
fear, I suppose, get more clicks than fairy lights and Black volunteers.
It will take an even bigger scale of imagination and work, in and beyond Detroit, to make the city a place of safe, affordable, and occupied
homes—not just a portfolio of investment assets. The backlog of need
is tremendous, but Detroit's people have gotten to work anyway. Law
and government will have to keep finding ways to help, or at least get
out of their way.

RES MIRANDA POPULO

The Art of Survival

During Detroit's bankruptcy, lawyers battled over whether the collection at the Detroit Institute of Arts could and should be liquidated. If
it had been sold, an art expert testified to the court, most of the artworks would be sold into private hands because "museums are unable
to compete against the formidable spending power of today's wealthy
private collectors." Artworks purchased by private estates would likely
vanish from public view entirely. Selling the collection according to the
timing of the litigation would also yield only "a fraction" of its full
market value. Buyers with enough capital to secure the art on short
notice would then be able to turn a profit by later selling the works "in
a less urgent, strategic fashion over a multiyear time frame." If museums
could not compete to buy at the front end, they definitely couldn't compete after a price jump. A collection like the DIA's, the expert warned,
could never be assembled in public hands again.

One of the pieces at risk of sale was a Renaissance painting from
1615 by Peter Paul Rubens called "Saint Ives of Treguier, Patron of Lawyers, Defender of Widows and Orphans." A poor mother clutches a baby
beside her little son, who reaches toward the saint. The saint hands the

widow a paper with good news—relief from eviction perhaps, or forgiveness of debts? The Saint depicted is associated with the Latin phrase, *Sanctus Ivo erat Brito, Advocatus et non latro, Res miranda populo.* It means "An advocate and not a bandit, a marvelous thing for the people."

The City of Detroit doesn't technically own the painting anymore, after the DIA's art collection was transferred to a nonprofit, though it is still on public display in the museum. The painting is a bittersweet reminder that the kind of sale averted for the DIA was not averted for tens of thousands of homeowners in Detroit—the widows and orphans of several generations of profiteering and abandonment. Too often across the city's history, law, lawyers, and government have been handmaidens of the destruction, suppression, or theft of Black wealth: marking segregation boundaries limiting where Black Detroit could live, indulging suburban expansion with exclusionary zoning, enabling extractive housing practices that targeted vulnerable residents, and restarting tax collection without shielding the poorest residents from displacement.

The art expert's warning—that the city's artworks would be sold for less than they were worth, then resold strategically after a jump in value—is what happened to too much of the city's housing. It was important to stabilize and restore land values in Detroit, attracting buyers back to the city. But there was so much vacant land to go around that the same could have happened without foreclosures of occupied homes. Displacing residents on the eve of recovery let the gains from the rising housing market land in the hands of too few people. Detroit's ten-year foreclosure crisis turned America's capital of the middle class into our capital of inequality.

The lawyers who defended the city and its assets, including the art collection, reduced Detroit's debt and gave it time to rebuild its administration. But it says something about our culture that the City of Detroit paid its bankruptcy lawyers and financial advisors $170 million (plus uncounted millions paid to creditors' lawyers). The total annual budget of UCHC, the biggest nonprofit legal aid office defending homeowners in a freefall housing crisis, was about $2 million. After our biggest city bankruptcy, moral debts to Black Detroit remain unpaid. In the end though, I think it is true to the city's deeper history that Detroit's world-class art collection remained open to the local public.

Art, music, and culture have helped the city's people make it through terrible hardships.

As the Allied Media Conference puts it, in words that are uncomfortable and also true, "Detroiters teach the rest of the world about how to survive and thrive in the wake of white supremacist economic violence and industrial collapse." One of those lessons, I think, is that housing security is a necessary component of any urban "recovery." Black Detroit's history of landownership has cycled through proud gains and damaging losses. But maybe history is the source of the city's courage today, too, teaches Detroit-based writer and social justice leader adrienne maree brown. When the wider nation was going through "impossible times," with mass shootings, natural disasters, and broken politics, she offered up that wisdom on her blog: "our visions are ropes through the devastation. look further ahead, like our ancestors did, look further. extend, hold on, pull, evolve."

Facing Forward

Inequality and the Problem of Border-to-Border Poverty

In 1907 and 1908, at age seventeen, Elizabeth Gurley Flynn traveled across the country as a labor organizer for the Industrial Workers of the World. In New York, she met a policeman weeping after a fire in a textile factory, where 146 workers jumped from eighth-story windows or burned to death because the exits were locked to prevent them from stealing. She visited Pittsburgh, an unforgettable landscape she described as "great flaming mills on both sides of the Ohio River, the roar and crash of the blast furnaces, the skies lit up for miles around at night, the smoke, gas-laden air, the grime and soot that penetrated every corner." In Butte, Montana, she visited a copper mine and an adjacent burn site with poisonous fumes that populated the cemetery with dead residents faster than the town attracted living ones. In the lumber camps of Washington and the coal mines of eastern Pennsylvania, she saw workers' "dreary and monotonous" existence far from families, with less than little invested in their sanitation, health, or education. Flynn recognized this world from her own childhood in the tenements of the South Bronx, where heat and hot water were rare, but bedbugs and cockroaches were not.

Most of the labor leaders of Flynn's era were exiled, imprisoned, or executed, including Joe Hill, the movement songwriter who nicknamed Flynn the "Rebel Girl," before he was killed by a Utah state firing squad. Nonetheless, in the forty years after Flynn's travels, relentless political advocacy by her and others yielded reforms and public investments that remade industrial communities.

Those generations confronted the disease and dangers of American poverty not just for moral reasons, but because fire, cholera, and political rage obey no borders. Taxpayers invested in opportunity and safety through public education, water treatment, sewage and transportation infrastructure, and modern fire protection. The interracial equality that Flynn fought for did not begin to progress until much later, but legal and political changes brought much higher levels of both "bread and roses" to the white working class. The harshest places became more like gateway cities, where immigrants who had arrived foreign and penniless could die as Americans, with optimism for their children.

In the postwar world of America's newly invented middle class, people could attain all kinds of things without paying extra for them: enroll a child in a baseball league, read books, picnic at a beach, call an ambulance, train for a trade, kick an addiction, put out the trash, learn English, watch a parade. Nine out of ten children born in 1940 had a higher household income when they turned thirty (adjusted for inflation) than their parents had enjoyed at the same age. In terms of income mobility, the 1940s were the best decade to be born in American history.

By the 1980s, the systems that had raised the working class from poverty to prosperity had begun to pull them back down. Both across and within states, income inequality widened. Communities of color skipped over in the first era of gateway cities found those investments declining just as the era of civil rights began. The share of Americans living in poor neighborhoods doubled between 1970 and 2009. The multi-decade convergence in incomes and standards of living between rich and poor regions came to an end. As machines replaced men and employers chose global markets for raw materials and manufacturing, hundreds of thousands of pink slips cut through families dependent on Pennsylvania steel, Alabama iron, West Virginia coal, Michigan manufacturing, Oregon timber, and the Pacific Naval Fleet. "[G]eography," writes journalist Phillip Longman, "has come roaring back as a determinant of economic fortune."

The Great Recession marked the one hundredth anniversary of

Flynn's travels. The post-recession recovery made inequality worse. In thirty-three states, including all four background states in this book, the top 1 percent of income earners took at least half (and up to all) income growth in their state between 2009 and 2012. By 2013, families in the top 10 percent of the national wealth distribution held 76 percent of all family wealth, while those in the bottom half held only 1 percent.

Poverty did not, of course, regress to a world Flynn would recognize. A child growing up poor now is more likely to lose her parent to a homicide or a prison term than to an industrial accident. We have more consumer goods and winter clothes, but the fear of shootings in high-poverty neighborhoods pumps residents' bodies with adrenaline and other stress hormones that are physically toxic to health. Starvation and food-borne illnesses are in retreat, but the illicit drugs that plague poor urban and rural areas today make moonshine look harmless. These places have better wages than they once did for full-time, over-the-table employment, but such jobs are hard to find. Children have better access to school, but to make it out of poverty, they need a bigger skill set than early schoolhouses had to teach. It is the extremity of hardship, not its precise forms, that is recognizable.

It is the same for local governments. After the recession, they seemed depleted in a way that echoed the past without repeating it. Broke cities started making international headlines: children poisoned by drinking water in Flint, debtor's prisons in the St. Louis suburbs, aging gas lines exploding in Allentown and Lawrence. Small towns and rural areas such as Obion County, Tennessee, drew attention as early adopters of cost-cutting practices that later became common. Obion officials resorted to subscription-based fire protection services, and showed they meant it when firefighters let a non-subscriber's mobile home burn to the ground—dogs, cat, and all. Signage along the scenic waterfronts of the Allegheny, Monongahela, and Ohio rivers spoiled the view with warnings such as this one: "These waters receive sewage from sewer overflows as a result of rain, snowmelt, and other events. Please limit contact with waters during these times."

Growing numbers of municipalities and counties struggle with concentrated poverty combined with a weak median income, which this book calls citywide poverty. Revenues decline while needs rise.

But it was not poverty alone that made local governments broke. A web of austerity measures constrained local authority to raise money and spend it. Since the 1980s, local governments have also needed to raise a growing share of their budget from their "own source revenue" (money they have raised locally), rather than revenues shared by federal or state governments. Anti-tax revolts, funded by wealthy individuals and businesses in most states, drained funding away from state and local government by setting strict voter approval requirements for any new taxes. Congressman Dan Kildee, U.S. Representative for Michigan's 5th congressional district, put it to me this way: "We're not offsetting the real drivers of decline. We have only applied one tool: Take a city with high service demand and low capacity. Then cut the capacity. It only increases the need for public services."

For a while, local governments for poor areas papered over steep losses in revenue. They cut costs by laying off staff and canceling programs. They postponed costs by taking expensive and high-risk loans, neglecting local infrastructure, and deferring compensation to public employees. They invented desperate, sometime oppressive, paths to new revenues. Now, almost fifty years after the "pay for what you get" era of local finance began, the future has arrived. Balloon payments are due on infrastructure, housing, education, pensions, and more.

Border-to-border low-income places are divided by differences in scale, politics, race, and more. Some are impoverished pockets within economically strong regions, others are surrounded by poor, broke places. Residents of some struggle most with finding a job, others with finding a home they can afford. In many majority-minority places, racial and ethnic discrimination in employment and credit markets helps explain not only why households are so poor, but also why they can't move away. Implicit and explicit bias that associates poverty with race and race with crime discourages public or private investment in cities of color, which has driven their deterioration. That same stigma then blocks coalition building and a sense of linked fate across historic manufacturing areas of all racial compositions. Poor, white strongholds of anti-elite populism rarely admit common ground with African American cities like Detroit or Camden. Neither type of community seems to realize how much they have in common with the primarily Latino or multiracial hubs of manufacturing and food production across the southwest.

This book has deliberately juxtaposed disparate places to build a foundation for future research and advocacy on citywide poverty. "If we have learned nothing else" from our recent history, writes urban scholar Kate Ascher, "it is that our biggest, bluest urban centers—and the outsize challenges they face—should not be the sole lens through which we look at America's future."

BROKEN COMPACTS

Systems Failure

"[I]f there has been a single problem facing contemporary democracies, whether aspiring or well established," writes political scientist Francis Fukuyama, "it has been centered in their failure to provide the substance of what people want from government: personal security, shared economic growth, and quality of basic services like education, health, and infrastructure that are needed to achieve individual opportunity." So it is with our local democracies. When they fail to provide basic services, we blame them—not because they are irrelevant, but because they are important.

Undoubtedly, there is criticism to go around. Many readers, I expect, will want more cathartic anger. This book is littered with past misdeeds, management mistakes, and overreaches by local governments. Public officials ended up in jail for misconduct ranging from sexting to bribery, kickbacks to nepotism. Favoritism and cronyism by some elected leaders undermined the interests of residents. They failed to fund pension commitments as they made them.

Places of citywide poverty, including those in this book, have signed unaffordable, giveaway deals on redevelopment projects like sports stadiums, shopping complexes, and market-rate housing to attract new, wealthier residents. They have displaced low-income and working-class people in the name of clearing out unsafe housing or lowering crime, only to have made those people more poor, consigned to worse housing. In the name of job creation, they have written deals that could never

survive a cost-benefit analysis, in which the tax incentives given to recruit business are scandalously out of proportion to what workers will
earn or other local gains. They have taken out high cost and high-risk
loans, such as swap derivatives and pension obligation bonds, which
investment banks increasingly market to desperate cities.

Scholarship and politics hotly debate the blameworthiness of these
choices and the numbers quantifying their harms. But I think a bigger problem amplified the effects of all those other errors: we failed
to invest in the people who live in poor places—their K-12 schools,
their community colleges, their housing, their neighborhoods. Local
and state systems largely ignored the mental health and family dissolution impacts of the crack and heroin epidemics. Courts and politics
systemically neglected segregated cities and neighborhoods of color. We
answered violence and addiction with little more than police, costing
society a fortune in broken families, lost potential, and taxpayer money.
Popular culture waited for the people of struggling rural places to move
away and scorned them when they didn't.

It's not that we didn't spend public money on broke places. Residents there live with the hardest edges of government power. I'm reminded of this by a makeup compact that I long carried in a Ziploc bag
because it no longer has a top.

This compact dates back to November 2019, when I visited Detroit's
eviction court in the central civil courthouse. Lawyers and judges can
enter the court through an expedited line with different rules, but I hadn't
traveled to Detroit with my bar card. I joined one of the public lines
crawling toward a metal detector and x-ray machine. An audio recording
welcomed us, then recited an exhaustive list of objects conceivably usable
as weapons to let us know they were all forbidden in court. As our line
inched forward, a man behind me verbalized the insult it conveyed to
hear this list droning on repeat. "Rocks and stones?! Really?!"

When I reached the front of the line, the security guard turned me
away. I had been warned that cell phones were prohibited, but I had
other objects that were not allowed: headphones, a couple of pens, a
bottle of water, an apple. With no lockers on site and no car, I left. I
came back the next day. My second time through that line, a guard
turned me away again for an item they had not noticed on the first pass:

a make-up compact, forbidden because of its mirror. I stepped out of the building and considered my compact—this cheap object, yet pricey to toss. Annoyed, I twisted the mirrored top until the hinge snapped. I dropped the mirror into a trash can full of other useful items that some of the poorest people in America had been forced to discard. I waited in line all over again.

All in all, even excluding travel time to the courthouse, it took me two hours over two days to make it into that courthouse. How often did people take an hour-long bus ride from somewhere across Detroit's 140 square miles only to be turned away for something they could not afford to throw away? Even if they did make it through security, how often did people miss their scheduled court appearances?

When I made it into a packed elevator on the second day, an older woman greeted us all, as if to calm her own nerves: "Good morning, everyone. Good luck on your cases." A twenty-something woman answered on our behalf. "Lord Jesus, stand by us." Two hours later, when her case was finally called in housing court, I saw our elevator prayer leader evicted. She thanked God aloud for the two extra days she got to live in her home because she had made it to court in person. Like 95 percent of tenants called into that court, she did not have an attorney to represent her.

Dozens of default judgments were entered against tenants who had not made it to court. But there were so many cases that the court door clicked open and closed constantly. Tenants waited on benches for their cases, holding paperwork in loose stacks or plastic bags. When their cases were called, one tenant spoke about not having hot water in months, another of flooding in his unit, another about his roof about to cave in from leaks and water damage. Another said her landlord had refused to repair her front door after a break-in, so she had moved out and withheld rent. She still wanted to move back in. The judge I watched wished every tenant good morning and good luck. She tried to be kind, sometimes encouraging tenants to find another place. But I didn't see a single tenant get any kind of relief other than extra time to move out.

Detroit has been infamous for its lack of local government services. That reputation is true. But that courthouse is also government in action. What if mornings like that were your main experience of public services? That courthouse processes about 30,000 eviction filings per year, which are judged and enforced by uniformed public officers. They take place in Michigan's busiest court, which was so notorious for poor customer service and case backlogs that the Michigan Supreme Court intervened in 2013.

Government is alive and well in policing too. Nearly 12,000 people per year are arrested in Detroit. Yet the criminal and civil systems that should process these arrests with integrity have faced layoffs, and they rely on ancient equipment in aging public buildings. Technically speaking, most of this work (other than police officers' pay) in criminal and civil justice is funded by Wayne County and the State of Michigan. But the general public knows little about who funds what in government. It should be no surprise that other than Josephine County, the lowest levels of faith I saw in the government were in Detroit.

The face of government in many border-to-border poor places has long been the police, the courts, and the child welfare system connected to both. Federal immigration enforcement belongs on this list too, as I was reminded on a trip to Lawrence, when U.S. Immigration and Customs Enforcement (ICE) officers conducted a round of arrests of people arriving for scheduled appointments to legalize their immigration status. All systems of law enforcement have the power to enact an unforgettable change in a person's life—to lose liberty, a child, or a home—which gives them an outsize role in forming public perceptions of the state.

In too many places for too long, state and local officials have triangulated a losing strategy for managing citywide poverty: "Attract New Residents, Subsidize Large Businesses, Defer Costs, Enforce Leases, Arrest People." This plan is a broken social compact with the people of poor places.

"FIRST WHO, THEN WHAT"

Resident-Centered Governance

"Designing a dream city is easy," Jane Jacobs writes. "Rebuilding a living one takes imagination." I am not going to try to offer a transformative vision of local politics, as if we could start over. We have a long road of reform ahead, and I intend to walk it the rest of my career. This book has tried to share the work of people rebuilding living places. Even though I have no master plan to offer, there is one theme that I learned from just about every person I spoke to for this book.

There can be no "recovery" for a city or county without prioritizing the safety and flourishing of the people who live there now. That means not just focusing on commuters, tourists, or future residents. Former mayor Daniel Rivera of Lawrence put it this way: "First who, then what." It's a reminder that his staff's work was for and about residents, not for outsiders or their perceptions. It's not always easy or obvious to nail the "what" part. For decades, we have done more to pursue the interests of people outside poor communities than those inside. Mayor Rivera had a wide dry-erase board in his office, near the conference table where he met with staff and constituents. He had written a message off to the side—part of his method for the "what" part. He laughed to show me how it's been there so long, he can't wipe it off. "Do something! Can we do it today!" it says in blue. In red, it says: "Stop explaining the problem, start explaining the solution!" For good measure, in green, the bottom reads: "Keep your head up!"

Examples of resident-centered good governance can be found all over the country. The idea that cities and counties should focus on shaping comfort, safety, and opportunity for their people should not sound radical. It sounds like democracy (governments should serve constituents), or even like family (take them as they are and go from there). It is both fiscally rational and humane. Poor places need, above all, an anti-poverty agenda that wraps around local people to provide stable, safe, nurturing, and challenging public schools; workforce training and development; trauma counseling for adults and children who have been victims and witnesses to violent crime; more compassionate and effective public safety efforts; safe, stable housing; and mental health and drug rehabilitation services.

Angela Glover Blackwell, head of the research organization Policy-Link, captures a similar lesson this way. Equitable policy, she says, means always investigating: "Who benefits? Who pays? Who decides?" These are the right questions every time state money is heading toward a local fisc, whether the government recipient is rich or poor.

To develop projects that benefit residents, in which they have a role in decisions, cities and counties must rebuild the networks undermined by concentrated poverty. "Trust and Relationships" would make a dull book title, but those words came up so often in my interviews that some days that title seemed most true. Again and again, people described how nothing could progress in their community unless they could repair trust in neighborhoods, trust in government, trust within families. They described how concentrated poverty and crime undermined cooperation and fueled the cycle of toxic stress. Higher rates of housing turnover means more strangers on every street. Fewer people sit on their front porches, walk to the park, and use public space. Less time in public reinforces social isolation and offers fewer chances to grow one's network of familiar faces. For low-income households who cannot afford to buy everything they need with money, damaged networks give people fewer chances to depend on one another for childcare, eldercare, and an emergency safety net.

In Stockton, advocates began facing this hardest problem, trying to heal the trauma driving fear, violence, and family dissolution. In Josephine, public officials faced the deep rot in locals' trust in government by hearing locals' grievances in town halls and offering straight facts, without tricks, in answer to assumptions that the government had spending problems, not revenue ones. In Lawrence, city leaders and anchor nonprofits worked to resew the social fabric of relationships upon which all the other work depends. They built social movements that lift good people into elected office and also hold them accountable; and circuits for information about new opportunities and resources. In Detroit, networks investigated the complex origins of local problems, then developed and pursued strategies for reform. There is no shortcutting the work of building trust among residents, forging networks of cooperation among shared institutions, and earning back public trust in local officials.

This book focused on the 2016 to 2020 period, never imagining what would follow it. When the COVID-19 pandemic hit, the importance of the resident-centered progress in these places became even more clear. Public and private leaders had to turn their systems toward urgent public health and economic needs. The cooperation and trust built in prior years was the backbone of these efforts. In Stockton, Maria Alcazar of STAND and her small staff of trustbuilders already knew the residents in their area, which allowed them to visit elderly people with food supplies, reassurance, and information. In the first months of the pandemic, social networks forged through soccer teams, farmworker advocates, low-rider clubs, and personal friendships allowed them to distribute PPE to undocumented farmworkers and food production workers exposed to COVID-19 but too poor to compete for protective supplies in the early supply crunch. Jerry Ann Hebron of Oakland Avenue Farms and her urban agricultural partners in Detroit were also central to emergency food aid across the pandemic, serving as an intermediary between restaurants' excess supply or former suppliers and laid-off workers. During pandemic lockdowns, the Josephine Community Library developed programs to move books, laptops, mobile hotspots, and virtual storytimes into residents' homes. At Lawrence Community Works, staff helped people apply for unemployment benefits, navigating paperwork problems as residents got snarled in overloaded, fast-changing safety nets. Across all these places, frontline organizations and people proved critical for distributing information that vulnerable residents would trust related to health risks, eviction moratorium rules and rent relief, vaccine safety, and more. Mutual aid became a better-known concept across the pandemic, but it has always been a strategy for survival in poor communities.

On the front of Stockton's city hall, a water-stained inscription reads: "To Inspire a Nobler Civic Life, To Fulfill Justice, To Serve the People." It will take some work to help local governments do that for a living. To start, we should judge and celebrate their progress on the civic engagement, quality of life, and life chances of those currently living in their borders. I think Mayor Michael Tubbs was the best mayor to occupy that city hall in several generations. But he was clear-eyed about the limits of his role. "Change is not going to happen because one person is elected," he said. "It's going to happen because one person is elected as a catalyst to bring a whole lot of people to become engaged in the process of creating change."

NETWORKS WITH UNICORNS

Seeing a Town for Its People

On a research trip to Flint in 2016, I visited a printmaker's shop downtown. I bought a gumdrop-pink shirt with a unicorn standing on a rainbow bursting into hearts. "Flint," it says in all caps, "now with unicorns."

I would not wear that shirt if I lived in Flint and my daughter had been poisoned by tap water. I would not wear that shirt if I had been the victim of a crime in the city. Flint has wounded some of its people, and they surely don't want to fly the city's flag. But I find meaning in the drawing and message anyway. Not just because it's rebellious, spunky, and hopeful, but because it's true. Flint does have unicorns.

One, named Debra Morgan, is a social worker who works with low-income elderly people. She helps them in small ways, like providing incontinence pads, and big ones, like utility assistance. Her husband is a pastor, and they have lived in the city since back when it had an industrial job base. After the water and lead poisoning crisis, their church and nonprofit Well of Hope was central to the city's humanitarian response. They host festivals and backpack giveaways to support local children and a giant community Thanksgiving. Morgan told me:

> We've heard the air being sucked out of the city. For the people who remain here, it costs a lot of money to stay in Flint. We could have left. Our friends ask: "Why do you all stay?" In our neighborhood, kids don't see their parents go to work, but they see us do that. We've bought coats, boots, and prom dresses for neighborhood kids. They sleep on our floors. The city may never come back. But we can't lose it from here. [She touches her heart.] We can't lose it from the heart. When you've seen what real community is, you can't settle for less than that.

Morgan is helping to provide a stable base on which the people of Flint can stand. She is helping those who are rooted in Flint as well as those whose most fervent wish is to leave.

This book has enabled me to meet many unicorns like Debra Morgan. I've often daydreamed about including portrait photography of them. Some are barely twenty years old, some middle-aged, some past retirement. Their skin colors are every shade. They have all kinds of body types. Some have tattoos or nose rings. Others would never wear pants without a tidy belt. Some would want to be photographed in front of a classic car, others in front of a street mural. Others would prefer to appear in a public park or a church. Some dropped out of high school, others attended elite graduate schools. Some worked inside government, some worked in the private sector, some moonlighted outside their day job. Some live in the town where they put their efforts, others don't. The work these towns need comes from many different kinds of people.

I know very well, as do they, that individuals aren't good enough. Local efforts aren't good enough. I googled a zillion scattered details to research this book, but my favorite was this question: "What do you call a group of unicorns?" The first answer was this: *Seeing a unicorn is believed to bring good luck and fortune, which is why a group of unicorns is called a blessing.*

The United States will need a lot of blessings to create twenty-first–century gateway cities. That work starts, I believe, with seeing these places for their unicorns, not just their poverty. It starts with listening to them and following their lead. "It is hard to know where to start on problems this overwhelming," one of my students commented after reading this book's introduction. "We don't have to know that," another student said. "They know what to do." I thought of Jasmine, Hector, Alfonso, Jimmy, Dave, Ken, Kate D., Jess, Dan, Luz, Shannon, Bernadette, Tepfirah, Raquel, and so many others in these pages. They set to work. Good government and a strong civil society grow from people who make them that way.

In Honor of a Gateway City

In their twenties, Joanne Peña and two of her brothers had made it out of postindustrial New England and into steady jobs in the Sun Belt. After a tour of duty with the U.S. Army, her brother Juan had become a homicide detective at the Prince George's County Police Department. Carlos was in the U.S. Marines in San Diego. Juan and Joanne were tight—"twins of the soul," as he liked to say. So Peña had followed him to a suburban town in Virginia.

With her GED and bilingual language skills, Peña landed the best-paying job of her life as a property manager for a real estate company. She had a toddler son whose father lived in the Dominican Republic. Her $42,000 annual salary seemed to her like a fortune, though in reality it could not sustain the cost of living. Her studio cost $1,200 in rent plus utilities. She couldn't reach her job without a car, so she took on payments to pay back $2,500 plus interest for her own "little hooptie," a well-loved Honda Civic. Even with childcare at an impossibly low cost—an elderly Guatemalan lady who took Peña's son for $25 a day—Peña's monthly after-tax income was more than spoken for. Some months she took out payday loans to keep up with her bills.

Getting to that point felt triumphant for the three siblings. Peña's mom had fled a U.S.-backed regime of poverty and terror in the Dominican Republic at age twelve; desperate to create roots in a new life, she'd had three children before she was eighteen and two more in the years soon after. She moved them across high-poverty towns in search of some kind of stability that never materialized: to Providence, Rhode

Island; to Lawrence, Massachusetts; to the Roxbury/Dorchester neighborhoods of Boston; sometimes back to Santo Domingo. Peña never
lived with her father. As the last born, Peña was generally ignored unless
she was being punished, and as a high school sophomore she was func-
tionally abandoned in Boston to live with a string of relatives and youth
programs. Peña's mother would later tell her children, in something like
an apology for the severe physical abuse across their childhoods: "Sometimes it wasn't that you guys were bad kids, it was just that I was so
angry. I felt powerless, uneducated, trapped."

During their years in Virginia, Peña and her brother Juan tried to
hold each other up, each struggling to become a more loving parent
than they had known themselves. But Juan died suddenly, and the floor
fell out from under Peña's life. She tried to keep her routine going in
Virginia after his death. She drove herself hard at work. She managed
to get herself and her son dressed neatly every day, but she fell into a
dangerous depression. Small acts of self-care, like doing dishes and taking out the trash, stopped. Her apartment went to hell. After a while,
she realized that "happiness was not living in Virginia." Happiness was
not earning $42,000 a year and listening to people talk about their new
shelving. Happiness, she said, was being closer to her family, "getting
back to roots and places that I know."

Peña moved with her son, then age five, back to Boston, but her
mother had no space, emotionally or physically, to take them in. Peña
applied for emergency housing, but with some of the nation's highest
rates of homelessness and poverty, Boston had no shelter beds in its own
metro area. The nearest spot was in Lawrence, so Peña ended up back in
one of the cities of her childhood. For a while, a homelessness program
gave her and her son cots to sleep on, located in the waiting room of
a dental office serving unhoused families. A room opened in a Lawrence family shelter, and Peña found a temp job commuting to Boston.
Just as the job wrapped up, her car brakes failed and her registration
expired. She couldn't afford either problem, so she left her hooptie in
street parking, where it was repossessed. The loan and abandonment
fees stacked up, eventually saddling her with $12,000 in debt. She with-
drew into herself. Her son was in kindergarten. "If I felt like taking him
to school," she said, "I'd take him. If I didn't, I'd stay in bed." She missed

several mandatory counseling meetings at the shelter. Non-compliance warnings accumulated unread in the mailbox she had stopped checking. A shelter staffer laid an eviction notice on top.

Peña was in a bad way. Nothing about it was exceptional for American poverty, and it would have been unsurprising for Peña and her son to end up on the street. But Peña was fortunate to have landed back in Lawrence. In part, that was true because the city held some good memories for her. She had spent relatively happy childhood years there with her brother: sledding in parks, getting strawberries at the grocery store where he worked, learning how to roller skate. Being there, in its own time, was helping her heal.

And Peña had landed in a city trying to do right by its most vulnerable residents. Enrolling her son in school linked her to Arlin Santiago, a social worker for homeless families at the Family Resource Center, built into the district by nonprofit and public agencies. Santiago helped Peña save her room at the shelter, then move into a studio with a state housing subsidy. She helped get Peña's son set up for school with shoes and a backpack, and called Peña when he missed class. Peña took steps on her own too, finding a job at a small business downtown called Heavenly Donuts. At Heavenly, Peña took home $200 per week for thirty hours (the after-tax minimum wage for Massachusetts), and she was mostly able to cover her son's childcare. Her apartment cost $850 per month, plus $80 in utilities, but the housing subsidy paid for $400 of those costs. "Me and my son, we'll make it work," she told herself.

On the second-year anniversary of her brother's death, by coincidence, Santiago came to find Peña at Heavenly. She was excited to tell Peña about a job posting: the city planning department needed an administrative assistant. It was perfect, Santiago stressed, given Peña's experience in property management. Peña wasn't so sure. But later that day, another person came in to tell Peña about that same job: a Lawrence police officer she chatted with from time to time at Heavenly. Her brother Juan had also been a police officer, so when the officer told her about the same job, she felt that Juan had made himself clear. She applied. She was hired.

Peña had moved to Santiago's side of the table, hustling hard for Lawrence and its future. She comes to life talking about plans for the city—this or that local investor buying real estate downtown, a database she is adopting that can make it easier for people to develop property there. In the months after settling into her job, she created a LinkedIn profile that said: "It does not matter how long it has taken me to get to this point, but I am exactly where I need to be."

She was excited to be behind the scenes for the city's future, her son's future. "The only thing that I'm putting out there into the world is my son. I can do little things here and there to better myself, but he's the one that's carrying the baton." She tried to build good memories for him. They went to all-you-can-eat wing night at the El Taller cafe. When the weather was decent, they walked along the greenway trail Groundwork Lawrence built to reach downtown. Sometimes she feels so impressed with him that she forgets he is still a little boy. "He was having a rough week at school," Peña tells me, "and I asked him, 'How can I be a better mom for you? What can I do so that you have a good day?' He said, 'I just want you to give me more hugs. And more kisses. And when I talk to you, I want you to listen.'" Peña is trying to do all of that, to climb out of the dark moments to be present for him. As she recounts this story to me, she pauses. "I wanted that too. Did I know to put that in words?"

During the COVID-19 pandemic, and after a building fire displaced her from her apartment, Peña ended up making her way to an affordable apartment with a yard in a Boston-area school district with smaller class sizes. She's too far from Lawrence to commute back to her old city job, and she can't afford a car, but she often thinks of Lawrence to restore her confidence. She thinks not only of her memories with her big brother, but also of the city's history. There is a seat by a canal where she used to sit to look at the site of a devastating fire in 1860, which she had learned about in school. "It physically hurts," she says, when she thinks of what happened there at the Pemberton Mill, when a five-story building collapsed and buried 670 workers. After a six-hour rescue effort, a lantern spilled and set the remains of the building, and all survivors of the collapse, on fire. She remembers those immigrant families before her who struggled—the heritage of Lawrence soil.

Peña explains why she had gone back to Lawrence to gather herself up again in the first place. "Everything is precarious. You buy anything at a store," she gestures to her shirt, "it's not meant to last." Even living situations, she says, don't last. So "you suffer through it," she says, and try to keep the weight off your children's shoulders. "You make it not seem like it's hard, so that they can have a Lawrence to come back to, like I did. The things that hurt when I was a kid—yeah, they hurt, but there were other things that were good. I was able to come back here and live in my own little pool of happy memories." She and Lawrence both suffered through hardship and abandonment. Both have some scar tissue. But it seems right, the way she and her gateway city looked out for each other.

When she was a child in Lawrence, Peña attended Wetherbee School, which was named for a local teacher and poet named Emily Greene Wetherbee. In 1898, Wetherbee wrote a poem about the city's mill workers, and maybe about the many others who were yet to come to Lawrence:

> There stands a busy city,
> I need not give its name.
> 'Tis young and enterprising,
> and not unknown to fame.
>
> . . . .
>
> And here from morn to even,
> at many a busy loom,
> stand patient toiling maidens
> who've found with us a home.
>
> . . . .
>
> And you, O favored sisters,
> who live a life of ease,
> lilies which toil and spin not,
> A lesson learn from these.

Author's Note

The roots of this book date back to my first job after college. I was a grant writer for Leadership, Education, and Athletics in Partnership (LEAP), a youth program in the public housing complexes of New Haven, Bridgeport, Hartford, Waterbury, and New London, Connecticut. These neighborhoods were hypersegregated, with thousands of Black and Latino families isolated in bleak housing and underperforming schools. But at LEAP, we got to see laughter and learning, too: middle schoolers writing stories in computer labs, teenagers reading to children, families cheering after dance performances, and camping trips in regional forests. LEAP was doing hand-to-hand anti-poverty work: the irreplaceable work of investing in people.

Soon after I left, government budget cuts forced terrible losses at the organization. The federal tax cuts of 2001 and 2003 caused dramatic funding reductions for AmeriCorps, which paid LEAP's high school and college student counselors. Other federal cuts led Connecticut to downsize its grants to programs serving children and families. In order for the state's wealthiest households to take home significant tax breaks, LEAP lost much of its funding to serve the state's poorest children.

LEAP had a strong base of philanthropy and other private funding, but most of those donors were connected to New Haven. That city had devastating levels of poverty, but as Yale University's unmovable home, New Haven still had some wealthier households. Strong social networks linked New Haven to suburban towns and donors. In LEAP's other cities, little private wealth remained within their borders. Their prosperous suburbs were gated by social walls. LEAP was forced to close its programs in every city other than New Haven.

Back then, I didn't know the word "disinvestment" or recognize that all five of these cities were citywide poor (as defined in the introduction) in a way that was distinct from poor neighborhoods in more mixed-income cities. But I saw what both of those problems looked like. I saw good anti-poverty work, and how hard it is to fund that work.

Unanswered questions from those days laid the research path to this book. How do local governments and nonprofits keep improving in spite of austerity, spatial inequality, and citywide poverty? So much is beyond their control, yet there is still urgent work to do locally, today. By the time I started this book, I felt overwhelmed by the forces of inequality and climate change, so I was drawn to people who *keep progressing anyway*. This project reflected my personal needs—my longing to recover the meaning and mission-driven community I experienced working at LEAP.

My plan was to write narrative portraits of border-to-border poor places through the people who care for them. That goal was elusive, I learned quickly, because a *place* has infinite depth, with heritage and history, complex physical and institutional environments, a state-specific legal context, and changing networks of people. I am a legal scholar (rather than a historian or social scientist), but my work was guided by Sara Lawrence-Lightfoot's qualitative methods for "portraiture," as well as practices from participatory action research and urban history. Over time, I narrowed the frame for each place to focus on a single advocacy theme.

This book's website includes a detailed methodology. The quick version is that I conducted about 250 interviews, nearly all of which took place in person during research trips between 2016 and 2020. In each city, I found people who believed in this project and introduced me to their networks, which in turn helped me connect to others. These early, instrumental navigators included Hector Lara, Kate Dwyer, Jess Andors, Maggie Super Church, Howard Davis, Alicia Alvarez, and John Philo. On research trips, I conducted interviews, attended community meetings, toured neighborhoods, observed programs, visited local/regional history museums, and chatted with locals. When I had complete drafts, I shared quotations, sections, or whole chapters with most of the interviewees named in the text. These conversations caught errors, gave people ownership of their own stories, and immensely increased the personal rewards of a project like this.

Early on, I felt self-conscious coming into a new town asking questions. Again and again, I was stunned by people's generosity and openness. In every city other than Detroit, the problem is not one of too many outside journalists and researchers, it's too few—or at least, too few who seem to care about good work in the town rather than just problems. All four communities here have been humiliated by bad press, and yet people there trusted me anyway—especially when they heard the hopeful title *The Fight to Save the Town*. People in Detroit (who have been relentlessly picked on and exploited by outside writers) had earned the right to slam the door on me. Instead, Detroiters were open and supportive as soon as they knew I was there to learn from the city, not to pathologize it. Aaron Foley wrote a terrific book called *How to Live in Detroit Without Being a Jackass*. I often imagined that my goal was similar: to write about Detroit without being a jackass. I figured that meant trying to understand the city's history, to acknowledge its contributions to American culture, and to show up for its modern-day strengths rather than just its sorrows.

I have worked hard to do justice to these places and their people, even as I'm all too aware of my limited angle of view. I'm a white woman living in San Francisco and a law professor at a privileged university, with no family ties to these places. I am an outsider to the events, hardships, and hard work recounted here. At times I have felt paralyzed by that separation and distance, unworthy to write about these places. But I believe that writing has a role to play in social change, and I believe in the work being done in communities that are not my own. I had something I wanted to contribute: the time to help lift up others' wisdom and connect work across towns.

Two dozen students left their mark on this book. Some answered research questions. Some commented on drafts or edited citations. Some transcribed interviews. Others workshopped ideas and challenges. Each one earned my admiration, which in turn pushed me to make something worthy of them and future students. Several Stanford Law School librarians chased down sources, facts, and data as though we were on a scavenger hunt together.

This research gathered more treasures than I could share in these pages. Every quote or name here stands for others who also taught me something. The cutting room floor is crowded with exceptional people doing exceptional work. *For every person named in this book, there are ten more who could have been named, deserved to be named, deserve to be supported.* Same for the endnotes, which stand in for the fuller list of written source material listed on this book's website. Some days, the four towns discussed here felt like exhibits to help prove the ideas of a few books in particular, including: Ian Haney López's *Dog Whistle Politics* and *Merge Left*, Jerry Frug's *City Making*, David Dante Troutt's *Price of Paradise*, Patrick Sharkey's *Uneasy Peace*, and Alan Mallach's *The Divided City*. Writing by Sheryll Cashin, Matt Desmond, Sheila Foster, and Richard Thompson Ford has also helped me understand the world I see.

I could not have battled my inner critic to publish this book without colleagues, friends, and family. Ian Haney López gave me challenging feedback and honored me with the license to speak with my own voice. Across COVID-19, Ian and his wife, Debbie Cortez, kept me and my family sane. So too, for three years and hundreds of hours, Julia Mendoza's friendship was part of my daily life and writing schedule. We laughed, cried, and kept working. Her forthcoming ethnography of the school-to-prison pipeline in Stockton will be a gift to the city. Detailed feedback from Nicole Allan, Solomon Greene, Scott Cummings, Richard Schragger, and Jerry Frug (plus workshop participants at a dozen law schools) pushed my ideas and text. My deans and colleagues at Stanford Law School believed in this project and gave me the time I needed to write it.

My agent, Wendy Strothman, guided my book proposal with rigor and purpose, leaving me with a debt to pay forward. She helped me find the just-right editor, Ben Loehnen at Avid Reader Press. Several formative conversations with Ben early on made my ideas and writing better. He gave me the freedom I needed to find my way, then applied his gentle genius as a line editor. After I implemented his redlines, I thought about how it annoys me when there is dog hair drifting in dusty tufts across my floor. I had given Ben a manuscript like that, with extra words tumbling across most pages. He helped me vacuum them up. Thanks to him, and to his terrific team of Carolyn Kelly, Phil Metcalf, and others at Avid, I'm less embarrassed to have readers' fine company in my house.

The fact of my family is inseparable from the fact of this book. Sometimes, my husband, Sade, engaged with the ideas here. Other days he just let me work through challenges out loud. He cut me short when I was looping through the same issues. Sometimes I thought my biggest problem was that he didn't do enough dishes, but now I see how much that missed the point. I see a single set of footprints as I look back over the journey of this project, but Sade was not carrying me. I was not carrying him. The single set is because after more than twenty years together, he is one of the two feet I put down on the earth each day. As the places here became my teachers, they became part of our daughter's childhood. She is richer for having learned from Detroit, Stockton, Lawrence, and Josephine, and this book is richer for her questions and ideas. My dad's confidence in me is the foundation on which all of my work stands.

My family passed through some hard times during this project, and I will always feel some sadness printed between the lines here. But so too, I'll think of the doctors and nurses who put several of us back together. Firefighters battled three rounds of catastrophic wildfire to count my family members among the living and their homes among the saved. Alzheimer's took so much of my mom away, but those years of loss and caregiving revealed my sister Jennifer's bottomless love and loyalty. My mom gave all of herself to raise both of us, but we had each other to hold her as she fell. My mom and my Grandma Lil could have been writers, if their lives had gone other ways. I write this book for them and because of them.

Notes

A full bibliography can be found at https://law.stanford.edu/michelle-wilde-anderson. Quotations not captured in these notes come from author interviews that took place between 2016 and 2021. The Author's Note contains more information about sources.

Prologue

ix *"If you think about it"*: David Lang, "Symphony for a Broken Orchestra," movie trailer by Temple Contemporary, video, 2:42, *http://symphonyforabrokenorchestra.org/about/*.

ix *"I don't want to abolish"*: Grover Norquist, "Conservative Advocate," interview by Mara Liasson, *Morning Edition*, NPR, May 25, 2001, audio, 7:30, *http://www.npr.org/templates/story/story.php?storyId=1123439*.

Introduction

3 *a for-profit company owned by*: Lisa Whiting, "Private Firms Protecting Josephine County," *Mail Tribune*, February 28, 2017, *https://web.archive.org/web/20170302183738/http://www.mailtribune.com/news/20170227/private-firms-protecting-josephine-county*; Laura Keeney, "Envision Healthcare's Acquisition of Rural/Metro Complete," *The Denver Post*, October 28, 2015, last modified April 21, 2016, *https://www.denverpost.com/2015/10/28/envision-healthcares-acquisition-of-ruralmetro-complete/*.

3 *second-poorest county*: "A picture of poverty in Oregon," *The Oregonian*, August 14, 2014, *https://projects.oregonlive.com/maps/poverty/*. Josephine's countywide poverty rate improved during the 2015-2019 period, but its rural areas continued to have some of the highest poverty rates in the state.

3 *opioid use outpaces*: "Prescription Drug Dispensing in Oregon, January 1, 2012-December 31, 2012: Schedules II-IV Medications Dispensed

in Oregon: Josephine County," Oregon Health Authority, November 2013, *http://www.orpdmp.com/orpdmpfiles/PDF_Files/Reports/Josephine.pdf*; "Prescribing and Drug Overdose Data Dashboard," Oregon Health Authority, *https://www.oregon.gov/oha/ph/PreventionWellness/Substance Use/Opioids/Pages/data.aspx.*

3 *county voters went to the polls*: "Past Election Results," Josephine County, *https://www.co.josephine.or.us/Page.asp?NavID=754.*

3 *murder of two elderly people*: Melissa McRobbie, "Details Emerge in Double-Slaying," *Mail Tribune*, June 18, 2015, *https://www.mailtribune .com/news/top-stories/details-emerge-in-double-slaying/.*

4 *"consider relocating to an area"*: Amelia Templeton, "Loss of Timber Payments Cuts Deep in Oregon," *All Things Considered*, NPR, May 21, 2013, transcript and audio, 2:38, *http://www.npr.org/2013/05/21/185839248 /loss-of-timber-payments-cuts-deep-in-oregon.*

5 *these metrics describe*: This definition is a combination of how sociologists define "places" (as a municipality or rural county government), how they define "place-based poverty" (where at least 20 percent of the population lives under the poverty line), and the typical measure for a "low-income median income" (a median income below two-thirds of the state number). When the place-based poverty defined by sociologists combines with a low median income, it becomes an even harder governance problem. This "place" unit of analysis is most salient to me as a scholar of law and government because places have their own elected officials, employees, and tax bases. They have legal duties to a specific territory and its residents.

5 *a 31 percent increase*: Daniel T. Lichter, Domenico Parisi, and Michael C. Taquino, "The Geography of Exclusion: Race, Segregation, and Poverty," *Social Problems* 59, no. 3 (2012): 373.

5 *$26,246 per year*: U.S. Census Bureau, "Poverty Thresholds: 2020," *https://aspe.hhs.gov/topics/poverty-economic-mobility/poverty-guidelines /prior-hhs-poverty-guidelines-federal-register-references/2020-poverty -guidelines (family of four with two minor children).*

6 *Others are rural*: Janet L. Wallace and Lisa R. Pruitt, "Judging Parents, Judging Place: Poverty, Rurality, and Termination of Parental Rights," *Missouri Law Review* 77, no. 1 (2012): 95–147, 117; Daniel T. Lichter and Kenneth M. Johnson, "The Changing Spatial Concentration of America's Rural Poor Population," *Rural Sociology* 72, no. 3 (2007): 331–358, 338. Rural residents are even more likely than urban residents to live in counties where at least one in every five people lives in poverty.

6 *low rates of college attainment*: David Autor, "The Faltering Escalator of Urban Opportunity," MIT Work of the Future, 2020, *http://workofthefuture .mit.edu/wp-content/uploads/2020/09/2020-Research-Brief-Autor.pdf.*

6 *the way people sort at bigger scales . . . and at smaller ones*: Richard Florida, *The New Urban Crisis: How Our Cities Are Increasing Inequality, Deepening Segregation, and Failing the Middle Class—and What We Can Do About It* (New York: Basic Books, 2017); Alan Mallach, *The Divided City: Poverty and Prosperity in Urban America* (Washington: Island Press, 2018); David Dante Troutt, *The Price of Paradise: The Costs of Inequality and a Vision for a More Equitable America* (New York: New York University Press, 2013).

6 *Since 1980, the wealthiest regions*: Robert Manduca, "The Contribution of National Income Inequality to Regional Economic Divergence," *Social Forces* 98, no. 2 (December 2019): 622–648.

6 *In thirty-one states*: "U.S. Metro Economies GMP and Employment Report: 2015–2017," U.S. Conference of Mayors, last modified January 20, 2016, *https://www.usmayors.org/2016/01/20/u-s-metro-economies -gmp-and-employment-report-2015-2017/*; Alan Berube and Carey Anne Nadeau, *Metropolitan Areas and the Next Economy: A 50-State Analysis* (Washington, D.C.: Brookings, February 2011), *https://www.brookings .edu/wp-content/uploads/2016/06/02_states_berube_nadeau.pdf*.

7 *Weak regions lacked*: Michael Storper, *Keys to the City: How Economics, Institutions, Social Interaction, and Politics Shape Development* (Princeton: Princeton University Press, 2013), 92–103.

7 *crowd into low-income suburbs*: Elizabeth Kneebone and Alan Berube, *Confronting Suburban Poverty in America* (Washington, DC: Brookings Institution Press, 2013).

7 *sociologists have shown*: Robert J. Sampson, "Neighbourhood Effects and Beyond: Explaining The Paradoxes of Inequality in the Changing American Metropolis," *Urban Studies* 56, no. 1 (January 2019): 3–32.

8 *depress a child's lifetime income*: Raj Chetty, Nathaniel Hendren, and Lawrence F. Katz, "The Effects of Exposure to Better Neighborhoods on Children: New Evidence from the Moving to Opportunity Experiment," *American Economic Review* 106, no. 4 (April 2016): 855–902; Ruth Gourevitch, Solomon Greene, and Rolf Pendall, *Place and Opportunity: Using Federal Fair Housing Data to Examine Opportunity across U.S. Regions and Populations* (Washington, D.C.: Urban Institute, 2018), *https:// www.urban.org/research/publication/place-and-opportunity-using-federal -fair-housing-data-examine-opportunity-across-us-regions-and-populations*.

8 *Federal and state governments*: *Policy Basics: Federal Aid to State and Local Governments* (Washington, D.C.: Center on Budget Priorities, 2018), *https://www.cbpp.org/research/state-budget-and-tax/federal-aid-to-state -and-local-governments*; Megan Randall, Tracy Gordon, Solomon Greene, Erin Huffer, *Follow the Money: How to Track Federal Funding to Local Governments* (Washington, DC: Urban Institute, 2018), *https://*

www.urban.org/research/publication/follow-money-how-track-federal -funding-local-governments.

8 *bundle subsidies and tax breaks*: Timothy J. Bartik, *Making Sense of Incentives: Taming Business Incentives to Promote Prosperity* (Kalamazoo: W.E. Upjohn Institute, 2019).

9 *broke local governments typically spend*: Michelle Wilde Anderson, "The New Minimal Cities," *Yale Law Journal* 123, no. 5 (March 2014): 1118–1227; Michelle Wilde Anderson, "The Western, Rural Rustbelt: Learning from Local Fiscal Crisis in Oregon," *Willamette Law Review* 50, no. 4 (2014): 465–513; Michelle Wilde Anderson, "Who Needs Local Government Anyway? A Consideration of Dissolution in Pennsylvania's Distressed Cities," *Widener Law Journal* 24 (2015): 149–180; Michelle Wilde Anderson, "Democratic Dissolution: Radical Experimentation in State Takeovers of Local Governments," *Fordham Urban Law Journal* 39, no. 3 (2012): 577–623; Mark Davidson and Kevin Ward, eds., *Cities Under Austerity: Restructuring the U.S. Metropolis* (New York: SUNY Press, 2018).

10 *among local government functions*: Michelle Wilde Anderson, "The New Minimal Cities," *Yale Law Journal* 123, no. 5 (March 2014): 1122–23.

10 *But they often share*: Michael B. Katz, *Why Don't American Cities Burn?* (Philadelphia: University of Pennsylvania, 2012), 155–161; David Brooks, "America Is Having a Moral Convulsion," *The Atlantic*, October 5, 2020, *https://www.theatlantic.com/ideas/archive/2020/10/col lapsing-levels-trust-are-devastating-america/616581/*; Megan Brenan, "Americans' Trust in Government Remains Low," *Gallup*, September 30, 2021, *https://news.gallup.com/poll/355124/americans-trust-government -remains-low.aspx*.

11 *curve of the number of manufacturing jobs*: Robert E. Scott, *Manufacturing Job Loss: Trade, Not Productivity, Is the Culprit* (Washington, D.C.: Economic Policy Institute, 2015), *http://www.epi.org/publication/manu facturing-job-loss-trade-not-productivity-is-the-culprit/*.

11 *number of manufacturing jobs*: Enrico Moretti, *The New Geography of Jobs* (Boston: Mariner Books, 2012).

11 *hubs of steel production*: Jon C. Teaford, *Cities of the Heartland: The Rise and Fall of the Industrial Midwest* (Indianapolis: Indiana University Press, 1993), 211.

12 *"Today an American"*: Moretti, *New Geography*, 22.

12 *took some of the hardest losses*: Ben Rooney, "Rust and Sun Belt cities lead '07 foreclosures," CNNMoney.com, February 13 2008, *https://money .cnn.com/2008/02/12/real_estate/realtytrac/*.

12 *a "lost decade"*: "'Lost Decade' Casts a Post-Recession Shadow on State Finances," (Washington, D.C.: Pew Charitable Trusts, 2019), *https://www.pewtrusts*

*.org/en/research-and-analysis/issue-briefs/2019/06/lost-decade-casts-a-post
-recession-shadow-on-state-finances.*

14 *most diverse city in America*: Deidre McPhillips, "How Racially and Ethnically Diverse Is Your City?" *U.S. News & World Report*, January 22,
2020, *https://www.usnews.com/news/cities/articles/2020-01-22/measuring
-racial-and-ethnic-diversity-in-americas-cities.* Stockton ranked as the
number one most diverse city in America in a 2018 index. Detroit
ranked first for the rate of increase in its racial diversity. For a rich analysis of "islands of integration" like Stockton and soon Detroit, see Sheryll
Cashin, *The Failures of Integration: How Race and Class Are Undermining
the American Dream* (New York: Public Affairs, 2004).

13 *representative group of twenty residents*: United States Census Bureau,
*American Community Survey Demographic and Housing Estimates, Stock-
ton, California,* 2019, *https://data.census.gov/cedsci/table?q=Stockton
%20city%20Race%20and%20Ethnicity&tid=ACSDP1Y2019.DP05*;
Gretchen Livingston, *In U.S. Metro Areas, Huge Variation in Intermarriage Rates,* Pew Research Center, May 18, 2017, *http://www.pewresearch
.org/fact-tank/2017/05/18/in-u-s-metro-areas-huge-variation-in-inter
marriage-rates/.*

14 *higher rate of foreclosures*: Ben Rooney, "Rust and Sun Belt cities lead
'07 foreclosures," CNNMoney.com, February 13 2008, *https://money.cnn
.com/2008/02/12/real_estate/realtytrac/.*

15 *"We all celebrate"*: Margaret LaPlante, *Images of America: Josephine County*
(Charleston, S.C.: Arcadia Publishing, 2016), 27.

16 *"Ever the velvet slippers"*: Elizabeth Gurley Flynn, *The Rebel Girl: An Autobiography, My First Life* (1906–1926) (New York: International Publishers, 1955), 127.

16 *blamed Lawrence for the regional opioid crisis*: Marc Fortier and Mike Pes-
caro, "Mayor Fires Back After Trump Blames Lawrence for NH Opioid Problem," *NBC Boston*, March 19, 2018, *https://www.nbcboston.com
/news/local/president-trump-singles-out-lawrence-as-source-of-new-hamp
shire-opioid-problem/125432/.*

19 *national study of all the local governments*: Anderson, "The New Minimal Cities"; Anderson, "The Western, Rural Rustbelt"; Anderson, "Who
Needs Local Government Anyway?"; Anderson, "Democratic Dissolution." These states include Michigan, Rhode Island, Oregon, Pennsylvania, California, New York, and Tennessee.

21 *"the darkest evening . . . miles to go"*: Robert Frost, "Stopping by Woods
on a Snowy Evening," in *The Poetry of Robert Frost*, ed. Edward Connery
Lathem (New York: Henry Holt and Company, 1923).

25 *"City of Ruins"*: Chris Hedges, "City of Ruins," *The Nation*, November 4,
2010; Matt Taibbi, "Apocalypse, New Jersey: A Dispatch From America's

Most Desperate Town," *Rolling Stone*, December 11, 2013; Donald Trump, "The Inaugural Address," January 20, 2017, Trump White House, transcript and video, 34:00-34:46, *https://trumpwhitehouse.archives .gov/briefings-statements/the-inaugural-address/*.

25 Forbes *magazine*: Kurt Badenhausen, "America's Most Miserable Cities," *Forbes*, February 2, 2011, *https://www.forbes.com/2011/02/02/stockton -miami-cleveland-business-washington-miserable-cities.html?sh=d3 3244479f3b*.

27 *"pernicious circular logic"*: Mitchell Duneier, *Ghetto: The Invention of a Place, the History of an Idea* (New York: Farrar, Straus & Giroux, 2016).

27 *"quite how to pick rural America up"*: Allan Golombek, "Sorry *New York Times,* Rural America Cannot Be Saved," *Real Clear Markets*, December 18, 2018.

27 *39 percent of the country*: "Report on the Economic Well-Being of U.S. Households in 2018," Board of Governors of the Federal Reserve System, May 2019, *https://www.federalreserve.gov/publications/2019-economic -well-being-of-us-households-in-2018-dealing-with-unexpected-expenses .htm*; Kim Parker, Juliana Menasce Horowitz, and Anna Brown, "About Half of Lower-Income Americans Report Household Job or Wage Loss Due to COVID-19," *Pew Research Center*, April 21, 2020, *https:// www.pewresearch.org/social-trends/2020/04/21/about-half-of-lower-income -americans-report-household-job-or-wage-loss-due-to-covid-19/#many -adults-have-rainy-day-funds-but-shares-differ-widely-by-race-education -and-income*. At the start of the COVID-19 pandemic, only 47 percent of adults had emergency funds to last three months. That number was only 29 percent for Latino adults, 27 percent for Black adults, and 23 percent for lower income adults, no matter their race.

29 *"Obsolescence is the very hallmark of progress"*: Thomas J. Sugrue, *The Or- igins of The Urban Crisis: Race and Inequality in Postwar Detroit* (Prince- ton: Princeton University Press, 1996), 125.

29 *That 1971 plan*: Michelle Wilde Anderson, "Cities Inside Out: Race, Poverty, and Exclusion at the Urban Fringe," *UCLA Law Review* 55 (2008): 1095–1160; Laura Bliss, "Before California's Drought, a Cen- tury of Disparity," *CityLab*, October 1, 2015.

30 *Fifty years later*: Camille Pannu, "Drinking Water and Exclusion: A Case Study from California's Central Valley," *California Law Review* 100, no. 1 (2012): 223–268; "The Town That Refuses to Die," KALW, 91.7 FM, San Francisco, July 10, 2019, transcript and audio, *https://www.kalw .org/podcast/crosscurrents-podcast/2019-07-10/the-town-that-refuses-to-die*. Pannu notes that Tulare County marked Allensworth, for example, as lacking a future. Allensworth remains populated and proudly marks its heritage as the first Black town in California.

30   *Today, among those states*: Anderson, "Democratic Dissolution."

30   *Atrophy has yielded*: Kimberlé Williams Crenshaw, "The Unmattering of Black Lives," *The New Republic*, May 21, 2020, *https://newrepublic.com /article/157769/unmattering-black-lives*. Race propels this legacy of dangerous atrophy. A powerful recent piece juxtaposed the loss of Black lives from police and vigilante violence and the ways in which environmental racism and health care disparities have driven mortality rates in Black communities. Kimberlé Crenshaw challenges readers to witness the connection "between the intentional killings and the left-dyings[.]"

31   *"You can't say"*: Sonia Sotomayor, *My Beloved World* (New York: Vintage Books, 2014), 95.

32   *His incumbent opponent*: Richard Winton, "Stockton mayor arrested, accused of playing strip poker with a minor and giving them alcohol," *Los Angeles Times*, August 4, 2016, *https://www.latimes.com/local/lanow/la-me-ln -stockton-mayor-20160804-snap-story.html*.

CHAPTER ONE: *Stockton*

35   *Judhromia Johnson, Jr.*: "Edison High Student Shot Thursday Dies at Hospital," *The Record*, February 9, 2010, *https://www.recordnet.com/article /20100209/A_NEWS/2090320*.

35   *Fernando Aguilar, sixteen*: "Pair Arrested in Shooting Deaths of Two Teens at Party," *The Record*, July 13, 2011, *https://www.recordnet.com /article/20110713/a_news02/107130321*.

35   *Juan Juarez-Martinez, seventeen*: "Crime Stoppers (April 27, 2015)," *The Record*, April 26, 2015, *https://www.recordnet.com/article/20150426 /NEWS/150429709*.

35   *Xavier Javier Plascencia, eighteen*: Christian Burkin, "Family Disputes Gang Tie in Latest Slaying," *The Record*, June 16, 2011, *https://www .recordnet.com/article/20110616/A_NEWS/106160323*.

35   *Joe Xiong, fifteen*: Derek Shore, "Victim Recounts Stockton Backyard Birthday Shooting," *CBS Sacramento*, July 25, 2011, *https://sacramento .cbslocal.com/2011/07/25/victim-recounts-stockton-backyard-birthday -shooting/*.

35   *Jorge Angulo . . . was shot*: "Pedestrian Killed by Car Identified," *The Record*, November 15, 2011, *https://www.recordnet.com/article/20111115/A_NEWS 02/111119943*.

35   *Alejandro Vizcarra, sixteen*: Roger Phillips, "Tragic List Keeps Growing," *The Record*, January 5, 2012, *http://www.recordnet.com/article/20120104 /A_NEWS/201040314*.

35   *an eighteen-year-old named Angelo Peraza*: Barbara Zumwalt, "Four Killed

in Two Week Spree," *The Record*, September 14, 2011, *https://www.record net.com/article/20110914/a_news/109140316*.

35   *three other students*: Phillips, "Tragic List."

35   *a funeral home's online guestbook*: "Angelo 'Lolo' Peraza," *Tribute Archive*, *https://www.tributearchive.com/obituaries/3113018/Angelo-LOLO-Mark -Peraza/wall*.

36   *"Nothing ever prepares you"*: Roger Phillips and Christian Burkin, "Edison High in Shock," *The Record*, February 6, 2010, *https://www.recordnet .com/article/20100206/a_news/2060327*.

36   *With just one counselor*: "ACLU Releases New Data on Stockton Unified's Pattern of Wrongly Arresting Students," News, ACLU, June 6, 2017, *https://www.aclunc.org/news/aclu-releases-new-data-stockton-unified-s -pattern-wrongly-arresting-students*; University of California at Davis, Analysis of SUSD Data commissioned by the ACLU of Northern California, June 6, 2017, *https://www.aclunc.org/sites/default/files/Analysis _June-2017-Stockton-USD-Data-Report.pdf*.

36   *2,000 arrests of students*: *Over-Policing in Stockton Schools: A Report Card*, Stockton Education Equity Coalition, 2017, *https://www.aclunc.org /sites/default/files/Report_Card_SEEC.pdf*; SUSD Data Analysis, 4.

37   *1989, when a white man opened fire*: "Five Children Killed as Gunman Attacks a California School," *The New York Times*, January 18, 1989, *https://www.nytimes.com/1989/01/18/us/five-children-killed-as-gunman -attacks-a-california-school.html*.

37   *It was the worst K-12*: "List of School Shootings in the United States (before 2000)," *Wikipedia*, *https://en.wikipedia.org/wiki/List_of_school_shoot ings_in_the_United_States_(before_2000)*.

38   *Two boom boxes*: Lisa Fernandez, "Punjabis and Mexican Dance Together on July 4 and the Internet Goes Crazy," *FOX KTVU*, July 19, 2017, *http://www.ktvu.com/news/punjabis-and-mexican-dance-together-on-july -4-and-the-internet-goes-crazy*.

38   *Some families have centuries*: "San Joaquin Valley, Part of Foothills Home of Yokut Tribe," *Escalon Times*, October 13, 2020, *https://www.escalon times.com/209-living/san-joaquin-valley-part-foothills-home-yokut-tribes/*; Terry Jones and Kathryn Klar, eds., *California Prehistory: Colonization, Culture, and Complexity* (Lanham, MD: Alta Mira Press, 2010).

38   *Some locals of Mexican and Spanish descent*: George Tays, "Pio Pico's Correspondence with the Mexican Government, 1846–1848," *California Historical Society Quarterly*, 13, no. 2 (June 1934): 124, *http://www.mil itarymuseum.org/PioPicoCorrespondence.pdf*. Commodore Stockton spared no blood in conquering California, but afterward he proclaimed, "All persons of whatever religion and whatever nation who freely adhere to the new Government, shall be considered as citizens of the territory,

and as such shall be zealously and completely protected in their liberty of conscience, persons and property."

39 *They would cram into stagecoach*: R. Coke Wood, "The Rise of Stockton," *San Joaquin Historian* 9, no.1 (January-March 1973): 2, 4.

39 *People say that nearly every*: Michael Bennett, "On Lock Sam: In the Heart of the Third City," *San Joaquin Historian* 14, no. 3 (2000): 1–9, *http://www.sanjoaquinhistory.org/documents/HistorianNS14-3.pdf.*

39 *Thousands fled their island nation*: Dawn Bohulano Mabalon, *Little Manila Is in the Heart: The Making of the Filipina/o American Community in Stockton, California* (Durham: Duke University Press, 2013), 56. By World War II, Stockton was home to the largest community of Filipinas/os living outside the Philippines, earning the city's downtown the nickname "Little Manila."

39 *Filipino farmworkers migrated*: Maya Abood, San Joaquin Valley Fair Housing and Equity Assessment (Sacramento, CA: California Coalition for Affordable Housing, 2014), 30, *https://www.frbsf.org/community-development/files/SJV-Fair-Housing-and-Equity-Assessment.pdf.*

39 *as labor rotations brought workers back*: Mabalon, *Little Manila Is in the Heart*.

39 *where boosters claimed*: Mark Arax and Rick Wartzman, *The King of California: J.G. Boswell and the Making of a Secret American Empire* (New York: Public Affairs, 2003), 257.

40 *One hundred years of systematic recruitment*: Mabalon, *Little Manila Is in the Heart*, 69.

40 *From 1975 to the late 1980s*: Don Walker, "A Short History of the Southeast Asian Immigration to San Joaquin County," *San Joaquin Historian* 17, no. 2 (Summer 2003): 5, *https://web.archive.org/web/20190326134038/http://www.sanjoaquinhistory.org/documents/HistorianNS17-2.pdf.*

40 *embodies the racial violence*: Robert V. Hine and John M. Faragher, *The American West: A New Interpretive History* (New Haven & London: Yale University Press, 2000), 248–249; Lori Gilbert, "Our Diversity: Native Americans First to Call Stockton Home," *The Record*, November, 29, 2014, *http://www.recordnet.com/article/20141129/ENTERTAINMENT LIFE/141129569*; Benjamin Madley, *An American Genocide: The United States and the California Indian Catastrophe, 1846–1873* (New Haven: Yale University Press, 2016), 62. Treaties in 1848 and then in 1851 extinguished Mexican and Native land rights. On August 17, 1846, Commodore Robert Stockton issued a proclamation that "[t]he only effectual means of stopping [Indian] inroads on the property of the country, will be to attack them in their villages." The proclamation escalated calls for violence against native Californians, who were killed at numbers classified by historians as a genocide.

40 *The Ku Klux Klan*: Mabalon, *Little Manila Is in the Heart*, 94–95.

40 *Public officials assembled*: Brian Niiya, "Stockton (Detention Facility)," *Densho Encyclopedia*, *http://encyclopedia.densho.org/Stockton%20%28de tention%20facility%29/*. The Stockton Assembly Center detained more than 4,000 Japanese-Americans who lived across the county over a 160-day period in 1942. Nearly all families were then moved to an internment camp in Rohwer, Arkansas.

40 *Banks used racially restrictive covenants*: Mabalon, *Little Manila Is in the Heart*, 272–275, 335–342.

40 *City leaders bulldozed homes*: Mabalon, *Little Manila Is in the Heart*, 278–296.

40 *there are no plaques*: Javier Padilla Reyes, "What Has Changed? From Segregation to Discrimination," *Placeholder*, May 25, 2021, *http://www .placeholdermag.com/culture/2017/08/17/from-segregation-to-discrimination -what-has-changed.html*. Reyes shows how the historical consequences of redlining are easily visible in Stockton using CalEnviroScreen, a tool that produces scores for census tracts based on environmental, health, and socioeconomic factors. Formerly redlined Stockton neighborhoods are some of the most polluted and unhealthy in the entire state.

41 *federal funding allocated*: Brett Theodos, Christina Plerhoples Stacy, and Helen Ho, *Taking Stock of the Community Development Block Grant* (Washington, D.C.: Urban Institute, 2017), 3, *https://www.urban.org /sites/default/files/publication/89551/cdbg_brief.pdf*; Roger Biles, *The Fate of Cities: Urban America and the Federal Government, 1945–2000* (Lawrence: University of Kansas Press, 2011), 190, 316, 325, 332. The modern era of federal funding for local improvements such as water and sewer infrastructure, flood control, public facilities for children and the elderly, parks, and historic preservation began with the establishment of the Community Development Block Grant (CDBG) Program in 1974. The federal government slashed funding for this program from 1981 to 1992. The federal urban agenda in the 1990s focused on investing in police for crime control and tax incentives for businesses.

41 *Stockton is a big city*: *2019 San Joaquin County Crop Report* (Stockton, CA: Office of the Agricultural Commissioner, San Joaquin County, 2019), *https://www.sjgov.org/WorkArea//DownloadAsset.aspx?id=33165*.

41 *Two freeways and a railroad*: Lange Luntao, "A City With No Center," *Placeholder*, September 3, 2014, *https://www.placeholdermag.com/cul ture/2014/09/03/a-city-with-no-center.html*. Stockton native and community leader Lange Luntao wrote an exceptional history of how the city's major transportation infrastructure, especially its segments of Route 99 and Interstate-5, exacerbated the urban development character that the

city is now infamous for: segregated, deteriorated older neighborhoods; a struggling downtown; and the "unsightly and unsustainable" sprawl.

41 *has mostly lost its better-paid manufacturing*: Abbie Langston and Justin Scoggins, *Stockton in Transition: Embedding Equity in an Emerging Megaregional Economy* (Oakland, CA: PolicyLink, 2019), 2–4.

42 *that land is used*: Darrah, *Getting Political*, 216.

42 *Even in the national growth years*: U.S. Bureau of Labor Statistics, "Unemployment: Stockton City, CA (U)," *Local Area Unemployment Statistics*, BLS Data Viewer, accessed January 23, 2022, *https://beta.bls.gov /dataViewer/view/timeseries/LAUCT067500000000003*.

42 *One in four people*: U.S. Census Bureau, "Poverty Status in the Past 12 Months," *2015–2019 American Community Survey 5-Year Estimates*, accessed January 23, 2022, *https://data.census.gov/cedsci/table?q=Poverty%20 Stockton&tid=ACSST5Y2019.S1701*.

42 *Well over half of the tenants*: U.S. Census Bureau, "Financial Characteristics," *2015–2019 American Community Survey 5-Year Estimates*, accessed January 23, 2022, *https://data.census.gov/cedsci/table?q=housing%20 income%20stockton&tid=ACSST5Y2019.S2503*.

42 *More than one-third*: U.S. Census Bureau, "Financial Characteristics for Housing Units with a Mortgage, *2015–2019 American Community Survey 5-Year Estimates*, accessed January 23, 2022, *https://data.census.gov /cedsci/table?q=housing%20income%20stockton&tid=ACSST1Y2019 .S2506*.

42 *living wage income*: Philip Martin, Brandon Hooker, and Marc Stockton, "Employment and Earnings of California Farmworkers in 2015," *California Agriculture* 72, no. 2 (2017): 110, *http://calag.ucanr.edu/archive /?type=pdf&article=ca.2017a0043*.

42 *seven of the ten counties*: Cassie Hertzog et. al., *California's San Joaquin Valley: A Region and Its Children Under Stress* (January 2017), 5, *https://regionalchange.ucdavis.edu/report/region-and-its-children-under -stress*.

42 *Too many parents*: Adam Brinklow, "SF Driving Up Commute Times in Northern California," *Curbed*, April 25, 2018, *https://sf.curbed.com /2018/4/25/17280190/cars-traffic-commuter-commute-san-francisco-bay -area*.

42 *Nearly one in ten working adults*: Mike McPhate, "California Today: The Rise of the Super Commuter," *New York Times*, August 21, 2017, *https://www.nytimes.com/2017/08/21/us/california-today-super-commutes -stockton.html*.

43 *city's homicide rate*: David Bennett and Donna Lattin, *Stockton California Marshall Plan: A Violence Reduction Strategy*, Lecture, Stockton Violence

Reduction Symposium, February 8, 2013, *https://crime-data-explorer*
.app.cloud.gov/pages/explorer/crime/crime-trend to find more recent info?
Slides=1985-2012].

43   *one of the highest rates of incarceration*: California Sentencing Institute,
Total Incarceration Rate 2016, http://casi.cjcj.org/Adult/2016. County
courts vary in their use of incarceration relative to other ways of handling criminal justice matters (such as addiction treatment through a
drug court program or probation) and the length of sentences.

43   *transferring youths to adult criminal court*: California Sentencing Institute,
Juvenile State Prison Population 2016, http://casi.cjcj.org/Juvenile/2016.

43   *city's police department ranked twelfth*: Mapping Police Violence, *Police
Accountability Tool, https://mappingpoliceviolence.org/cities.*

44   *local news station reported*: "Man Shot, Killed Outside Stockton Movie
Theatre," *CBS 13 Sacramento*, April 25, 2014, *http://sacramento.cbslocal
.com/2014/04/25/man-shot-outside-stockton-movie-theater/.*

44   *more than $190 million in capital projects*: City's Brief in Support of State-
ment of Qualifications, *In re* City of Stockton (June 29, 2012), 33.

44   *"phantasmagoria of worn-out, mangled faces"*: Leonard Gardner, *Fat City*
(New York: New York Review Books, 1969), 122.

45   *One journalist wrote*: Joan Darrah, *Getting Political: Stories of a Woman
Mayor* (Sanger, California: Quill Driver Books, 2003), 221 (quoting Michael Fitzgerald of *The Stockton Record*).

45   *the "uncontrolled development"*: Darrah, *Getting Political*, 158.

46   *major raise in 2020*: Cassie Dickman, "Stockton City Council, Mayor,
Getting a Pay Raise in January," *The Record*, December 2, 2020, *https://
www.recordnet.com/story/news/local/2020/12/02/pay-raises-approved-stockton
-city-council-mayor/3796764001/.*

46   *By comparison, the city of Riverside*: Budget analysis on file with author.

46   *Stockton's housing prices fell*: California Common Sense, *How Stockton
Went Bust: A California City's Decade of Policies and the Financial Crisis that Followed* (July 1, 2012), 4, *https://www.heartland.org/_template
-assets/documents/publications/how_stockton_went_bust.pdf.*

46   *By 2011, 56 percent of mortgages*: Robbie Whelan, "Second-Mortgage
Misery," *Wall Street Journal*, June 7, 2011, *https://www.wsj.com/articles
/SB10001424052702304906004576369844062260756.*

46   *Reuters called Stockton*: Michelle Conlin and Jim Christie, "Stockton:
The town the housing boom broke" Reuters, March 19, 2012, *https://
www.reuters.com/article/us-usa-economy-stockton/stockton-the-town
-the-housing-boom-broke-idUSBRE82I0EJ20120319.*

46   *Property tax revenues*: *In re* City of Stockton, California, Debtor, 493
B.R. 772, 778 (Bankr. E.D. Cal. 2013).

46   *city cut nearly $90 million*: *City of Stockton*, 493 B.R. 772, 780.

46 *"Stockton committed"*: *City of Stockton*, 493 B.R. 772, 779.

46 *unaffordable pension obligations*: *City of Stockton*, 493 B.R. 772, 779; "How Stockton Went Bust," 8–9.

47 *By 2010, Stockton faced*: City's Brief in Support of Statement of Qualifications, *In re* City of Stockton (June 29, 2012), 33–35.

47 *Podesto also signed a twenty-year*: Gary Wolff, *Independent Review of the Proposed Stockton Water Privatization* (Oakland: The Pacific Institute for Studies in Development, Environment and Security, 2003), *https://www .inthepublicinterest.org/wp-content/uploads/stockton_privatization _review1.pdf*; Gary Wolff et al., "Private Sector Participation in Water Services: Through the Lens of Stockton," *Hastings Law Journal* 57 (2006): 1328-31; *Concerned Citizens Coalition of Stockton v. City of Stockton*, No. CV020397, 2006 WL 6111277 (Cal. Super. 2006).

47 *That deal did not stand up in court*: *Hidden Costs: The High Cost of Water Privatization Before It Even Starts* (Oakland: Public Citizen, 2014), *https://www.citizen.org/wp-content/uploads/acf2a8.pdf.*

47 *Layoff notices went home*: *City of Stockton*, 493 B.R. 772, 780.

47 *Remaining employees took benefit cuts*: *City of Stockton*, 493 B.R. 772, 779–80.

48 *police union rented a billboard*: Jeffrey Michael, "Do Stockton Police Care About Their City?" *Valley Economy* (blog), May 31, 2010, *http://valleye con.blogspot.com/2010/05/do-stockton-police-care-about-their.html.*

48 *"Homicides were at"*: *City of Stockton*, 493 B.R. 772, 780.

48 *The year 2012*: Joe Goldeen, "Epidemic of Violence," *The Record*, January 13, 2013, *https://www.recordnet.com/article/20130113/a_news 02/301130317.*

48 *Officers adapted to staffing shortfalls*: Tom DuHain, "Stockton police to focus on violent crime," *KCRA* 3 (Jun. 1, 2012), *http://www.kcra.com /article/stockton-police-to-focus-on-violent-crime/6397012.*

48 *"Arm yourself or get out"*: J. Joe Stiglich, "Oakland A's Pitcher Dallas Braden Goes Ballistic at Stockton Town Meeting," *Mercury News*, September 27, 2012, *https://www.mercurynews.com/2012/09/27/oakland-as -pitcher-dallas-braden-goes-ballistic-at-stockton-town-meeting/.*

48 *By 2012*: Kurt Badenhausen, "America's Most Miserable Cities," *Forbes*, February 2, 2011, *http://www.forbes.com/2011/02/02/stockton-miami -cleveland-business-washington-miserable-cities.html.*

49 *San Joaquin County Grand Jury Report*: San Joaquin County Grand Jury, *South Stockton Quality of Life: As the South Side Goes, So Goes Stockton*, Case Number 1414, 2015, 1, *http://standaffordablehousing.org/wp-con tent/uploads/2015/06/Grand-Jury-Report-on-South-Stockton-5-13-15 .pdf?44cce4.*

49 *"Lord, please help us."*: Michelle Conlin and Jim Christie, "Stockton: The

Town the Housing Boom Broke," *Reuters*, March 19, 2012, *https://www
.reuters.com/article/us-usa-economy-stockton/stockton-the-town-the-housing
-boom-broke-idUSBRE82I0EJ20120319.*

49   *city council voted*: City of Stockton, "City of Stockton Files for Chapter
      9 Bankruptcy Protection," news release, June 28, 2012, *http://www.stock
      tonca.gov/files/News_2012_6_28_BankruptcyPetition.pdf.*

50   *Stockton's high-income Lincoln Village*: Joint Center for Political and Eco-
      nomic Studies, *Place Matters for Health in the San Joaquin Valley: Ensur-
      ing Opportunities for Good Health for All*, March 2012, 17, *https://www
      .nationalcollaborative.org/wp-content/uploads/2016/02/PLACE-MAT
      TERS-for-Health-in-San-Joaquin-Valley.pdf;* Joe Goldeen, "Two Neigh-
      borhoods, Years Apart," *Record*, March 1, 2012, *https://www.recordnet
      .com/article/20120301/A_NEWS/203010317.*

50   *women's walking group*: Roger Phillips, "Crimes Rattle Victory Park," *Rec-
      ord*, September 25, 2012, *https://www.recordnet.com/article/20120925/a
      _news/209250318.*

51   *after Lara's arrival*: "We Can Solve Crimes and Take Care of Our Com-
      munity," Media Center, United States Congressman Jerry McNerney,
      February 22, 2013, *https://mcnerney.house.gov/media-center/in-the-news
      /we-can-solve-crimes-and-take-control-of-our-community.*

51   *According to court documents*: Petition for Nuisance Abatement and Receiv-
      ership at 1-9, *City of Stockton v. Singh*, No. STC-CV-UMCP-2016-5206
      (May 31, 2016).

51   *business was open to the public*: Petition for Nuisance Abatement and Re-
      ceivership at 8, *City of Stockton v. Singh*, No. STC-CV-UMCP-2016-5206
      (May 31, 2016).

51   *The store captured the paradox*: Alexandra Natapoff, "Underenforcement,"
      Fordham Law Review 75, no. 3 (2006), *https://ir.lawnet.fordham.edu
      /cgi/viewcontent.cgi?article=4241&context=flr.* This is a rich explanation
      of how under-policing in low-income communities of color often runs
      in tandem with excessive criminalization, punishment, and police shows
      of force.

52   *a tough place to run a nonprofit*: City of Stockton & Reinvent South
      Stockton Coalition, *Stockton Reinvention Tour*, June 2018, *https://ncg.org
      /sites/default/files/files/pages/ReinventStockton_June1_2018_Summary.pdf.*

52   *southside library closed*: City memo on file with author.

53   *early speeches rallied*: *True Son*, directed by Kevin Gordon (California:
      Jahanu Films & True Son Productions, 2014).

53   *church-based volunteers*: Kevin Parrish, "Faith, Hope, and Solidarity," *The
      Record*, March 21, 2012, *https://www.recordnet.com/article/20120321/A
      _NEWS/203210321.*

56   *Easy access to alcohol*: Rachel Davis, Howard Pinderhughes, and Myesha

Williams, *Adverse Community Experiences and Resilience: A Framework for Addressing and Preventing Community Trauma*, February 2016, *https:// www.preventioninstitute.org/publications/adverse-community-experiences -and-resilience-framework-addressing-and-preventing*. A recent report funded by the Kaiser Foundation, based in part on evidence from Stockton, defines "community trauma" in three dimensions: the socio-cultural environment, the physical/built environment, and the economic environment (including education).

58 *Two shootings at the store*: Petition for Nuisance Abatement and Receivership, *City of Stockton v. Singh,* No. STC-CV-UMCP-2016-5206 (May 31, 2016): 2.

59 *"in any sustained and meaningful way"*: *South Stockton Quality of Life*, 1.

59 *Stockton tied for first place*: Martha Hostetter, Sarah Klein, and Douglas McCarthy, *Health Care Improvement in Stockton, California: Collaboration, Capacity-Building, and Medicaid Expansion* (New York: The Commonwealth Fund, July 2017), *https://www.commonwealthfund.org/ publications/case-study/2017/jul/health-care-improvement-stockton-california -collaboration-capacity*.

59 *first mayor elected after bankruptcy*: Nashelly Chavez and Bill Lindelof, "Stockton Mayor Arrested, Accused of Holding Strip Poker Game at Youth Camp," *Sacramento Bee*, August 4, 2016, *https://www.sacbee.com /news/local/crime/article93717602.html*.

61 *supplemental metric developed at UCSF*: "Screening Tools," Aces Aware, *https://www.acesaware.org/learn-about-screening/screening-tools/*. Researchers developed an updated tool called the Pediatric ACEs and Related Life-Events Screener (PEARLs). California became the first state in the nation to reimburse health care providers for screening Medi-Cal patients for ACEs.

61 *revealed the scope of child abuse*: Kathryn Collins et al., *Understanding the Impact of Trauma and Urban Poverty on Family Systems: Risks, Resilience and Interventions* (Baltimore: Family-Informed Trauma Treatment Center, 2010), 4, *https://www.nctsn.org/sites/default/files/resources /resource-guide/understanding_impact_trauma_urban_poverty_family _systems.pdf*.

62 *these worrisome high scores*: Cecilia Chen and Nadine Burke Harris, *A Hidden Crisis: Findings on Adverse Childhood Experiences in California* (Center for Youth Wellness, February 2020), *https://centerforyouthwell ness.org/wp-content/uploads/2020/02/hidden-crisis-errataversion.pdf:6*. White and Black adults have roughly the same rate of ACE scores at or above four. Latinos have a slightly higher rate, and a group defined as "Asian, Pacific Islanders, or other races" has a slightly lower rate.

62 *an ACE score of six or more*: Ibid., 4.

62   *odds go up*: Ryan C. Meldrum et al., "Are Adverse Childhood Experiences Associated with Deficits in Self-Control? A Test Among Two Independent Samples," *Criminal Justice & Behavior* 47, no. 2 (2020): 166, 167; Joshua Mersky, James Topitzes, and Arthur Reynolds, "Unsafe at Any Age: Linking Childhood and Adolescent Maltreatment to Delinquency and Crime," *Journal of Research in Crime and Delinquency* 49, no. 2 (2012): 295, 298.

62   *an ACE score of four or more*: Devika Bhushan et al., *Roadmap for Resilience: The California Surgeon General's Report on Adverse Childhood Experiences, Toxic Stress, and Health* (Office of the California Surgeon General, 2020), Table 1, *https://www.acesaware.org/wp-content/uploads/2020/12/Roadmap-For-Resilience_CA-Surgeon-Generals-Report-on-ACEs-Toxic-Stress-and-Health.pdf.*

62   *more than five times as likely*: Chen and Burke Harris, *A Hidden Crisis*, 10, 12.

62   *risk of social outcomes*: Devika Bhushan et al., Roadmap for Resilience, 156.

62   *three violent ACEs*: Chen and Burke Harris, *A Hidden Crisis*, 14.

62   *drives a person's likelihood*: Bryanna Hahn Fox et al., "Trauma changes everything: Examining the relationship between adverse childhood experiences and serious, violent and chronic juvenile offenders," *Child Abuse & Neglect* 46 (August 2015), 165; Mersky et al., "Unsafe at Any Age," 298–99, 306–9; David Eitle and R. Jay Turner, "Exposure to Community Violence and Young Adult Crime: The Effects of Witnessing Violence, Traumatic Victimization, and Other Stressful Life Events," *Journal of Research in Crime and Delinquency* 39, no. 2 (May 2002): 226, 231–32.

62   *exposure to a toxin*: Devika Bhushan et al., *Roadmap for Resilience*, 7.

63   *They evolved to flood the body*: Gayla Margolin and Elana B. Gordis, "The Effects of Family and Community Violence on Children," *Annual Review of Psychology* 51, no. 1 (February 2000): 459–461, 462–464; Nadine Burke Harris, *The Deepest Well: Healing the Long-Term Effects of Childhood Adversity* (Boston: Mariner Books, 2019), 57–76.

63   *stress levels can become toxic*: Burke Harris, *The Deepest Well*, 54–55.

63   *adversity can trigger*: Charles F. Gillespie et al., "Trauma exposure and stress-related disorders in inner city primary care patients," *General Hospital Psychiatry* 31 (2009): 506.

63   *Trauma commonly triggers depression*: Keisha Carr Paxton et al., "Psychological Distress for African-American Adolescent Males: Exposure to Community Violence and Social Support as Factors," *Child Psychiatry and Human Development* 34 no. 4 (Summer 2004): 290–91.

63   *overeating or drug use*: Sunghyun Hong and Inger Burnett-Ziegler, "The

Frequency of PTSD and Subthreshold PTSD among African-American Women with Depressive Symptoms in a Disadvantaged Urban Neighborhood: Pilot Study," *Journal of Racial and Ethnic Health Disparities* 4 no. 6 (2017): 1069. Trauma can cause disorders other than PTSD or induce symptoms that fall below the clinical line for PTSD (known as subthreshold PTSD). In one study, 70 percent of women from disadvantaged neighborhoods who had experienced trauma show some degree of PTSD symptomatology.

63 *learn to wear a mask of aggression*: Kenneth Dodge, J.E. Bates, and G.S. Pettit, "Mechanisms in the Cycle of Violence," *Science* 250, no. 4988 (December 1990): 1678, 1681; Christopher M. Adams, "The Consequences of Witnessing Family Violence on Children and Implications for Family Counselors," *The Family Journal* 14, no. 4 (October 2006): 334–37.

63 *Patterns of harmful events*: Davis, Pinderhughes, and Williams, *Adverse Community Experiences and Resilience*, 12.

63 *feelings that a person is not safe*: Collins et al., *Understanding the Impact of Trauma and Urban Poverty on Family Systems: Risks, Resilience and Interventions*, 11–12.

64 *Even when a child or adolescent*: Karyn Horowitz, Stevan Weine, and James Jekel, "PTSD Symptoms in Urban Adolescent Girls: Compounded Community Trauma," *Journal of the American Academy of Child and Adolescent Psychiatry* 34, no. 10 (October 1995): 1357–58, *https:// doi.org/10.1097/00004583-199510000-00021.*

64 *"Hearing about violent events"*: Ibid., 1358.

64 *school performance goes down*: Christopher M. Adams, "The Consequences of Witnessing Family Violence on Children and Implications for Family Counselors," *The Family Journal* 14, no. 4 (October 2006): 334, 337. This describes developmental delays and lower academic achievement in children who have observed domestic violence against their mother.

64 *Trauma can affect*: Collins et al., *Understanding the Impact of Trauma and Urban Poverty on Family Systems*, 11.

64 *the natural "egocentrism"*: Burke Harris, *The Deepest Well*, 101.

64 *secondary health harm*: Emma Barrett, Katherine Mills, and Maree Teesson, "Hurt People Who Hurt People: Violence Amongst Individuals with Comorbid Substance Use Disorder and Post Traumatic Stress Disorder," *Addictive Behaviors* no. 36 (2011): 721, 723.

64 *major regional public health assessment . . . the city's highest-poverty neighborhoods*: San Joaquin County 2016 Community Health Needs Assessment, 39, 64, *https://healthiersanjoaquin.org/pdfs/2016/2016_CHNA_full_doc ument-narrative_and_health_profiles.pdf.*

65 *number of domestic violence*: Ibid., 13.

65 *More than 18 percent*: Ibid., 64.

65 *high school juniors reported*: Ibid., 66.

65 *Fifteen percent reported*: Ibid., 39, 64

65 *Yet San Joaquin County*: Ibid., 63.

65 *One-third of people who were abused*: Collins et al., *Understanding the Impact of Trauma and Urban Poverty on Family Systems*, 4.

65 *Parents' own trauma*: Collins et al., *Understanding the Impact of Trauma and Urban Poverty on Family Systems*, 1-2; Mark Assink et al., "The Intergenerational Transmission of Child Maltreatment: A Three-Level Meta-Analysis," *Child Abuse and Neglect* 84 (August 2018): 131, 132, 142. In a meta-analysis of eighty-four studies of child maltreatment, researchers found that the odds of child maltreatment (including physical, sexual, and emotional abuse, as well as neglect) were nearly three times higher in families of parents with their own history of child maltreatment. The study found that factors such as parents' social isolation, parents' young age, stress, poverty, attachment insecurity, maternal substance abuse, and parents' current violence victimization all compounded the risk of intergenerational transfer of mistreatment.

65 *Traumatized adults*: Collins et al., *Understanding the Impact of Trauma and Urban Poverty on Family Systems*.

65 *"buffering adults" can transform outcomes*: Assink et al., "Intergenerational Transmission," 142. Supportive relationships with non-abusive adults in both childhood and adulthood (along with other social support and an escape from poverty) are associated with lower intergenerational transmission of child mistreatment.

66 *Supportive relationships, nutrition*: Collins et al., *Understanding the Impact of Trauma and Urban Poverty on Family Systems*, 22.

66 *Mothers who suffered abuse*: Egeland et al., "Breaking the Cycle of Abuse," 1087.

66 *The crack . . . epidemic*: Donovan X. Ramsey, *When Crack Was King* (New York: One World/Random House, 2022).

67 *some of those traumatized children*: Matthew Phelan, "The History of 'Hurt People Hurt People,'" *Slate*, September 17, 2019, https://slate.com/culture/2019/09/hurt-people-hurt-people-quote-origin-hustlers-phrase.html. The phrase "hurt people hurt people" seems to have been popularized by self-help books, religious figures, and media. The psychological and biological truth of trauma is not that simple.

67 *an $850,000 grant*: St. Joseph's Medical Center, "Initiative to Address Trauma in South Stockton Receives $850K," August 1, 2016, https://www.dignityhealth.org/central-california/locations/stjosephs-stockton/about-us/press-center/initiative-to-address-trauma-in-south-stockton-receives-$850k.

68 *held out as a model*: Harold Pierce, "Stockton Emerging as Public Health Model for Toxic Stress Intervention," *Bakersfield Californian*, September 16, 2017, *https://www.bakersfield.com/news/stockton-emerging-as-public-health-model-for-toxic-stress-intervention/article_9d0c3d90-94d3-11e7-96f4-6b3d30fae5a8.html*.

69 *how to recognize the signs of trauma*: Maria Lotty et al., "Effectiveness of a Trauma-Informed Care Psychoeducational Program for Foster Carers—Evaluation of the Fostering Connections Program," *Child Abuse and Neglect* 102 (2020): 9. In a study of foster parents, for example, researchers found that those who received TIC training reported less child behavioral and emotional difficulties by the fifteenth month.

69 *Apu was proud to report*: *https://www.urban.org/sites/default/files/publication/100707/impact_of_the_national_initiative_for_building_community_trust_and_justice_on_police_administrative_outcomes_2.pdf*.

71 *police solved more cases*: Dan Lawrence et al., *Impact of the National Initiative for Building Community Trust and Justice on Police Administrative Outcomes* (Washington, D.C.: Urban Institute, 2019): 4, 36; *https://www.urban.org/sites/default/files/publication/100707/impact_of_the_national_initiative_for_building_community_trust_and_justice_on_police_administrative_outcomes_2.pdf*; Michael Friedrich, "A Police Department's Difficult Assignment: Atonement," *Bloomberg CityLab*, October 23, 2019.

71 *the office's civilian Ceasefire and Peacekeeper*: Jesse Jannetta et al., *Learning to Build Police-Community Trust* (Washington, D.C.: Urban Institute, 2019): 46–47.

71 *Mayor Tubbs recruited and secured*: Steve Lopez, "Column: Stockton's Young Mayor Has Bold Turnaround Plan: Basic Income and Stipends for Potential Shooters," *Los Angeles Times*, May 26, 2018, *https://www.latimes.com/local/california/la-me-lopez-stockton-money-05272018-story.html*; "The Solution," Advance Peace, *https://www.advancepeace.org/about/the-solution/*.

71 *medical care to treat gunshot injuries*: Mike McLively, October 17, 2017, letter of support for Funding Agreement with Advance Peace to Implement the Peacemaker Fellowship Program, *https://stockton.granicus.com/MetaViewer.php?view_id=63&clip_id=6064&meta_id=526071*.

72 *build an evidence-based plan*: Clese Erikson and Lydia Mitts, *South Stockton Promise Zone* (Washington: Funders Forum on Accountable Health, George Washington University, 2018), 5–6, *https://accountablehealth.gwu.edu/sites/accountablehealth.gwu.edu/files/CA%20-%20South%20Stockton.pdf*.

76 *This barrier dates back*: "About the Board," California Victim Compensation Board, *https://victims.ca.gov/board/*; Lily Dayton, "Most Survivors Want More Rehab, Less Punishment for Victimizers," Rosenberg

Foundation, August 23, 2016, *https://rosenbergfound.org/most-survivors-want-more-rehab-less-punishment-for-victimizers/*; Cal. Govt. Code § 13963.1. The Reagan Administration created a federal Victims of Crime Act Fund, which sets aside the fines and penalties levied against federal offenders, then distributes those funds to state victim support programs. California also uses substantial fines and fees generated by the criminal justice system for a victim compensation fund to help pay victims' expenses. In 2013, California began a competitive grant program to use surplus victim compensation funds to pay for trauma recovery centers, which offer counseling and a broad range of support to the victims of sexual assault, shootings, and other crimes; and the surviving family members of homicide.

76 *principles of freedom under law*: Lois Herrington and Ronald Reagan, "Remarks on Signing Executive Order 12360, Establishing the President's Task Force on Victims of Crime," April 23, 1982, *https://www.reaganlibrary.gov/research/speeches/42382b*.

77 *database is not publicly accessible*: "911 Calls," *The Record*, October 28, 2010, *https://www.recordnet.com/article/20101028/A_NEWS0201/10280315*.

77 *A 2016 state audit of this database*: The CalGang Criminal Intelligence System (California State Auditor, August 11, 2016), *https://www.voiceofsandiego.org/wp-content/uploads/2016/08/CalGangs-audit.pdf*.

77 *more than 100,000 people were listed*: Attorney General's Annual Report on CalGang (California Department of Justice, 2017) 3, *https://oag.ca.gov/sites/all/files/agweb/pdfs/calgang/ag-annual-report-calgang-2017.pdf*.

77 *dropped to 45,000*: California Department of Justice, Attorney General's Annual Report on CalGang, 2020, 1–4, *https://oag.ca.gov/sites/all/files/agweb/pdfs/calgang/ag-annual-report-calgang-2020.pdf*.

78 *wait five years after his last entry*: Retention Period for Adult Records, 11 C.C.R. §§ 754.4(a)(6-7) (2021); Criteria to be Designated as a Gang Member or Associate, 11 C.C.R. § 752.4(a) (2021).

78 *"Healing For All" bill*: Healing for All Act of 2017, A.B. 1639, August 20, 2018, *https://leginfo.legislature.ca.gov/faces/billNavClient.xhtml?bill_id=201720180AB1639*.

79 *She embarked on an ambitious campaign*: December 2020 Surgeon General report: "Roadmap for Resilience: The California Surgeon General's Report on Adverse Childhood Experiences, Toxic Stress, and Health," *https://health.ucdavis.edu/crhd/pdfs/resources/roadmap-for-resilience-ca-surgeon-generals-report-on-aces-toxic-stress-and-health-12092020.pdf*.

79 *she visited Stockton*: "New California Surgeon General Joins Community Groups in Stockton to Discuss Health Disparities," *California Pan-Ethnic Health Network*, January 22, 2019, *https://cpehn.org/about-us/blog*

/new-california-surgeon-general-joins-community-groups-in-stockton-to-discuss-health-disparities/.

80 *A local blog*: "The Chaos Machine: An Endless Hole," Invisibilia Season 7, Episode 2, April 29, 2021, *https://www.npr.org/2021/04/29/992017530/the-chaos-machine-an-endless-hole*; David Siders, "The Fall of Michael Tubbs," *Politico*, December 23, 2020, *https://www.politico.com/news/magazine/2020/12/23/the-fall-of-michael-tubbs-449619*.

CHAPTER TWO: *Josephine*

83 *The creek is named after*: Stephanie Flora, "Emigrants to Oregon in 1846," *http://www.oregonpioneers.com/1846.htm*; "The Applegate Trail Interpretive Center," Rogue Web, *http://www.rogueweb.com/interpretive/*. Crowley was part of an early party traveling on the Applegate Trail, which was intended as a less dangerous route than the Oregon Trail. For decades, Crowley's grave served as a trail marker for travelers crossing the region's forested mountains, and later to the gold miners who laid claim to Grave Creek's banks.

83 *According to a detective on the case*: "Suspect sought in death of girlfriend," *The Bulletin*, July 23, 2009, *https://www.bendbulletin.com/localstate/suspect-sought-in-death-of-girlfriend/article_3076ffa8-0f42-5ccc-a27a-9c608b52c025.html*; Chris Conrad, "Wolf Creek man charged in girlfriend's killing," *Mail Tribune*, August 29, 2009, *https://www.mailtribune.com/crime-courts-and-emergencies/2009/08/29/wolf-creek-man-charged-in-girlfriends-killing/*.

83 *When O'Dell was a boy*: "Suspect sought," Associated Press.

83 *His mother was then killed*: Ibid.

84 *On the cover of a history*: Ibid.

84 *Teddy Roosevelt's speech celebrating*: "The Man in the Arena Speech," The Theodore Roosevelt Center, *https://www.theodorerooseveltcenter.org/Blog/Item/The%20Man%20in%20the%20Arena*.

84 *The federal government had been sending*: "Governor's Task Force on Federal Forest Payments and County Services," *Final Report* (State of Oregon: 2009), 4, 12, 30, 78, *https://digital.osl.state.or.us/islandora/object/osl%3A18897*. The term "timber counties" can broadly refer to the thirty-three counties in Oregon that receive some share of the federal timber payments described later in this chapter. In several of these counties, including Josephine, at least 60 percent of the land is federally owned. These counties are most at risk of severe losses of general fund revenues when federal direct subsidies fall or terminate.

85 *the area around Grave Creek was governed*: Doyce B. Nunis, Jr., ed., *The*

Golden Frontier: The Recollections of Herman Francis Reinhart, 1851-1869 (Austin: University of Texas Press, 1962), 48 n.32.

85   *The Umpqua and Rogue River watersheds*: "The Cow Creek Story," Cow Creek Band of Umpqua Tribe of Indians, *https://www.cowcreek-nsn.gov /tribal-story/*.

85   *Coastal forests nurtured a rich Umpqua tradition*: Patricia Whereat-Phillips, *Ethnobotany of the Coos, Lower Umpqua, and Siuslaw Indians* (Corvallis, OR: Oregon State University Press, 2016).

85   *They lost more than half of their community*: George W. Riddle, *History of Early Days in Oregon* (Riddle, OR: Reprinted from the Riddle Enterprise, 1920), 56.

86   *In 1852, settlers accused the son*: Ibid.; Nunis, *Golden Frontier*, 47–48. According to a settler reporting on this event, "to the Indians, the boy's fault would not compare with the treatment their women had received from drunken white men."

86   *a vigilance committee—a group of white volunteers*: Hubert Howe Bancroft and Frances Fuller Victor, *History of Oregon* (San Francisco: The History Company, 1888), 369–79. In southern Oregon and northern California at this time, volunteer militiamen tracked and killed Native Americans deemed hostile or "annoying" to white settlers.

86   *The chief's son was easy to recognize*: Nunis, *Golden Frontier*, 47–48.

86   *Within four hours*: Ibid., 48; Riddle, *Early Days*, 56.

86   *They hanged the chief's son*: Ibid.

86   *The chief himself was subsequently murdered*: Cow Creek Band, "Cow Creek Story."

86   *settlers forced tribal members on a 160-mile journey*: Robert H. Ruby, John A. Brown, and Cary C. Collins, *A Guide to the Indian Tribes of the Pacific Northwest*, 3rd ed. (Norman, OK: University of Oklahoma Press, 2010), 107.

86   *Oregon legally established 1,642 square miles*: "Josephine County History," Oregon Secretary of State, *https://sos.oregon.gov/archives/records/county /Pages/josephine-history.aspx*.

86   *The county elected eight public officers*: Ibid.

86   *bands of volunteers continued to patrol*: Bancroft and Victor, *History of Oregon*, 369-79. For a general overview of the history and origins of posse comitatus in the West, see David B. Kopel, "The 'Posse Comitatus' and the Office of Sheriff: Armed Citizens Summoned to the Aid of Law Enforcement," *Journal of Criminal Law & Criminology* 104, no. 4 (Fall 2014): 761–850.

86   *Like most western counties at that time*: James J. Chriss, *Beyond Community Policing: From Early American Beginnings to the 21st Century* (London: Routledge, 2011), 50. The "continuing heavy presence" of the military in

western states—which was full of volunteer militiamen committing vigilante violence against Native Americans—suppressed the development of formal cities and towns with social services, such as fire and police.

87 *the rural township of Wolf Creek*: "Endangered gray wolf is found dead in Northern California," *Los Angeles Times*, February 6, 2020, *https://www.latimes.com/california/story/2020-02-06/endangered-gray-wolf-found-dead-in-northern-california*. Like many other places called Wolf Creek across the Pacific Northwest, Josephine's Wolf Creek township was named for the gray wolves who visited the riverbanks for water at night. Somehow those wolves seem symbolic. Every wolf in the state had been shot or poisoned through eradication programs by 1947. But sixty years later, wolves had crossed back into the state from the east, and northeast Oregon had its first new wild wolf pack. In 2011, one of its young members (tracked on GPS as OR-7 but nicknamed Journey) made a 1,200 mile trek across Oregon, into California, and back home again. He had become the first wolf in California in ninety years. He later sired a female, tracked as OR-54, who traveled 8,712 miles across the forest and mountain ranges of Oregon and California. She was shot in Shasta County in 2020, but the species had progressed across impossible odds. They refused to be wiped off the land that bore their names.

87 *a resurgent back-to-the-land movement*: James J. Kopp, *Eden Within Eden: Oregon's Utopian Heritage* (Corvallis, OR: Oregon State University Press, 2009). Southern Oregon and northern California had long been a place for seeking utopia, with one of the richest histories of communes in the country. In the early decades of the twentieth century, the region was home to agricultural and labor cooperatives offering an alternative to bursting industrial cities. In the Great Depression, a "back to the land" movement in the region focused more on survival, as people struggled to find a "place where a man stood a chance." Mid-century, at the peak of postwar anticommunism and the rise of suburbia, cooperatives and communes faded away, only to roar back to life in the region during the 1960s and 1970s. In those decades, new waves of seekers (including "refugees from affluence") established new communities of alternative religions, nontraditional family structures, communal housing, and sustainable lifestyles.

87 *Josephine County landed on the cover of* Life *magazine*: "The Youth Communes: New Way of Living Confronts the U.S.," *LIFE* magazine, July 18, 1969, 21.

87 *Leaders there published* WomanSpirit: Heather Burmeister, "Women's Lands in Southern Oregon: Jean Mountaingrove and Bethroot Gwynn Tell Their Stories," *Oregon Historical Quarterly* 115, no. 1 (Spring 2014): 61–62, 79, *https://doi.org/10.5403/oregonhistq.115.1.0060*.

87 *"verdant comfort of the gentle"*: "Spiritual Gathering of Radical Faeries," Nomenus, *https://nomenus.org/2018/07/sgrf-gathering-july-13-23/*.

87 *Masters started a radio show*: Howard Kurtz, "The Evangelist's New Pulpit," *The Washington Post*, November 29, 1990, *https://www.washingtonpost.com/archive/lifestyle/1990/11/29/the-evangelists-new-pulpit/46dd60c0-b2ca-4a07-8f2a-b9dab0e27eb3/*.

87 *For several decades, he counseled*: Roy Masters, "Cancer and Energy Loss," *Advice Line Radio Program*, January 4, 2018, produced by Foundation of Human Understanding, podcast, *https://www.blogtalkradio.com/roy-masters/2018/01/05/cancer-and-energy-loss-k9139*. As recently as January 2018, for instance, Masters was warning online radio listeners about, "What doctors don't tell you about Asthma Attacks! Every Mother's incessant impatience drains the adrenaline of her child to the point of breathless exhaustion and even passing out."

88 *Many locals in Josephine thought of Masters*: Edith Decker, "Preacher Roy Masters brought controversy, uproar to Josephine," *Daily Courier*, April 1, 2010, *http://web.thedailycourier.com/eedition/2010/04/01/Progress/3.pdf*.

88 *Masters broadcasted a show*: "About Mark Masters," Talk Radio Network, *http://markmasterstrn.com/*; "The Godfather of Right-Wing Radio," The Daily Beast, *https://www.thedailybeast.com/the-godfather-of-right-wing-radio*.

88 *after their operations had emptied the forests*: James Stevens, *Green Power: The Story of Public Law* (Seattle: Superior Publishing Company, 1958), 273, 25. The big forests of the Great Lakes region had been so heavily logged and swept by fire by 1920 that a first-hand account described their forests as an "abomination of desolation."

88 *"more dangerous than war"*: James LeMonds, *Deadfall: Generations of Logging in the Pacific Northwest* (Missoula, Montana: Mountain Press Publishing Company, 2001), 156–57. The industry promoted tales of Paul Bunyan—the "mythical boss logger" who "pulled the stumps with his teeth"—to teach that a real timber man wears a "dented hard hat" and is "too tough to feel pain, too brave to voice his fears, too stoic to complain about hazardous conditions."

88 *the "flannel-shirt frontier"*: Michael Hibbard and James Elias, "The Failure of Sustained-Yield Forestry and the Decline of the Flannel-Shirt Frontier," *Forgotten Places: Uneven Development and the Loss of Opportunity in Rural America*, ed. Thomas A. Lyson and William W. Falk (Lawrence, Kansas: University Press of Kansas, 1993).

88 *Most timber-related workers manufactured products*: Josh Lehner, *Timber Counties*, Oregon Office of Economic Analysis, May 28, 2013, *http://oregoneconomicanalysis.com/2013/05/28/timber-counties/*; Josh Lehner,

Historical Look at Oregon's Wood Product Industry, Oregon Office of Economic Analysis, January 23, 2012, *http://oregoneconomicanalysis.com /2012/01/23/historical-look-at-oregons-wood-product-industry/.*

88   *aligned Oregon towns with the rise and fall of the Rust Belt:* Amy Glasmeier and Priscilla Salant, "Low-Skill Workers in Rural America Face Permanent Job Loss," *Carsey Institute Policy Brief* no. 2 (Spring 2006): 2, *http://files.eric.ed.gov/fulltext/ED536116.pdf; Strengthening the Rural Economy,* prepared by the Executive Office of the President Council of Economic Advisers (Washington, D.C., 2010), 4, *https://www.agri-pulse .com/ext/resources/pdfs/r/u/r/1/0/RuralAmericaRpt27Apr10.pdf.* Rural areas experienced heavy job losses in the manufacturing sector between 1997 and 2003.

88   *But blue-collar jobs in southern Oregon were mostly nonunionized:* LeMonds, *Deadfall,* xviii, 70–73.

89   *At an Argentine sawmill:* Stevens, *Green Power,* 23. By 1933, a U.S. Senate report presciently warned that the success of foreign mills could lead to "far-reaching and utterly demoralizing economic and social losses to dependent [domestic] industries, to local communities, and to entire forest regions."

89   *In the earliest years of Western logging:* LeMonds, *Deadfall,* 46; Nathan Rice, "Seeking Balance in Oregon's Timber Country," *High Country News,* April 29, 2013, *http://www.hcn.org/issues/45.9/45.7/seeking-bal ance-in-oregons-timber-country.*

89   *Modern feller bunchers do the work of ten to fifteen men:* "Feller Bunchers Specs and Charts," Construction Equipment Guide, *https://www.con structionequipmentguide.com/charts/feller-bunchers.*

89   *During the recession of the early 1980s:* Vincent Adams and Dawn Marie Gaid, "Federal Land Management and County Government: 1908–2008," working paper RSP 0804, (Corvallis, Oregon: Oregon State University, Rural Studies Program, 2008), *https://ir.library.oregonstate.edu /concern/technical_reports/mk61rn05n;* Michael Blumm & Tim Wigington, "The Oregon & California Railroad Grant Lands' Sordid Past, Contentious Present, and Uncertain Future: A Century of Conflict," *Boston College Environmental Affairs Law Review* 40, no. 1, (February 2013): 63, *https://lawdigitalcommons.bc.edu/cgi/viewcontent.cgi?article=2094 &context=ealr.*

89   *the Pacific Northwest's timber industry laid off 20 percent:* Ibid., 206; Hibbard and Elias, *The Failure of Sustained-Yield Forestry,* 195–96. Even as timber-related *employment* fell steeply across the 1970s, Oregon timber *production and profits* continued to grow until a 1989 peak.

89   *a 22 percent cut in real earnings:* Hibbard and Elias, *The Failure of Sustained-Yield Forestry,* 206–7, 207; Nick Beleiciks, *Oregon Labor Trends:*

Oregon Sees Third Month of Modest Job Gains, Worksource Oregon Employment Department, December 2011. Measured in constant dollars, hourly manufacturing wages in Oregon fell from $10.68 to $8.38 from 1978 to 1990. Timber-related jobs continued to vanish even during the housing boom that preceded the 2008 recession because technology kept advancing. By 1988, before the timber wars of the 1990s, real per capita income in rural areas of Oregon was 77 percent of the state's urban areas, and educational attainment rates severely lagged the state's urban areas. Like all manufacturing economies, these differences set the region up for particularly big losses as the service and knowledge economy eclipsed the industrial one.

91   *the federal government shares 50 percent*: Blumm and Wigington, "Grant Lands' Sordid Past," 21.

91   *nearly three-fourths of the forests*: "Josephine County," Oregon Forest Resources Institute, last modified 2019, *https://knowyourforest.org/sites /default/files/documents/Josephine-state-economic-19.pdf#overlay-context=*.

91   *While the federal government did not otherwise pay . . . property taxes*: OR. REV. STAT. § 321.272; Governor's Task Force, *Final Report*, 14; Oregon Secretary of State, Audits Division, *Oregon's Counties: 2012 Financial Condition Review* (2012), 10 (hereafter cited in text as *2012 Financial Condition Review*), *http://www.cooscountywatchdog.com/uploads/8/7/3/0/8730508/sos _or_counties_2012_financial_condidtion_review_2012-17.pdf*. The federal government pays "payments in lieu of taxes" to cover any local services the forests might require. These formal PILT payments make up a smaller share of local funds.

91   *sharply discounted property taxes*: Oregon Department of Revenue, "How forestland is taxed in Oregon," accessed January 23, 2022, *https://www .oregon.gov/dor/programs/property/Pages/timber-forestland-tax.aspx*.

91   *Until 1990, there were few constraints*: Rice, *Seeking Balance*; Hibbard and Elias, *The Failure of Sustained-Yield Forestry*. In 1990, a laid-off timber worker said, "You talk to the old timers here and they'll tell you that [the timber company] said they had enough timber to last them for the next hundred years. Then they got greedy in the last four or five years and literally raped the ground, took all the trees and did very little planting. I've gone through two back surgeries from working in this mill. Now this happens [the mill closes]. Sure, I'm disgusted."

92   *nicknamed the "Department of Nothing Remaining"*: LeMonds, *Deadfall*, 169.

92   *tree farms take decades of growing time*: Rice, *Seeking Balance*; LeMonds, *Deadfall*, 22–23; Hibbard and Elias, *The Failure of Sustained-Yield Forestry*, 201–3; Dawn Marie Gaid, "Changing Federal County Payments and Rural Oregon Counties: Analysis of Policy Impact and Responses

from Loss of Secure Rural Schools Funding in Selected Oregon Counties," working paper No. RSP 0904, (Corvallis, Oregon: Oregon State University, Rural Studies Program, 2009), 14, *https://ir.library.oregon state.edu/concern/graduate_projects/f4752j29r*. "Sustained-yield forestry" promised to level out cutting with new planting—a big change from the old system when timber companies would leave behind a "stump farm" for a tax foreclosure or a firesale transfer. But sustained-yield tree farming never took hold widely enough, and most companies kept moving into virgin forest. Clear-cut logging meant that when land was replanted, it was "managed more like plantations than forests," with heavy use of herbicides to limit growth only to replanted trees.

92 *The U.S. Fish and Wildlife Service listed the owl*: Blumm and Wigington, "Grant Lands' Sordid Past," 26–39; Michelle W. Anderson, "The Western, Rural Rustbelt: Learning from Local Fiscal Crisis in Oregon," *Willamette Law Review* 50, (2014): 473.

92 *Between 1989 and 1999, 45 percent of the sawmills*: LeMonds, *Deadfall*, 170.

92 *By 2000, timber harvests on 24 million acres*: Jean M. Daniels, *The Rise and Fall of the Pacific Northwest Log Export Market*, General Technical Report PNW-GTR-624, (Portland, OR: U.S. Department of Agriculture, Forest Service, Pacific Northwest Research Station, 2005).

92 *"Some people think we're a bunch of dumb hicks"*: Hibbard and Elias, *The Failure of Sustained-Yield Forestry*, 210.

93 *Shops in the Pacific Northwest sold bumper stickers*: Jennifer Sherman, *Those Who Work, Those Who Don't: Poverty, Morality, and Family in Rural America* (Minneapolis: University of Minnesota Press, 2009), 36.

93 *President Bill Clinton and Vice President Al Gore's Northwest Forest Plan*: "Northwest Forest Plan Overview," Regional Ecosystem Office (REO), *https://www.fs.fed.us/r6/reo/overview.php*; Governor's Task Force, *Final Report*, 13. The president's Northwest Forest Plan (NWFP) was "a landscape approach to federal land management designed to protect threatened and endangered species while also contributing to social and economic sustainability in the region." The NWFP has been challenged again and again in efforts to increase harvest levels. Environmentalists and the timber industry are still, so to speak, at loggerheads.

93 *putting $1.2 billion into five years of funding*: Harriet H. Christensen, Terry L. Raettig, and Paul Sommers, tech. eds., "Northwest Forest Plan: outcomes and lessons learned from the Northwest economic adjustment initiative," General Technical Report PNW-GTR-484 presented to a forum (Portland, OR: July 29–30, 1997), 2 (hereafter cited in text as "Lessons learned from the NEAI"), *https://www.fs.fed.us/pnw/pubs/pnw_gtr484.pdf*; Elisabeth Grinspoon, PhD, Delilah Jaworski, and

Richard Phillips, *Social and Economic Status and Trends*, special report prepared for the U.S. Department of Agriculture, February 2016, 45, 74, *https://www.fs.fed.us/r6/reo/monitoring/downloads/socioeconomic/Nwfp 20yrMonitoringReportSocioeconomic.pdf*. These funds comprised the Northwest Economic Adjustment Initiative. Unemployment hit highs in 1992 and 2003 in the Oregon regions covered by the Plan, but then spiked to its highest level following the 2007–2008 recession.

93 *The job-training programs showed gains*: Rebecca McLain and Will Kay, *Northwest Economic Adjustment Initiative Assessment, Cave Junction, Illinois Valley, Oregon*, (Sierra Institute, 2007) (hereafter cited as *NEAI Report*), *https://web.archive.org/web/20071007231129/http://www.sierrain stitute.us/neai/OR_case_studies/Cave_Junction_OR.pdf*. As part of the Northwest Economic Adjustment Initiative, the U.S. Department of Labor directed a special grant stream between 1994 and 2000 for dislocated timber workers. A regional Jobs Council operated retraining and education services for 661 workers during this time. More than 75 percent of those workers did place in new jobs, but their new positions took home average hourly wages of between $8 to $10 per hour (approximately double the federal minimum wage at that time, but less than experienced timber and mill workers had earned).

93 *limited literacy and math skills*: McLain and Kay, *NEAI Report*, 27–31. A comprehensive evaluation of the retraining efforts found that the program was bogged down by the number of displaced wood workers with limited reading, writing, and math skills, which required using months of their time in the program on basic education rather than job skills. In addition, the retraining funds available for each worker did not last long enough: unemployment benefits and supportive services (like counseling and child care) lasted only six months or one year, but workers needed two years to complete a skills track at Rogue Community College.

93 *"Cussing at computers"*: LeMonds, *Deadfall*, 147.

94 *Meanwhile, the tax breaks and federal deficits*: McLain and Kay, *NEAI Report*, 30; Deborah A. Verstegen, "Education Fiscal Policy in the Reagan Administration," Educational Evaluation and Policy Analysis 12, no. 4 (December 1990): 368, *https://doi.org/10.3102/01623737012004355*. By the end of Reagan's second term, in 1988, vocational and adult education programs were funded 27 percent lower than in 1980.

94 *it did try to replace some of the public revenues*: Secure Rural Schools and Community Self-Determination Act of 2000, Pub. L. 106–393, 114 Stat. 1607, 2000; Bruce Sorte, Paul Lewin, and Bruce Weber, "Economic Impacts on Oregon Counties of the Termination of the Secure Rural Schools and Community Self-Determination Act (P.L. 106–393)," Working Paper No. RSP 0805 (Corvallis, Oregon: Oregon State

University, Rural Studies Program, 2008), 3, *https://ir.library.oregonstate.edu /concern/technical_reports/tm70n070r?locale=en*; Governor's Task Force, *Final Report*, 16. In 1993, through the so-called "spotted owl safety net," Congress decoupled federal subsidies in the region from harvest revenues in western counties with the Omnibus Reconciliation Act of 1993, and then statewide with the Secure Rural Schools and Community Self-Determination Act of 2000, or "SRS Act."

94 *In 1993, Congress began*: Gaid, *Changing Federal County Payments and Rural Oregon Counties*, 10.

94 *Oregon's timber counties took home a full half*: Ibid.

94 *Federal funding has been saved*: Bruce Weber, Paul Lewin, and Bruce Sorte, "Economic Impacts on Oregon of the Termination of Secure Rural Schools Payments to Counties: 2011 Update 2–3," Working Paper No. RSP 1101 (Corvallis, Oregon: Oregon State University, Rural Studies Program, 2011), *https://ruralstudies.oregonstate.edu/biblio/economic-impacts-oregon-termination-secure-rural-schools-payments-counties-2011-update*; Governor's Task Force, *Final Report*, 16; "FAQs for Title I-Secure Payments for States and Counties," U.S. Forest Service, last modified November 25, 2013, *http://www.fs.usda.gov/main/pts/securepayments/faqs*; "Secure Rural Schools Reauthorization," U.S. Forest Service, *https:// www.fs.usda.gov/pts/*. Even during this ramp-down period, the subsidies were substantial: In 2007–2008, federal subsidies for roads and discretionary spending in thirty-three Oregon counties totaled $230.2 million, with another $35.8 million for county schools. Since 2013, the federal funds have been reauthorized as unrelated amendments and additions to separate legislative packages.

94 *But backwoods recreation, fixed incomes*: Anne A. Riddle, *The Outdoor Recreation Economy*, Congressional Research Service report prepared for Congress, October 22, 2019, *https://fas.org/sgp/crs/misc/R45978.pdf*. In 2017, the United States made $1.6 trillion through tourism, of which only $427 billion (or 27 percent) was through outdoor recreation.

94 *Some say the county's best shot*: Lehner, *Timber Counties*.

95 *young people in particular have left*: Oregon Secretary of State, *2012 Financial Condition Review*, 45. In 1950, one out of four Josephine residents were older than age fifty; rising to about half of the population in 2010. This shift could drive demand for health and social services while the local workforce is shrinking.

95 *Josephine's population is substantially older*: U.S. Census Bureau, "Population Estimates: July 1, 2019, (V2019)," accessed October 15, 2021, *https://www.census.gov/quickfacts*.

95 *One in five families with minor children in Josephine live below the poverty line*: Oregon Secretary of State, *2012 Financial Condition Review*, 45.

U.S. Census Bureau, "Poverty Status in the Past 12 Months," *2015–2019 American Community Survey 5-Year Estimates*, accessed January 23, 2022, *https://data.census.gov/cedsci/table?t=Poverty&g=0500000US41033&tid=ACSST5Y2019.S1702*.

95 *Only 17.5 percent of the population*: U.S. Census Bureau, "Population Estimates: July 1, 2019, (V2019)," accessed October 15, 2021, *https://www.census.gov/quickfacts*.

95 *Jay Williams, a former mayor*: Nick Carey, "Special Report: America's route to recovery," *Reuters*, December 29, 2009, *https://jp.reuters.com/article/instant-article/idUKTRE5BS2I620091229*.

95 *Many millworkers and loggers*: LeMonds, *Deadfall*, xviii, 70–73.

95 *When Washington state passed a law*: LeMonds, *Deadfall*; McLain and Kay, *NEAI Report*, 30. Truckers typically work as independent contractors rather than employees, heightening their economic vulnerability.

95 *"In the middle of winter"*: LeMonds, *Deadfall*, 132.

96 *a rare liberal to hold office there*: Like most local government races, Josephine County elections are technically nonpartisan. As the first Democrat elected to the county in two decades, however, Toler believes he won because his Republican opponent was effectively disqualified.

96 *In Oregon, drought conditions*: "Drought in Oregon, 2000 to the present," National Integrated Drought Information System, *https://www.drought.gov/states/oregon*.

96 *The average annual temperature in the region*: R.S. Vose, et al., "Temperature changes in the United States," *Climate Science Special Report: Fourth National Climate Assessment, Volume I*; D.J. Wuebbles, et al., ed., U.S. Global Change Research Program (2017): 185–206, *https://science2017.globalchange.gov/chapter/6/#:~:text=The%20largest%20changes%20were%20in,in%20the%20Northern%20Great%20Plains*. Based on average annual temperatures in the recent period between the years 1986–2016, as compared to average annual temperatures for the first half of the twentieth century, 1901–1960.

96 *further weakening the trees' resistance*: Thomas Kolb et al., "Observed and anticipated impacts of drought on forest insects and diseases in the United States," *Forest Ecology and Management* 380, (2016): 321–34, *https://www.fs.fed.us/rm/pubs_journals/2016/rmrs_2016_kolb_t001.pdf*.

96 *One million acres of Oregon land burned*: "911 Dispatchers Slammed With Calls About Qanon-Backed False Claims About Wildfires," *KEZI 9 ABC News*, September 11, 2020, *https://www.kezi.com/content/news/572381892.html*; Shane Dixon Kavanaugh, "Rash of Oregon arson cases fuels fear, conspiracy theories during devastating wildfires," *The Oregonian*, September 19, 2020, *https://www.oregonlive.com/wild*

fires/2020/09/rash-of-oregon-arson-cases-fuel-fear-conspiracy-theories
-during-devastating-wildfires.html.

96 *A new flank in the timber wars*: Ibid.

97 *The northern spotted owl remains threatened*: Brooke Jarvis, "A shot in the dark," *California Sunday Magazine*, February 4, 2016, *https://story.cali forniasunday.com/barred-owl-removal/.*

97 *With less restrictive diets*: Ibid.

97 *"Shoot an owl" is now an official task*: Craig Welch, "The Spotted Owl's New Nemesis," *Smithsonian Magazine*, January 2009, *https://www.smith sonianmag.com/science-nature/the-spotted-owls-new-nemesis-1316 10387/.*

97 *Meanwhile, ongoing lawsuits over demands to resume*: "Oregon," Pacific Northwest Research Station, U.S. Forest Service, last modified December 12, 2016, *https://www.fs.fed.us/pnw/rma/fia-topics/state-stats/Oregon /index.php*; Jes Burns, "Jordan Cove Would Be Oregon's Top Carbon Polluter If Built," *Oregon Public Broadcasting*, May 3, 2019, *https://www .opb.org/news/article/jordan-cove-oregon-lng-carbon-pollution/.*

97 *That approach would have managed wildfire risk*: Tony Schick and Jes Burns, "Efforts to Reduce Wildfire Risk Fall Short, Buck Science," *Oregon Public Broadcasting*, July 24, 2018, *https://www.opb.org/news/article /west-wildfire-risks-fuels-treatment-thinning-burning/.*

97 *And the United States has never enacted a federal climate change statute*: Jody Freeman and Kate Konschnik, "U.S. Climate Change Law and Policy: Possible Paths Forward," *Global Climate Change and U.S. Law*, 2nd ed., ed. Jody Freeman and Mike Gerrard (Washington, D.C.: American Bar Association Book Publishing, 2014).

98 *By 2005, the industry was attracting people*: "Oregon resumes issuing medical marijuana cards," *News on 6*, Associated Press, June 20, 2005, *https:// www.newson6.com/story/5e368b6d2f69d76f620a26d7/oregon-resumes -issuing-medical-marijuana-cards*; Noelle Crombie, "Legal marijuana in Oregon: A look at the state's pot history," *OregonLive*, November 7, 2014, *https://www.oregonlive.com/marijuana/2014/11/legal_marijuana_in _oregon_a_lo.html.*

99 *Wages, in freefall from dwindling grower profits*: Oregon Liquor Control Commission, *2019 Recreational Marijuana Supply and Demand Legislative Report* (Oregon, 2019), 7–8, *https://www.oregon.gov/olcc/marijuana /Documents/Bulletins/2019%20Supply%20and%20Demand%20Legis lative%20Report%20FINAL%20for%20Publication(PDFA).pdf.* "Increased supply has resulted in consumer prices falling from more than $10 per gram of usable marijuana in October 2016 to less than $5 per gram in December 2018."

99 *Rumor has it that tobacco conglomerates*: Chris Roberts, "Sensing Big Bucks, Tobacco Companies Pivot Toward Marijuana," *Observer*, March 2, 2018, *https://observer.com/2018/03/legalization-has-tobacco-companies-interested-in-marijuana-industry/*.

100 *Rates of homelessness soared*: Hanna Merzbach, "Desperation in Josephine County: On the brink of homelessness," Street Roots, February 3, 2021, *https://www.streetroots.org/news/2021/02/03/desperation-josephine-county-brink-displacement*. From 2017 to 2019, the county's homeless population nearly doubled.

100 *Mistrust of government generates reluctance*: Edward W. Morris, "'Snitches End Up in Ditches' and Other Cautionary Tales," *Journal of Contemporary Criminal Justice* 26, no. 3 (August 2010): 254, 262–264, *https://doi.org/10.1177%2F1043986210368640*. The criminologist Edward Morris, for instance, compared anti-snitching culture at a predominately white, low-income rural school to that of a predominately black, low-income urban school. Views of the police in the first setting, he found, stemmed from "reputation-based distrust" that the police treated kids from "bad families" worse than kids from "good families." In the second setting, "race-based distrust" expected the criminal justice system to be racially discriminatory.

100 *Where a wrongdoer or his family is known personally*: Ralph A. Weisheit, David Falcone, and L. Edward Wells, *Rural Crime and Rural Policing*, special report prepared for the U.S. Department of Justice, Office of Justice Programs, National Institute of Justice, September 1994, 7–8, *https://www.ojp.gov/pdffiles/rcrp.pdf*; Alexandra Natapoff, *Snitching: Criminal Informants and the Erosion of American Justice* (New York: NYU Press, 2010).

101 *Research shows that people care*: Tracey L. Meares and Peter Neyroud, *Rightful Policing*, New Perspectives in Policing Bulletin NCJ 248411 (Washington, D.C.: U.S. Department of Justice, National Institute of Justice, 2015), *https://www.ncjrs.gov/pdffiles1/nij/248411.pdf*; Tracey L. Meares, "The Path Forward: Improving the Dynamics of Community–Police Relationships to Achieve Effective Law Enforcement Policies," *Columbia Law Review* 117, no. 5 (June 2017): 1355, *https://www.jstor.org/stable/44288101*.

101 *By spending years as a community-based deputy*: Quint C. Thurman and Edmund F. McGarrell, eds., *Community Policing in a Rural Setting*, 2d ed., (London: Routledge, 2014). David Alan Sklansky, "Police and Democracy," *Michigan Law Review* 103, no. 7 (2005): 1699, 1779, *https://repository.law.umich.edu/mlr/vol103/iss7/1/*.

101 *Between 2008 and 2012*: *2012 Financial Condition Review*, 42. Federal funds accounted for 22 percent of the county's governmental fund

revenues in 2011. In that year, before federal funding started falling, Josephine County generated only $177 per capita in locally generated revenues, compared with $122 per capita in federal timber subsidies.

101 *Josephine still relied on these subsidies*: Ibid.

101 *He laid off all detectives*: Kelly Jarvis and Lisa Lucas, *Study of the Reduction in Law Enforcement Funding in Josephine County 2010–2018* (Portland: NPC Research, 2019), 4.

102 *Same for the records staff*: Ibid., 5–6.

102 *The number of dispatch staffers*: Ibid., 4, 22, 50.

102 *One told dispatch that a gunshot wound*: Ibid.

102 *their staffing dropped from twenty-three local officers*: Ibid., I.

102 *The sheriff's office dropped from eighty-five people*: Ibid., 4.

102 *The hours of the sheriff's office fell*: Ibid., 5; Shane Dixon Kavanaugh, "Unsolved Josephine County Deaths Illustrate Small-Town Crisis Stemming from Law-Enforcement Cutbacks," *The Oregonian*, March 11, 2014, *https://www.oregonlive.com/pacific-northwest-news/2014/03/crime _cave_junction_josephine.html*.

102 *could respond only to "life-threatening calls"*: Jarvis and Lucas, *Study of the Reduction in Law Enforcement Funding*, 4. In 2012, an average of twenty calls per day "did not receive a deputy response due to limited resources."

103 *The case offered tragic confirmation*: Anderson, *New Minimal Cities*, 1, n.3. In the aftermath of the Great Recession, he was not the only sheriff making such an announcement. Similar press releases came out of other rural Oregon counties. In Milwaukee, the county sheriff warned the public that his resources were so denuded that they should arm themselves. In many other struggling cities, public leaders were not so candid (or foolish, depending on your view), but the reality was no different.

103 *"consider relocating to an area with adequate law enforcement"*: Amelia Templeton, "Loss of Timber Payments Cuts Deep in Oregon," *NPR*, May 21, 2013, *http://www.npr.org/2013/05/21/185839248/loss-of-timber -payments-cuts-deep-in-oregon*.

103 *"whole system has crumbled"*: Ibid.

103 *Instead, they were staying with abusers*: Ibid.

103 *Even compared to the severity*: Lisa R. Pruitt, "Place Matters: Domestic Violence and Rural Difference," *Wisconsin Journal of Law, Gender and Society* 23, no. 2 (2008): 347, 351.

103 *Nearly one in five homicides*: T. K. Logan, Lisa Shannon, and Robert Walker, "Protective Orders in Rural and Urban Areas: A Multiple Perspective Study," *Violence Against Women* 11, no. 7 (July 2005): 876, 899, quoted in Pruitt, "Place Matters," 350, 362, 379–80.

103 *Yet rural areas have fewer law enforcement officers*: Ibid.

103 *A study of rural and urban counties*: Pruitt, "Place Matters," 381.

103   *91 percent of restraining orders*: Ibid.

103   *The county already had the highest rate of auto theft*: Jarvis and Lucas, *Study of the Reduction in Law Enforcement Funding*, 21.

104   *Laurie Houston lost her twenty-one-year-old son*: Kavanaugh, "Unsolved Josephine County Deaths."

104   *Witnesses said the driver*: Ibid.

104   *"I won't let my son"*: Ibid.

104   *"He was somebody"*: Ibid.

104   *When these cuts went into effect*: Jarvis and Lucas, *Study of the Reduction in Law Enforcement Funding*, II.

104   *Alternative incarceration programs also closed*: Governor's Task Force, *Final Report*, 78.

105   *It also closed the non-secure juvenile residential facility*: Jarvis and Lucas, *Study of the Reduction in Law Enforcement Funding*, 7.

105   *The district attorney's office lost 40 percent*: Ibid., 8.

105   *These "cite and release" policies*: Governor's Task Force, *Final Report*, Ex. E; Jarvis and Lucas, *Study of the Reduction in Law Enforcement Funding*, II.

105   *all three of the stages of prison abolition*: This framework, known as the "Attrition Model," dates back to the Prison Research Education Action Project in a 1976 pamphlet called "Instead of Prisons: A Handbook for Abolitionists."

105   *The county's mental health court reports impressive success*: Options for Southern Oregon, "Mental Health Court," *http://www.optionsonline.org /mental-health-court*.

106   *The Oregon State Police*: Jarvis and Lucas, *Study of the Reduction in Law Enforcement Funding*, 9.

106   *But governors have long warned Josephine*: Dave Hogan, "Loss of Timber Payments Cuts Across Oregon," *The Oregonian*, June 25, 2008; Matt Cooper, "Timber Counties Make Plea to Salem," *The Register Guard*, December 20, 2011, *https://www.registerguard.com/article/20111220/NEWS /312209999*; Eric Mortenson, "Loss of Federal Forest Payments Has Oregon Counties Looking for Revenue While Having Millions that Can't be Tapped," *The Oregonian*, January 21, 2012, *https://www .oregonlive.com/environment/2012/01/loss_of_federal_forest_pay ment.html*.

106   *State-level governmental task forces*: Eric Mortenson, "Legislature Considers Rescue of Oregon Timber Counties if Services Fall Through the Crack," *The Oregonian*, September 12, 2012, *https://www.oregonlive.com /business/2012/09/legislature_considers_rescue_o.html*.

106   *a journalist reported a drug dealer "hawk[ing] meth"*: Kavanaugh, *Unsolved Josephine County Deaths*.

106   *Oregon has the sixth highest rate*: Rachel N. Lipari et al., *State and*

Substate Estimates of Nonmedical Use of Prescription Pain Relievers from the 2012–2014 National Surveys on Drug Use and Health, The CBHSQ Report (Rockville, MD: Center for Behavioral Health Statistics and Quality, Substance Abuse and Mental Health Services Administration, 2017), *https://www.samhsa.gov/data/sites/default/files/report_3187/ShortReport-3187.html.*

106 *Josephine County had the highest rate: Prescription Drug Dispensing in Oregon: January 1, 2012–December 31, 2012 Schedules II—IV Medications Dispensed in Oregon: Josephine County,* prepared by the Oregon Health Authority, Public Health Division, Prescription Drug Monitoring Program (Oregon, 2013), 21, table 20, *http://www.orpdmp.com/orpdmpfiles/PDF_Files/Reports/Josephine.pdf.* Data for 2012 is the most recent year for which county-level prescription data is available.

106 *nearly two and a half times as many prescriptions:* Oregon Health Authority, *Prescription Drug Dispensing in Oregon,* 21 table 20. In 2012, 202,818 prescriptions were filled for the county's total population—including kids—of 82,775. See also "Prescribing and Overdose Data for Oregon," Opioid Overdose and Misuse, Oregon Health Authority Public Health Division, *https://www.oregon.gov/oha/ph/PreventionWellness/SubstanceUse/Opioids/Pages/data.aspx.* To use this tool, click "Prescribing by Drug Class"; then scroll to "Prescribing by County" and filter for Josephine County.

106 *Drug overdose mortality rates:* Oregon Health Authority Public Health Division, "Prescribing and Overdose Data for Oregon." See also the 2010-2014 data profile of Josephine County, Oregon, in "Drug Overdose Deaths in the United States," NORC, *https://opioidmisusetool.norc.org/.*

107 *"Inside the cab of his pickup truck": Town of Castle Rock, Colorado v. Gonzales,* 545 U.S. 748, 754 (2005).

107 *"No State shall . . . deprive any person":* U.S. Constitution, amend. XIV, sec. 1.

108 *Indeed, nothing in the Constitution:* Years before its decision in *Castle Rock,* the Supreme Court decided that the Due Process Clause does not affirmatively require the state to protect citizens against private actors if the state itself did not create those harms. *DeShaney v. Winnebago County Dept. of Social Servs.,* 489 U.S. 189 (1989). Other cases affirm that citizens do not enjoy the right to a variety of discretionary government services. See *Harrington v. City of Suffolk,* 607 F.3d 31, 35 (2d Cir. 2010) (police investigations); *Moses v. D.C.,* 741 F. Supp.2d 123, 125 (D.D.C. 2010) (emergency medical care); and *Jackson v. Byrne,* 738 F.2d 1443, 1447 (7th Cir. 1984) ("the Constitution does not guarantee to members of the public at large the adequacy of elementary protective services [including firefighting services]."). In 1973, the Supreme Court rejected

claims for a federal right to education. *San Antonio Independent School District v. Rodriguez*, 411 US 1 (1973).

108 *Oregon has established a "mandatory arrest" law*: *Nearing v. Weaver*, 670 P.2d 137 (Or. 1983).

108 *Budget-strapped municipalities cannot order employees*: States have their own versions of these laws, but federal law demonstrates how tricky these issues can become. On the one hand, the Anti-Deficiency Act means Congress cannot authorize spending that has not yet been appropriated. On the other, the Fair Labor Standards Act, or FLSA, means that no one besides FLSA-exempt workers can be made to work without pay. Those laws came into conflict after a Trump Administration shutdown over the border wall in 2018. Current litigation is wrestling with whether it is legal for the federal government to force workers to continue working during shutdowns in which their pay has not yet been appropriated. See *Rowe v. United States*, 151 Fed. Cl. 268 (2020).

108 *syphilis, a dangerous but treatable STD*: "National Overview—Sexually Transmitted Disease Surveillance, 2019," Sexually Transmitted Disease Surveillance 2019, Centers for Disease Control and Protection, *https:// www.cdc.gov/std/statistics/2019/overview.htm#Syphilis*. The rates of primary and secondary syphilis have increased almost every year since 2002, increasing 11.2 percent from 2018 to 2019 alone. *https://www.oregon .gov/oha/PH/ABOUT/Documents/sha/state-health-assessment-full-report .pdf*, page 150.

109 *Although it found that the sheriff*: Melissa McRobbie, "Called in for questioning: The sheriff's changing resume," *Grants Pass Daily Courier*, November 1, 2014.

109 *Tax opponents and other critics*: Jonn Lilyea, "Daryld 'Gil' Gilbertson; embellishing Sheriff in Oregon," *This Ain't Hell* (blog), October 30, 2014, *https://valorguardians.com/blog/?p=56124&cpage=1*; Adrian Black, "Sheriff Gilbertson," Rogue Territory: In Rural Southern Oregon, Josephine County's Public Safety Crisis, last modified 2014, *http://www.rogueterritory .org/sheriff-gilbertson.html*; "Remove and prohibit any image of Sheriff Gil Gilbertson wearing the Master EOD badge," *https://www.change.org/p /the-commissioners-of-josephine-county-oregon-remove-and-prohibit-any -image-of-sheriff-gil-gilbertson-wearing-the-master-eod-badge*.

110 *The retired manager of a marina*: "Armed Posse Patrols Timber Lands in Sheriff's Place," *Fox News*, October 17, 2012, *https://www.foxnews .com/us/after-budget-cuts-reduce-sheriff-force-armed-posse-patrols-oregon -county*.

111 *State and national media took hold*: Stephanie McNeal, "Citizens take law into own hands after cash-strapped Ore. county guts sheriff's office,"

FoxNews, December 28, 2013, *https://www.foxnews.com/politics/citizens-take-law-into-own-hands-after-cash-strapped-ore-county-guts-sheriffs-office.*

111 *concealed carry permits reached historic highs*: Jarvis and Lucas, *Study of the Reduction in Law Enforcement Funding,* 21. After 2012, concealed carry permits doubled from 712 to 1,382. Numbers continued to rise in subsequent years, and ultimately peaked at 2,147 in 2016. Permits last for four years in Oregon, so the number of new permits only represents a fraction of registered gun-carriers.

113 *common in Josephine as well*: Jarvis and Lucas, *Study of the Reduction in Law Enforcement Funding,* 54–55. The major local private security company saw its business increase 252 percent between 2012 and 2014.

113 *The United States has a long history*: " 'Policing the Police': How the Black Panthers Got Their Start," *WBUR,* September 23, 2015, *https://www.wbur.org/npr/442801731/director-chronicles-the-black-panthers-rise-new-tactics-were-needed*; David A. Sklansky, "The Private Police," *UCLA Law Review* 46, no. 4 (April 1999): 1165n125, *https://law.stanford.edu/publications/the-private-police/*; Steven A. Holmes, "As Farrakhan Groups Land Jobs from Government, Debate Grows," *New York Times,* March 4, 1994, *https://www.nytimes.com/1994/03/04/us/as-farrakhan-groups-land-jobs-from-government-debate-grows.html.*

113 *these groups described their work*: Joshua Bloom and Waldo E. Martin, *Black against Empire: The History and Politics of the Black Panther Party* (Oakland, California: University of California Press, 2016).

113 *Oregon law grants citizens*: Or. Rev. Stat. § 133.225 (2017) (granting private persons the power to arrest a person with probable cause or for crimes committed in their presence, and allowing that private person to use physical force under some circumstances).

113 *a second category*: David H. Bayley and Clifford D. Shearing, "The Future of Policing," *Law and Society Review* 30, no. 3 (1996): 585, 587, *https://www.jstor.org/stable/3054129.* "[T]he acceptability of volunteer policing has been transformed in less than a generation. While once it was thought of as vigilantism, it is now popular with the public and actively encouraged by the police. Because these activities are uncoordinated, and sometimes ephemeral, it is hard to say how extensive they are."

113 *the full responsibilities and constitutional limitations*: Gloria Hillard, "In Tight Times, L.A. Relies on Volunteer Police," *NPR,* May 19, 2011, *https://www.npr.org/2011/05/19/136436405/in-tight-times-l-a-relies-on-volunteer-police.* The International Association of Chiefs of Police estimates that 2,100 police departments have volunteer programs of this kind.

114 *State law requires*: "How to be a reserve police officer," *Police One,* May 1,

2011), *https://www.policeone.com/police-jobs-and-careers/articles/4046999 -How-to-be-a-reserve-police-officer/*; Peter J. Gardner, "Arrest and Search Powers of Special Police in Pennsylvania: Do Your Constitutional Rights Change Depending on the Officer's Uniform?," *Temple Law Quarterly* 59, no. 2 (Summer 1986): 519–21, *https://heinonline.org/HOL/P?h=hein .journals/temple59&i=529*. Courts hold volunteer police to the same constitutional standards as regular police, but with more limited power to conduct searches and collect evidence on private property. In *Commonwealth v. Eshelman,* 477 Pa. 93, 383 A.2d 838 (1978), the Pennsylvania Supreme Court held that evidence seized pursuant to a warrantless search by auxiliary police is subject to exclusion under the fourth amendment. Notably, Eshelman treats auxiliary police as traditional police for Fourth Amendment purposes even when they are not on active duty and thus have no statutory authority.

114   *draw upon "merchant's privilege statutes"*: David A. Sklansky, "Private Police and Democracy," *American Criminal Law Review* 43, no. 1 (Winter 2006): 89, 93.

114   *Josephine's previous sheriff tried to expand*: Reserve Police Officer, City of Grants Pass, Oregon, volunteer class certification posting prepared by City of Grants Pass, June 22, 2018. In Josephine, reserve deputies have typically responded to car crashes, property crimes, and other calls for service. Reserve corrections deputies help run the county jail.

114   *Speaking on public radio*: "Think Out Loud," Oregon Public Broadcasting, April 8, 2014, *https://www.opb.org/radio/programs/thinkoutloud/seg ment/josephine-county-sheriff-asking-volunteers-to-help-investigate-crime/*.

114   *In 2011, a California Highway Patrol*: Gund v. County of Trinity, 24 Cal. App.5th 185 (Cal. Ct. App. 2018).

114   *The county argued, and the court agreed*: Cal. Lab. Code § 3366 (West). The law is California Labor Code § 3366, which provides the exception to the general rule that workers' compensation is not available for people providing voluntary services to a public agency.

115   *David Sklansky, a scholar*: David Sklansky, *Democracy and the Police* (Stanford, CA: Stanford University Press, 2007), 128–131.

117   *Concerned Fathers Against Crime*: Bob Just, "Homeland defense: A call to the churches," *WorldNetDaily*, January 8, 2002, *https://www.wnd.com /2002/01/12290/*.

118   *700 volunteers passed through*: Tay Wiles, "Sugar Pine Mine, the other standoff," *High Country News,* February 2, 2016, *https://www.hcn.org /issues/48.2/showdown-at-sugar-pine-mine article*; Ashley Powers, "The Renegade Sheriffs," *New Yorker*, April 23, 2018, *https://www.newyorker .com/magazine/2018/04/30/the-renegade-sheriffs*.

118   *When self-appointed volunteers*: Joseph Margulies, "How the Law Killed

Ahmaud Arbery," *Boston Review*, July 7, 2020, *http://bostonreview.net
/race-law-justice/joseph-margulies-how-law-killed-ahmaud-arbery*; Sharon
Finegan, "Watching the Watchers: The Growing Privatization of Criminal Law Enforcement and the Need for Limits on Neighborhood Watch
Associations," *University of Massachusetts Law Review* 8, no. 1 (2013):
88, *https://scholarship.law.umassd.edu/umlr/vol8/iss1/3*; Adeoye Johnson, "Neighborhood Watch: Invading the Community, Evading Constitutional Limits," *University of Pennsylvania Journal of Law and Social
Change* 18, no. 5, (2016): 459, *https://scholarship.law.upenn.edu/jlasc
/vol18/iss5/3/*. Ahmaud Arbery, a twenty-five-year-old African American
out jogging not far from his home, was followed and murdered by armed
white men in a south Georgia neighborhood on February 23, 2020.
Trayvon Martin, a seventeen-year-old African American teen walking
home from a convenience store, was killed by a neighborhood watch
volunteer on patrol on February 26, 2012.

118 *In Jackson County, just forty-five minutes*: April Ehrlich, "Oregon Town
Grapples with Shooting Death of 19-Year-Old Aidan Ellison," NPR,
December 4, 2020, *https://www.npr.org/2020/12/04/942946598/oregon
-town-grapples-with-shooting-death-of-19-year-old-aidan-ellison*.

118 *health and elder care industry*: Global Diversity Rankings by Country,
Sector and Occupation (New York, NY: Forbes Insights, 2012), 19,
*https://images.forbes.com/forbesinsights/StudyPDFs/global_diversity_rank
ings_2012.pdf*.

118 *There is no indication that*: Ryan Lenz, "Leader of Josephine County
Oath Keepers Breaks with Stewart Rhodes Over Leadership Style,"
Southern Poverty Law Center, May 16, 2017, *https://www.splcenter.org
/hatewatch/2017/05/16/leader-josephine-county-oath-keepers-breaks-stew
art-rhodes-over-leadership-style*.

119 *higher rate of food stamps, welfare, and Medicaid*: "A picture of poverty
in Oregon," *Oregonian*, August 14, 2014, *https://projects.oregonlive.com
/maps/poverty/*. Recently available data from 2019 and 2020 shows that,
just as in 2014, Josephine County residents continue to rely on public
benefits at a higher rate than their Jackson County neighbors. "Data and
Reports," Oregon Department of Human Services, *https://www.oregon
.gov/dhs/assistance/pages/data.aspx*.

120 *Given increases in closed and open-carry weapons*: Jarvis and Lucas, *Study
of the Reduction in Law Enforcement Funding*, 54. The county issued 712
concealed carry permits in 2012, but that number kept climbing after
the cuts, rising to a peak of 2,147 new permits issued in 2016. The totals from 2012–2016 mean that more than 10 percent of the eligible,
over-eighteen population in Josephine got a new permit between 2012–
2016.

120 *Sheriff Daniel and the school district*: Josephine County, Oregon, *Primary Election Results*, prepared by the County Clerk and Recorder, May 17, 2016, 7, *https://www.co.josephine.or.us/Files/16MAYPRIMARY.pdf*. The levy results were reported as Question 17–71.

121 *Josephine's rate was the lowest*: Oregon Secretary of State, *2012 Financial Condition Review*, 7–8.

122 *After the deep cuts in 2012*: Jarvis and Lucas, *Study of the Reduction in Law Enforcement Funding*, 6.

122 *county still had to release one-third*: Ibid., 38.

122 *After the cuts of 2012*: Ibid., II.

124 *Back in 2012, Josephine's sheriff*: Jeff Barnard, "Josephine County accelerates sentences to avoid jail releases," *Mail Tribune*, May 30, 2012, *https://mailtribune.com/archive/josephine-county-accelerates-sentences -to-avoid-jail-releases*.

127 *Voters had passed two other tax levies as well*: Shaun Hall, "Passage of Tax Measures Surprises Many," *Mail Tribune*, May 18, 2017, *https://www .mailtribune.com/top-stories/2017/05/18/passage-of-tax-measures-surprises -many/*; Josephine County, Primary Election Results, *https://www.co.jose phine.or.us/Files/16MAYPRIMARY.pdf*.

CHAPTER THREE: *Lawrence*

131 *More than one hundred relatives and friends*: I attended this graduation on June 6, 2019.

132 *Thirty percent of the workforce*: "Commuting Characteristics by Sex," 2019 American Community Survey 5-Year Estimates, Subject Table S0801, *https://data.census.gov/cedsci/table?q=commuting&t=Commuting &g=1600000US2534550&tid=ACSST5Y2017.S0801&hidePreview =true*.

133 *Nearly one of every four Lawrence residents*: "QuickFacts: Lawrence City, Massachusetts," U.S. Census Bureau, *https://www.census.gov/quickfacts /lawrencecitymassachusetts*.

133 *median monthly rent*: "Financial Characteristics," 2015–2019 American Community Survey 5-Year Estimates, Subject Table S2503, *https://data .census.gov/cedsci/table?q=housing&g=1600000US2534550&tid=ACSS T5Y2019.S2503&hidePreview=true*.

134 *Bread and Roses Strike of 1912*: Bruce Watson, *Bread & Roses: Mills, Migrants, and the Struggle for the American Dream* (New York: Penguin Books, 2005), 1–4, 163–77.

135 *"My people are not in America"*: Watson, *Bread & Roses*, 26.

135 *In the late 1800s and early 1900s*: Ibid., 22.

135 *On so-called "coffin ships"*: Donald B. Cole, *Immigrant City: Lawrence,*

Massachusetts 1845–1921 (Chapel Hill: University of North Carolina Press, 1963) 11, 68.

135 *Soon came exiles of poverty*: Ibid.

136 *these migrants produced*: Thomas S. Dublin, *Lowell: The Story of an Industrial City* (Washington, D.C.: Dept. of the Interior, 1992); Sven Beckert, *Empire of Cotton: A Global History* (New York: Vintage Books, 2014), 147, 280–92; Schinto, *Huddle Fever*, 86. As producers of cotton cloth, early industrialists in Massachusetts (particularly the founders of the town of Lowell, but also Abbott Lawrence) spent the nineteenth century tied to Southern slavery. Massachusetts Senator Charles Sumner called it an "unholy union" between "the cotton-planters and flesh-mongers of Louisiana and Mississippi and the cotton-spinners and traffickers of New England—between the lords of the lash and the lords of the loom." Clergy and millworkers in Lowell made their city a hub for antislavery activism in the state and supported the Union war effort, though Massachusetts mills continued to purchase cotton generated through systems of debt peonage, sharecropping, convict leasing, and racial violence.

136 *a few inches smaller*: "The Ayer Mill Clock Tower," Essex Family Community Foundation, *http://eccf.org/ayer-mill-clock-tower/*. The Ayer Mill belltower and weathervane are 267 feet tall.

136 *conditions in the textile industry killed*: Watson, *Bread & Roses*, 9.

136 *The deafening machines*: Dublin, *Lowell: The Story of an Industrial City*, 85–89. At the Boott Cotton Mill Museum in the Lowell National Historical Park, staff will turn on a few of the machines in the weavers' room for visitors to hear. I found the sound shocking—like jackhammers sped up to a blur, at a volume so loud it hurt inside my brain. A sign on the wall quotes a millworker poet named Lucy Larcom, who wrote in 1889 that she trained herself to tune out the "incessant discords" so "that it became like a silence . . . And I defied the machinery to make me its slave."

136 *one report in 1912*: Francis McLean et al., *The Report of the Lawrence Survey: Studies in Relation to Lawrence, Massachusetts, Made in 1911* (Lawrence: The Andover Press, 1912), 63.

136 *The mortality record*: Robert Forrant and Susan Grabski, *Images of America: Lawrence and the 1912 Bread and Roses Strike* (Charleston: Arcadia Publishing, 2013), 26.

136 *Giant pipes shot*: McLean et al., *Lawrence Survey*, 226–36.

136 *An innovative water treatment system*: David Sedlak, *Water 4.0: The Past, Present, and Future of the World's Most Vital Resource* (New Haven: Yale University Press, 2014), 48, 52. Emblematic of the region's technological prowess, in 1896 Lawrence became the first city in the United States to install drinking water filtration that minimized typhoid fever bacteria.

136 *a 1912 report*: McLean et al., *Lawrence Survey*, 39.

136 *The richest one percent*: Watson, *Bread & Roses*, 132.

136 *average wages in Lawrence mills*: Ibid., 72, 132.

137 *a single party*: Ibid., 133.

137 *Billy Wood*: Watson, *Bread & Roses*, 20, 24; Edward G. Roddy, *Mills, Mansions, and Mergers: The Life of William M. Wood* (Lowell: American Textile History Museum, 1997), 34–38, 122, 125. Billy Wood funded a senior citizen's home and an elite planned community in Andover, but otherwise spent his fortune on family homes and possessions. Wood was admired, however, for his humble origins. He grew up in a poor immigrant family and began working in mills at age twelve, but he managed to teach himself math at the public library and move into an office job. He married the daughter of the mill owner and went on to build a multimillion dollar empire of woolen mills. Being an uneducated, Roman Catholic, second-generation American made Wood an outsider in the world of his wife and wealthy contemporaries, to the point that he denied the truth of his upbringing.

137 *after sixty years of debate*: Watson, *Bread & Roses*, 32. As early as the 1840s, elites in Boston considered actions to improve the working conditions of, as Thoreau put it, the "wage slaves" of the Merrimack River.

137 *A new law*: Ibid., 12.

137 *mill owners implemented the law*: Ibid., 13.

137 *record-setting low temperatures*: Ibid., 123.

137 *Marches featured American flags*: Ibid., 91, 183.

137 *as broke as its people*: Ibid., 25. The year of the strike, Lawrence was heading toward bankruptcy, unable to pay its bills.

137 *"We will either break this strike"*: Forrant and Grabski, *Lawrence and the 1912 Bread and Roses Strike*, 44.

137 *The state dispatched armed militia*: Watson, *Bread & Roses*, 110–11.

137 *The U.S. Marines*: Ibid.

137 *Elizabeth Gurley Flynn*: Elizabeth Gurley Flynn, *The Rebel Girl: An Autobiography, My First Life (1906–1926)* (New York: International Publishers, 1955), 128.

138 *As the strike dragged on*: Ibid.

138 *"pale, emaciated, dejected" state*: Ibid., 142.

138 *Facing cavalry, billy clubs*: Watson, *Bread & Roses*, 78, 108, 111, 156.

138 *one woman flashed*: Ibid., 177.

138 *At a 1912 Congressional hearing*: Ibid., 194.

138 *They debated*: Ibid., 196.

138 *Education was important*: Ibid.

138 *Carmela Teoli testified*: Ibid., 192–93.

138 *"foreign operatives"*: Ibid., 47.

138 *"a war against"*: Ibid., 174.

138 *"[W]e were not considered"*: Forrant, *Lawrence and the 1912 Bread and Roses Strike*, 45; Katherine Paterson, *Bread and Roses, Too* (Boston: Houghton Mifflin Harcourt, 2006), 64. In Katherine Paterson's young adult novel set during the Lawrence strike, a child tries to stop her mother from marching, afraid that she'll end up in jail. The mother reassures her: "Can they put ten, twenty thousand peoples in jail?" the mother asks. "Only jail big enough is the mills, and we already been in those."

139 *15 percent average wage increase*: Watson, *Bread & Roses*, 205–6, 208.

139 *The settlement required*: Ibid., 94–95, 210. Labor leader Emma Goldman delighted in sending Teddy Roosevelt a telegram that read "Undesirable citizens victorious. Rejoice!" It was a comeuppance for Roosevelt's reference to Big Bill Haywood as an "undesirable citizen," which provoked labor activists to wear buttons proclaiming themselves undesirable citizens.

139 *The phrase was first published in*: Helen M. Todd, "Getting Out the Vote," *American Magazine*, May/October 1911, 611, 619. Todd's speech argued that women's votes "will go toward helping forward the time when life's Bread, which is home, shelter and security, and the Roses of life, music, education, nature and books, shall be the heritage of every child that is born in the country, in the government of which she has a voice."

139 *Oppenheim's poem describes*: James Oppenheim, "Bread and Roses," *American Magazine*, November/April 1911–12, 214.

139 *a man was fatally crushed*: Watson, *Bread & Roses*, 214.

139 *"We are a new people"*: Forrant, *Lawrence and the 1912 Bread and Roses Strike*, 9.

139 *By 1921, these ideas*: Cole, *Immigrant City*, 10. Cole describes prejudiced reactions to the strike, their connection to Madison Grant's 1914 book *Passing of the Great Race*, and anti-immigrant legal reform.

139 *Most of the strike's leaders*: Watson, *Bread & Roses*, 244-46. Strike leaders such as Flynn, Emma Goldman, Joe Ettor, and Auturo Giovannitti went on to lead similar but unsuccessful strikes in other states, ultimately scattering. Flynn was arrested repeatedly for labor organizing and opposition to World War I, leading her to help establish the American Civil Liberties Union (ACLU) to defend people accused of political crimes. Goldman was later convicted under the Espionage Act for speaking out against World War I. Ettor, after being booted out of Lawrence and then falling out with other organizers, retired to start a wine business in California. Giovannitti turned to poetry and ultimately sunk into a depression.

139 *Strike leader Big Bill Haywood*: Ibid., 247-48; "Big Bill Haywood Weds; Can't Speak Russian and Russian Wife Can't Speak English," *New York Times*, January 14, 1927, *https://www.nytimes.com/1927/01/14/archives /big-bill-haywood-weds-cant-speak-russian-and-russian-wife-cant.html*.

139 *survived by a Russian wife*: Ibid.

139 *Billy Wood*: Watson, *Bread & Roses*, 24, 252–53.

139 *In the years after the strike*: Ibid.

139 *In 1926, grief-stricken*: Ibid., 252–53.

140 *Lawrence did nothing*: Ibid., 255–56; "Strikers' Monument (Lawrence, MA)," Queen City, MA, *https://queencityma.wordpress.com/2014 /09/08/strikers-monument-lawrence-ma/*; Cole, *Immigrant City*, 195–96. In 1912 and the decade following, citizen and business groups in Lawrence tried to distance the city from the strike, for instance with a pamphlet calling for readers to see "Lawrence As It Really Is, Not As Syndicalists, Anarchists, Socialists, Suffragists, Pseudo Philanthropists and Muckraking Yellow Journalists Have Painted It." A 1962 "God and Country" parade protested the IWW and its perceived association with atheism and anarchism. The first city event celebrating the strike took place in 1980, and the first memorial to it (the Strikers' Monument on the central common) was unveiled in 2012.

140 *first public playground*: Watson, *Bread & Roses*, 219, 221.

140 *Regulations reduced child labor*: John A. Fliter, *Child Labor in America: The Epic Legal Struggle to Protect Children* (Lawrence: University of Kansas, 2018), 69–220. After the strike, Congress established the Children's Bureau to investigate child welfare. In the years following, federal laws progressed and regressed in restricting child labor, until finally the Fair Labor Standards Act of 1938 prohibited child labor before age fourteen, excluding on farms.

140 *built civic infrastructure*: "Projects in Lawrence," The Living New Deal, *https://livingnewdeal.org/us/ma/lawrence-ma/*; "Bridges (Lawrence, MA)," Queen City Massachusetts, last modified July 1, 2014, *https://queenci tyma.wordpress.com/category/bridges/page/2/*. These projects included Den Rock Park, the Gilbert Memorial Bridge across the North Canal, and the Kershaw Bridge spanning the South Canal.

140 *Racial discrimination*: Ira Katznelson, *When Affirmative Action Was White: An Untold History of Racial Inequality in Twentieth-Century America* (New York: W.W. Norton & Company, 2005); Ta-Nehisi Coates, "The Case for Reparations," *Atlantic*, June 2014, *https://www.theatlantic .com/magazine/archive/2014/06/the-case-for-reparations/361631/*. Throughout the 1930s and 1940s, public works programs and social reforms incorporated and enabled racial discrimination.

140 *The Lawrence mills remained*: Edward G. Roddy, *Mills, Mansions, and Mergers: The Life of William M. Wood* (Lowell: American Textile History Museum, 1997), 79.

140 *"rich in the aroma of leather"*: Louise L. Schiavone, letter to the Editor, "A City's Better Days," *New York Times*, June 4, 2012, *https://www.nytimes .com/2012/06/05/opinion/lawrence-mass-a-citys-better-days.html*.

140 *In his closing speech*: Watson, *Bread & Roses*, 207.

141 *Laws there permitted*: John F. Kennedy, "New England and the South," *Atlantic*, January 1954, 33.

141 *Southern state regulations*: James C. Cobb, *The Selling of the South: The Southern Crusade for Industrial Development, 1936–1990* (Urbana: University of Illinois Press, 2d ed. 1993), 28–29, 214–15; Kennedy, "New England and the South," 36. One town, for example, offered a $51 million incentive package to one company, which amounted to more than $5,000 in public debt per capita (counting every town resident, including children), even though that number was more than double the annual income of a minimum wage worker at that time.

141 *18,000 textile jobs*: Llana Barber, *Latino City: Immigration and Urban Crisis in Lawrence, Massachusetts, 1945–2000* (Chapel Hill: University of North Carolina Press, 2017), 43.

141 *One in five Lawrence workers*: Kennedy, "New England and the South," 36.

141 *John F. Kennedy admonished Southern officials*: Cobb, *Selling of the South*, 42; Ibid., 33.

141 *"their newfound (industrial) benefactors"*: Cobb, *Selling of the South*, 43.

141 *the textile industry has hemorrhaged*: David Koistinen, "The Causes of Deindustrialization: The Migration of the Cotton Textile Industry from New England to the South," *Enterprise & Society*, September 2002, 502–3; Alexander Von Hoffman, *House by House, Block by Block: The Rebirth of America's Urban Neighborhoods* (Oxford University Press, 2003), 232–34.

141 *forty-two countries*: Elizabeth L. Cline, *Overdressed: The Shockingly High Cost of Cheap Fashion* (New York Portfolio/Penguin, 2012), 52, 48–56.

141 *Ayer Mill's grand bell tower*: Essex Family Community Foundation, "The Ayer Mill Clock Tower."

141 *rang for the last time*: Ibid.

141 *publicly traded textile giant*: Textron helped invent and popularize synthetic materials such as rayon for parachutes, clothing, and lingerie. It also devised new ways to reduce production costs, becoming one of the first sizable American companies to relocate its manufacturing strategically in a game of global leap-frog for tax advantages.

141 *By the end of the 1950s*: Cobb, *Selling of the South*, 42.

141 *Ownership of the American Woolen Company*: "Our Story," American Woolen, *https://americanwoolen.com/our-story.*

141 *For most of the late twentieth century*: Ibid.

142 *someone stole the tower's*: Keith Eddings, "Ayer Mill Clock Tower, a Lawrence Icon, Turns 100," *Eagle Tribune*, September 18, 2010, *https://www.eagletribune.com/news/local_news/ayer-mill-clock-tower-a-lawrence-icon-turns/article_f541a790-2975-528b-b148-f4489fb2ac45.html.*

142 *In the thirty-five years*: Eddings, "Ayer Mill Clock Tower."

142 *When a hazardous waste company*: Ibid.

142 *"Among workers there is only one"*: Watson, *Bread & Roses*, 66.

143 *New York City's conditions*: Kim Phillips-Fein, *Fear City: New York's Fiscal Crisis and the Rise of Austerity Politics* (New York: Metropolitan Books, 2017), 21–22, 35, 54.

143 *Caribbean trail*: Dávila, *Barrio Dreams*, 6; Ramon Borges-Mendez, "Migration, Settlement and Incorporation of Latinos in Lawrence, Massachusetts," *The Making of Community: Latinos in Lawrence, Massachusetts*, ed. Jorge Santiago and James Jennings (2005), 232; Juan Gonzalez, *Harvest of Empire: A History of Latinos in America* (New York: Penguin Books, 2000), 83. Nearly half of Puerto Rico's active workforce migrated from the island to the mainland between 1945 and 1965. Theodore Roosevelt, Jr., who was the island's governor from 1929–1932, observed the poverty of Puerto Rican landowners reduced to "lean, underfed women and sickly men" barely subsisting as seasonal sugar workers.

144 *language, music, food, and culture*: Junot Díaz, illustrations by Leo Espinosa, *Islandborn* (New York: Penguin Young Readers Group, 2018). In this moving children's book, a Dominican-American schoolgirl gathers remembrances of her family's lost nation. Family members tell stories of "[b]at blankets, more music than air, fruit that makes you cry, beach poems, and a hurricane like a wolf."

144 *Rafael Trujillo's thirty-one-year reign of terror*: Frank Moya Pons, *The Dominican Republic: A National History* (Princeton: Markus Wiener Publishing, 2010), 320–61.

144 *Trujillo rose to power*: Ibid.

144 *"He was our Sauron"*: Junot Díaz, *The Brief and Wondrous Life of Oscar Wao* (New York: Penguin Random House, 2007), 2.

144 *U.S. military again invaded*: Pons, *Dominican Republic*, 381–404.

144 *under U.S. command*: For a history of the U.S. entanglement in the island's turbulent history, see ibid., 279–444.

144 *400,000 other Dominicans fled*: Gonzalez, *Harvest*, 117–19.

144 *Decades of terror*: Pons, *Dominican Republic*, 361–67, 378–79, 434. Describing the Trujillo years as "deformed economic growth," with "a very poor, large working and peasant class, a very rich and very small upper class, and a total lack of democratic institutions," Pons also describes the doubling of the number of households living under the poverty line between 1984 and 1989.

144 *"harvest of empire"*: Gonzalez, *Harvest*.

145 *A video of the factory*: "Lawrence Maid Footwear," Boston TV News Digital Library, Ten O'Clock News, March 7, 1977, *http://bostonlocaltv.org /catalog/V_6CRTUZHVUDNUU38*.

145   *Lawrence Maid paid*: Barber, *Latino City*, 77–79.

145   *decades of steady wage decline*: Lawrence Mishel, Elise Gould, and Josh Bivens, "Wage Stagnation in Nine Charts," Economic Policy Institute, January 6, 2015, *https://www.epi.org/publication/charting-wage-stag nation/#:~:text=Ignored%20is%20the%20easy-to,workers%20over%20 the%20past%20generation*, Figure 4. The authors define low-wage workers as workers whose wages fall in the bottom 10 percent nationally.

145   *Middle-wage workers also*: Ibid. The authors define middle-wage workers as falling in the fiftieth percentile nationally.

145   *Latinos in Massachusetts*: Barber, *Latino City*, 186.

145   *Their median household income*: Ibid. Latino household income was also diverging further downward from that of white households. In 1979, Latino households made half of what the average white household made; within ten years, they were making only a quarter for every white household's dollar.

145   *the income of high-wage earners*: Mishel et al., "Wage Stagnation in Nine Charts," Figure 4.

145   *Llana Barber documents*: Barber, *Latino City*, 27, 90–120. Barber offers lessons larger than Lawrence, presenting a compelling urban history for understanding postindustrial, multiracial America in general.

145   *the Dominican share of Lawrence's population*: Ramona Hernández and Glenn Jacobs, "Beyond Homeland Politics: Dominicans in Massachusetts," *Latino Politics in Massachusetts: Struggles, Strategies, and Prospects*, ed. by Carol Hardy-Fanta and Jeffrey N. Gerson (New York: Routledge, 2002), 283; A.K. Sandoval-Strausz, *Barrio America: How Latino Immigrants Saved the American City* (New York: Basic Books, 2019). The growth of its Latino population across this period situates Lawrence among a number of American cities, suburbs, and rural areas where Latinos were instrumental in stabilizing or expanding areas in decline. Sandoval-Strausz focuses on Dallas and Chicago, but relates them to changes nationwide.

146   *Throughout two nights*: Barber, *Latino City*, 127–28, 130.

146   *"We can't even ride"*: Ibid., 151.

146   *"police officers treat us"*: Ibid.

146   *Only two of Lawrence's ninety-six*: Ibid., 139.

146   *One white religious leader suggested*: Ibid., 165.

146   *Hate crimes and white nativism*: Ibid., 124.

146   *Lawrence city officials resisted*: Ibid., 137.

146   *reinforce anti-Latino narratives*: Anna Adams, *Hidden From History: The Latino Community of Allentown, Pennsylvania* (Allentown: Lehigh County Historical Society, 2000), 1. In this, Lawrence is similar to other smaller northeastern cities such as Allentown and Lancaster, Pennsylvania, and

Hartford, Connecticut, where a poorly paid supply of Puerto Rican workers supported the cities' postwar economies, which in turn attracted Latino newcomers from the 1980s to 1990s even as manufacturing sectors shrank. "Economic decline," writes Adams, "is causing xenophobic feelings among the longtime Anglo natives who identify violence, noise and litter with the arrival of Latinos."

147 *"Giving the city back"*: Barber, *Latino City*, 167.

147 *"If you work"*: Ibid.

147 *the "undeserving poor" script*: Schinto, *Huddle Fever*, 194. In a first-person account of Lawrence in the 1980s and 1990s, the journalist Jeanne Schinto observed that white people classified Lawrence's Puerto Ricans and Dominicans as Black, regardless of whether those groups saw themselves that way. Schinto quoted the poet Martín Espada's "From an Island You Cannot Name": ". . . grabbing at the plastic / identification bracelet / marked Negro, / shouting 'I'm not! / Take it off! / I'm Other!' "

147 *"most vicious population"*: Cole, *Immigrant City*, 33.

147 *In 1856, the* Lawrence American *described*: Ibid., 40; Schinto, *Huddle Fever*, 213. In light of this history, I found it especially poignant to read the following account from Terri Kelley, a Lawrence High School teacher in the 1990s, recalling a Vietnamese student who had changed his name to Patrick: " 'I want to have an American name,' he said. 'Patrick is an Irish name, you know,' Terri told him. 'Yes, that, too,' said Patrick."

147 *an assistant principal*: Barber, *Latino City*, 178.

147 *Lawrence's immigrant history intensified*: Ibid., 145.

147 *Such claims overlooked*: Ibid., 146–47.

147 *"They forget, too"*: Ibid., 173.

148 *favor suburbs over cities*: Barber, *Latino City*, 23–32, 44–49, 170. Barber describes the rise of "a distinctly suburban political agenda" from the 1970s through mid-1990s, and "rejected shared responsibility for what were considered urban problems."

148 *Yet in the suburbs*: L. Owen Kirkpatrick and Chalem Bolton, "Austerity and the Spectacle," *Cities Under Austerity: Restructuring the U.S. Metropolis*, ed. Mark Davidson and Kevin Ward (Albany: SUNY Press 2018), 50. Federal money, for example, was often funneled instead to suburban projects like the construction of highways.

148 *The Massachusetts suburbs of the Route 128 area*: Lily Geismer, *Don't Blame Us: Suburban Liberals and the Transformation of the Democratic Party* (Princeton: Princeton University Press, 2015), 1. Historian Lily Geismer tells the story of this political transition with great care in her history of five wealthy suburbs in the Route 128 economy.

148 *"Anti-Snob Zoning Act"*: Barber, *Latino City*, 30.

148 *only about 8 percent*: Geismer, *Don't Blame Us*, 196–97, 284.

149   *Proposition 2 ½*: Ibid., 261–62.

149   *Lawrence took deep cuts*:

149   *fallen ever since*: Ibid., 266–67; Municipal Finance Task Force, Local Communities at Risk: Revisiting the Fiscal Partnership Between the Commonwealth and Cities and Towns (2005). An override provision of Proposition 2½ required municipalities to obtain voter approval to raise taxes over a set limit, which has further intensified the inequality in municipal services funding between smaller, wealthier suburbs able to obtain such approval and poorer or larger cities that lack a voter majority that is able or willing to fund public investments.

149   *Massachusetts ranked forty-seventh*: Municipal Finance Task Force, Local Communities at Risk, xiii.

149   *eleventh lowest state income tax*: Jared Walczak, Scott Drenkard, and Joseph Bishop-Henchman, *2019 State Business Tax Climate Index*, Tax Foundation, *https://files.taxfoundation.org/20180925174436/2019-State -Business-Tax-Climate-Index.pdf*, 29 (ranking based on 2019 figures).

149   *one-fifth of spending per pupil*: Barber, *Latino City*, 159–62. Per pupil spending dropped from $2,307 to $1,839.

149   *funding for the state's gateway cities*: Ibid., 176.

149   *City staff started taping*: Schinto, *Huddle Fever*, 230.

150   *"Massachusetts Miracle"*: Barber, *Latino City*, 42, 45–46.

150   *exuberant, colorful light displays*: Schinto, *Huddle Fever*, 44.

150   *John J. Buckley*: Barber, *Latino City*, 115–16.

151   *"Lawrence cannot afford"*: Ibid.

151   *speculative real estate investment*: Schinto, *Huddle Fever*, 220.

151   *increasingly absentee set of landowners*: Ibid. Lawrence-based journalist Jeanne Schinto described how her local paper in the early 1990s identified the owners of these dilapidated, unsafe "nuisance properties." Each owner's primary address was listed too, and they seemed to live just about anywhere except Lawrence.

151   *Deep budget cuts*: Barber, *Latino City*, 162.

151   *Arson offered an answer*: Ibid., 188–91.

151   *In 1989, a businessman invented*: Schinto, *Huddle Fever*, 34.

151   *Then he abandoned*: Ibid.

151   *Lawrence became known*: Barber, *Latino City*, 161, 188, 190.

152   *2 percent of the city's jobs*: U.S. Department of Census, *General Population Characteristics, Massachusetts, https://www2.census.gov/library/publi cations/decennial/1990/cp-1/cp-1-23.pdf*, D-1, 224; Barber, *Latino City*, 165.

152   *An antiquated city council system*: Barber, *Latino City*, 162–63.

152   *"rotten with patronage"*: Ibid.

152   *"Nothing speaks louder"*: Ibid., 165; William A. Lindeke, "Latino Political

Succession and Incorporation: Lawrence," *Latino Politics in Massachu-setts: Struggles, Strategies, and Prospects*, edited by Carol Hardy-Fanta and Jeffrey N. Gerson (New York: Routledge, 2002), 79. The few Latinos who made it into public administration were rarely Dominican or Puerto Rican. As a sizable share of the Lawrence electorate, these groups would pose a greater threat to the political status quo if they became city leaders.

152 *"Ethnic Tensions in Lawrence"*: "Ethnic Tensions in Lawrence," *Boston TV News*, filmed March 28, 1991, *http://bostonlocaltv.org/catalog/V_DLJ0D BUKV6TTYAO.*

153 *"Southern bigotry"*: Ian Haney López, *Dog Whistle Politics: How Coded Racial Appeals Have Reinvented Racism & Wrecked the Middle Class*, (Oxford: Oxford University Press, 2014). The clip is like a textbook case of "strategic racism" from Ian Haney López's book. López offers a detailed account of how politicians regularly deploy coded racial appeals to obtain support for policies that entrench inequality.

154 *major nonprofit educational organization*: "About Us," Right Question Institute, *https://rightquestion.org/about/*. Santana is the co-director of The Right Question Institute, an educational and advocacy organization that empowers people to advocate for themselves.

155 *ethnic clubs*: Dengler et al., *Images of America: Lawrence*, 110. Between 1847 and 1947, for example, a network of more than 600 immigrant organizations established in Lawrence a "network of mutual aid [that] served as medical, life, and unemployment insurance for many years."

155 *"Where rows of textile"*: Schinto, *Huddle Fever*, 214.

155 *By 2000, services*: "SOCDS Census Data: Output for Lawrence City, MA," U.S. Department of Housing and Urban Development State of the Cities Data Systems (SOCDS), *https://socds.huduser.gov/Census/indus try.odb?msacitylist=14460*2500934550*0.0&metro=cbsa.*

155 *Centro and other Latino organizations helped create ties*: Laura E. Gómez, *Inventing Latinos: A New Story of American Racism* (New York: New Press, 2020); Arlene Dávila, *Barrio Dreams*, 169–73. These books offer a rich and textured portrayal of the way that citizenship status, cultural stereotypes, scarcity, and skin color have operated to segment the Latino community.

155 *faced colorism and anti-Black bias*: Tanya Katerí Hernández, "The Afro-Latino Story of Latino Anti-Blackness," *Al Día News* (Feb. 19, 2020), *https://aldianews.com/articles/politics/opinion/afro-latino-story-latino -anti-blackness/57664*; Tanya Katerí Hernández, *On Latino Anti-Black Bias: "Racial Innocence" & The Struggle for Equality* (Boston: Beacon Press, 2022). Among legal scholars, Tanya Katerí Hernández has been an important analyst of anti-Black bias within the Latino community and its negative socio-economic effects on Latinos of African descent.

NOTES

311

155 *Lawrence residents from Latin America*: Ana Gonzalez-Barrera, "Hispanics with Darker Skin Are More Likely to Experience Discrimination than Those with Lighter Skin," Pew Research Center, July 2, 2019, *https:// www.pewresearch.org/fact-tank/2019/07/02/hispanics-with-darker-skin -are-more-likely-to-experience-discrimination-than-those-with-lighter-skin/*.

156 *Centro's diverse mix of caseworkers and clientele*: Rodolfo O. De La Garza and Alan Yang, *Americanizing Latino Politics, Latinoizing American Politics* (New York: Routledge, Taylor & Francis Group, 2020). Across the country, the 1990s and early 2000s were important years in the process of Latino political and identity formation across sub-groups based on national origin.

156 *shared communications like* Rumbo: Lindeke, *Latino Political Succession*, 81; G. Cristina Mora, *Making Hispanics: How Activists, Bureaucrats, and Media Constructed a New American* (Chicago: University of Chicago Press, 2014).

156 *Latinos began winning elected offices*: Lindeke, *Latino Political Succession*, 73–74.

156 *civil rights lawsuit*: Lindeke, *Latino Political Succession*, 90; "Cases Raising Claims Under Section 2 of the Voting Rights Act," U.S. DOJ, *https:// www.justice.gov/crt/cases-raising-claims-under-section-2-voting-rights -act-1*. The U.S. Department of Justice lawsuit against Lawrence successfully invoked the Voting Rights Act of 1965 to establish that Lawrence's district boundaries weakened Latino voting power, and that the city had made inadequate efforts to translate campaign materials, hire Latino pollworkers, and prevent interference with Latino voting. In a 1999 settlement, the city agreed, among other reforms, to hire new Latino pollworkers and establish better procedures for bilingual election information.

156 *Two additional voting rights lawsuits*: These cases were, respectively, *United States v. City of Lawrence*, No. 1:98-cv-12256 (D. Mass. Nov. 5, 1998) and *Morris v. City of Lawrence*, 01-CIV-11889 (Prelim. Injunction Nov. 5, 2001).

157 *Andors, Kotelchuck, and Harol, along with Maggie Super Church*: LCW remained home for Andors, and she is now its executive director. Kotelchuck, Harol, and Church ended up leaving LCW and Groundwork to support Lawrence from within other organizations. Kotelchuck helps lead the Boston Federal Reserve's research and support for Massachusetts Gateway Cities. Harol is the president of the Life Initiative, an impact investment fund that supports Lawrence and other communities in Massachusetts. Church authored the city's current land use plan and is now fighting to clean up the city's canals (as well as supporting infrastructure and climate resilience) as vice president of Conservation Law

Foundation. After more than a decade as the executive director of LCW, Traynor left Lawrence in 2011 to start up a network organizing project called Trusted Space Partners.

158   *an article for* Shelterforce *magazine*: Jessica Andors and William Traynor, "Network Organizing: A Strategy for Building Community Engagement," *Shelterforce*, March 1, 2005, *https://shelterforce.org/2005/03/01 /network-organizing-a-strategy-for-building-community-engagement/*.

158   *LCW began setting up three-part group dinners*: The first NeighborCircles dinner is mostly a social event, structured around a map exercise in which participants share how their family came to Lawrence, often revealing common origins abroad or common patterns (such as similar jobs held by an older Italian-American and a younger Puerto Rican). At the second dinner, hosts facilitate a discussion about neighborhood quality of life and ways to improve it. At the third dinner, groups plan a small action or event to improve their block.

159   *In 1921, Robert Frost had described it*: Robert Frost, "A Brook in the City"; Schinto, *Huddle Fever*, 30–31. Literary criticism links the poem to the Spicket River.

160   *Italian multinational company*: Jon Chesto, "Lawrence Dam Owner Faces Federal Complaint Over Dilapidated Canals," *Boston Globe*, June 7, 2017, *https://www.bostonglobe.com/business/2017/06/07/lawrence-dam-owner -faces-federal-complaint-over-dilapidated-canals/Wh2l7hmg3lMvYa5aFq ByqO/story.html*. Italian company Enel Green Power acquired the canals as part of its purchase of a hydroelectric plant on the Merrimack River.

160   *"place to dispose"*: Keith Eddings, "New Life for an Empty Red Brick Relic, 73 affordable apartments planned for historic Duck Mill," *Eagle Tribune*, July 12, 2015, *https://www.eagletribune.com/news/new-life-for-an-empty -red-brick-relic/article_3dbd355e-1ec6-5da6-a614-f6f8caad4806.html*.

161   *The city elected its first Latino mayor*: Barber, *Latino City*, 248.

161   *"City of the Damned"*: Jay Atkinson, "Lawrence, MA: City of the Damned," *Boston*, February 28, 2012, *https://www.bostonmagazine.com /news/2012/02/28/city-of-the-damned-lawrence-massachusetts/*. The article's opening reads like a caricature of poverty-as-spectacle writing: "Crime is soaring, schools are failing, government has lost control, and Lawrence, the most godforsaken place in Massachusetts, has never been in worse shape. And here's the really bad news: it's up to controversial Mayor William Lantigua to turn it all around."

162   *a "hollow prize"*: H. Paul Friesema, "Black Control of Central Cities: The Hollow Prize," *Journal of the American Institute of Planners* 35 (1969): 75. Historian H. Paul Friesema first coined this term, but wider and deeper empirical analysis of its truth arose in later work. Here are some other sources: Neil Kraus and Todd Swanstrom, "Minority Mayors and

the Hollow Prize Problem," *PS: Political Science and Politics* 34 (2001): 99; Robert O. Self, *American Babylon: Race and the Struggle for Postwar Oakland* (Princeton: Princeton University Press, 2003), 313–27.

162 *"A regular pattern of overestimating revenues"*: Locke Lord LLP, Bond Counsel, "Preliminary Official Statement and Notice of Sale," August 8, 2019 (City of Lawrence, Massachusetts General Obligation Bonds).

162 *During Lantigua's first year*: Chris Camire, "Along with Lantigua probe, Lawrence confronts fiscal, crime struggles," *Lowell Sun*, June 12, 2011, *https://www.lowellsun.com/2011/06/12/along-with-lantigua-probe-lawrence -confronts-fiscal-crime-struggles/*.

162 *The city police staffing ratio*: City of Lawrence Police Department and State of Massachusetts police-to-population ratio, 1985–2019, on file with author, created from FBI Uniform Crime Reporting Police Employee data, *https://ucr.fbi.gov/crime-in-the-u.s/2019/crime-in-the-u.s.-2019/topic -pages/police-employee-data*.

162 *The state of Massachusetts intervened*: While not as strong as a control board or a receivership, both of which have been deployed before in Massachusetts, the overseer did have the power to trigger the appointment of a control board if the city refused to work constructively with the overseer.

163 *misusing campaignn funds*: Travis Andersen, "AG Sues Mayor William Lantigua over Donations," *Boston Globe*, August 28, 2013, *https://www .bostonglobe.com/metro/2013/08/27/lawrence-mayor-william-lantigua -sued-over-alleged-campaign-finance-violations/7gvRSHEb0qFKUbXch QboPM/story.html*; Alex Bloom, "Outrage, Cynicism over Fuel Aid for Mayor's Low-Income Housing," *Eagle-Tribune*, May 15, 2011, *https:// www.eagletribune.com/news/outrage-cynicism-over-fuel-aid-for-mayors -low-income-housing/article_baf14a0e-2805-594c-a56c-a924893ceebd .html*; Anthony Pappalardo, "Is William Lantigua the Most Corrupt Mayor in America?" *Vice*, August 18, 2012, *https://www.vice.com/en /article/5gwkbk/is-william-lantigua-the-most-corrupt-mayor-in-america*.

163 *The rally drew hundreds*: Jess Bidgood, "After Seeing a Dismal Reflection of Itself, a City Moves to Change," *New York Times*, May 23, 2012, *https://www.nytimes.com/2012/05/30/us/a-massachusetts-city-tries-to -change-its-image.html*.

164 *In 2014, Massachusetts senator Elizabeth Warren*: Maria Cramer, "Daniel Rivera Sworn in as Lawrence Mayor," *Boston Globe*, January 5, 2014, *https://www.bostonglobe.com/metro/2014/01/04/dan-rivera-sworn -lawrence-new-mayor/J0oLtCfQByFlPsJrkIYO0I/story.html*.

164 *As would also happen*: Editorial Board, "Lawrence Should Scrap Mayoral Recount Vote," *Boston Globe*, September 14, 2015, *https://www.boston globe.com/opinion/editorials/2015/09/13/lawrence-should-scrap-rivera-recall*

-vote/LfExmsJDFENLNcef08rK8K/story.html; Lisa Kashinsky, "Mayor Responds to Recall Effort: Affidavits Filed," *Eagle-Tribune*, September 3, 2015, *https://www.eagletribune.com/news/mayor-responds-to-recall -effort-affidavits-filed/article_e4cd56fd-1c62-5397-b736-d0bf29fdc1c6 .html.*

164 *In 2015, a group called*: Ibid.

164 *The group included*: Ibid.

165 *Signature collectors for the recall*: Keith Eddings, "From the Dominican Republic, Lantigua joins effort to recall Rivera," *Eagle-Tribune*, November 25, 2015, *https://www.eagletribune.com/news/from-the-dominican-rep ublic-lantigua-joins-effort-to-recall-rivera/article_34a96fdb-2fed-5aef -865a-4e7634b73e8c.html.*

165 *The recall failed*: Daniel Rivera, "Rivera: Lawrence is Strong, People Are Talking about City," *Commonwealth Magazine*, February 5, 2016, *https://commonwealthmagazine.org/politics/rivera-lawrence-is-strong-people -are-talking-about-city/.*

165 *This included the addiction crisis*: Anise Vance and Luc Schuster, "Opioid Addiction Is a National Crisis. And It's Twice as Bad in Massachusetts," 2018, *https://www.bostonindicators.org/reports/report-website-pages/opioids -2018* This documents the addiction and overdose crisis across all six New England states and shows the statewide spike in deaths from opioid overdoses from 2012 to 2016, pages 2–6.

165 *reported twice in* The New York Times: Katharine Q. Seelye, "Addicted Parents Get Their Fix, Even with Children Watching," *New York Times*, September 27, 2016, *https://www.nytimes.com/2016/09/28/us/addicted -parents-get-their-fix-even-with-children-watching.html.*

165 *The woman depicted in the Family Dollar overdose video*: Katharine Q. Seelye, Julie Turkewitz, Jack Healy, and Alan Blinder, "How Do You Recover After Millions Have Watched You Overdose?" *New York Times*, December 11, 2018, *https://www.nytimes.com/2018/12/11/us/overdoses-you tube-opioids-drugs.html.*

165 *She later told the* Times: Ibid.

166 *Lawrence became a popular scapegoat*: "Gov. LePage: Non-White Dealers From Lowell And Lawrence Are Fueling Maine's Drug Problems," *WBUR News*, August 29, 2016, *http://www.wbur.org/news/2016/08/29 /lepage-lowell-lawrence-drug-problems.* Mayor Rivera responded: "The governor would be better off finding a solution for the many people in his state that are in desperate need of detox beds, counseling and treatment." Keith Eddings, "Rivera Blasts Maine Governor for Blaming Lawrence for Opioid Crisis," *Eagle-Tribune*, August 30, 2016, *http://www .eagletribune.com/news/rivera-blasts-maine-governor-for-blaming-lawrence -for-opioid-crisis/article_d91de160-6ec5-11e6-ab88-474a10579e31.html.*

166 *Paul LePage blamed Lawrence*: Ibid.

166 *"The heroin-Fentanyl arrests"*: Ibid.

166 *"They're Hispanic"*: Ibid.

166 *New Hampshire governor*: KCRA Staff, "New England Gov. Blames Mass. City for Majority of Drugs," *WCVB*, last modified March 1, 2017, *https://www.wcvb.com/article/new-england-gov-blames-mass-city-for-majority-of-drugs/9081009*.

166 *Then–President Trump in a speech blamed*: Nik DeCosta-Klipa, "Donald Trump Blamed Two Massachusetts Cities for New Hampshire's Opioid Problem. Their Mayors Shot Back," *Boston.com*, March 19, 2018, *https://www.boston.com/news/local-news/2018/03/19/donald-trump-blamed-two-massachusetts-cities-for-new-hampshires-opioid-problem-their-mayors-shot-back*.

166 *police staffing levels*: FBI Uniform Crime Reporting Police Employee data, on file with author, *https://ucr.fbi.gov/crime-in-the-u.s/2019/crime-in-the-u.s.-2019/topic-pages/police-employee-data*. City of Lawrence Police Department and State of Massachusetts police-to-population ratio, 1985–2019.

167 *Ingesting lead is extremely hazardous*: Mona Hanna-Attisha, *What the Eyes Don't See: A Story of Crisis, Resistance, and Hope in an American City* (New York: One World, 2018), 156, chapter 11. As Mona Hanna-Attisha explains in her study on lead poisoning caused by toxic water in Flint, Michigan, lead paint has a sweet taste that attracts children. But science has concluded "there is no safe level of lead in the human body" and lead paint's developmental effects have been linked to school dropout rates and crime.

167 *lead abatement*: Jill Harmacinski, "Lawrence Receives $5.1M in Lead Paint Removal Grant Money," *Eagle-Tribune*, October 6, 2020, https://www.eagletribune.com/news/merrimack_valley/lawrence-receives-5-1m-in-lead-paint-removal-grant-money/article_cf732677-a7b9-5a87-b36a-50f501877124.html; Vilma Martínez-Dominguez and Daniel Rivera, *City of Lawrence FY2020 Action Plan (Draft)* (2020), *https://cityoflawrence.com/DocumentCenter/View/10448/HUDs-Annual-Action-Plan-FY2020-PDF*. Vilma Martínez-Dominguez has been working to reduce lead paint in the city's housing, including while she served as the city's community development director.

167 *police told* The New York Times: Katharine Q. Seelye, "One Son, Six Hours, Four Overdoses: A Family's Anguish," *New York Times*, January 21, 2018, *https://www.nytimes.com/2018/01/21/us/opioid-addiction-treatment-families.html*.

168 *A man walking his dog along the Merrimack*: Spencer Buell, "Beheaded Lawrence Teenager Identified as Missing 16-Year-Old," *Boston Magazine*,

December 2, 2016, *http://www.bostonmagazine.com/news/blog/2016 /12/02/beheaded-teenager-lawrence/.*

168 *Investigation and prosecution later revealed*: Elizabeth Llorente, "Massachusetts Teen Beheaded Classmate in Jealous Rage: Prosecutor," *Fox News*, May 1, 2019, *https://www.foxnews.com/us/massachusetts-teen-beheaded -classmate-jealous-rage.* Police determined that a fifteen-year-old teenager had killed the victim, his high school classmate, over a petty conflict about a girl.

171 *Crime fell dramatically*: Lawrence Police Department 2019 Annual Report, January 29, 2020, *https://www.cityoflawrence.com/DocumentCenter /View/27328/2019_Annual-Report-.*

171 *Murthy explains that we*: Vivek H. Murthy, *Together: The Healing Power of Human Connection in a Sometimes Lonely World* (New York: HarperCollins, 2020), 12–13, 28–41.

171 *Loneliness and social isolation*: Ibid.

171 *They also build on themselves*: Ibid., 37–41.

171 *Low-income immigrants living*: Ibid., 126.

171 *deepest gains in people's health and well-being*: Ibid., 8.

171 *"[t]he real therapeutic synergy"*: Ibid., 167.

171 "doing good makes us feel good": Ibid., 167 (emphasis in original).

171 *Strong social networks also deliver*: Ibid., 51, 175, 241.

172 *social science research demonstrating*: Chris Benner and Manuel Pastor, *Equity, Growth, and Community: What the Nation Can Learn from America's Metro Areas* (Oakland: University of California Press, 2015). Here are some examples of how this kind of decentralized community engagement can bring economic growth and diverse local solutions to global problems.

174 *Working Cities Challenge (WCC) Initiative*: Federal Reserve Bank of Boston, *Working Cities Challenge, https://www.bostonfed.org/community -development/supporting-growth-in-smaller-industrial-cities/working-cities -challenge.aspx#:~:text=The%20Working%20Cities%20Challenge%20 (WCC,of%20their%20low-income%20residents.&text=This%20 ultimately%20led%20to%20the,after%20Living%20Cities'%20Integra tion%20Initiative.*

174 *intensive community collaboration*: Ibid.

175 *"civic and social crisis"*: Sean Safford, *Why the Garden Club Couldn't Save Youngstown: The Transformation of the Rust Belt* (Cambridge: Harvard University Press, 2009), 5.

176 *a "skills mismatch"*: Peter Cappelli, *Skill Gaps, Skill Shortages and Skill Mismatches: Evidence for the U.S.* (Cambridge: National Bureau of Economic Research, 2014).

177 *Tamar Kotelchuck cataloged*: Tamar Kotelchuck, *Less-Skilled Workers &*

the High-Technology Economy: A Regional Jobs Strategy for Lawrence, MA (MIT Libraries: 1999), https://ocw.mit.edu/courses/urban-studies-and-plan ning/11-423-information-and-communication-technologies-in-community -development-spring-2004/study-materials/kotelchuck1_28.pdf.

177 "skills predict growth": Edward L. Glaeser and Jesse M. Shapiro, "Urban Growth in the 1990s: Is City Living Back?" Journal of Regional Science 43, no. 1 (March 2003): 142.

177 Dozens of empirical analyses: Yolanda K. Kodrzycki and Ana Patricia Muñoz, "Economic Distress and Resurgence in U.S. Central Cities: Concepts, Causes, and Policy Levers," Economic Development Quarterly 29, no. 2 (January 2015) (cataloguing sources).

177 labor economist Enrico Moretti: Moretti, New Geography, 222–31.

183 Even in the ordinary case: Dengler et al., Images of America, 68. Rodriguez's tailored, culturally informed approach to teaching is reminiscent of the adaptation and investment that went into earlier generations of immigrants to Lawrence. Lawrence's school system in the late 1800s required "a very flexible educational system" in multiple lanuguages, adapted to the "large number of immigrants with no English skills and the need for many children to go to work."

173 "weighs a lot on our children": Ibid.

184 released from ten years of state fiscal oversight: Shira Schoenberg, "State Ends Oversight of City of Lawrence's Finances," Mass Live, October 24, 2019, https://www.masslive.com/news/2019/10/state-ends-oversight-of-city -of-lawrences-finances.html.

184 more than half the city's police officers: Lawrence Police Department, Quarterly Report, July–September 2020, October 1, 2020, https://lawpd.com /DocumentCenter/View/41171/Third-Quarter-Report.

185 A formal evaluation: Mt. Auburn Associates/Lawrence Evaluation Case Study, 8.

CHAPTER FOUR: Detroit

187 58 percent of the children . . . and one-third of the housing: "Highland Park, MI," Census Reporter, https://censusreporter.org/profiles /16000US2638180-highland-park-mi/.

187 built in 1911: "George Ferris School," Detroiturbex, http://www.detroit urbex.com/content/schools/ferris/index.html.

188 bought it for $2,000 . . . trying to raise: J.C. Reindl, "Entrepreneur's big vision for empty Highland Park schools may die," Detroit Free Press, January 28, 2019, https://www.freep.com/story/money/business/2019 /01/28/detroit-arts-highland-park/2656154002/.

188 15 million Model Ts: "Ford Highland Park Plant," Detroit Historical

Society, *https://detroithistorical.org/learn/encyclopedia-of-detroit/ford-high land-park-plant*.

188 *zip code: 48203*: The film *Detroit 48202: Conversations Along a Postal Route* is a tender, insightful portrait of the adjacent area. *America Re-Framed*, season 7, episode 3, "Detroit 48202: Conversations Along a Postal Route," directed and produced by Pam Sporn, aired January 29, 2019, on PBS, *https://www.pbs.org/video/detroit-48202-conversations-along -a-postal-route-tzx2ee/*.

189 *120,000 Black homeowners*: Edward Lynch et al., "The State of Economic Equity in Detroit," Detroit Future City, May 2021, 98, *https:// detroitfuturecity.com/wp-content/uploads/2021/05/The-State-of-Eco nomic-Equity-in-Detroit.pdf*; "Progress Report 2016–2019," Wayne County Treasurer's Office, *https://www.waynecounty.com/elected/treasurer /wayne-county-treasurer-s-progress-report.aspx*.

189 *64 percent lower*: "Detroit City, Michigan: 2019 Population Estimates," U.S. Census Bureau, *https://www.census.gov/quickfacts/detroitcitymichigan*.

189 *twenty square miles*: *Detroit Future City*, 11.

189 *fell from 900,000 to 171,000*: "Analysis of the Detroit, Michigan Housing Market," Department of Housing and Urban Development, October 1966, ii, *https://www.huduser.gov/portal/publications/pdf/scanned /scan-chma-DetroitMichigan-1966.pdf*; "Detroit City, Michigan," U.S. Census Bureau.

189 *a 25 percent fall in the number of homeowners*: *Detroit Future City: 2012 Strategic Framework Plan* (Detroit: Inland Press, 2013), 210.

190 *53 percent of its Black residents*: *Growing Detroit's African-American Middle Class*, (Detroit: Detroit Future City, 2019).

190 *eighty tenants were evicted per day*: Robert Goodspeed, Margaret Dewar, and Jim Schaafsma, "Michigan's Eviction Crisis," University of Michigan Poverty Solutions, May 2020, *https://poverty.umich.edu/files/2020/05 /Michigan-Eviction-Project-policy-brief.pdf*.

190 *10,000 people a year*: "2019 State of Homelessness," Homeless Action Network of Detroit, *https://static1.squarespace.com/static/5344557fe4b 0323896c3c519/t/5fa051f37ccdd221587af2d9/1604342268391/2019 _HAND+ANNUAL+REPORT+%281%29.pdf*.

190 *one-third*: "Detroit City, Michigan: 2019 Population Estimates," U.S. Census Bureau.

190 *the following business model*: Joshua Akers and Eric Seymour, The Eviction Machine: Neighborhood Instability and Blight in Detroit's Neighborhoods (Ann Arbor: Poverty Solutions at the University of Michigan, 2019), *https://poverty.umich.edu/files/2019/07/Akers-et-al-Eviction -Machine-Revised-June-18.pdf*.

190 *a median price of $1,300*: Ibid.

190 *median Detroit rents of $820 per month*: U.S. Census Bureau, "Population Estimates: July 1, 2019 (V2019)," accessed October 15, 2021, *https:// www.census.gov/quickfacts/.*

191 *a thousand low-wage jobs*: Adrienne Roberts, "Amazon Looks to Open $400-Million Distribution Center at Michigan State Fairgrounds in Detroit," *Detroit Free Press*, August 11, 2020.

192 *"Detroit was, above all"*: Thomas Sugrue, *The Origins of the Urban Crisis* (Princeton, N.J.: Princeton University Press, 2014), 21, 23.

192 *Helicopter photography*: Alex S. MacLean, "Detroit by Air," *New York Times*, December 7, 2014, *https://www.nytimes.com/interactive/2014/12 /07/opinion/sunday/exposures-detroit-by-air-alex-maclean.html.*

192 *an award-winning video*: "Detroit '67," music video by Sam Roberts Band, October 8, 2009, on YouTube, *https://www.youtube.com/watch ?v=wgNenEe0VcE.* The video won the 2009 Video of the Year from the JUNO Awards, the Canadian Grammys.

193 *"Blacks went crazy"*: "Reporter Charlie LeDuff Discovers His Black History," accessed October 22, 2021, *https://www.dailymotion.com/video /x31q5t3.* Herb Boyd, *Black Detroit: A People's History of Self-Determination* (New York: HarperCollins Publishers, 2017), cover. In his blurb reviewing Herb Boyd's exceptional history of the city, Ta-Nehisi Coates put it this way: "Detroit has become a code for urban failure, which is to say, black failure." For a vivid example of Detroit cast as urban failure, see Glen Beck, "Beck TV: Hiroshima vs. Detroit—Which City Really Embraced the 'American Dream'?" *The Blaze* (Feb. 28, 2011), *http://www .theblaze.com/stories/2011/02/28/beck-tv-hiroshima-vs-detroit-which-city -really-embraced-the-american-dream/.*

193 *the white gaze on Detroit*: Hadas Gold, "Detroit, the right's perfect pinata," Politico, August 18, 2013, *https://www.politico.com/story/2013/08 /detroit-michigan-conservatives-095630;* "Detroit at Crossroads 50 Years After Riots Devastated City," NBC News, July 17, 2017, *https:// www.nbcnews.com/news/nbcblk/detroit-crossroads-50-years-after-riots -devastated-city-n783631.* There is a cottage industry of writing that blames Black Detroit for ruining the city. From the right, figures like Ann Coulter (speaking on FoxNews) say things like: "[Detroit was] the gem of the United States of America. First, it was destroyed by the mob with the race riots. Then it was destroyed by the unions driving the jobs abroad." More centrist writings similarly assume 1967 was the city's demographic tipping point.

193 *"My city got a black eye"*: Tawana "Honeycomb" Petty, "Black City," *Coming Out My Box* (Detroit: CreateSpace Independent Publishing Platform, 2016), 5.

193 *shelter for . . . 5,000 people*: "Doorway to Freedom—Detroit and the

Underground Railroad," Detroit Historical Society, *https://detroithistorical
.org/learn/encyclopedia-of-detroit/underground-railroad.*

194 *Two-thirds of the 1,400 men*: Boyd, Black Detroit, 36, 47; "Michigan in
the American Civil War," Michigan Legislature, October 2015, *https://
www.legislature.mi.gov/Publications/CivilWar.pdf.*

194 *Ten percent would not survive*: "1864: First Michigan Colored Infantry
Mustered Into Service," Michigan Day by Day, February 17, 2018,
*http://harris23.msu.domains/event/1864-first-michigan-colored-infantry
-mustered-into-service/.*

194 *"Colored Waiting Room"*: "One-Way Ticket: Jacob Lawrence's Migration
Series," Museum of Modern Art, accessed October 22, 2021, *https://www
.moma.org/interactives/exhibitions/2015/onewayticket/panel/12/history/.*

194 *Detroit's Black population grew more than 700 percent*: Sugrue, *The Origins
of the Urban Crisis*, 29.

194 *"Five Dollar Day" . . . allowed Ford to grow*: Beth Tompkins Bates, *The
Making of Black Detroit in the Age of Henry Ford* (Chapel Hill: The University of North Carolina Press, 2012), 23, 48–50.

194 *thirty-acre foundry*: "Henry Ford's Rouge," The Henry Ford, accessed
October 22, 2021, *https://www.thehenryford.org/visit/ford-rouge-factory
-tour/history-and-timeline/fords-rouge/.*

194 *tuberculosis, deafness, dismemberment, or death*: Bates, *Making of Black
Detroit*, 64–65.

194 *"up South"*: Gerald Van Dusen, *Detroit's Sojourner Truth Housing Riot of
1942* (Charleston: The History Press, 2020), 12. "Up South" was not
just a general nickname to capture Detroit's culture. By World War II,
white migrants from the South were the second-largest group in Detroit.

194 *"if they were white"*: Dan Georgakas and Marvin Surkin, *Detroit: I Do
Mind Dying*, 3rd edition, (Chicago: Haymarket Books, 2012), 153.

194 *Segregation cut across daily life*: Jeremy Williams, *Detroit: The Black Bottom Community* (Charleston: Arcadia Publishing, 2009), 45; Ernest Borden, *Detroit's Paradise Valley* (Charleston: Arcadia Publishing, 2003), 9.

194 *"ethnic hodgepodge"*: Williams, *Detroit: The Black Bottom Community*, 11,
49.

195 *up to 150 percent of what white tenants paid*: Bates, *Making of Black Detroit*, 33.

195 *most dilapidated buildings*: Bates, *Making of Black Detroit*, 97; Van Dusen,
Detroit's Sojourner Truth Housing Riot, 21, 25–30, 38–41.

195 *by 1926 about a third*: Williams, Detroit: *The Black Bottom Community*,
50–52.

195 *a photograph from the eve of*: Ibid., 31.

195 *In 1925, a man named Dr. Ossian Sweet*: Kevin Boyle, *Arc of Justice: A
Saga of Race, Civil Rights, and Murder in the Jazz Age* (New York: Picador,

2004). The facts of the Sweet trial are widely reported, but this is the richest telling of the story.

195   *"When I opened the door"*: Ibid., 290.

195   *As a five-year-old*: Ibid., 68.

195   *In closing arguments*: Ibid., 334. After the second trial, Darrow told the jury: "These people are the children of slavery. If the race that we belong to owes anything to any human being, or to any power in this Universe, they owe it to these black men."

196   *The case was one of*: Ibid., 344–46. Ms. Sweet and one of their children, however, subsequently died from tuberculosis, which they had contracted while held in jail pending trial. Dr. Sweet went on to enjoy wide professional success, but troubled by grief and trauma, he took his own life in 1960.

196   *Black families purchased these lots*: Van Dusen, *Detroit's Sojourner Truth Housing Riot*, 57.

196   *West Eight Mile*: Gerald Van Dusen, *Detroit's Birwood Wall: Hatred & Healing in the West Eight Mile Community* (Charleston: The History Press, 2019), 29; Andrew Wiese, *Places of Their Own: African American Suburbanization in the Twentieth Century* (Chicago: University of Chicago Press, 2004). West Eight Mile is one of hundreds of Black semi-rural and suburban communities that persevered in spite of exclusion from banking and infrastructure investments.

196   *In a photograph*: Van Dusen, *Detroit's Birwood Wall*, 117.

197   *the opinion cited*: Brown v. Board of Education of Topeka, 347 U.S. 483, 494 n.11 (1954).

197   *The Birwood Wall*: Van Dusen, *Detroit's Birwood Wall*, 170–72. The Birwood Wall is now a long line of murals along one side of the Alfonso Wells Memorial Playground, which honors a West Eight Mile resident who adopted and fostered neighborhood babies, obtained grants to renovate the homes of local senior citizens, and spent his own elder years active in local politics and civil rights causes.

197   *June 22, 1938*: Kieran Mulvaney, "When Joe Louis Boxed Nazi Favorite Max Schmeling," June 2, 2021, *https://www.history.com/news/joe-louis-max-schmeling-match*. Truth, as they say, is more interesting than fiction. Schmeling used the Nazi salute and socialized with Hitler and other Nazi officers, but he also refused to fire his Jewish-American manager and (just months after his fight with Louis) he sheltered two Jewish boys from the terrorism of Kristallnacht. Schmeling and Louis became friends after the war, and Schmeling was one of the pallbearers at Louis's funeral in 1966.

197   *"White Americans"*: Ibid.

197   *more than one hundred*: Van Dusen, *Detroit's Sojourner Truth Housing Riot*, 114, 124.

197 *It took two months*: Ibid., 131.

197 *One infamous photograph*: I learned the back story of this picture from a presentation by Jamon Jordan, the official historian for the City of Detroit, who has an encyclopedic knowledge of the city and an actor's gift for bringing history to life. Black Scroll Network History & Tours, *https://blackscrollnetwork.weebly.com/*.

197 *Some white Detroiters were killed*: Sugrue, *The Origins of the Urban Crisis*, 29.

198 *Black veterans gave up on their hometowns*: David H. Onkst, "'First a Negro . . . Incidentally a Veteran': Black World War Two Veterans and the G.I. Bill of Rights in the Deep South, 1944–1948," *Journal of Social History* 31, no. 3 (Spring 1998): 517–543.

198 *In the Second Great Migration from 1940 to 1970*: Sugrue, *The Origins of the Urban Crisis*, 23 (Table 1.1). By 1970, African-Americans represented 44 percent of the city's total population.

198 *By the late 1940s, approximately 80 percent*: Van Dusen, *Detroit's Sojourner Truth Housing Riot*, 20.

198 *"This property shall not be used"*: Sipes v. McGhee, 316 Mich. 614, 620 (Mich. 1947).

198 *"I have seen Mr. McGhee"*: Ibid., 621. This case resonates with Ian Haney López's groundbreaking argument in *White by Law: The Legal Construction of Race* (New York: New York University Press, 1996).

198 *The NAACP and Thurgood Marshall*: In *Shelley v. Kraemer,* 334 U.S. 1 (1948), the Supreme Court overturned *Sipes v. McGhee* as well as the eponymous companion case from Missouri.

198 *Blues, writes city historian Herb Boyd*: Boyd, Black Detroit, 3.

198 *John Lee Hooker, the son of a Mississippi sharecropper*: John Sinclair, "Mother City Blues through the Ages," *Heaven Was Detroit: From Jazz to Hip-Hop and Beyond*, ed. M. L. Leibler (Detroit: Wayne State University Press, 2016), 93.

199 *A segregated Black middle and high school*: "Motown legacy eclipses a larger story about black music in Detroit," NPR, February 15, 2017, *https://www.michiganradio.org/post/motown-legacy-eclipses-larger-story-about-black-music-detroit*.

199 *Langston Hughes called a "minor miracle"*: Borden, *Detroit's Paradise Valley*, 30.

199 *"OWN and MANAGE"*: Ibid.

199 *For most of the neighborhood's history*: Wilson and Cohassy, *Toast of the Town: The Life and Times of Sunnie Wilson* (Detroit: Wayne State University Press, 2018), 102.

199 *A middle-class housing development*: "Mies van der Rohe, Lafayette Park," Detroit Historical Society, accessed October 22, 2021, *https://detroit*

*historical.org/learn/encyclopedia-of-detroit/mies-van-der-rohe-residential
-district-lafayette-park.* This housing development, called Lafayette Park, was designed by Mies van der Rohe. It remains an architectural jewel, and it served as an early experiment in racially integrated housing. But the small number of high-cost units open to African Americans could not replace the wealth and housing that was lost in Black Bottom.

199 *Black families moved:* Van Dusen, *Detroit's Birwood Wall,* 59.

200 *Detroit lost more than half:* Sugrue, *The Origins of the Urban Crisis,* 144 (table 5.2); Sugrue, *The Origins of the Urban Crisis,* 137.

200 *82,000 defense-industry jobs:* Sugrue, *The Origins of the Urban Crisis,* 140–41.

200 *Black unemployment nearly doubled:* Sugrue, *The Origins of the Urban Crisis,* 146, 151.

200 *most decentralized of any big city:* Elizabeth Kneebone, *Job Sprawl Revisited: The Changing Geography of Metropolitan Employment* (Washington, D.C.: Brookings Institution, 2009), 8. As a practical matter, what this means is that Metro Detroit had the highest share of jobs located more than ten miles from the urban center.

200 *On childhood trips:* Diana Ross, *Secrets of a Sparrow* (New York City: Villard Books, 1993), 82.

200 *Dearborn's mayor from 1942 to 1978:* "Orville Hubbard–the ghost who still haunts Dearborn," Detroit News, July 17, 2020, *http://blogs.detroitnews.com/history/2000/07/17/orville-hubbard-the-ghost-who-still-haunts-dearborn/.*

200 *Detroit chapter of the NAACP:* Heather Ann Thompson, *Whose Detroit? Politics, Labor, and Race in a Modern American City* (Ithaca: Cornell University Press, 2001), 20–21.

200 *Aretha Franklin's father:* "Franklin, Clarence LaVaughn," Detroit Historical Society, accessed October 22, 2021, *https://detroithistorical.org/learn/encyclopedia-of-detroit/franklin-clarence-lavaughn.*

201 *League of Revolutionary Black Workers:* Georgakas and Surkin, *Detroit: I Do Mind Dying.*

201 *James and Grace Lee Boggs:* James Boggs and Grace Lee Boggs, "The City Is the Black Man's Land," *Racism and the Class Struggle: Further Pages from a Black Worker's Notebook,* ed. James Boggs (New York: Monthly Review Press, 1970), 40.

201 *The death toll of forty-three:* Sugrue, *Origins of the Urban Crisis,* 259.

201 *telegraphed 3-777:* Jon Lowell, "A Time of Tragedy," *Detroit News,* August 11, 1967, 4, *https://lsa.umich.edu/sid/detroiters-speak/detroiters-speak-archive/_jcr_content/par/download_1667472917/file.res/%22A%20Time%20of%20Tragedy%22%20Article%20from%20the%20Detroit%20News.*

201 *More than two thousand buildings*: Sugrue, *Origins of Urban Crisis*, 259.

201 *Seventeen thousand federal, state, and local*: Thomas J. Sugrue, "Foreword," *Detroit 1967: Origins, Impacts, Legacies*, ed. Joel Stone (Detroit: Wayne University Press, 2017), ix.

201 *a summary of the problem*: Georgakas and Surkin, *Detroit: I Do Mind Dying*, 14.

202 *STRESS unit alone killed twenty-two*: Thompson, *Whose Detroit?*, 81–82, 91.

202 *protested police brutality . . . pro-police rallies*: Thompson, *Whose Detroit?*, 94–98.

202 *Ninety percent*: Heather Ann Thompson, "Rethinking the Politics of White Flight in the Postwar City, Detroit 1945–1980," *Journal of Urban History* 25, no. 2 (January 1999): 163–98, 189. Thompson's extraordinary article analyzes the development of Detroit's city politics in the 1950s, 60s, and 70s, including the racial polarization that resulted from white Detroit's reliance on harsh, anti-Black policing as an answer to rising unemployment.

202 *Black share of Detroit's population grew*: Thompson, "Rethinking the Politics of White Flight," 163.

202 *Starting in the 1970s and consistently as late as 2018*: Van Dusen, *Detroit's Birwood Wall*, 121–23, 162–64.

202 *more than 20 percent of Detroiters*: *Detroit Future City: 2012 Strategic Framework Plan*, 42, 160.

203 *In* Milliken v. Bradley: 418 US 717 (1974).

203 *meaningless remedy*: Joyce A. Baugh, *The Detroit School Busing Case: Milliken v. Bradley and the Controversy of Desegregation* (Lawrence: University Press of Canvas, 2011).

203 *a systematic analysis of city finances from 1950 to 2013*: Nathan Bomey and John Gallagher, "How Detroit Went Broke: The Answers Mmay Surprise You–and Don't Blame Coleman Young," *Detroit Free Press*, September 15, 2013, updated July 18, 2018, *https://www.freep.com/story/news/local/michigan/detroit/2013/09/15/how-detroit-went-broke-the-answers-may-surprise-you-and/77152028/*.

203 *When a city is at least 50 percent African American*: Zoltan L. Hajnal and Jessica Trounstine, "Who or What Governs?: The Effects of Economics, Politics, Institutions, and Needs on Local Spending," *American Politics Research* 38, no. 6, 1130, 1152 (2010).

203 *Hurricane HUD*: Roger Biles, *The Fate of Cities: Urban America and the Federal Government, 1945–2000* (Lawrence: University of Kansas Press, 2011), 213.

203 *Housing legislation in the 1950s and 1960s*: Keeanga-Yamahtta Taylor,

Race for Profit: How Banks and the Real Estate Industry Undermined Black Homeownership (Chapel Hill: University of North Carolina Press, 2019), 42–89, 171.

203   *Speculators took advantage*: Taylor, *Race for Profit*, 145.

203   *A Detroit Free Press survey*: Ibid., 182.

204   *"predatory inclusion" in these homeownership programs*: Ibid., 5, 179.

204   *Real estate agents typically*: Ibid., 181.

204   *Lenders' losses were backstopped*: Jennifer Szalai, "Two Histories of Financiers Profiting from Real Estate While Homeowners Go Belly Up," *New York Times*, Oct. 31, 2019, *https://www.nytimes.com/2019/10/31/books /review-homewreckers-aaron-glantz-race-for-profit-keeanga-yamahtta -taylor.html*.

204   *More than one hundred speculators*: Taylor, *Race for Profit*, 198–200.

204   *Owners on fixed income*: Ibid., 175.

204   *Foreclosures spiked*: Ibid., 170.

204   *By the mid-1970s*: Ibid., 224–225.

204   *Hoping to build a future*: Jenny Nolan, "Auto plant vs. neighborhood: The Poletown battle," *Detroit News*, January 26, 2000, *http:// blogs.detroitnews.com/history/2000/01/26/auto-plant-vs-neighborhood -the-poletown-battle*.

204   *After the resistance vigils*: Thompson, *Whose Detroit?*, 208.

205   *"John's Carpet House"*: NPR, September 28, 2015, *https://www.michigan radio.org/post/detroit-locals-love-neighborhood-blues-festival-city-not -so-much*; William Schambra, "Saving John's Carpet House, Saving Civil Society?" *Nonprofit Quarterly*, August 12, 2014, *https://nonprofit quarterly.org/saving-john-s-carpet-house-saving-civil-society/*.

205   *The Allied Media Conference*: "The Black Lives Matter Convenes at AMC2015," Allied Media Projects, August 4, 2015, *https://alliedmedia .org/news/black-lives-matter-movement-convenes-amc2015*.

205   *Caregivers at the New Light*: Robert B. Jones, Sr., "Searching for the Son: Delta Blues Legend Son House in Detroit," *Heaven Was Detroit: From Jazz to Hip-Hop and Beyond*, ed. M. L. Leibler (Detroit: Wayne State University Press, 2016), 74.

205   *Wilson . . . established the Forest Club*: Wilson and Cohassy, *Toast of the Town*, 104, 107.

205   *Staffed by Wilson and his last waitress*: Ibid., 167–75.

206   *"why some people be mad"*: Lucille Clifton, *Blessing the Boats: New and Selected Poems 1988–2000* (Rochester: BOA Editions, Ltd., 2000), 38.

207   *18 percent of people*: *Detroit Future City*, 210.

204   *French photographers*: Sean O'Hagan, "Detroit in ruins: the photographs of Yves Marchand and Romain Meffre," *The Guardian*, January 1, 2011.

207   *the city had lost 25 percent of its population*: Joshua Akers and Eric

Seymour, *The Eviction Machine: Neighborhood Instability and Blight in Detroit's Neighborhoods* (Ann Arbor: Poverty Solutions at the University of Michigan, 2019), 8, *https://poverty.umich.edu/files/2019/07/Akers-et-al-Eviction-Machine-Revised-June-18.pdf.*

207 *"prolonged collapse":* Robert E. Scott, Manufacturing Job Loss: Trade, Not Productivity, Is the Culprit, Issue Brief #402 (Washington, D.C.: Economic Policy Institute, 2015), 1–2, *https://files.epi.org/2015/ib402-manufacturing-job-loss.pdf;* U.S. Bureau of Labor Statistics, *All Employees, Manufacturing [MANEMP], FRED, Federal Reserve Bank of St. Louis, https://fred.stlouisfed.org/series/MANEMP.* Between 1970 and 2000, the total number of manufacturing jobs rose and fell modestly within a range of 16.8 to 19.6 million jobs.

207 *2014 manufacturing jobs total:* Ibid.

207 *400,000 jobs: Detroit Future City,* 44.

207 *unemployment rate nearly quadrupled: In re* City of Detroit, Mich., 504 B.R. 97, 119 (Bankr. E.D. Mich. 2013).

207 *more likely to live in poverty: Detroit Future City,* 44.

207 *Total tax revenues sank:* Wallace C. Turbeville, *The Detroit Bankruptcy* (New York: Demos, 2013), 17, *https://www.demos.org/research/detroit-bankruptcy.* The city's total tax revenues fell 20 percent between 2008 and 2013.

207 *Municipal income tax revenues fell:* City of Detroit, 504 B.R. 97, 118.

207 *Sales tax revenues fell:* Turbeville, *The Detroit Bankruptcy,* 18.

207 *a 35 percent drop in property tax revenues:* Ibid.

207 *the state cut aid to Detroit:* Turbeville, *The Detroit Bankruptcy,* 20; City of Detroit, 504 B.R. 97, 118. The city's falling population drove more than one-third of these state aid cuts, due to a population-based state aid formula. The balance of the cuts to state aid were discretionary state political choices.

207 *These reductions were not worse:* Nathan Bomey, *Detroit Resurrected: To Bankruptcy and Back* (New York: W. W. Norton & Company, 2016), 13. This source documents state aid reductions to all municipalities by 31 percent between 2000 and 2010.

208 *"[T]he City lost":* City of Detroit, 504 B.R. 97, 116.

208 *Some lawyers and financial analysts:* Turbeville, *The Detroit Bankruptcy,* 5.

208 *$300 million in termination payments:* City of Detroit, 504 B.R. 97, 114–18; Turbeville, *The Detroit Bankruptcy,* 26–32; Bomey, *Detroit Resurrected,* 21–29, 91–93.

208 *$1 billion to $3.5 billion:* City of Detroit, 504 B.R. 97, 113–14.

208 *$18,000 per year . . . $30,000 for police and fire:* City of Detroit, 504 B.R. 97, 113–14.

208 *an additional $4.3 billion:* Oral Opinion on the Record of Judge Steven

Rhodes, *In Re* City of Detroit, November 7, 2014, *https://www.mied .uscourts.gov/pdffiles/dboralopinion.pdf.*

208   *twice as many retirees*: Steven Yaccino and Monica Davey, "Detroit's Emergency Manager Offers Dire Report on City," *New York Times*, May 12, 2013,   *https://www.nytimes.com/2013/05/13/us/detroit-fiscal-problems-are -severe-report-says.html.*

208   *fallen by 77 percent*: Nathan Bomey and John Gallagher, "How Detroit Went Broke: The Answers May Surprise You—and Don't Blame Coleman Young," *Detroit Free Press*, Sept. 15, 2013, *https://www.freep.com /story/news/local/michigan/detroit/2013/09/15/how-detroit-went-broke-the -answers-may-surprise-you-and/77152028/.*

208   *Seventy-two sites qualified for the federal Superfund program*: Ibid.

208   *Detroit entered bankruptcy*: City of Detroit, 504 B.R. 97, 120.

209   *Sixty-one percent of employed city residents*: Detroit Future City, 42.

209   *In 2011, the city's violent crime rate*: Ibid., 210.

209   *more than doubled*: Mark Hatzenbuehler et al., "The Collateral Damage of Mass Incarceration: Risk of Psychiatric Morbidity Among Nonincarcerated Residents of High-Incarceration Neighborhoods," *American Journal of Public Health* 105, no. 1 (January 2015):138–143.

209   *an average of sixty-nine per year*: Tresa Baldas, "Detroit Police Finally Rid of Federal Oversight," *Detroit Free Press*, March 31, 2016, *https:// www.freep.com/story/news/local/michigan/detroit/2016/03/31/detroit -police-finally-rid-federal-oversight/82491776/.*

209   *50 percent more likely to die*: Detroit Future City, 210.

209   *Detroit cut its public workforce*: Michelle Wilde Anderson, "Needing and Fearing Billionaires in Cities Abandoned by Wealth," *Yale Law & Policy Review* 35, no. 1 (2016): 235.

209   *The city closed*: Detroit Future City, 272; City of Detroit, 504 B.R. 97, 120.

209   *only 35,000 of the city's 88,000 street lights . . . 27 percent of its roads*: Detroit Future City, 160.

209   *about one-third . . . 250,000 miles . . . Archaic IT systems*: City of Detroit, 504 B.R. 97, 120–21.

210   *Unpaid income taxes*: Turbeville, *The Detroit Bankruptcy*, 20.

210   *controversial law . . . 57 percent*: Michelle Wilde Anderson, "Democratic Dissolution: Radical Experimentation in State Takeovers of Local Governments," *Fordham Urban Law Journal* 39, no. 3 (2012): 577–623. As I wrote even before the Flint Water Crisis, the reforms raised serious concerns about accountability. The law gave an unelected official new powers that the displaced elected officials had lacked. Misappropriations and conflict-of-interest concerns about emergency managers in Pontiac and Highland Park had offered a grim reminder that everyone, including state officials, needed checks and balances.

210 *Just about every decision*: Bankruptcy litigation is highly technical, as the court confirms how much each creditor is owed, the city assets that can be sold or transferred to creditors, and what percentage of the city's debt will be forgiven. In Detroit's case, creditors disputed nearly every one of these decisions. In *Detroit Resurrected*, cited above, reporter Nathan Bomey memorializes the full chronology of the bankruptcy's participants and controversies.

211 *cut dramatically*: Susan Tompor, "Even 5 years later, retirees feel the effects of Detroit's bankruptcy," *Detroit Free Press*, July 18, 2018, *https:// www.freep.com/story/money/personal-finance/susan-tompor/2018/07/18 /detroit-bankruptcy-retirees-pension/759446002/*.

211 *Grand Bargain*: James M. Ferris, "Detroit's Grand Bargain: Philanthropy as a Catalyst for a Brighter Future," June 2017, *https://cppp.usc.edu/wp -content/uploads/2017/08/IHI_Digital_2017.pdf*.

211 *$50 million*: Aaron Mondry, "Big changes are in the works at Belle Isle, Detroit's favorite park," Detour Detroit, January 26, 2021, *https://detour detroiter.com/big-changes-are-in-works-at-belle-isle-detroits-favorite-park/*.

211 *Detroit's bankruptcy plan*: The Challenges of Meeting Detroit's Pension Promises (Washington, D.C.: Pew Charitable Trusts, March 2018), *https://www.pewtrusts.org/-/media/assets/2018/03/challenge_of_meeting _detroits_pension_promises_report_v6.pdf*; City of Detroit, "Overview of Detroit's Plan of Adjustment," release CLI-2187394v4, February 2014, *https://detroitmi.gov/Portals/0/docs/EM/Announcements/Summary_Plan OfAdjustment.pdf*.

211 *"I urge you"*: Oral Opinion on the Record of Judge Steven Rhodes, *In Re* City of Detroit, November 7, 2014, *https://www.mied.uscourts.gov /pdffiles/dboralopinion.pdf*.

212 *15 percent increase*: Christine Ferretti, "After Detroit Bankruptcy: Optimism, but 'challenges are real'," *Detroit News*, July 18, 2018, *https:// www.detroitnews.com/story/news/local/detroit-city/2018/07/18/detroit -bankruptcy-optimism-but-challenges-real/772729002/*.

212 *"skyscraper sale"*: David Segal, "A Missionary's Quest to Remake Motor City," *New York Times*, April 13, 2013, *http://www.nytimes.com/2013 /04/14/business/dan-gilberts-quest-to-remake-downtown-detroit.html*.

212 *fifty richest people*: "Bloomberg Billionaires Daily Index: Dan Gilbert," *Bloomberg*, accessed November 10, 2021, *https://www.bloomberg.com /billionaires/profiles/daniel-gilbert/*.

212 *fifteen buildings*: Michael Wayland, "Dan Gilbert Purchases Five More Detroit Buildings," MLive, December 18, 2012, *https://www.mlive.com /business/detroit/2012/12/dan_gilbert_purchases_five_mor.html*.

212 *"I made a prediction"*: Paige Williams, "Drop Dead, Detroit! The Suburban Kingpin Who Is Thriving off the City's Decline," *New Yorker*,

January 19, 2014, *http://www.newyorker.com/magazine/2014/01/27/drop-dead-detroit*.

213 *18 million*: "What We Do," Bedrock Detroit, accessed November 14, 2021, *https://www.bedrockdetroit.com/about/*.

213 *250 properties*: Anderson, "Needing and Fearing," 241.

213 *State and local taxpayers invested*: J.C. Reindl, "Ilitch Organization to Get $74M Bonus for Hitting Arena District Goal," *Detroit Free Press*, May 11, 2019, *https://www.freep.com/story/money/business/2019/05/11/ilitch-organization-arena-detroit-district-goal-bonus/1157439001/*.

213 *A third billionaire*: Akers, *Eviction Machine*, 22; Tom Perkins, "How the Morouns Became Detroit's Least Trustworthy Billionaire Family," Curbed: Detroit, January 6, 2020, *https://detroit.curbed.com/2020/1/6/21051665/moroun-family-detroit-history-michigan-central-station*.

216 *"Detroit hit rock bottom" . . . "Detroit finally had hope"*: Bomey, *Detroit Resurrected*, xv.

216 *A stunning 48 percent*: Akers, *Eviction Machine*, 10; Joshua Akers and Eric Seymour, "Instrumental exploitation: Predatory property relations at city's end," *Geoforum* 91 (May 2018), 132.

216 *The rate of homeownership*: Carl Hedman and Rolf Pendall, *Rebuilding and Sustaining Homeownership for African Americans* (Washington, D.C.: Urban Institute, 2018), 4, *https://www.urban.org/research/publication/rebuilding-and-sustaining-homeownership-african-americans*. This rate of decline was much higher than for white Detroiter or Michigan as a whole.

216 *a majority renter city by 2016*: Macdonald, Christine. "Black home ownership plunges in Michigan." *Detroit News*, July 10, 2018. *https://www.detroitnews.com/story/news/michigan/2018/07/10/black-home-owner ship-drop-largest-michigan/767804002/*.

216 *Discrepancies in subprime lending*: Debbie Gruenstein Bocian, Wei Li, and Keith S. Ernst, *Foreclosures by Race and Ethnicity: The Demographics of a Crisis* (Washington, D.C.: The Center for Responsible Lending, 2010), 8, *https://www.responsiblelending.org/mortgage-lending/research-analysis/fore closures-by-race-and-ethnicity.pdf*.

216 *Nearly half of the mortgages*: Ashton, Philip, "CRA's 'Blind Spots': Community Reinvestment and Concentrated Subprime Lending in Detroit," *Journal of Urban Affairs* 32, no. 5 (2010), 586–87.

217 *six times as high*: Joe Guillen, "Detroit leads the nation in reverse mortgage foreclosures," *Detroit Free Press*, June 14, 2019, *https://www.freep.com/story/news/investigations/2019/06/14/detroit-leads-nation-reverse-mort gage-foreclosures/1442186001/*.

217 *Homeowners used*: Ibid.

217 *"value gap"*: Alexa Eisenberg, Connor Wakayama, and Patrick Cooney,

Reinforcing Low-Income Homeownership Through Home Repair: Evaluation of the Make It Home Repair Program (Ann Arbor: Poverty Solutions at the University of Michigan, 2021), 3.

217 *Small purchase prices*: Matthew Goldstein, "Detroit: From Motor City to Housing Incubator," *New York Times*, November 4, 2017.

217 *As global real estate investment*: Josh Akers and Eric Seymour, "Instrumental exploitation: Predatory property relations at city's end," *Geoforum* 91, no. 1 (May 2018), 127–140.

217 *Demand grew in all kinds of broke towns*: Greg Jaffe, "The Strange Summer Land Rush in Peoria's Dying South End," *Washington Post*, August 14, 2021.

217 *A buyer could get land*: Akers, *Eviction Machine*, 19 (2005–2014 numbers).

218 *Average rents in the city*: Julie Cassidy, *Detroit: The Evolution of a Housing Crisis* (Lansing: Michigan League for Public Policy, 2019), 2, *https:// mlpp.org/detroit-the-evolution-of-a-housing-crisis/*.

218 *in weak land markets*: Desmond, *Evicted*, 74–76.

218 *speculator could clear a profit*: Akers, *Eviction Machine*, 6.

218 *The city's tax assessment office*: Bernadette Atuahene and Christopher Berry, "Taxed Out: Illegal Property Tax Assessments and the Epidemic of Tax Foreclosures in Detroit," *U.C. Irvine Law Review* 9 (2019): 862.

218 *Thirty years had passed*: Ibid.

218 *The city estimated*: Turbeville, *The Detroit Bankruptcy*, 20.

218 *A majority of Detroit homes*: Atuahene, "Predatory Cities," 109.

218 *The lower the property value*: Ibid., 113.

219 *Detroit has one of the highest*: Bob DeBoer and Adam H. Langley, *50-State Property Tax Comparison Study for Taxes Paid in 2020* (Cambridge, MA: Lincoln Institute of Land Policy, June 2021), 2, *https://www.lincolninst .edu/sites/default/files/pubfiles/50-state-property-tax-comparison-for-2020 -full_0.pdf*. Aaron Twait, *50-State Property Tax Comparison Study* (Cambridge, MA: Lincoln Institute of Land Policy, April 2015).

219 *relatively high tax rate*: Ibid.

219 *Wayne County was also teetering*: Eric D. Lawrence, "How Wayne County navigated its financial crisis," *Detroit Free Press*, October 20, 2016, *https:// www.freep.com/story/news/local/michigan/wayne/2016/10/20/wayne-county -ends-consent-agreement/92469844/*.

219 *If a landowner falls behind in Detroit*: Bernadette Atuahene and Christopher Berry, "Taxed Out: Illegal Property Tax Assessments and the Epidemic of Tax Foreclosures in Detroit," *U.C. Irvine Law Review* 9 (2019): 870–71 (enumerating these fees in detail).

219 *a "pageant of misery"*: Akers and Seymour, *Eviction Machine*, 21.

219   *$52.3 million*: Claire Herbert, *A Detroit Story: Urban Decline and the Rise of Property Informality* (Oakland: University of California Press, 2021), 213.

220   *most Detroit applicants*: Michele Oberholtzer, "Myth-busting the Detroit tax foreclosure crisis," *Detroit Metro Times*, September 13, 2017, *https:// www.metrotimes.com/detroit/myth-busting-the-detroit-tax-foreclosure-crisis /Content?oid=5552983.*

220   *started reappearing*: Rachel Monroe, "Gone Baby Gone," *The New Republic*, October 2017; Matthew Goldstein and Alexandra Stevenson, "Market for Fixer-Uppers Traps Low-Income Buyers," *New York Times*, February 20, 2016.

220   *In Detroit, land-installment contracts*: Akers and Seymore, *Eviction Machine*, 12.

220   *generally treated as an eviction*: Ibid.

220   *After a protracted battle to regulate . . . Texas is home*: Monroe, "Gone Baby Gone"; Genevieve Hébert Fajardo, "'Owner Finance! No Banks Needed!' Consumer Protection Analysis of Seller-Financed Home Sales: A Texas Case Study," *Georgetown Journal on Poverty Law & Policy* 20, no. 1 (Spring 2013): 429–48.

220   *Local scholars Joshua Akers and Eric Seymour*: Joshua Akers and Eric Seymour, *The Eviction Machine: Neighborhood Instability and Blight in Detroit's Neighborhoods* (Ann Arbor: Poverty Solutions at the University of Michigan, 2019).

220   *In a multiyear study*: Ibid.

221   *"Exit Strategy April 2013, LLC"*: Oberholtzer, "Myth-busting the Detroit tax foreclosure crisis."

221   *"tax-wash" their inventory*: Akers and Seymour, *Eviction Machine*, 9.

221   *150,000 Detroit properties*: Hedman and Pendall, *Rebuilding and Sustaining Homeownership*, 8.

221   *45,000 parcels . . . 41% of them*: Detroit Future City, 272.

221   *Nearly 30 percent*: Carl Hedman and Rolf Pendall, *Rebuilding and Sustaining Homeownership for African Americans* (Washington, D.C.: Urban Institute, 2018), 8.

221   *Another 70,000 households*: Seymour and Akers, "Building the Eviction Economy," 43.

221   *Nearly 30 percent*: Ibid.

221   *between 2013 and 2017*: Joe Guillen, "Detroit leads the nation in reverse mortgage foreclosures," *Detroit Free Press*, June 14, 2019, *https://www .freep.com/story/news/investigations/2019/06/14/detroit-leads-nation-reverse -mortgage-foreclosures/1442186001/.*

221   *As the mortgage market dried up*: Joel Kurth, "Land contracts trip up would-be homeowners," *Detroit News*, February 29, 2016, *https://www*

*.detroitnews.com/story/news/local/detroit-city/2016/02/29/land-contracts
-detroit-tax-foreclosure-joel-kurth/81081186/.*

222   *grew more in Detroit . . . and were disproportionately concentrated*: Eric Sey-
      mour and Joshua Akers, "Portfolio solutions, bulk sales of bank-owned
      properties, and the reemergence of racially exploitative land contracts,"
      Cities 89 (June 2019): 51, 54.

222   *nearly 30,000 eviction filings per year*: Robert Goodspeed, Margaret
      Dewar, and Jim Schaafsma, "Michigan's Eviction Crisis," University
      of Michigan Poverty Solutions, May 2020, *https://poverty.umich.edu
      /files/2020/05/Michigan-Eviction-Project-policy-brief.pdf.*

222   *Countywide, more than one in five*: Ibid., table 1.

222   *By 2019, nearly half*: Alexa Eisenberg, Connor Wakayama, and Patrick
      Cooney, *Reinforcing Low-Income Homeownership Through Home Repair:
      Evaluation of the Make it Home Repair Program* (Ann Arbor: Poverty
      Solutions at the University of Michigan, 2021).

222   *An estimated 24,000 homes*: Ryan Ruggiero, Josh Rivera, and Patrick
      Cooney, *A Decent Home: The Status of Home Repair in Detroit* (Ann
      Arbor: Poverty Solutions at the University of Michigan, 2020), 8–9, 14,
      *https://poverty.umich.edu/files/2020/10/The-Status-of-Home-Repair-in-De
      troit-October-2020.pdf.*

222   *nearly 9 percent*: Christine MacDonald, "Detroit kids' lead poisoning
      rates higher than Flint," *Detroit News*, November 14, 2017, *https://
      www.detroitnews.com/story/news/local/detroit-city/2017/11/14/lead-poisoning
      -children-detroit/107683688/.*

222   *In one ZIP code, 22 percent*: Ibid.

222   *Asthma rates*: *Detroit Future City*, 160.

222   *An aging housing stock*: Alexa Eisenberg, Eric Seymour, Alex B. Hill,
      Joshua Akers, "Toxic structures: Speculation and lead exposure in De-
      troit's single-family rental market," *Health & Place* 64 (July 2020).

223   *Between 2014 and 2019, 141,000 people*: Joel Kurth, "Detroit says no
      proof water shutoffs harm health. Get real, experts say," Bridge Michi-
      gan, February 26, 2020, *https://www.bridgemi.com/michigan-health-watch
      /detroit-says-no-proof-water-shutoffs-harm-health-get-real-experts-say.*

223   *households below the poverty line*: Dahlia Rockowitz, Chris Askew-Mer-
      win, Malavika Sahai, Kely Markley, Cria Kay, and Tony Reames, *House-
      hold Water Security in Metropolitan Detroit: Measuring the Affordability
      Gap* (Ann Arbor: Poverty Solutions at the University of Michigan, 2018),
      *https://poverty.umich.edu/10/files/2018/08/PovertySolutions-PolicyBrief
      -0818-r2.pdf.*

223   *an average of about 3,800 people*: Homeless Action Network of Detroit,
      "Sheltered Homeless Persons in Detroit (MI) 10/1/16–9/30/2017," 6,
      https://static1.squarespace.com/static/5344557fe4b0323896c3c519/t/5a7c

*751608522985c2a3c780/1518105882011/2017+AHAR+All+Persons
+Report+FINAL+from+HDX.pdf.*

223 *195 Detroit Public Schools closed*: John Grover and Yvette van der Velde, *A School District in Crisis Detroit's Public Schools 1842–2015* (Detroit: Loveland Technologies, 2016), *https://app.regrid.com/reports/schools*.

223 *During the 2015–2016 school year*: Erin Einhorn and Chastity Pratt Dawsey, "The children of 8B: One classroom, 31 journeys, and the reason it's so hard to fix Detroit's schools," *Chalkbeat Detroit*, October 2, 2018, *https://detroit.chalkbeat.org/2018/10/2/21106013/the-children-of-8b -one-classroom-31-journeys-and-the-reason-it-s-so-hard-to-fix-detroit-s -schools*.

224 *Less than 5 percent of Detroit tenants*: Christine MacDonald, "Study: Tenants in 1 out of 6 Rentals Faced Evictions in Michigan," *Detroit News*, May 20, 2020, *https://www.detroitnews.com/story/news/local/michigan /2020/05/20/study-tenants-one-out-six-rentals-faced-eviction-michigan /5227452002/*.

224 *a "predatory city"*: "Predatory Cities," *California Law Review* 108, no. 1 (2020): 107–82.

225 *"Detroit has had"*: Joel Kurth and Christine MacDonald, "Volume of Abandoned Homes 'Absolutely Terrifying,'" *Detroit News*, May 14, 2015, *http://www.detroitnews.com/story/news/special-reports/2015/05/14/detroit -abandoned-homes-volume-terrifying/27237787*.

225 *other transformative long-form*: For example, see: Mark Betancourt, "Detroit's Housing Crisis Is the Work of Its Own Government," *VICE News*, December 29, 2017, *https://www.vice.com/en/article/kznzky /detroits-housing-crisis-is-the-work-of-its-own-government*; Ross Jones, "A Detroit Landlord Is Being Sued for 'Predatory Contracts.' The City Forgave $1M in Unpaid Property Taxes," ABC News: Detroit WXYZ, November 7, 2019, *https://www.wxyz.com/longform/a-detroit-landlord-is -being-sued-for-failing-to-maintain-homes-the-city-forgave-1m-in-un paid-property-taxes*.

225 *Detroit-based scholars*: Margaret Dewar, Eric Seymour, and Oana Drută, "Disinvesting in the City: The Role of Tax Foreclosure in Detroit." *Urban Affairs Review* 51, no. 5 (2015): 587–615; Lan Deng, Eric Seymour, Margaret Dewar, and June Manning Thomas, "Saving strong neighborhoods from the destruction of mortgage foreclosures: The impact of community-based efforts in Detroit, Michigan," *Housing Policy Debate*, 28, no. 2 (2018): 153–179; Bernadette Atuahene and Christopher Berry, "Taxed Out: Illegal Property Tax Assessments and the Epidemic of Tax Foreclosures in Detroit," *U.C. Irvine Law Review* 9 (2019): 847–886; *A People's Atlas of Detroit*, ed. Linda Campbell, Andrew Newman, Sara Safransky, and Tim Stallman (Detroit: Waye State University Press, 2020);

Claire W. Herbert, *A Detroit Story: Urban Decline and the Rise of Property Informality* (Oakland: University of California Press, 2021). Other examples of this important work are cited elsewhere in this chapter and in this book's bibliography.

226 *counseling and workshops*: "Tax Foreclosure Prevention," United Community Housing Coalition, *https://www.uchcdetroit.org/tax-foreclosure -prevention*.

227 *the Make It Home program*: "Make It Home," United Community Housing Coalition, *https://www.uchcdetroit.org/make-it-home*. To qualify, residents must live in a home being foreclosed by the Wayne County Treasurer as their primary residence, own no other homes, and pass a home inspection and a criminal background check, among other requirements.

226 *ranged from $2000 to $5600*: Roshanak Mehdipanah, Margaret Dewar, and Alexa Eisenberg, "Threats to and Opportunities for Low-Income Homeownership, Housing Stability, and Health: Protocol for the Detroit 2017 Make-It-Home Evaluation Study," *International Journal of Environmental Research and Public Health* 18 (October 2021): 3, *https://doi .org/10.3390/ijerph182111230*.

227 *1,100 occupied homes*: "Make It Home Helps 1,157 Detroit Families Stay in Their Homes," City of Detroit, February 27, 2020, *https://www .detroitnews.com/story/news/michigan/2018/07/10/black-home-owner ship-drop-largest-michigan/767804002/ https://detroitmi.gov/news/make-it -home-helps-1157-detroit-families-stay-their-homes*.

227 *An accompanying repair program*: Eisenberg, et al, "Reinforcing Home-ownership," 4.

227 *a research foundation to understand*: Bernadette Atuahene and Timothy R. Hodge, "Stategraft," *Southern California Law Review* 91, no. 2 (2018): 263–302; Bernadette Atuahene, " 'Our Taxes Are Too Damn High': Institutional Racism, Property Tax Assessments, and the Fair Housing Act," *Northwestern University Law Review* 112, no. 6 (2018): 1501–64.

227 *pushing the Mayor's office*: Christine MacDonald, "Activists propose Detroit fund for overtaxed homeowners," *The Detroit News*, July 27, 2020, *https://www.detroitnews.com/story/news/local/detroit-city/2020/07/27/ac tivists-propose-detroit-fund-overtaxed-homeowners/5482828002/*.

227 *"Nobody Moves"*: "About," Detroit Eviction Defense, *https://www.detroit evictiondefense.net/about/*.

228 *DED organizers have proactively identified*: Joshua Akers, Eric Seymour, et al., "Liquid Tenancy: 'Post-crisis' Economies of Displacement, Community Organizing, and New Forms of Resistance," *Radical Housing Journal* 1, no. 1 (2019): 19–21, *https://radicalhousingjournal.org/2019 /liquid-tenancy/*.

228   *DED has developed campaigns*: Akers and Seymour, *Eviction Machine*, 23–28.

228   *protest outside the private home*: Christine Ferretti and Christine Mac-Donald, "Protesters Call on Treasurer to Save Family Homes," *Detroit News*, August 21, 2017, *https://www.detroitnews.com/story/news/local /detroit-city/2017/08/31/protesters-assessments-wayne-county-treasurer /105151692/.*

228   *23,000 eligible households*: Seymour and Akers, "Building the Eviction Economy," 45.

228   *property tax exemption program*: "Housing Information Portal," accessed April 21, 2021. *https://hip.datadrivendetroit.org/pages/info-action-briefs/what -do-we-know-about-tax-foreclosures-and-evictions-detroit/.*

228   *fell 94 percent*: Louis Aguilar, "New Detroit Tax fforeclosure Data Reveal Hopeful Signs—with One Exception," *Bridge Detroit*, January 25, 2021, *https://www.bridgedetroit.com/new-detroit-tax-foreclosure-data-reveal -hopeful-signs-with-one-exception/*; *Neighbor to Neighbor: The First Detroit Property Tax Foreclosure Census* (Detroit: Quicken Loans Community Fund, 2019), *https://www.foreclosureoutreach.org/wp-content/themes/fore closure-outreach/resources/neighbor_to_neighbor-detroit.pdf.*

229   *took three years and cost $10 million*: Charles E. Ramirez, "Tax Justice Group Calls on Detroit to Fix 'Unfair' Property Assessments," *Detroit News*, July 7, 2021, *https://www.detroitnews.com/story/news/local/de troit-city/2021/07/07/tax-justice-group-calls-detroit-fix-unfair-property-as sessments/7881010002/.*

228   *an average total of $3,800*: Christine MacDonald and Mark Betancourt, "Detroit Homeowners Overtaxed $600 Million," *Detroit News*, January 9, 2020, *https://www.detroitnews.com/story/news/local/detroit-city/housing/2020 /01/09/detroit-homeowners-overtaxed-600-million/2698518001/.*

228   *assessed her house as worth $57,000*: Ibid.

229   *In 2018 and 2019 . . . She began to advocate for*: Kat Stafford, "Detroit City Council Aims to Address Big Issues Facing Detroiters with 'People's Bills,'" *Detroit Free Press*, September 30, 2019, *https://www.freep.com /story/news/local/michigan/detroit/2019/09/30/detroit-city-council-water -affordability-plan/3814833002/.*

229   *Janee Ayers*: Sarah Cwiek, "Detroit 'Bans the Box' on Most Rental Applications," *Michigan Radio*, February 14, 2019, *https://www.michiganradio .org/politics-government/2019-02-14/detroit-bans-the-box-on-most-rental -applications.*

229   *15 percent of adults*: City of Detroit, Fair Chance Ordinance Overview, April 2018, *https://detroitmi.gov/sites/detroitmi.localhost/files/2018-04/Fair ChanceOrdinance.pdf.*

229   *one-fifth of its general fund*: Kristen Jordan Shamus, "Michigan Spending

One-Fifth of Its General Fund Budget on Prisoners," *Detroit Free Press*, December 12, 2019, *https://www.freep.com/story/news/local/michigan /2018/12/19/prison-michigan-corrections-jail/2230794002/*; Heather Ann Thompson, "Unmaking the Motor City in the Age of Mass Incarceration," *Journal of Law in Society* 15 (December 2014): 41–61.

230 *eventually raising $65,000*: Rhonda J. Smith, "Detroit Black Farmers Land Fund Selects 30 Farmers for Cash Grants to Buy Land," *Planet Detroit*, October 28, 2020, *https://planetdetroit.org/2020/10/detroit-black -farmers-land-fund-selects-30-farmers-for-cash-grants-to-buy-land/*.

231 *It has not been easy*: Annamarie Sysling, "Detroit Black Farmer Land Fund Launches Second-Year Crowdfunding Campaign," *WDET*, June 22, 2021, *https://wdet.org/2021/06/22/detroit-black-farmer-land-fund-launches -second-year-crowdfunding-campaign*.

231 *An estimated 2,400 owner-occupied homes*: "Wayne County Circuit Court Extends Redemption for Occupied Properties Until March 2022," Wayne County Treasurer's Office, accessed January 23, 2022, *https:// www.waynecounty.com/elected/treasurer/wayne-county-treasurer-s-office -halts-property-tax.aspx*.

231 *"Halloween in the D"*: Meira Gebel, "So Long Angels' Night: Halloween Fun Returns to Detroit," *Detroit Free Press*, October 10, 2018, *https:// www.freep.com/story/news/local/michigan/detroit/2018/10/10/halloween -detroit-angels-night/1593180002/*.

231 *"Angels' Night"*: City of Detroit, accessed October 22, 2021, *https:// web.archive.org/web/20131029191414/http://www.ci.detroit.mi.us/angels night/default.htm*.

232 *Groups of orange-clad volunteers*:"Angels' Night Poster and Oratorical Contest," City of Detroit, accessed October 22, 2021, *https://web.archive .org/web/20131030022348/http://www.ci.detroit.mi.us/angelsnight/Contest Guidelines07.htm*.

232 *"museums are unable to compete"*: Expert Witness Report of Michael Plummer, *In re* City of Detroit (July 8, 2014): 25–26, *https://detroitmi.gov /sites/detroitmi.localhost/files/2018-05/Expert%20Witness%20Report%20 of%20M%20Plummer.pdf*.

232 *Buyers with enough capital*: Ibid., 26.

233 *associated with the Latin phrase*: "Catholic Prayer: Litany of Saint Yves," *Catholic Culture*, accessed December 15, 2021, *https://www.catholicculture .org/culture/liturgicalyear/prayers/view.cfm?id=1477*.

233 *"An advocate and not a bandit"*: *https://www.catholicculture.org/culture /liturgicalyear/prayers/view.cfm?id=1477*.

233 *says something about our culture*: Nathan Bomey, Joe Guillen, and Brent Snavely, *Detroit Free Press*, *https://www.freep.com/story/news/local/detroit*

-bankruptcy/2014/12/30/detroit-bankruptcy-advisers-jones-day-miller-buck
fire-ernst-young-conway-mackenzie/21072715/.

233 *about $2 million*: "About Us: Our Financials," *https://www.uchcdetroit.org
/who-we-are.*

234 *"Detroiters teach the rest of the world"*: "History," Allied Media Conference, *https://amc.alliedmedia.org/about/history.*

Chapter 5: Facing Forward

235 *traveled across the country as a labor organizer*: Elizabeth Gurley Flynn,
The Rebel Girl: An Autobiography, My First Life (1906–1926) (New York:
International Publishers, 1955), 37, 83, 81–83, 97, 102, 125.

236 *"bread and roses"*: This is a reference to a poem and a strike, described in
greater detail in Chapter 3.

236 *Nine out of ten children*: Raj Chetty, David Grusky, Maximilian Hell, et
al, "Executive Summary: The Fading American Dream: Trends in Abso-
lute Income Mobility Since 1940," *Equality of Opportunity Project* (Palo
Alto: Stanford, 2016), *http://www.equality-of-opportunity.org/assets/docu
ments/abs_mobility_summary.pdf.*

236 *Both across and within states*: Estelle Sommeiller and Mark Price, "The
Increasingly Unequal States of America Income Inequality by State, 1917
to 2011," Economic Analysis and Research Network, February 19, 2014,
https://www.epi.org/publication/unequal-states/.

236 *Communities of color skipped over*: Ira Katznelson, *When Affirmative
Action Was White: An Untold History of Racial Inequality in Twentieth-
Century America* (New York: W.W. Norton & Company, 2005).

236 *The share of Americans living*: Mallach, *The Divided City*, 37.

236 *"[G]eography," wrote journalist*: Phillip Longman, "Bloom and Bust: Regional Inequality Is Out of Control. Here's How to Reverse It," *Washington Monthly*, November 2015, 29.

237 *In thirty-three states*: Estelle Sommeiller and Mark Price, *The Increasingly Unequal States of America: Income Inequality by State, 1917 to 2011*
(Washington, D.C.: Economic Analysis and Research Network, 2014), 4.

237 *By 2013*: *Trends in Family Wealth, 1989–2013* (Washington, D.C.:
Congressional Budget Office, 2016), 1, *https://www.cbo.gov/sites/default
/files/114th-congress-2015-2016/reports/51846-familywealth.pdf.*

237 *Obion officials had resorted*: "No Pay, No Spray: Firefighters Let Home
Burn," NBCNews, October 5, 2010, *https://www.nbcnews.com/id/wbna
39516346.*

237 *"These waters receive sewage"*: Michelle Wilde Anderson, "Losing the War
of Attrition: Mobility, Chronic Decline, and Infrastructure," *Yale Law*

Journal Forum 127 (2017), *https://www.yalelawjournal.org/forum/losing -the-war-of-attrition*; Michael Lynch, "ALCOSAN Creates Subcommittee to Develop Customer Assistance Program," *90.5 WESA, http:// wesa.fm/post/alcosan-creates-subcommittee-develop-customer-assistance -program* (March 27, 2015). Thomas Jefferson called the Ohio River "the most beautiful river on earth. Its current gentle, waters clear, and bosom smooth and unbroken." *Notes on the State of Virginia* (1781).

239   *"If we have learned nothing"*: Kate Ascher, "Has the Pandemic Changed Cities Forever?" *New York Times Book Review*, September 10, 2021.

239   *"[I]f there has been a single problem"*: Francis Fukuyama, *Political Order and Political Decay: From the Industrial Revolution to the Globalization of Democracy* (New York: Farrar, Straus and Giroux, 2014).

242   *Michigan Supreme Court intervened*: "In Detroit, 36th District Court Reform a Success Story," *Detroit News*, October 6, 2014, *https://www .detroitnews.com/story/opinion/editorials/2014/10/06/detroit-th-district -court-improves/16824031/*.

242   *Nearly 12,000 people*: Federal Bureau of Investigation, "Arrests Offense Counts in Detroit Police Department: 2019" accessed December 15, 2021, *https://crime-data-explorer.app.cloud.gov/pages/explorer/crime/arrest*.

242   *Federal immigration enforcement*: Milton J. Valencia, "Five arrested at Lawrence immigration office," *Boston Globe*, March 31, 2017, *https:// www.bostonglobe.com/metro/2017/03/31/five-arrested-lawrence-immigration -office/SUeBGCVTiNxKerc1C84nhM/story.html*.

Index

Federal Bureau of Investigation
(FBI), 96
federal government
bias about government
dependence, 119
Bureau of Land Management,
118
Department of Justice, 311n156
Federal Housing Administration,
196
Fish and Wildlife Service, 92, 97
Fourteenth Amendment, 107–8
Immigration and Customs
Enforcement, 242
suburbia and financial support,
145–46, 148–51, 177
timber revenues and, 91–98
Federal Reserve Bank of Boston,
174, 179
The Fight to Save the Town (Wilde
Anderson), 20–21, 244
Fink, Susan, 173–74
fire protection, subscription-based,
237
Flint (Michigan), 113, 237, 246,
315n167, 327n210
Flynn, Elizabeth Gurley, 16, 137,
139, 235–36, 303n139
Forbes magazine, 25–26
Ford, Henry, 194
Ford, Henry, II, 29
Ford Field, 199
Ford Rouge Complex, 194
Forest Club, 205
Fortman, Candice, 225
Foundation for Human
Understanding, 87–88
Foundation for Transparency in
Government, 164–65
Fourteenth Amendment, 107–8
Frost, Robert, 21, 159
Fukuyama, Francis, 239

The Gap, Inc., 141
Gardner, Leonard, 44–45
gateway cities, 21–24, 31–33, 134
General Motors, 204
Gilbert, Dan, 212, 213
Gilbertson, Gil, 101–3, 107, 109,
114, 124
Gilbertville, 213
glass cliff, 162n
Glenn, Lane, 133–34, 177–78, 180
Goldilocks and the Three BARS
(children's book), 119–20
Goldman, Emma, 303n139
Gomez, Yesenia, 73
Gomez, Zoila, 174, 181–82
Gonzales, Jessica, 107
González, Juan, 144
Gore, Al, 93
Gorman, James, 54
Gorman, Virginia, 52, 53–54
"Gospel of Wealth" (Carnegie),
137
Grand Bargain deal, 211
Grants Pass Daily Courier (Oregon),
109
Greater White Rose church, 55
Great Recession
citywide poverty problem prior
to, 5–6
Detroit bankruptcy and housing
foreclosures, 18, 49, 189–91,
206–24, 233
Foreclosure Crisis of, overview, 6
income inequality following,
237
Josephine County service cuts,
1–5, 83–85, 101–9
Lawrence budget deficit and,
162–65, 184
lost decade following, 12
Stockton municipal bankruptcy,
42, 44–50

About the Author

Michelle Wilde Anderson is a law professor at Stanford University, where she teaches in the areas of local government, property, and environmental justice. Her writing has appeared in *The New York Times*, *Los Angeles Times*, *Chicago Tribune*, *Yale Law Journal*, and other publications. The American Law Institute (ALI) awarded her their Early Career Scholars Medal in 2019. Anderson came up through thirteen years of public education in California and served as a proud member of the law faculty of the University of California, Berkeley for six years. She has also taught as a visiting professor at Harvard and Columbia Law Schools. Anderson chairs the Board of Directors of the National Housing Law Project and has served as a board member for the East Bay Community Law Center in Oakland for more than a decade. She lives with her family in San Francisco.

🐦@MWILDEANDERSON